Typographic Composition

TEXT & TABLE LAYOUT DESIGN CONTENTS PAGES · TEXT PAGES FIGURE/PLATE CAPTIONS · TABLES

P·I·E BOOKS
Villa Phoenix Suite 301, 4-14-6, Komagome, Toshima-ku, Tokyo 170-0003 Japan
Tel: 03-3940-8302 Fax: 03-3576-7361
e-mail: editor@piebooks.com sales@piebooks.com

ISBN4-89444-136-5 C3070

Printed in Japan

The jacket design uses artwork contributed by:

Black + White Magazine, **Cahan & Associates**, **Colors Magazine**, **Synopsis Magazine**, and **Zacharko Design Partnership**.

Editorial Notes

Credit Format (クレジットフォーマット)	
MEDIUM (媒体名) TITLE (タイトル) YEAR (年度) COUNTRY (国名)	
CL:	Client (クライアント)
PB:	Publisher (出版社)
E:	Editor (編集) ※
AD:	Art Director (アートディレクター)
Chief D:	Chief Designer (チーフデザイナー)
D:	Designer (デザイナー)
P:	Photographer (カメラマン)
I:	Illustrator (イラストレーター)
TY:	Typographer (タイポグラファー)
CW:	Copywriter (コピーライター)
ST:	Stylist (スタイリスト)
HM:	Hair & Make-up (ヘア&メイク)
DF:	Design Firm (デザイン会社)

※EDITOR(編集)：雑誌の場合は基本的に編集長の名前を記入していますが、
複数の名前が記載されている場合は、先頭に明記されているのが編集長となります。
The managing editor is credited for magazines;
where multiple names appear,the first is the managing editor.

※提供者の意向によりクレジットデータの一部を記載していないものがあります。
Please note that some credit data has been omitted at the request of the submittor.

はじめに

文字の可読性への挑戦や新しいスタイルの追及がさかんだった傾向が少し落ち着き、最近では、読みやすく、またビジュアルを引き立てるシンプルな文字組が好まれているようです。テキストを読みやすく組むとつまらないデザインになりがち、という考え方はもはや過去の物で、シンプルなレイアウトでも、デザイナーの力量次第で洗練された新しいスタイルを生み出すことができるのです。本書では、主張の強すぎるデザインではなく、シンプルでありながらさりげなく個性的な『美しい文字組・表組』を紹介します。

また、本書では冊子形態の作品のみを紹介しています。フリーフォームの要素が強すぎるポスターや広告、フライヤーといった１面で完結する作品ではなく、全体のデザイン・バランスの統一を図らなくてはならないブローシャーや雑誌の文字・表レイアウトに焦点を絞りました。そして、以下の4つのカテゴリー別に作品を分類しています。

– 目次のレイアウト：
  本文への導入部として、機能的でデザイン性の高い作品を紹介。
– テキストのレイアウト：
  テキスト主体のレイアウトで、シンプルで洗練された作品を紹介。
– 少ない文字とビジュアルのレイアウト：
  ビジュアル主体のレイアウトで、文字とのバランスが優れた作品を紹介。
– 表組のレイアウト：
  文字と罫線、また時には罫線を使わずに構成された美しい作品を紹介。

テキストとビジュアルのバランスを絶妙に保つ難しさ、いかに余白を生かし、多くの要素をすっきりと読みやすくまとめるのか。
これらのハードルを超え、会社案内、カタログ、雑誌、書籍といった多様な媒体の中で、それぞれのコンセプトや個性を表現する優れたレイアウトの数々を、堪能していただけたら幸いです。

最後に、忙しい中ご協力いただいた出版社の方々、そして快く作品をご提供いただいたクリエイターの方々にこの場を借りてお礼を申しあげます。

FOREWORD

The tendency to defy readability in pursuit of style has waned. These days easy-to-read, simple type composition that sets off the visuals is preferred. The belief that making type readable renders dull design is a past misnomer; with the power of design, the simplest of layouts can be refined and stylistically fresh. This volume presents beautiful typographic composition that while simple, displays subtle, unassertive individuality.

The range of work shown is limited to bound book(let)s. Unlike advertising-related posters with over-powering, spontaneous elements, or fliers, that are complete as single pages, we have focused on typographic composition for brochures and magazines—layouts designed considering the balance and unity of the book as a whole. The works are organized in four categories:

Contents pages, works exemplary as functional and well-designed introductions to the main text;
text pages, simple and refined layouts composed primarily of text;
figure/plate captions, well-balanced examples of type used on primarily visual layouts;
and tables, beautifully composed combinations of type and rules, or other graphic devices.

Maintaining an exquisite balance between type and visuals, making white space come alive, organizing multiple elements into a clear and readable form—we are pleased to present numerous examples of outstanding layouts that not only resolve these design challenges, but express the concepts and personality of a variety of applications and mediums including company brochures, catalogues, magazines, and books.

Finally, we would like to express our gratitude to the publishers for their cooperation, and the designers for their contributions—thank you all.

VORWORT

Die Tendenz, bei der Gestaltung weniger auf Lesbarkeit als auf Stil zu achten, läßt nach. Heutzutage werden wieder leicht zu lesende, einfache Schriftkompositionen bevorzugt. Diese sollen die visuellen Komponenten unterstützen und zur Geltung bringen. Der Glaube, daß allein die Lesbarkeit von Schrift ein langweiliges Design aufwertet, gehört der Vergangenheit an. Durch die Kraft des Designs können auch einfachste Layouts verbessert und stilistisch aufgefrischt werden. Dieser Band präsentiert wunderbare typografische Kompositionen - oft in ihrer Art einfach, strahlen sie eine subtile, unangepasste Individualität aus.

Die gezeigten Arbeiten beschränken sich auf gebundene Drucksachen, Bücher und Broschüren. Anders als Werbe-Plakate mit ins Auge springenden, spontanen Elementen, und anders als Flyer, die als Einzelseite konzipiert sind, haben wir uns hier auf typografische Kompositionen beschränkt, deren Layouts unter dem Eindruck der Einheitlichkeit der Drucksache als Ganzes wohl ausbalanciert sind. Die Arbeiten sind in vier Kategorien eingeteilt:

Inhaltsübersichten - beispielhafte Arbeiten die funktional und gut gestaltet vor dem Hauptinhalt als Einleitung bzw.
Übersicht stehen; Textseiten - einfache und raffinierte Layouts, die im wesentlichen für Text komponiert sind;
Üerschriften, Unterzeilen und Bildtexte - wohl-balancierte Beispiele von Schrift in vorwiegend visuellen Layouts;
Tabellen, wunderbar komponierte Kombinationen von Schrift, Zahlen und Linien, sowie andere grafische Arbeiten.

Wir freuen uns, Ihnen eine Vielzahl von Beispielen herausragender Layouts präsentiern zu können, die eine exquisite Balance zwischen Schrift und Bild darstellen, bei denen Weißraum lebt, bei denen multiple Elemente in eine klare, lesbare Form gebracht sind. Zudem, daß die Herausforderungen der Gestaltungsaufgabe perfekt gelöst sind, weisen alle diese Broschüren, Kataloge, Magazine und Bücher ein eigenständiges Konzept und einen unverwechselbaren Charakter auf.

Wir danken allen Herausgebern der gezeigten Drucksachen für Ihre Kooperation und allen Designern für Ihre Beiträge recht herzlich.

Index

MAGAZINE 雑誌

BANG DECEMBER 1999 SWEDEN PB: bang E: Ulrika Lorentzi D: Paul Kühlhorn / Eva Liljefors P: Rineke Dijkstra DF: Fellow Designers

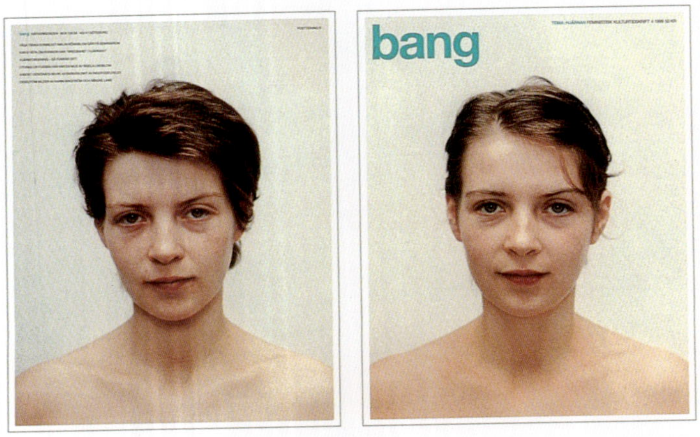

RINEKE DIJKSTRA
FÖDD 1959, SITTARD, HOLLAND
UTBILDAD 1981–1986 PÅ GERRIT REITVELD ACADEMIE, AMSTERDAM
AKTUELL MED UTSTÄLLNINGEN "FRA DET SKJULTE – 10 ÅRS ERHVERVELSER" PÅ DET NATIONALE FOTOMUSEUM I DANMARK. PÅGÅR TILL 22 JANUARI 2000
BILDERNA HETER TIA, LOCATION AMSTERDAM, NETHERLANDS, DATE JUNE 23 1994 OCH TIA, LOCATION AMSTERDAM, NETHERLANDS, DATE NOVEMBER 14 1994

innehåll

MEDVERKANDE: HEIDI BACKMAN ÖVERINSPEKTÖR/PRODUCENT / ANDERS W BERGGREN GENUSFORSKARE / FREDRIK BONDESTAM SKRIBENT / RINEKE DIJKSTRA KONSTNÄR / HELENA DREBER STUDERANDE / INGER EDELFELDT FÖRFATTARE / CARL-JOHAN DE GEER KONSTNÄR / KRISTINA HAGSTRÖM LITTERATURVETARE / KATARINA HAMBERG MED DR / EVA HELMENIUS LITTERATURVETARE / CHARLOTTE HOLGERSSON DOKTORAND PÅ HANDELSHÖGSKOLAN / MARIE HØEG FOTOGRAF / ERICA JONVALLEN LITTERATURVETARE / JENNY KEMPE SKRIBENT/ LEKTÖR / FILIPPA VON KRUSENSTJERNA KONSTNÄR / INEZ VAN LAMSWEERDE KONSTNÄR / ABIGAIL LANE KONSTNÄR / ANDERS LEDBERG DOKTORAND I NEUROVETENSKAP / SISELA LINDBLOM FÖRFATTARE / CLAUDIA LINDÉN DOKTORAND I LITTERATURVETENSKAP / GUNILLA NORDENFORS KVINNOJOUREN I UMEÅ / KAJSA NORELL JOURNALIST / EMELII OLSSON STUDE- RANDE / MALIN RÖNNBLOM DOKTORAND I STATSVETENSKAP / JENNY SAHLSTRÖM SOCIOLOGISTUDERANDE / ANN-SOFI SIDÉN KONSTNÄR / ELSE-MARIE STABERG FIL DR I PEDAGOGIK / CRISTINE SUNDBOM KVINNOJOUREN I UMEÅ / KARL VILHJALMSSON FOTOGRAF / STEFAN VILLKATT SKRIBENT / ULLA WIKANDER PROFESSOR I EKONOMISK HISTORIA / KARIN WIKSTRÖM KONSTNÄR / IKA ÖSTERBLAD ILLUSTRATÖR **TACK TILL:** SARA ARRHENIUS / ANDERS LEDBERG

3

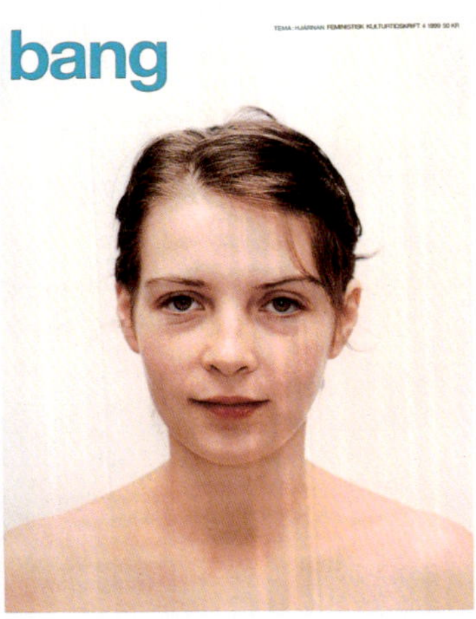

COVER

MAGAZINE 雑誌

SPACE MARCH 2000 SWEDEN

PB: SPACE Magazine E: Jonas Lindberg CD,AD,D,TY: Simina Astilean P: Tobias Sjodin I: Alvaro Tapia CW: Sonia Hedstrand DF: Anima Design Ltd. Contributors: Okko Oinonen / Dorinel Marc / Mauro Rongione / Mickadelica / Milou Allerholm / Peter Cornell / Terese Cedervret / Maiken Håverstein / Samuel Dahlberg

space #2

Redaktion
Chefredaktör och ansvarig utgivare:
Jonas Lindberg
0709-503102
fax: 08- 545 880 44
jonas@space-mag.com

Bildredaktör och formgivare:
Simina Astilean 0708-878 124
simina@space-mag.com

Textredaktör:
Sonia Hedstrand 0739-848788
sonia@space-mag.com

Christian Hörgren
christian@space-mag.com

Korrektur:
Clara Gustafsson
Kasper Paulig

Skribenter:
Sonia Hedstrand
Christian Hörgren
Jonas Lindberg
Milou Allerholm
Peter Cornell
Terese Cedervret
Maiken Håvarstein
Samuel Dahlberg

Fotografer:
Tobias Sjödin 070- 459 04 41
Peter Orevi 070- 772 81 86
Okko Oinonen +358 (0)50 567 53 42
Mauro Rongione 070-774 39 38
Dorinel Marc 0708- 82 69 32
Mikeadelica

Annonser:
Projekt Initiativ
Hanna Starck-Johnson
tel: 08- 459 23 20
fax: 08- 459 23 10
e mail: hanna.starck@projektinitiativ.se

Tryck:
Trydells Tryckeri AB

Space:
Space Art Expo
Rosenhill
115 25 Stockholm
e-mail: info@space-mag.com
hemsida: http://www.space-mag.com

Starfront
foto: Mikeadelica

innehåll 1.

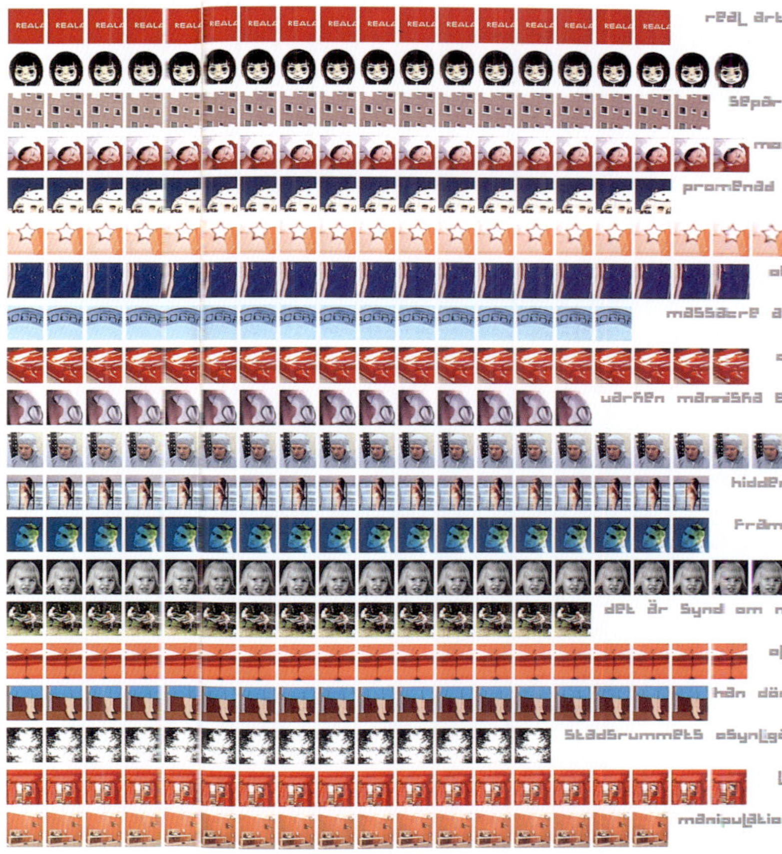

COVER

BLACK + WHITE No.33 OCTOBER 1998 AUSTRALIA

PB: Studio Magazine E, CD: Marcello Grand E: Karen-Jane Eyre AD,D: Cassidy Hall
P: Marino Parisotto Vay (COVER) / Effie Paleologou (CONTENTS)

BLACK + WHITE No.36 APRIL 1999 AUSTRALIA

PB: Studio Magazine E, CD: Marcello Grand E: Karen-Jane Eyre AD,D: Andrew Godfrey
P: Howard Schatz (COVER) / Arunas (CONTENTS)

REM

06. RAI BANDA 08. TYRONE BRANIGAN 10. REX DUPAIN 12. SYLVANA VAN DIJK 14. ROBYN LEA 16. CHRIS KINSER 18. HANS REITMEYER 20. TREVOR WORDEN 22. MARY WAGNER 24. HALLIE BURTON 26. JOHN KANANGHINIS 28. KIM ROTHBART 30. LOIS GREENFIELD

SAS (SHORT ATTENTION SPAN)

32. THE PEEP SHOW.
MAKING ART OF PORN.
34. HA-HA-HARD NEWS.
TV COMEDY'S SERIOUS PUNCH.
36. I WANT TO SCREEN.
THE TECHNOLOGY THAT'S PULLING PEOPLE APART.
38. GENRE BENDERS.
HOLLYWOOD'S KARAOKE CROWD.
128. PARTING SHOTS.
(NOT ONLY) REVIEWS.

FEATURES

40. RETRO FUTURISM.
THE FUTURE WAS THEN.
44. IRVINE WELSH.
THE FILTH INTERVIEW.
THE EROTIC MIRACLE.
TOKYO'S SOCIO-SEXUAL REVOLUTION.

RAW HYPE

48. BELINDA MCCLORY.
MISTRESS OF *THE MATRIX* UNCOVERED.
74. RICHARD GRIEVE.
AN ACTOR RUNNING AWAY FROM HOME.

GALLERIES

80. CARL AUSTIN HYATT 108. HISAKO SAKURAI

0:33

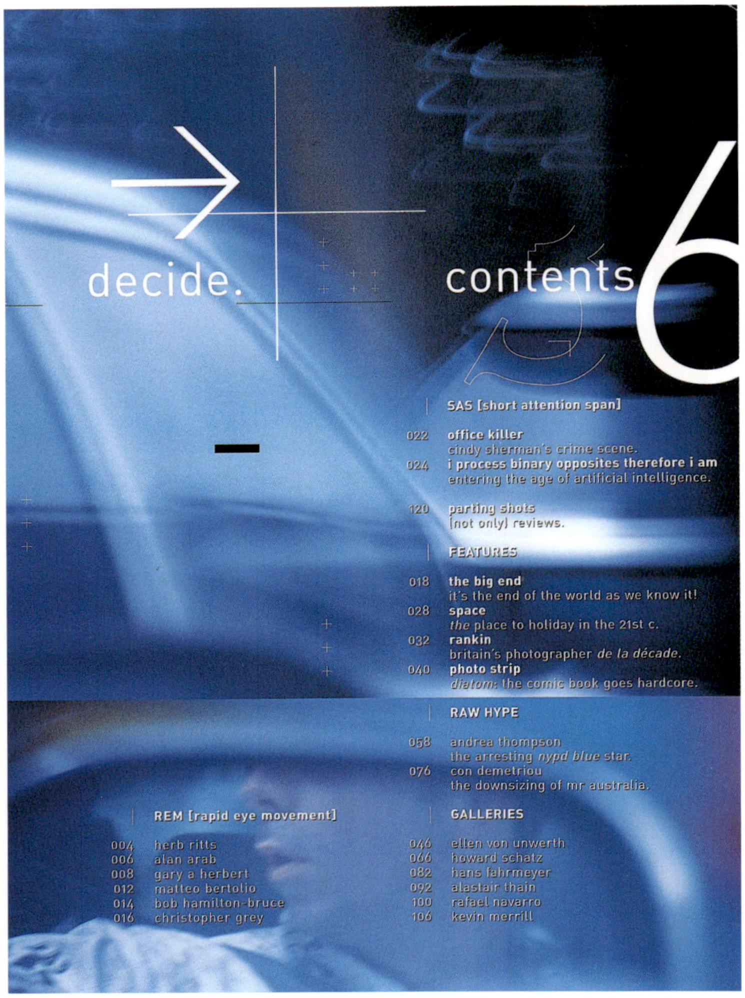

decide.

contents 36

SAS [short attention span]

022 **office killer**
cindy sherman's crime scene.
024 **i process binary opposites therefore i am**
entering the age of artificial intelligence.
120 **parting shots**
[not only] reviews.

FEATURES

018 **the big end**
it's the end of the world as we know it!
028 **space**
the place to holiday in the 21st c.
032 **rankin**
britain's photographer *de la décade*.
040 **photo strip**
diatom: the comic book goes hardcore.

RAW HYPE

058 andrea thompson
the arresting *nypd blue* star.
076 con demetriou
the downsizing of mr australia.

REM [rapid eye movement]

004 herb ritts
006 alan arab
008 gary a herbert
012 matteo bertolio
014 bob hamilton-bruce
016 christopher grey

GALLERIES

046 ellen von unwerth
066 howard schatz
082 hans fahrmeyer
092 alastair thain
100 rafael navarro
106 kevin merrill

No.33 COVER

No.36 COVER

BLACK + WHITE No.30 APRIL 1998 AUSTRALIA

PB: Studio Magazine E, CD: Marcello Grand E: Karen-Jane Eyre AD,D: Tim McIntyre
P: Stephane Sednaoui (COVER) / Sonny Vandevelde (CONTENTS)

[#30] CONTENTS →

No.30 COVER

MAGAZINE 雑誌

BLACK + WHITE NO.32 AUGUST 1998 AUSTRALIA

PB: Studio Magazine E,CD: Marcello Grand E: Karen-Jane Eyre AD,D: Tim McIntyre
P: Franco Lacosta (COVER) / Jez Smith (CONTENTS)

No.32 COVER

REM (RAPID EYE MOVEMENT)

0:32

SAS (SHORT ATTENTION SPAN)

FEATURES

RAW HYPE

GALLERIES

MAGAZINE 雜誌

BLACK + WHITE NO.28 DECEMBER 1997 AUSTRALIA
PB: Studio Magazine E,CD: Marcello Grand E: Karen-Jane Eyre AD,D: Tim McIntyre
P: Daniela Federici (COVER) / Jez Smith (CONTENTS)

BLACK + WHITE NO.29 FEBRUARY 1998 AUSTRALIA
PB: Studio Magazine E,CD: Marcello Grand E: Karen-Jane Eyre AD,D: Tim McIntyre
P: Dominique Derisbourg (COVER) / Jez Smith (CONTENTS)

[TABLE OF CØNTENTS] B/W ISSUE TWENTY 8

RAPID EYE MØVEMENT [REM]
08. CRAIG OWEN 10. WOLFGANG PIETRZOK
12. ROBERT ASMAN 14. ROXANN MILLS 16. JASON BENJAMIN
18. ROCHELLE WHATMAN 20. JEAN-MARIE BOTTEQUIN
22. PETER BALAZSY 24. ALEX DONNINI

SHØRT ATTENTIØN SPAN [SAS]
26. **POPULARITY BREEDS CONTEMPT:** THE PROBLEM WITH U2.
30. **MAD SEED:** THE 45-YEAR EVOLUTION OF A PUBLISHING INSTITUTION.
34. **F*#K S**T UP!:** RE-PUNCTUATING POP.
36. **HEROINE ADDICTION:** LOVING THE KILLER BABE.
124. **PARTING SHOTS:** (NOT ONLY) REVIEWS.

[FEATURES]
40. **JOHN CHRISTOPHER DEPP III:** INSIDE THE ENIGMA.
76. **TURNING TABLES:** THE VERY PUBLIC WORLD OF THE EROTIC DANCER.
114. **SURFACE TENSION:** WHY A PICTURE'S STILL WORTH A THOUSAND WORDS.

[GALLERIES]
44. DANIELA FEDERICI 62. OLIVIER [illegible]ALIN
70. JASON GOLTZ 80. ANDERSON & LOW 88. GEORGE [illegible]HOLZ
96. MIRANDA PENN TURIN 102. RICHAR[illegible] EGLI

[RAW HYPE]
56. SUSIE PORTER: OZ CINEMA'S NEW INGENUE.

[TABLE OF CONTENTS] [illegible]

RAPID EYE MOVEMENT [REM]
08. JAMIE GRAY
10. LOUISE LISTER
12. LISA BURNS
14. TINA GONSALVES
16. KAREN GRAFFEO
18. LOUDER THAN WORDS

SHORT ATTENTION SPAN [SAS]
26. ALL ABOUT ALICE: NEW WORDS FROM AM HOMES GIVE VOICE TO A PAEDOPHILE.
28. ANNIE SPRINKLE: LIFE'S TOUGH WHEN YOU'RE A PLEASURE ACTIVIST.
30. GENERATION GEEK: THE NERDING OF CULTURE.
32. AND NOW FOR SOME ART FROM OUR SPONSOR: BREAKING FROM THE BANALITY OF TV.
40. LOVE SEX INTELLIGENCE: IN SEARCH OF A FORUM FOR MALE EROTICA.
124. PARTING SHOTS: (NOT ONLY) REVIEWS.

[FEATURES]
3[illegible]. CORNUCOPIA: MARKY MARK GETS DOWN FOR *BOOGIE NIGHTS*.
42. GILLIAN ARMSTRONG: *OSCAR & LUCINDA*: THE AUSTRALIAN DIRECTOR'S CUT.
54. DUSTIN HOFFMAN: ACTING UP IN THE *MAD CITY*.
114. TIMES2: ANDREW HORTON TAKES A [illegible]2-HOUR BITE OF THE BIG APPLE.

[RAW HYPE]
58. ROBYN [illegible]: DUMPING GIRLFRIEND FOR A NEW SOUND.

[GALLERIES]
6[illegible]. BOB [illegible]
66. HOWARD SCHATZ
78. DEBORAH SAMUEL
84. DANIEL AESCHLIMANN
94. ADAM BRUZZONE
10[illegible]. ROBERT FARBER

No.28 COVER

No.29 COVER

No.07 COVER

+81vol.07 CONTENTS

"+81" is the international dialing code for Japan.
The combination of the number "81" and the innately positive plus sign makes for the a visual image that can be read by people all over the world regardless of how they would pronounce it.

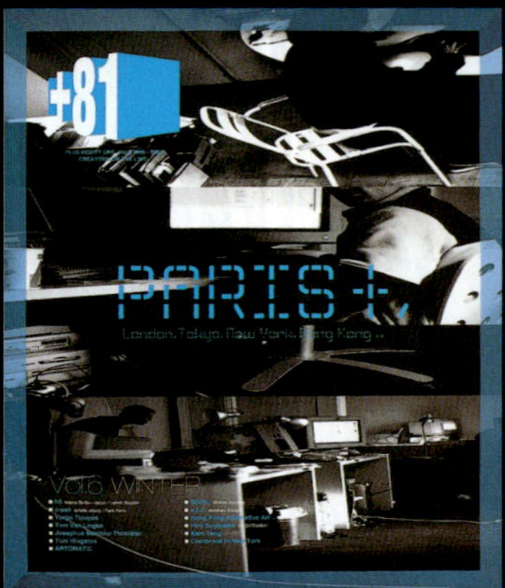

No.06 COVER

FACES +81.06 →

+81 vol.06 CONTENTS

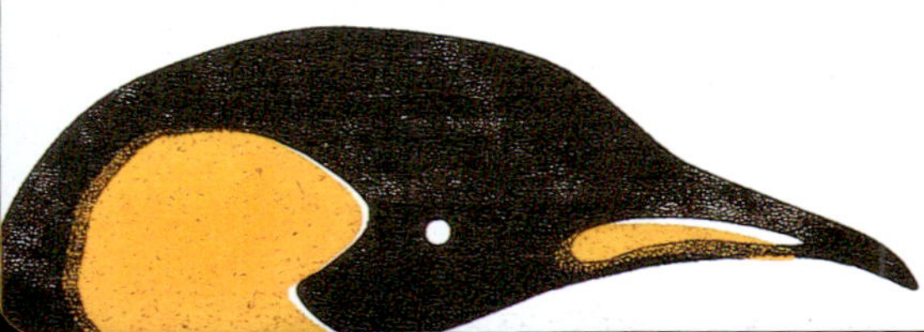

with complete control

009 JUNZO KURODA
-01/WASH MAN 2.0
-02/SENTOUKI (M)
-03/SENTOUKI (S)

010 FURNITURE DESIGN AGRA
-01/WHEEL
-02/WHEEL
-03/CHANGEABLE COVER

011 SOUP DESIGN
-01/WDH
-02/WDH S=1/10
-03/WDH S=1/10
-04/WDH S=1/10

COVER

MAGAZINE 雑誌

ECÍFFO VOL.33 AUTUMN 1998 JAPAN CL: KOKUYO Co., Ltd. CD: Akihiro Kishimoto AD: Shintaro Abe P: Roberto Carra

ECÍFFO VOL.34 SPRING 1999 JAPAN CL: KOKUYO Co., Ltd. CD: Akihiro Kishimoto AD: Shintaro Abe P: Francesco Radino

No.33 COVER

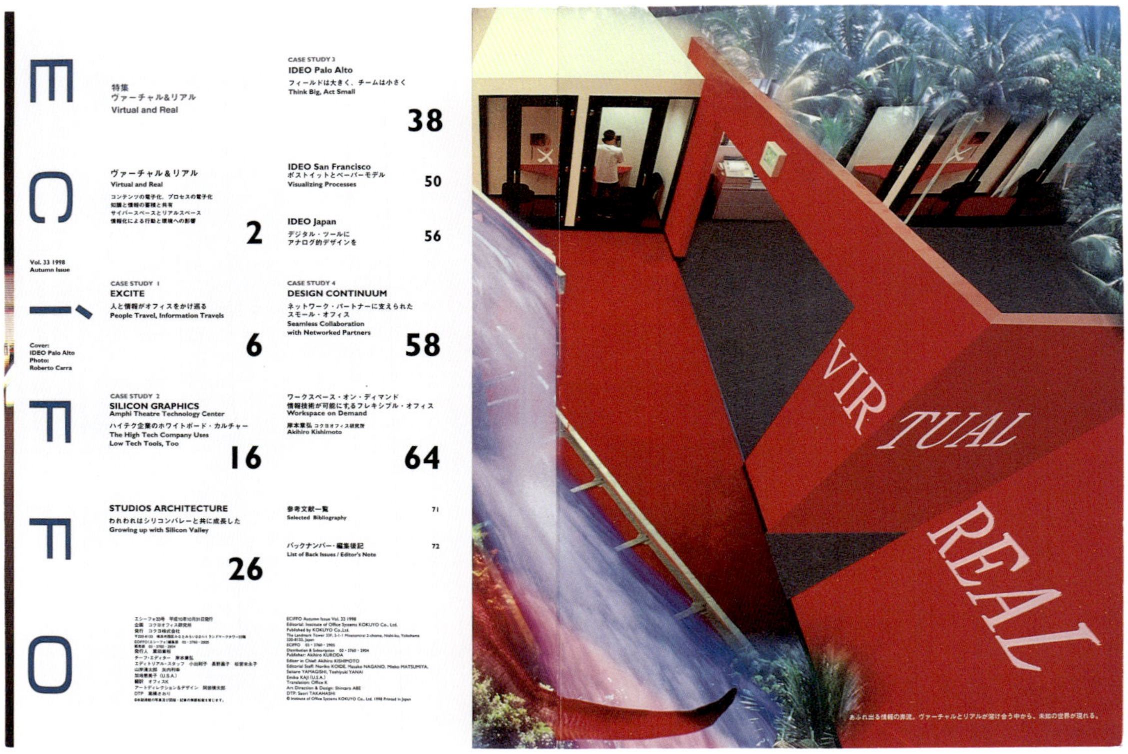

No.34 COVER

MAGAZINE 雑誌

ECÍFFO VOL.35　AUTUMN 1999　JAPAN　CL: KOKUYO Co., Ltd.　CD: Akihiro Kishimoto　AD: Shintaro Abe　P: Roberto Carra

ECÍFFO VOL.36　SPRING 2000　JAPAN　CL: KOKUYO Co., Ltd.　CD: Akihiro Kishimoto　AD: Shintaro Abe　P: Francesco Radino

No.35 COVER

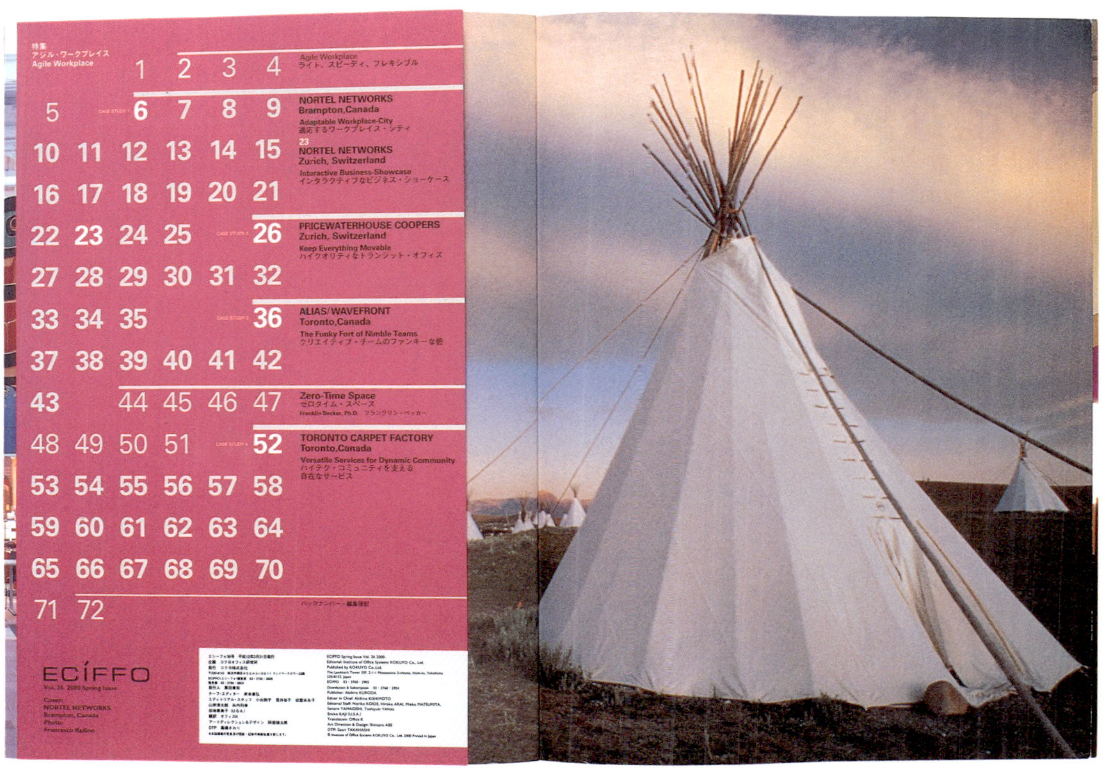

No.36 COVER

BROCHURE ブローシャー

ERNIE.EY.COM 1999 USA CL: Ernie Online AD,D: Mark Murphy DF: Murphy Design Inc.

COVER

KUNSTFEST AM KULTURFORUM 1999 GERMANY CL: Berliner Festspiele AD,D,CW,DF: Cyan

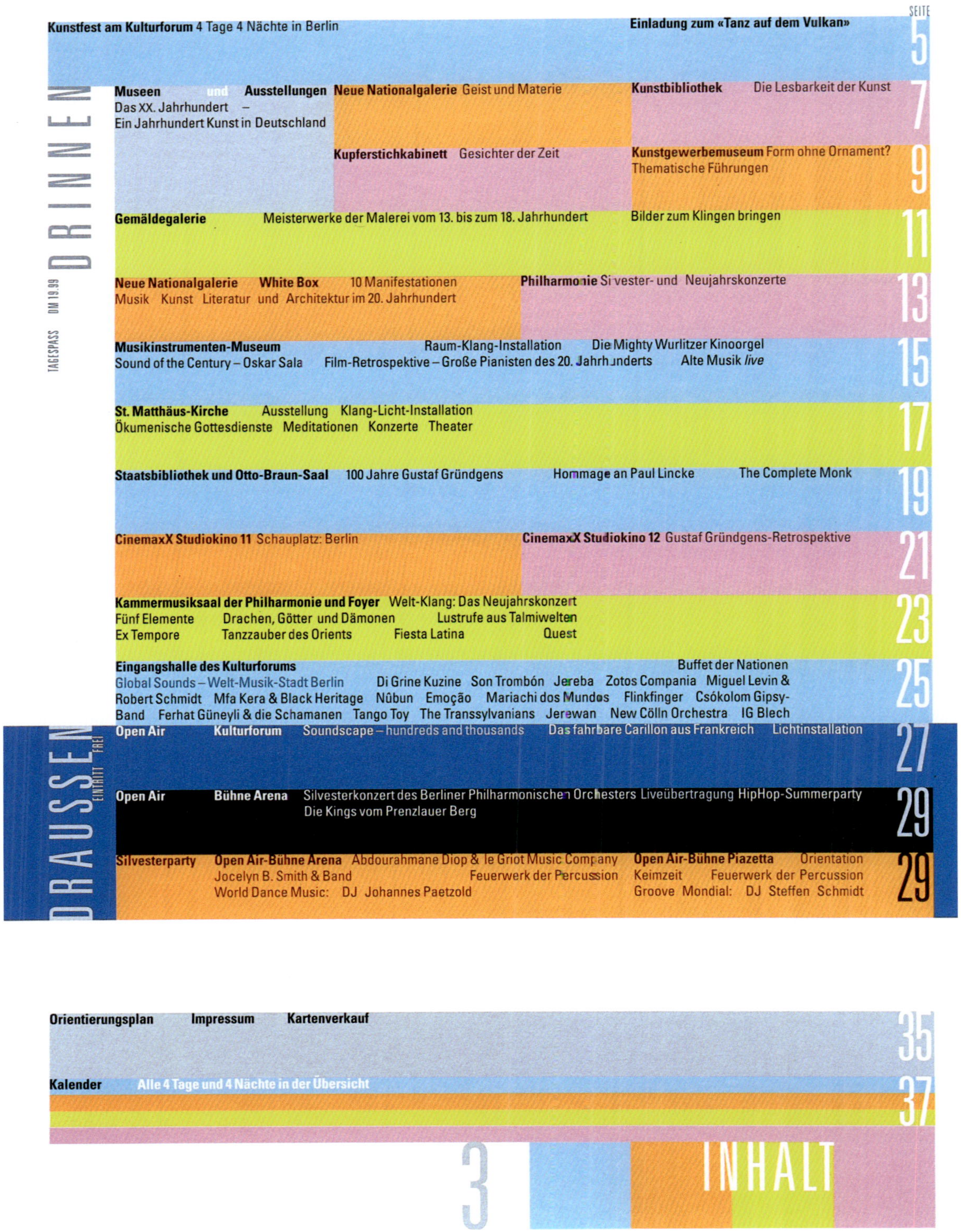

SEITE

Kunstfest am Kulturforum 4 Tage 4 Nächte in Berlin **Einladung zum «Tanz auf dem Vulkan»** 5

DRINNEN

Museen und **Ausstellungen** Das XX. Jahrhundert – Ein Jahrhundert Kunst in Deutschland **Neue Nationalgalerie** Geist und Materie **Kunstbibliothek** Die Lesbarkeit der Kunst 7

Kupferstichkabinett Gesichter der Zeit **Kunstgewerbemuseum** Form ohne Ornament? Thematische Führungen 9

Gemäldegalerie Meisterwerke der Malerei vom 13. bis zum 18. Jahrhundert Bilder zum Klingen bringen 11

Neue Nationalgalerie **White Box** 10 Manifestationen Musik Kunst Literatur und Architektur im 20. Jahrhundert **Philharmonie** Silvester- und Neujahrskonzerte 13

TAGESPASS DM 19.99

Musikinstrumenten-Museum Sound of the Century – Oskar Sala Raum-Klang-Installation Film-Retrospektive – Große Pianisten des 20. Jahrhunderts Die Mighty Wurlitzer Kinoorgel Alte Musik *live* 15

St. Matthäus-Kirche Ausstellung Klang-Licht-Installation Ökumenische Gottesdienste Meditationen Konzerte Theater 17

Staatsbibliothek und Otto-Braun-Saal 100 Jahre Gustaf Gründgens Hommage an Paul Lincke The Complete Monk 19

CinemaxX Studiokino 11 Schauplatz: Berlin **CinemaxX Studiokino 12** Gustaf Gründgens-Retrospektive 21

Kammermusiksaal der Philharmonie und Foyer Welt-Klang: Das Neujahrskonzert Fünf Elemente Drachen, Götter und Dämonen Lustrufe aus Talmiwelten Ex Tempore Tanzzauber des Orients Fiesta Latina Quest 23

Eingangshalle des Kulturforums Buffet der Nationen Global Sounds – Welt-Musik-Stadt Berlin Di Grine Kuzine Son Trombón Jereba Zotos Compania Miguel Levin & Robert Schmidt Mfa Kera & Black Heritage Nûbun Emoção Mariachi dos Mundos Flinkfinger Csókolom Gipsy-Band Ferhat Güneyli & die Schamanen Tango Toy The Transsylvanians Jerewan New Cölln Orchestra IG Blech 25

DRAUSSEN EINTRITT FREI

Open Air **Kulturforum** Soundscape – hundreds and thousands Das fahrbare Carillon aus Frankreich Lichtinstallation 27

Open Air **Bühne Arena** Silvesterkonzert des Berliner Philharmonischen Orchesters Liveübertragung HipHop-Summerparty Die Kings vom Prenzlauer Berg 29

Silvesterparty **Open Air-Bühne Arena** Abdourahmane Diop & le Griot Music Company Jocelyn B. Smith & Band Feuerwerk der Percussion World Dance Music: DJ Johannes Paetzold **Open Air-Bühne Piazetta** Orientation Keimzeit Feuerwerk der Percussion Groove Mondial: DJ Steffen Schmidt 29

Orientierungsplan **Impressum** **Kartenverkauf** 35

Kalender **Alle 4 Tage und 4 Nächte in der Übersicht** 37

3 INHALT

COVER

ANNUAL REPORT アニュアルレポート

KOWLOON-CANTON RAILWAY CORPORATION 1999 HONG KONG

CL: Kowloon-Canton Railway Corporation CD: Kan Tai-keung AD: Eddy Yu Chi Kong / Chau So Hing D: Lerry Ho P: Bob Davis I: Ng Cheuk Bong DF: Kan & Lau Design Consultants

Contents

COVER

ANNUAL REPORT アニュアルレポート

SOUND TRANSIT 1998 ANNUAL REPORT 1999 USA CL: Sound Transit CD,AD,D: Tony Secolo CW: Tim Healy

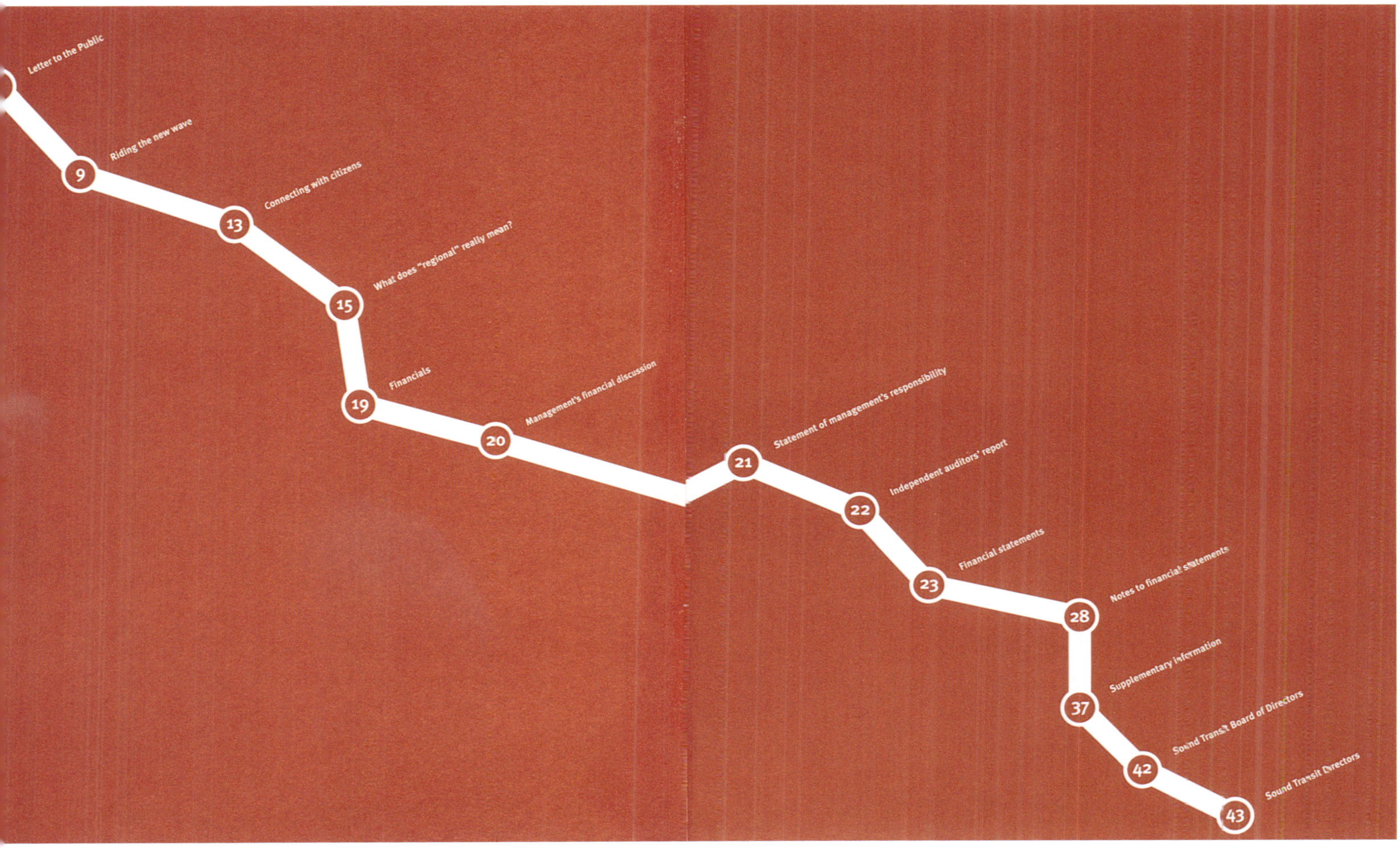

COVER

INS 1998 ANNUAL REPORT 1998 USA CL: INS CD,AD: Bill Cahan D: Lian Ng I: Kevin Ellsworth CW: Thom Elkjer DF: Cahan & Associates

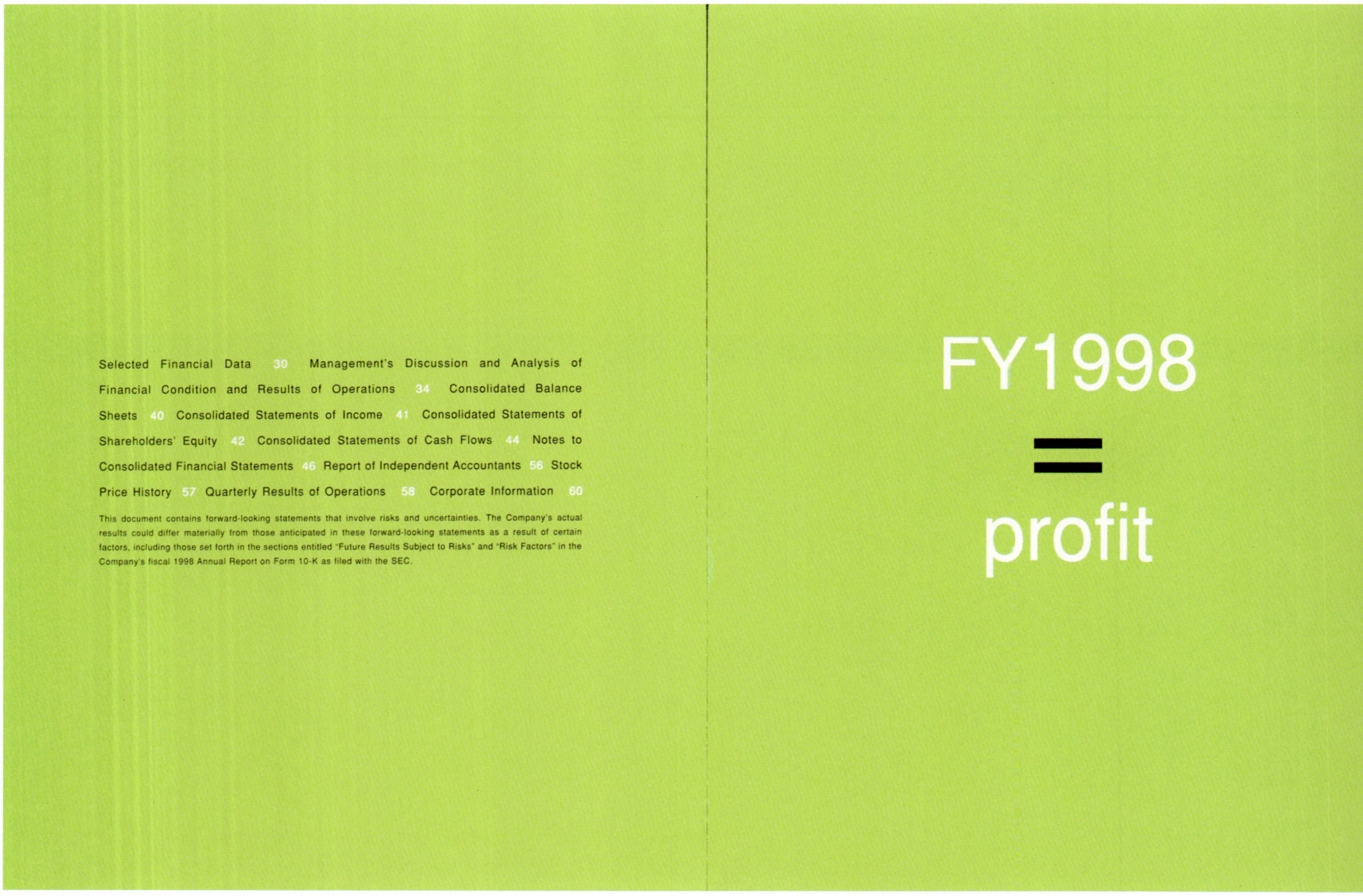

COVER

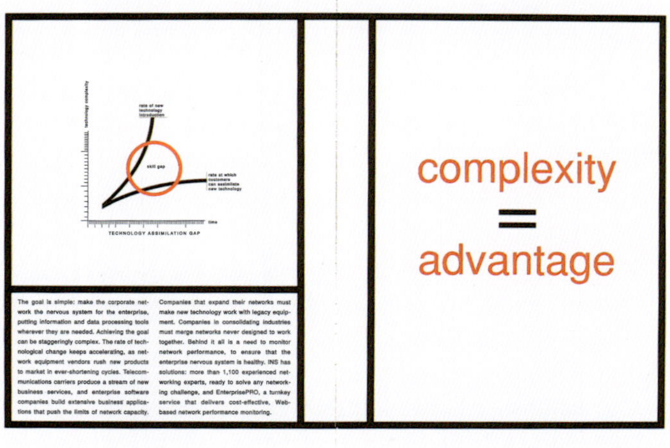

TEXT PAGES

MILIEUDIENST AMSTERDAM 1998 NETHERLANDS CL: Milieudienst Amsterdam D: Richard Niessen CW: Arnold Korporaal

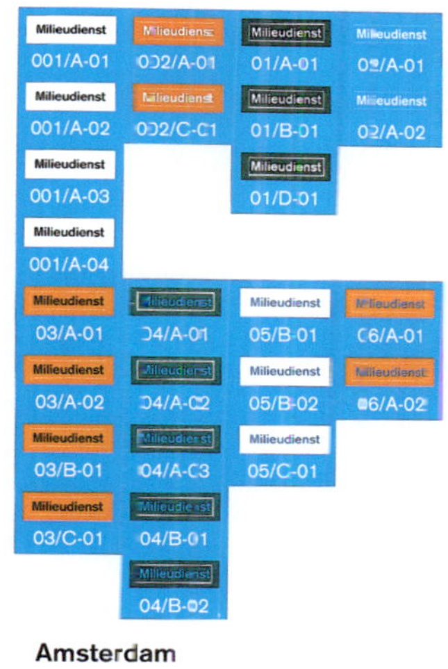

COVER

MARTHA STEWART BABY MARCH 2000 USA

PB,DF: Martha Stewart Omnimedia E: Alice Gordon AD: Deb Bishop / Barbara deWilde D: Angie Gubler P: Chris Baker / Frank Heckers (COVER & CONTENTS) / Gentle & Hyers / Dana Gallagher / Ken Kochey / Minh & Wass / Maria Robledo

contents baby

MARTHA STEWART BABY 2000

COVER
Agnès, 10 months old, is caught mid-laugh by photographer Frank Heckers.

4

5

COVER

MAGAZINE 雑誌

COLORS 37 PRAYER APRIL-MAY 2000 ITALY

PB: Colors Magazine S.r.l. Editorial Director: Oliviero Toscani E: Renzo di Renzo Creative Editor: Richard Christiansen AD: Tetsuya Tamano D: Anna Maria Stilllone

COLORS 29 TOYS DECEMBER-JANUARY 1998-99 ITALY

PB: Colors Magazine S.r.l. Editorial Director: Oliviero Toscani E: Adam Broomberg AD: Thomas Hilland

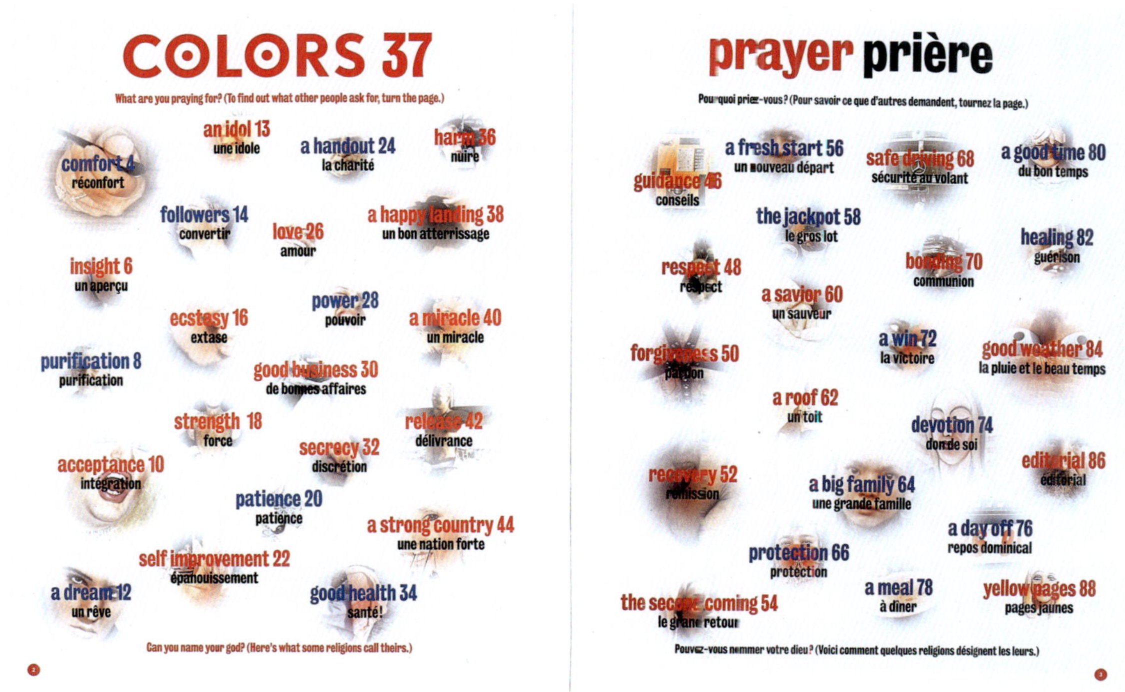

No.37 COVER

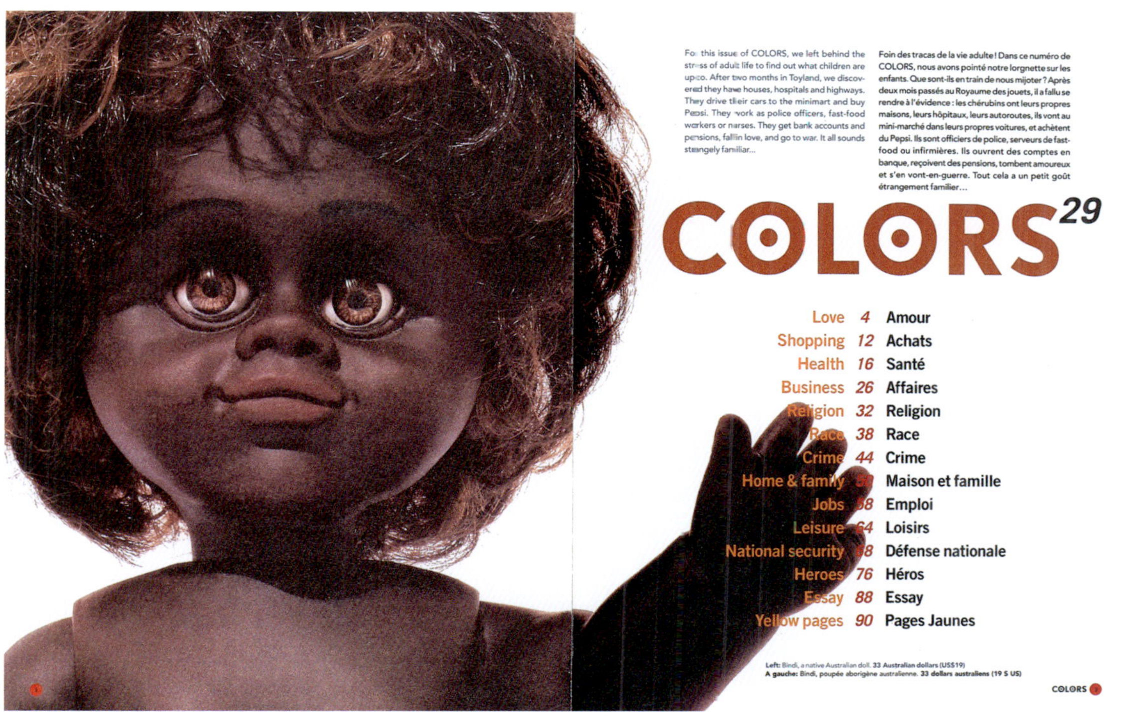

No.29 COVER

MAGAZINE 雑誌

CASA BRUTUS SUMMER 1999 JAPAN

PB: Magazine House E: Kazuhiro Saito / Chieko Yoshiie AD: Yasushi Fujimoto (cap) Chief D: Kazuyoshi Komatsu D: Emu Tsunematsu / Yusuke Nagumo / Mitsuko Watanabe I: Jean-Philippe Delhome(COVER) DF: Cap

CASA BRUTUS AUTUMN 1999 JAPAN

PB: Magazine House E: Kazuhiro Saito / Chieko Yoshiie AD: Yasushi Fujimoto (cap) Chief D: Kazuyoshi Komatsu D: Emu Tsunematsu / Yusuke Nagumo / Mitsuko Watanabe I: groovisions (COVER) DF: Cap

Casa BRUTUS

*features

012 Everybody's watching Northern Europe 今、世界中が北欧デザインに注目する理由。
●サローネで話題沸騰のデザイン集団はフィンランドの「スノークラッシュ」
●来日経験ゼロの建築家夫妻のモダン住宅は、なぜか日本風でした
●ヤコブセンがデザインした600万脚売れているデザインチェアからリゾートまで
●UFO住宅から宇宙人チェアまで、北欧は近未来デザインの宝庫です

045 the Tableware by Sori Yanagi 柳宗理の器はいかがですか？
●白磁土瓶や黒柄カトラリーが出来るまで、ロングインタビュー
●世界初、柳宗理のテーブルウェア全カタログ。しかも全商品プレゼント！

058 Tom Ford special interview トム・フォードとグッチをめぐる8人の建築家・デザイナー。

062 Salone Internazionale del Mobile '99 21世紀と暮らす家具を決めるミラノ・サローネ'99。

077 Fashion & Interior 海浜生活のニュースタンダード。

084 Grand Chef goes to the "DEPA-CHIKA" あのジョエル・ロブション氏もデパート食料品売場に驚く。

088 Everybody says "I love tofu" なにしろtofu好きなもので!!
●世界はすでに知っている。トーフは今やモードです
●いちばんおいしいのは？ 通の4人が絹・木綿・ざるを食べ較べ
●デパ地下で予約してまで豆腐を買う理由

151 Travel to Copenhagen, Denmark コペンハーゲン、北欧デザインのタイムカプセル。
●ウェグナー、ケアホルム……、椅子マニア垂涎の美術館、中古家具店
●ヤコブセンがデザインしたホテルへ
●デザイン好きが選んだ、コペンハーゲンで見るべき建築ベスト5

*regulars

007 Season's Greetings 世界各都市の夏を彩るお菓子。

037 News/on your fridge デザイン・建築etc.の最新ニュース。

109 a wall newspaper
●奈良智美のスペシャルイラストレーション
●速報／「スター・ウォーズ エピソード1」の家具&インテリア
●M・ヤング／X・ムラン／F・シモン／安藤忠雄×J・タレル／田辺誠一／松浦弥太郎／嶺川貴子／葉山考太郎／立川裕大／銅金裕司／都築響一／岸野正彦／A・マクドナルド／滝本 誠

121 Norimizu Ameya「owls room」「フクロウの頭部の3分の1くらいは目玉である」

128 Tokyo latest Movement フロム東京＃1。裏原宿を塗る、NGAP。

133 Living with Arts アートとしての器使い、陶磁器の壁と暮らす部屋。

139 a Fantastic Bookshelf & Cupboard 気になる本棚&食器棚「CHIC SIMPLE」編集者、キム・J＝グロス

143 Wine ワインセレブリティーに聞いた「20世紀を代表する銘柄、2000年を迎える銘柄」。

164 Home, where the beautiful rumors are. 世界の都市からの最新おバカ情報「いやん、バカンス♥」

166 Pet with Design パグ犬専用ルーム

1999 Summer/Renewal 3rd Issue
*3・6・9・12、各月1日発売（季刊）

Cover
illustration_Jean-Philippe Delhome
design_Yasushi Fujimoto+cap

© マガジンハウス 1999
禁・無断転載
©by King Features Syndicate, Inc.

「カーサ・ブルータス」「ブルータス」の出版情報は「BRUTUS ONLINE」でご覧になれます。
http://brutus.magazine.co.jp/

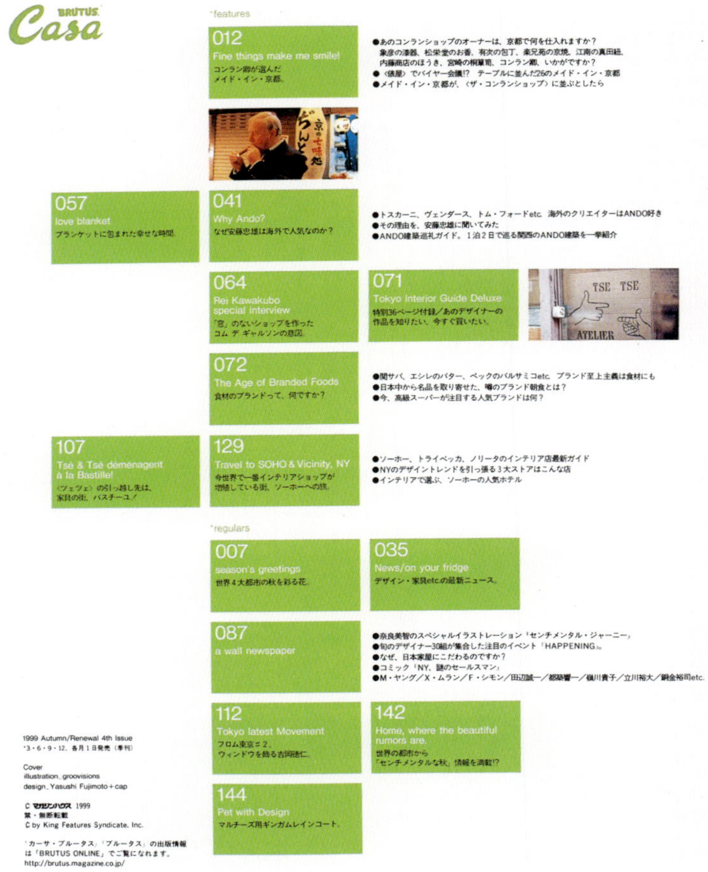
Casa BRUTUS

*features

012 Fine things make me smile! コンラン卿が選んだメイド・イン・京都。
●あのコンランショップのオーナーは、京都で何を仕入れますか？ 象彦の漆器、松栄堂のお香、有次の包丁、楽兄苑の京焼、江南の真田紐、内藤商店のほうき、宮崎の桐簞笥、コンラン卿、いかがですか？
●〈俵屋〉でバイヤー会議!? テーブルに並んだ26のメイド・イン・京都
●メイド・イン・京都が、〈ザ・コンランショップ〉に並ぶとしたら

057 love blanket ブランケットに包まれた幸せな時間。

041 Why Ando? なぜ安藤忠雄は海外で人気なのか？
●トスカーニ、ヴェンダース、トム・フォードetc. 海外のクリエイターはANDO好き
●その理由を、安藤忠雄に聞いてみた
●ANDO建築巡礼ガイド。1泊2日で巡る関西のANDO建築を一挙紹介

064 Rei Kawakubo special interview「窓」のないショップを作ったコム デ ギャルソンの意図。

071 Tokyo Interior Guide Deluxe 特別36ページ付録／あのデザイナーの作品を知りたい、今すぐ買いたい。

072 The Age of Branded Foods 食材のブランドって、何ですか？
●関サバ、エシレのバター、ペックのバルサミコetc. ブランド至上主義は食材にも
●日本中から名品を取り寄せた、噂のブランド朝食とは？
●今、高級スーパーが注目する人気ブランドは何？

107 Tsé & Tsé déménagent à la Bastille! 〈ツェツェ〉の引っ越し先は、家具の街、バスチーユ！

129 Travel to SOHO & Vicinity, NY 今世界で一番インテリアショップが増殖している街、ソーホーへの旅。
●ソーホー、トライベッカ、ノリータのインテリア店最新ガイド
●NYのデザイントレンドを引っ張る3大ストアはこんな店
●インテリアで選ぶ、ソーホーの人気ホテル

*regulars

007 season's greetings 世界4大都市の秋を彩る花。

035 News/on your fridge デザイン・家具etc.の最新ニュース。

087 a wall newspaper
●奈良美智のスペシャルイラストレーション「センチメンタル・ジャーニー」
●旬のデザイナー30組が集合した注目のイベント「HAPPENING」。
●なぜ、日本家屋にこだわるのですか？
●コミック「NY、謎のセールスマン」
●M・ヤング／X・ムラン／F・シモン／田辺誠一／都築響一／嶺川貴子／立川裕大／銅金裕司etc.

112 Tokyo latest Movement フロム東京＃2。ウィンドウを飾る吉岡徳仁。

142 Home, where the beautiful rumors are. 世界の都市から「センチメンタルな秋」情報を満載!?

144 Pet with Design マルチーズ用ギンガムレインコート。

1999 Autumn/Renewal 4th Issue
*3・6・9・12、各月1日発売（季刊）

Cover
illustration_groovisions
design_Yasushi Fujimoto+cap

© マガジンハウス 1999
禁・無断転載
© by King Features Syndicate, Inc.

「カーサ・ブルータス」「ブルータス」の出版情報は「BRUTUS ONLINE」でご覧になれます。
http://brutus.magazine.co.jp/

SUMMER 1999 COVER

AUTUMN 1999 COVER

CATALOG カタログ

LIFE WITH IDÉE VOL.2 1997 JAPAN CL: IDÉE Co., Ltd. AD: Kaoru Watanabe D: Katsunori Hironaka P: Noboru Morikawa

LIFE WITH IDÉE VOL.3 1999 JAPAN CL: IDÉE Co., Ltd. AD,D: Kaoru Watanabe D: Miya Nishio P: Masayuki Hayashi

Life with IDÉE
C O N T E N T S

Vol. 02 COVER

CONTENTS

VOL. 03 COVER

MAGAZINE 雑誌

RELAX VOL.38 APRIL 2000 JAPAN
PB: Magazine House E: Hitoshi Okamoto AD: Eisaku Ono (NANA) D: Hideyuki Yamano (NANA) I: Eric Haze (COVER)
P: Ivory Serra (CONTENTS)

RELAX VOL.40 JUNE 2000 JAPAN
PB: Magazine House E: Hitoshi Okamoto AD: Eisaku Ono (NANA) D: Hideyuki Yamano (NANA) / Yoko Komatsu (NANA)
I: Eric Haze (COVER) P: P.M.Ken (CONTENTS)

table of contents

001 cover artwork by mark gonzales
004 wanna relax ? ワナ・リラックス__ホンマタカシ
006 sit back, relax, and enjoy !
009 bad news バッド・ニュース__
スターバックス__ジェリー・スプリンガー__ルイジ・コラーニ__焼肉
018 man watching マン・ウォッチング
022 art for all みんなのアート__畠山直哉
026 a girl like you 君になりたい__奥菜 恵
030 i love t-shirts アイ・ラヴ・T-シャツ
046 mark gonzales マーク・ゴンザレス
060 best must hit shit ベスト・マスト・ヒット・シット__NB
066 grv numbers 今月のGRVナンバー__グルーヴィジョンズ
068 what the hell is lomo ? ロモ通信__ロンドン編
070 curiosity killed the ape 帰ってきたコーネリアスの惑星見学__小山田圭吾
074 victory road to uno shoten 宇野商店への道__宇野 薫
076 sunday people サンデー・ピープル__奥田民生
090 relax boy リラックス・ボーイ__渋谷直角
091 fab ! columns for man in café ファブ！
108 cinérelax シネ・リラックス__ストップ・メイキング・センス
112 nigo's general seminar ジェネラル・セミナー__NIGO
116 relaxin' with リラクシン・ウィズ__UES
122 fighting seminar 格闘センセイ__格闘するTシャツ
126 king of kings of kids 学級王__J-ロープ
128 welcome to my castle オレの城へようこそ__イケてる将棋バカの世界
130 racing journal レーシング・ジャーナル__AIR
132 freestyle フリースタイル__バブルス
134 nana なあなあ__サバンナ
136 see ya ! またネ！__若木信吾
138 how to make a relaxing place__リラックスな事の始末

38

relax

wasn't born to follow !
monthly
april 2000

www.relaxmag.com

table of contents

001 cover artwork by Eric Haze
004 wanna relax ? ワナ・リラックス__ホンマタカシ
006 sit back, relax, and enjoy !__五木田智央
009 bad news バッド・ニュース__
レゴ×SOPH.__シナモンロール__NASDA__焼肉
018 man watching マン・ウォッチング
022 art for all みんなのアート__エリック・ヘイズ
028 a girl like you 君になりたい__柴咲コウ
032 mobile life, modern life モバイル馬鹿
048 grv numbers 今月のGRVナンバー__グルーヴィジョンズ
050 what the hell is lomo ? ロモ通信__オシラセ、ホウコク編
052 curiosity killed the ape 帰ってきたコーネリアスの惑星見学__小山田圭吾
054 nigo's general seminar. ジェネラル・セミナー__NIGO
056 our favorite shop アワ・フェイヴァリット・ショップ__リリー・フランキー
058 i love sticker 貼って貼って貼りたおせ!
072 cinérelax シネ・リラックス__ハピネス
076 sunday people サンデー・ピープル__トミー・ゲレロ
090 ltd. edt. LTD. EDT.__ジェームス・ラヴェル
091 fab ! columns for man in café ファブ！
108 best must hit shit ベスト・マスト・ヒット・シット__吉田カバン
116 relaxin' with リラクシン・ウィズ__リトル・テンポ
122 fighting seminar 格闘センセイ__マッハvs.ごっちゃん
126 king of kings of kids 学級王__ロボカップ・トイズ
128 welcome to my castle オレの城へようこそ__デジタルペットたちの部屋
130 racing journal レーシング・ジャーナル__カート・ウォレイス、エリック・カーター
132 freestyle フリースタイル__岡野寛
134 nana なあなあ__松本零士
136 see ya ! またネ！__若木信吾
138 how to make a relaxing place__リラックスな事の始末

特別付録
シール×2シート 全49種類

40

relax

wasn't born to follow !

No.38 COVER

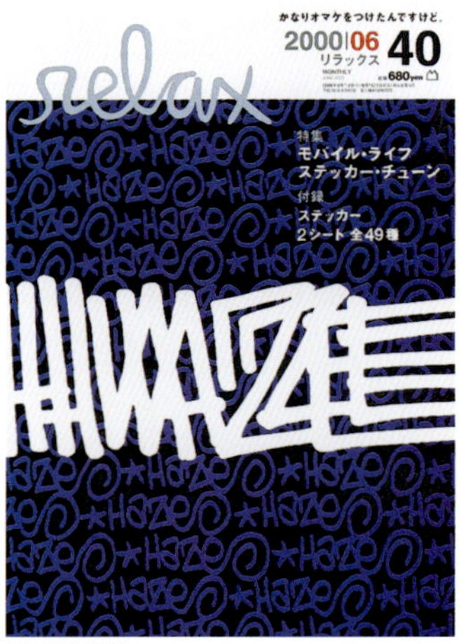

No.40 COVER

BOOK 書籍

GASBOOK 6　1999　JAPAN　PB: DesignEXchange Co., Ltd.　CD,AD: Akira Natsume　D: Hideki Inaba

MAGAZINE 雑誌

RELUCKS　1999　JAPAN　E: Chokkaku Shibuya / Shogo Kawabata / Masaru Kato　AD,D: tgb design

GASBOOK COVER

RELUCKS COVER

TRACE URBAN CULTURE MAGAZINE NO.3 1998 GREECE CL,CD,AD,DF: Altervision D: Tasos Efremidis / Apostolos Rizos / Dimitris Mitsiopoulos / Klimis Mastoridis

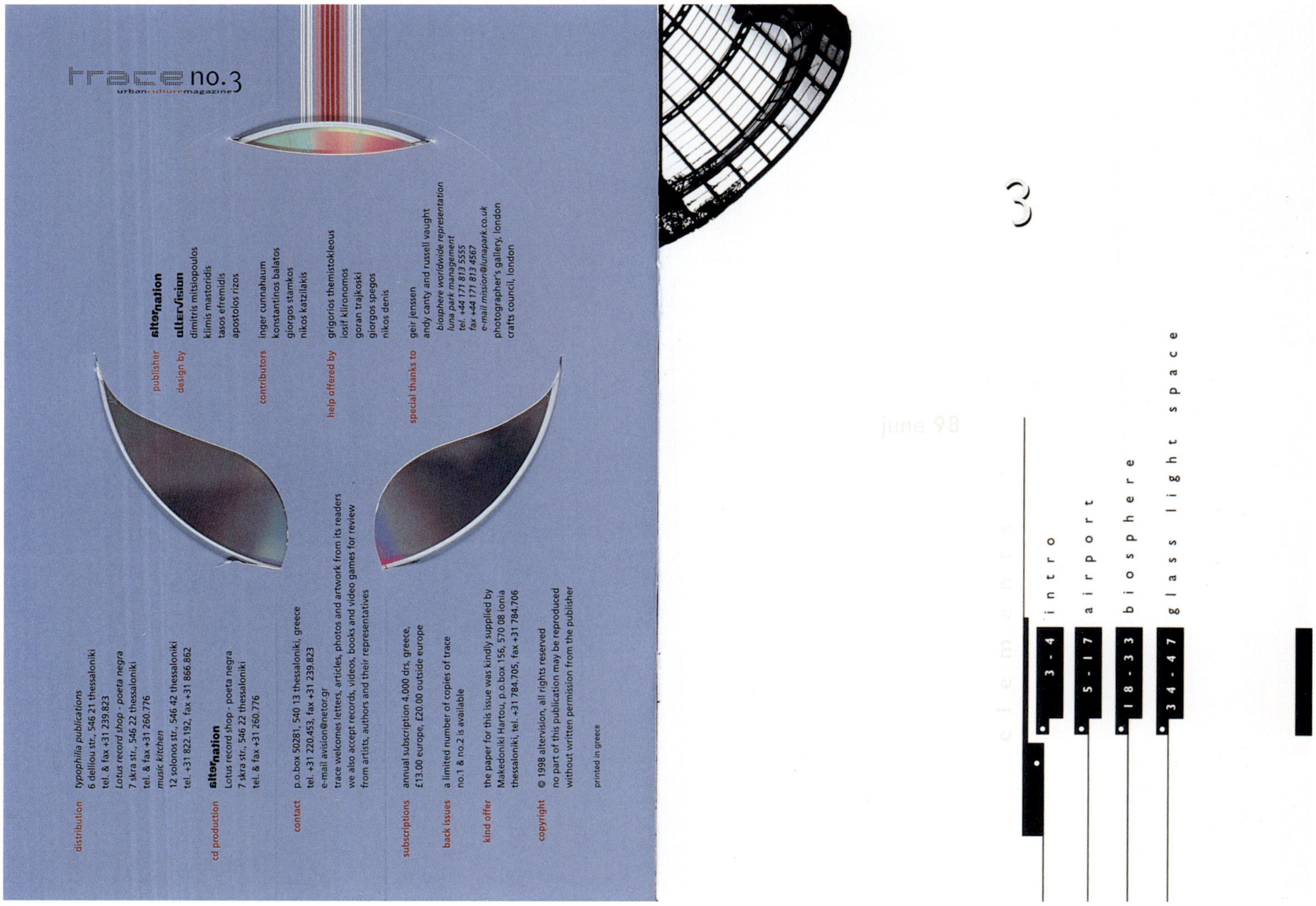

trace no.3
urban culture magazine

publisher alternation

design by altervision
dimitris mitsiopoulos
klimis mastoridis
tasos efremidis
apostolos rizos

contributors inger cunnahaum
konstantinos balatos
giorgos stamkos
nikos katzilakis

help offered by grigorios themistokleous
iosif klironomos
goran trajkoski
giorgos spegos
nikos denis

special thanks to geir jenssen
andy canty and russell vaught
biosphere worldwide representation
luna park management
tel. +44 171 813 5555
fax +44 171 813 4567
e-mail mission@lunapark.co.uk
photographer's gallery, london
crafts council, london

distribution *typophilia publications*
6 delliou str., 546 21 thessaloniki
tel. & fax +31 239.823
Lotus record shop - poeta negra
7 skra str., 546 22 thessaloniki
tel. & fax +31 260.776
music kitchen
12 solonos str., 546 42 thessaloniki
tel. +31 822.192, fax +31 866.862

cd production alternation
Lotus record shop - poeta negra
7 skra str., 546 22 thessaloniki
tel. & fax +31 260.776

contact p.o.box 50281, 540 13 thessaloniki, greece
tel. +31 220.453, fax +31 239.823
e-mail avision@netor.gr
trace welcomes letters, articles, photos and artwork from its readers
we also accept records, videos, books and video games for review
from artists, authors and their representatives

subscriptions annual subscription 4.000 drs, greece,
£13.00 europe, £20.00 outside europe

back issues a limited number of copies of trace
no.1 & no.2 is available

kind offer the paper for this issue was kindly supplied by
Makedoniki Hartou, p.o.box 156, 570 08 ionia
thessaloniki, tel. +31 784.705, fax +31 784.706

copyright © 1998 altervision, all rights reserved
no part of this publication may be reproduced
without written permission from the publisher

printed in greece

3

june 98

elements

3 - 4 intro
5 - 17 airport
18 - 33 biosphere
34 - 47 glass light space

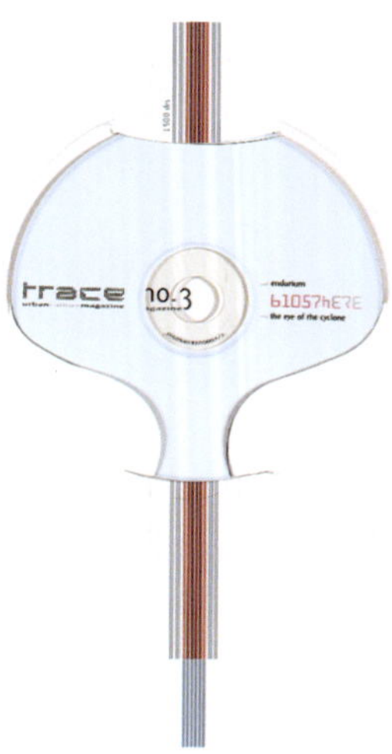

No.03 COVER

TRACE URBAN CULTURE MAGAZINE NO.2 1996 GREECE CL,CD,AD,DF: A tervision D: Tasos Efremidis / Apostolos Rizos / Dimitris Mitsiopoulos / Klimis Mastoridis

No.02 COVER

MAGAZINE 雑誌

SYNOPSIS NO.6 SPRING 2000 FRANCE PB,CW: Synopsis Sarl E: Hervé Lavergne CD,AD,D,TY: Stéphane Vrielinck AD,D,TY: Thierry Chapuy / Jean-Patrice Wattinne I: Di Marco (COVER) P: Dunn Meas (CONTENTS) CD,DF: L'Éclaireur

Sommaire synopsis

Actualités 8
14 Séries américaines
18 Cinéma américain
22 Scénaristes en action !
26 Concours et formations

30 Avant-première : le nouveau scénario de Jean-Jacques Beineix

36 Raconter une histoire vraie
Le fait divers à la télévision et au cinéma
38 A l'origine était le réel
46 Révéler l'invisible pour filmer le réel
52 L'affaire Romand
54 Faut-il être flic pour écrire un polar ?
57 La presse : un nouveau filon pour Hollywood

Cinéma
60 "Le Petit Voleur", un film uppercut
66 Maupassant scénariste ?
68 Quatre mains et deux scénarios
72 Les scénaristes au cinéma
74 Le petite fabrique du spectateur
76 Dominique Cabrera
80 Pasolini scénariste
82 Le scénario selon John Irving

5

Sommaire synopsis

84 Ecriture
Construire le temps du récit
88 Alain Minier
90 L'inceste
94 Raymond Scénar
96 Les amants du Petit-Pont
102 Ecriture publicitaire
106 Bande dessinée
108 Ecriture interactive

110 Edition
Eric-Emmanuel Schmitt
116 Bon anniversaire, Le Poulpe !
118 Coups de cœur des éditeurs
121 Contrats

122 Guide
Concours et aides
Formations
124 Bibliothèques
125 Droits
126 Abécédaire du scénariste
128 Scénarédités
129 Internet

130 Le mot de la fin
Bernard Loiseau

SYNOPSIS
LA REVUE DU SCENARIO
BIMESTRIEL
38, rue du faubourg Saint-Jacques, 75014 Paris.
Tél. : 01.53.10.20.70 - Fax : 01.53.10.20.71.
www.6nop6.com

Directeur de la publication : Alban Sauvanet.
Fondateurs-Comité éditorial : Laurent Daniélou, Patrice Hoffmann, Hervé Lavergne, Alban Sauvanet, Jean-Luc Seigle.
Rédacteur en chef : Laurent Delmas.
Rédactrice en chef adjointe : Béatrice de Mondenard.

Direction artistique : Stéphane Vrielinck, Thierry Chapuy, Jean-Patrice Wattinne (l'éclaireur) assistés de Mafalda.
Editeur : Hervé Lavergne.
Secrétaire de rédaction : Isabelle Alvaresse.
Editrice déléguée chargée de la communication : Sylvie Vallon.
Marketing et promotion : Mélanie Chandelier.
Développement : Micheline Oerlemans.
Evénements : Marie-France Chatrier, Sabrina Botbol.

Ont collaboré à ce numéro :
Cécile Berger, Séverine Biolatto-Gautier, Caroline Bongrand, Pascale Borenstein, Frédéric Bosser, Sandrine Bouillot, Marie-France Briselance, Angelo Cianci, Emmanuel Ethis, Guillemette Faure, Patricia de Figueirédo, Anna Fregonese, Valérie Ganne, David Haeberli, Patrice Hoffmann, Luc Jabon, Olivier du Jaunet, Laurie Laufer, Hervé Lavergne, Bernard Loiseau, Marie Marvier, Dominique Monrocq, Jean-Claude Morin, Ludovic Plon-Dumas, Julien Rappeneau, Véronique Richebois, Juliette Sales, Raymond Scénar.

SYNOPSIS abonnements :
Muriel du Serre-Telmon. Tél. : 01 44 84 84 89
D.I.P - 70, rue Compans, 75019 Paris.

Responsable du site www.6nop6.com :
Sandrine Bouillot. webmaster@6nop6.com

SYNOPSIS Publicité :
Marc Grand, Benoît de Maigret, Jean-Christophe Mikhaïloff (Institutionnel Médias).
23, rue Faidherbe - 75011 Paris.
Tél. : 01.40.24.16.67 - Fax : 01.40.24.25.64.

SYNOPSIS, la revue du scénario, est édité par la société Synopsis sarl au capital de 50 000 FF RCS B 420 167 660.
© Tous droits de reproduction réservés.
Commission paritaire : 0704 K 78941.
Dépot légal : à parution - **ISSN :** 1291-2328.
Distribution France et étranger : NMPP.
Ventes aux libraires : DIF'POP'.
Tél. : 01.40.24.21.31.
Impression : Dulac Imprimeries / Pacy-sur-Eure.
Flashage/photogravure : Quadratin.

Ce numéro comporte un encart abonnement 2 pages broché pour l'ensemble de la diffusion et un encart jeté pour la diffusion abonnement.

Couverture : Di Marco.
© Di Marco

La revue décline toute responsabilité quant aux manuscrits et photos qui lui sont envoyés.

Photo : © Dunn Meas

7

No.06 COVER

MAGAZINE 雑誌

SYNOPSIS NO.5 WINTER 2000 FRANCE

PB,CW: Synopsis Sarl E: Hervé Lavergne CD,AD,D,TY: Stéphane Vrielinck AD,D,TY: Thierry Chapuy / Jean-Patrice Wattinne
P: Marianne Rosenstiehl/H&K (COVER) / Jean-Marie Leroy/H&K (CONTENTS P.7) / Debra Kellner (CONTENTS P.9)
CD,DF: L'Éclaireur

CONTENTS P. 7

CONTENTS P. 9

No.05 COVER

MAGAZINE 雑誌

LINE SPRING 2000 UK PB: TIME Life Entertainment Group Ltd. E: Tyler Brûlé / Tim Clark CD: Herbert Winkler AD: Richard Spencer Powell D: Sam Wilson TY: Fidel Peugeot@RGB107-6.com P: Jimmy Backius ST: Eddie Schachnow HM: Sabrina B Paul (CONTENTS)

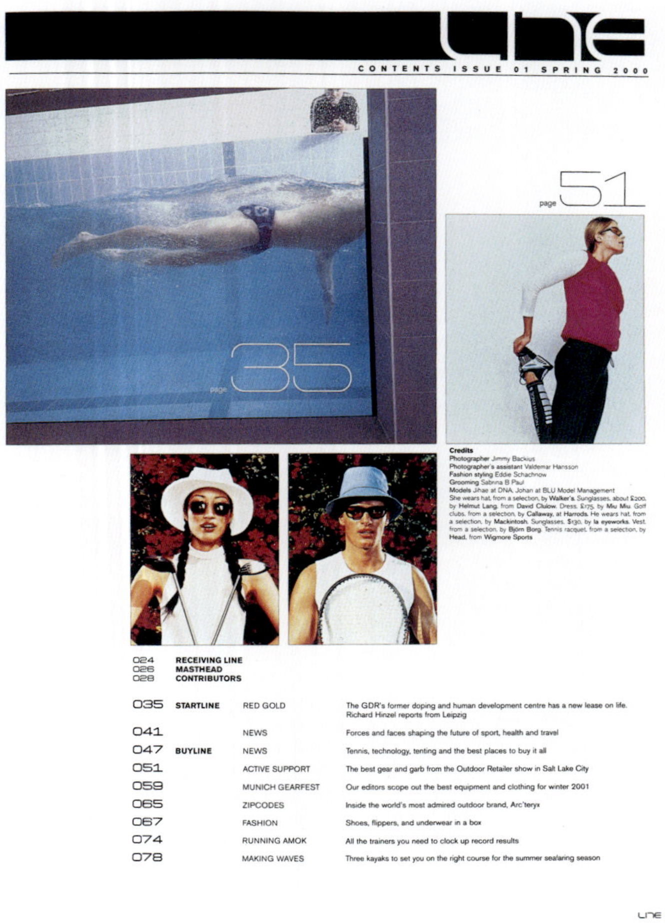

CONTENTS ISSUE 01 SPRING 2000

page 35

page 51

Credits
Photographer Jimmy Backius
Photographer's assistant Valdemar Hansson
Fashion styling Eddie Schachnow
Grooming Sabrina B Paul
Models Jihae at DNA, Johan at BLU Model Management
She wears hat, from a selection, by **Walker's**. Sunglasses, about £200, by **Helmut Lang**, from **David Clulow**. Dress, £175, by **Miu Miu**. Golf clubs, from a selection, by **Callaway, at Harrods**. He wears hat, from a selection, by **Mackintosh**. Sunglasses, $130, by **la eyeworks**. Vest, from a selection, by **Björn Borg**. Tennis racquet, from a selection, by **Head**, from **Wigmore Sports**

LINE 13

CONTENTS ISSUE 01 SPRING 2000

page 74

page 132

page 82

16 LINE

COVER

DAZED & CONFUSED VOL.66 JUNE 2000 UK PB: Dazed & Confused E: Jefferson Hack Photographic Director: Emma Reeves AD: Martin Bell P: Alexei Hay (COVER)
ST: Jason Farrer (COVER) HM: Marcos "Reggae" Smith (COVER)

CONTENT 66/01

WWW.CONFUSED.CO.UK
INDEPENDENT THINKING IN A DEPENDENT WORLD

MAIN CONTENTS

FASHION

PHOTOGRAPHY **ALEXEI HAY**
STYLING **JASON FARRER**
GROOMING **MARCOS** "REGGAE"
SMITH AT **4 LIFE BARBER STUDIO**
THANKS TO **CAROLINA GONZALEZ**

EMIMEM WEARS DENIM SHIRT BY
TRIPPLE FIVE SOUL

RETOUCHING ON BOTH COVERS **THE SHOEMAKERS ELVES**

INFORMATION

CONTENT 66/02

WWW.CONFUSED.CO.UK
INDEPENDENT THINKING IN A DEPENDENT WORLD

DISINFORMATION

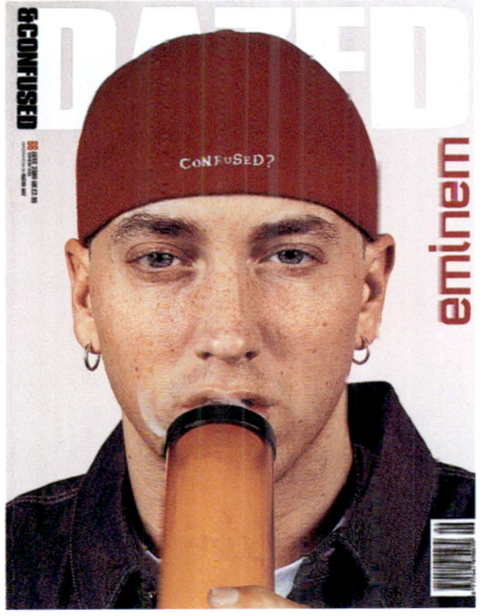

COVER

© 2000 20TH CENTURY FOX

CONTENTS

表紙の顔＝レオナルド・ディカプリオ
いよいよ4月22日に日本公開が迫りました、レオナルド・ディカプリオ主演の『ザ・ビーチ』！ 原作はベストセラー小説、監督は『トレインスポッティング』のダニー・ボイルという話題性もさることながら、やはり最大の見どころはレオが『タイタニック』以来はじめて出演作に選んだ映画だということでしょう。そこで今月のCUTでは、『ザ・ビーチ』の撮影秘話はもちろんのこと、知られざる子供時代、私生活、そして世界中の女性が熱狂する"レオ現象"にいたるまでをレオ自身が語り下ろした完全保存版インタビューを、美麗フォトの数々とともにお届けします！
© Cover Photograph by Patrick Demarchalier

Cut

CONTENTS

MAY 2000 NO.102 カット5月号／月刊／定価690円

発行人＝渋谷陽一
Publisher＝YOICHI SHIBUYA
編集人＝佐藤健
Editor in Chief＝KEN SATO
編集＝稲田浩／粉川しの／茂倉正樹／藤本敦子
Editors＝HIROSHI INADA / SHINO KOKAWA / MASAKI MOCHIKURA / ATSUKO FUJIMOTO
編集協力＝上田智子／小野寺佐登美
Associate Editors＝TOMOKO UEDA / SATOMI ONODERA
橋中佐和／中村明美／小田島久恵／佐藤久理子
SAWA HASHINAKA / AKEMI NAKAMURA / HISAE ODASHIMA / KURIKO SATO
高野裕子／小西未来／島田陽子／片岡さと美
YUKO TAKANO / MIRAI KONISHI / YOKO SHIMADA / SATOMI KATAOKA
岩田桃子／竹澤彩子／原口紀子
MOMOKO IWATA / AYAKO TAKEZAWA / NORIKO HARAGUCHI
翻訳＝内瀬戸久司
Translator＝HISASHI UCHISETO
協力＝ナナ通信／インペリアル・プレス・ジャパン
Co-operation＝NANA TSUSHIN / IPJ
ユニフォト・プレス／PPS通信社
UNIPHOTO PRESS / PPS
印刷＝大日本印刷株式会社
Printing＝DAINIPPON PRINTING CO., LTD.

アート・ディレクション＆デザイン＝中島英樹
Art Direction & Design＝HIDEKI NAKAJIMA for NAKAJIMA DESIGN CO.,LTD. TEL.03-5489-1757
デザイン＝中島デザイン：前田淳二
Design＝JUNJI MAEDA for NAKAJIMA DESIGN

発行＝（株）ロッキング・オン
〒150-8569 東京都渋谷区桜丘町20-1 渋谷インフォスタワー19F
Published by ROCKIN' ON INC.
Shibuya Infoss tower 19F, 20-1 Sakuragaoka-cho, Shibuya-ku, TOKYO, JAPAN ZIP 150-8569
TEL.03-5458-3031 FAX.03-5458-3040
http://www.rock-net.co.jp

COVER

photograph by Gen Inaba

photograph by Risaku Suzuki

Esquire 5
MAY. 2000 Vol.14 No.5
cover photograph by Risaku Suzuki
art direction by Hisashi Sakurai

COVER

MENSWORK MAGAZINE 1998 USA CL: American Crew CD,P: David Raccuglia AD: Marcos Chavez D: Aimee Sealfon CW: Kurt Kueffner / Terry Lane / Craig Hanson DF: Liska + Associates, Inc.

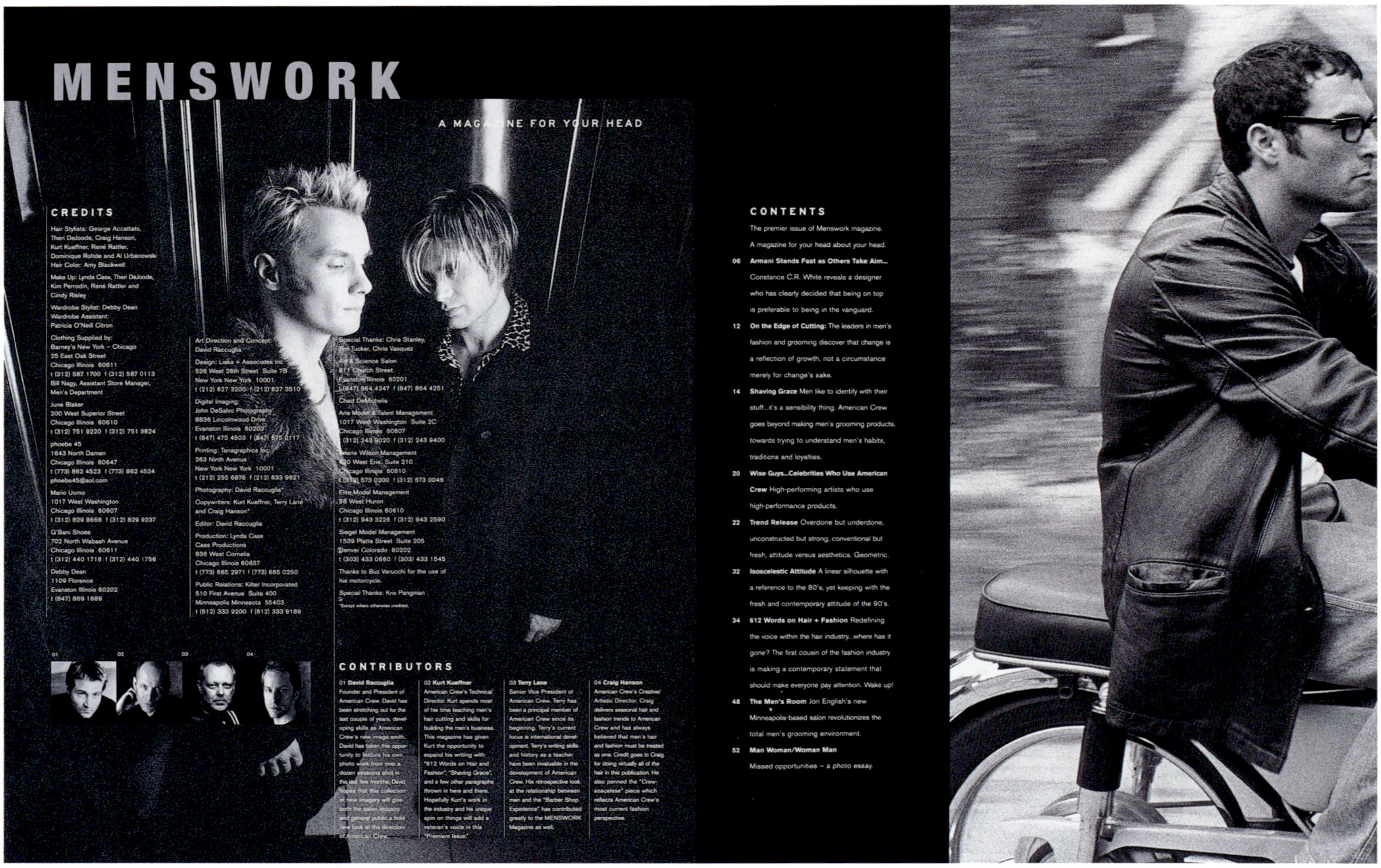

COVER

ASIA PACIFIC LEATHER FAIR '97 AUTUMN & WINTER COLLECTION 1997 HONG KONG

CL: Italian Trade Commission CD,AD: Eric Chan D,I: Lo Chi Ming
P: Stephen Cheung DF: Eric Chan Design Co. Ltd.

CONTeNTS

page no.

COVER

TOKION NO.18　MAY 2000　JAPAN　PB: Knee High Media Japan　E: Kaori Sakurai　AD,D: Takaya Toyama　P: Yoshiko Seino (COVER)

CONTENTS

ROOTS

Cover Credits
Photography: YOSHIKO SEINO
COVER DESIGN: TAKAYA TOYAMA (knowork)

JUICY FRUITS

Livingtype, Iwama Satoshi, Quietstorm, Love Fashion, Dario Robleto, Tokion 4×4 Bilboard Project, Blackalicious, Dublab, Mumbleboy

WOODY LIFE

"Trees sure are nice." I think about trees this way. I feel the spirit of trees. They are alive. Even after they're made into other things, they will continue to live and breath. As long as our world is around, and along as there are people who continue to think about them.....
Photography: Yasuhide Kuge

SIMPLY DELECTABLE

Edible clothes? Clothing from food? It's fashion with a scent. The kind of perfume that carries the passage of history. But it's not the kind that brings about relaxation, It's an immediate, real fragrance that comes floating in.
Photography: Dino Dinco

HIROSHI TOMURA

Cherry blossoms fluttter down like snowflakes, a beautiful sound from their continual fall. Everything is just right. And now it's Tom's turn. Through that door awaits the ever growing world of Hiroshi Tomura.
Photography: Kyoji Takahashi

STAN LEE

Strong, kind, an ally to the people. This has been the definition of "superhero" for a looooong time. But what kind of people are heros in real life? Let's find out from the source himself, Marvel Comics creator Stan Lee.

OVER GRAY, FIELD BLUE

We went looking for our roots, and came upon a series of unpredictable encounters. The scenery felt like the memory of a place long since passed. We took the clothing of Ozone Rocks to the people of the Naxi tribe. It was the overlap of our world and theirs, but everything seemed right.
Photography: Tetsuya Yamamoto

COLUMNS

Arty-Oni Koichi: Chida and Midori Araki
Tokion Kids Camera: Action Punch + Ema
Han-Ken: Yuki Fujita
Time Dokan: Masaomi Takaba
Salon de Apron: Sen Watanabe
3AP: 3 Art Project

Review: CD, Game, Web
Tokion News

目 次

ルーツ

Cover Credits
Photography: 清野賀子
COVER DESIGN: 遠山隆哉（knowork）

ジューシーフルーツ

岩間賢、Blackalicious、Dario Robleto、Quietstorm、Love Fashion、Dublab、Mumbleboy、Livingtype、Tokion 4+4 Bilboard Project

ウッディライフ

「木はいいなあ」本気でそんなことを考えました。本気で木の気を感じました。木は生きています。伐採されても、加工されても、木はいつまでも生きています。地球が存在するかぎり、木を想い続ける人間が地球に存在するかぎり‥‥。
写真：久家靖秀

シンプリーディレクティブ

食べられる服?! 食べ物の服?! 匂いのあるファッション企画。気どった香水の香りでも、リラクゼーション効果のある香りでもなく、とても身近でとても現実的な食べ物の匂い。プンプンプンプン漂ってきます。
写真：Dino Dinco

戸村 浩

ハラハラと舞う桜吹雪、淡々と流れる美しいサウンド。さ〜て、準備はOKです。あとはトムさんの出番を待つだけです。扉の向こうには造形美術家、戸村浩さんの世界が広がっています。
写真：高橋恭司

スタン・リー

強くって、やさしくって、正義の味方。これが古代からず〜っと守られ続けているヒーローの定義。でも一体本物のヒーローってどんな人? マーヴェル・コミックスのクリエーターの考える真のヒーローとは‥‥?

オーバーグレイ、フィールドブルー

ルーツ探しに出た旅は、思い掛けない偶然と思い掛けない出会いの連続でした。初めての地に広がる見覚えのある風景。OZONE ROCKSの洋服をさりげなく着こなすナシ族の人々。この旅の体験が前世の記憶にぴったり重なり合ったことは言うまでもありません。
写真：山本哲也

コラム

Arty-Oni：チダコウイチ+アラキミドリ
Tokyo Kids Camera：アクションパンチ+EMA
HAN-KEN：藤田雄己
タイムドカン：vol.1++++鷹羽正臣
salon de apron：渡辺宣
3AP：3 ART PROJECT
ATTIC：富樫信也+及川亘(LUNCH FOR EAR)
愛のセメント劇場：アントニオ・デザイン・サービス
Color Peace：浅野佳枝&住田芽衣+ピエール瀧
INNER TREASURE：石山義明(PHUNK INC.)
新婚ギリシャ神話：天明晃太郎+白根ゆたんぽ
Un apres-midi des messieurs：nonchalantes
漫画：佐々木「ドワーフ」三朗

レビュー：CD、ゲーム、ウェブ
トキオンニュース

COVER

TOKION

TOKION MAGAZINE / KNEE HIGH MEDIA / No.18

THE FOUNDERS

Publisher.................... Lucas Badtke-Berkow ルーカス・ビー・ビー
Co-Publisher............... Adam Glickman アダム・グリックマン

THE CREW

Editor-In-Chief............ Kaori Sakurai 櫻井香織
Editor.......................... Peter Wilson ピーター・ウイルソン
Art Director................. Takaya Toyama 遠山隆哉（knowork）
Designers.................... Jerry Ukai ジェリー鵜飼（antonio design service）
Hideaki Komiyama 小宮山秀明（TGB design）
Kevin Lyons ケビン・リオンズ
Office Manager........... Taku Harano, Lanha Hong-Porretta 原野拓、ランハ・ホン・ペレッタ
Printing Director.......... Yoshiya Sasou 佐宗良哉（DAI NIPPON PRINTING CO,LTD.）

TRANSLATORS

Kaori Yoshida, Miki Hayashi, Taro Nettleton, Kay Miyake, Haruna Ito

ADVERTISING

*JAPAN......................... Junko Sakamoto 坂本純子
telephone: +81-3-5469-9318 fax: +81-3-5469-5656

*USA .... Janet Halter ジャネット・ハルター
telephone: +1-213-626-7332 fax: +1-213-626-7521

CIRCULATION

*JAPAN
Resonance Publishing LTD.
6-19-3 J6 Building 8F Jingumae, Shibuya-ku 150-0001
TEL 03-5766-1171 FAX 03-5766-1177
e-mail: info@resonance.co.jp

*USA
Big Top
1990 Lombard St suite 100 SF, CA 94123.
TEL 415-447-4284
tracie@bigtoppubs.com

*HONG KONG
Seven Hills Limited
RM 701-4, Hang Seng Wanchai Building 200 Hennessy Road, Wanchai, H.K.
TEL 2893-1393 FAX 2838-8745
E-mail: contact@citymagazine.com.hk

*UK
K's Communications Inc.
lap@kscom.netkonect.co.uk
TEL/FAX 0181-983-4054

EDITORIAL OFFICES

KNEE HIGH MEDIA JAPAN, INC./ TOKION HEAD OFFICE
#101 Wood House 1-11-3 Higashi Shibuya-ku, Tokyo 150-0011 Japan
TEL: 81-3-5469-9318 FAX: 81-3-5469-5656
URL: http://www.tokion.com E-mail: tokion@ari.bekkoame.ne.jp

KNEE HIGH MEDIA US, INC./ TOKION US OFFICE
939 1/2 Chung King Rd. Los Angeles, CA 90012, USA
TEL: 1-213-626-7332 FAX: 1-213-626-7521
URL: http//:www.tokionusa.com E-mail: mail@tokionusa.com

HONG KONG DESK
Seven Hills Limited
RM 701-4, Hang Seng Wanchai Building 200 Hennessy Road, Wanchai, H.K.
TEL 2893-1393 FAX 2838-8745
E-mail: contact@citymagazine.com.hk

SUBSCRIPTIONS:

*JAPAN
1 year 10,000 Yen (6 issues + T-shirt) 1年契約：¥10,000
2 years 20,000 Yen (12 issues + T-shirt) 2年契約：¥18,000
Send Japanese Yen only via post office to: 郵便振替口座：10180-7421830
#101 Wood House 1-11-3 Higashi Shibuya-ku, Tokyo 150-0011 （有）ニーハイメディア・ジャパン

*USA/CANADA
1 year $30/ $45 (6 issues + CD)
2 years $55/ $85 (12 issues + CD)
Send US check or money order dollars only to: 939 1/2 Chung King Rd Los Angeles, CA 90012

ALL OTHER COUNTRIES
1 year $112 (6 issues + T-shirt)
2 years $199 (12 issues + T-shirt)
Send post office money orders only to: #101 Wood House 1-11-3 Higashi Shibuya-ku, Tokyo 150-0011.

TOKION ROOTS ISSUE 2000年6月1日 通巻18号
定価／国内 980円（税込）アメリカ 4,95ドル カナダ 6,50ドル イギリス 6,95ポンド
発行／ニーハイメディア・ジャパン
〒150-0011 東京都渋谷区東1-11-3ウッドハウス101 TEL:03-5469-9318 FAX:03-5469-5656
発売／（株）レゾナンス
〒150-0001 東京都渋谷区神宮前6-19-13J6ビル8F TEL:03-5766-1171 FAX:03-5766-1177
印刷／大日本印刷株式会社 ISBN4-947735-28-7 C0470 Y934E
©2000 Knee High Media Japan Inc. 禁無断転載

TCC high quality photographic printing　FUJIFILM

TOKION IS A FICTIONAL WORD MEANING THE SOUND OF NOW. TOKION IS PUBLISHED BIMONTHLY BY KNEE HIGH MEDIA KNEE HIGH MEDIA. REPRODUCTION IN WHOLE OR PART WITHOUT PRIOR WRITTEN PERMISSION FROM THE PUBLISHERS IS STRICTLY PROHIBITED. TOKION WELCOMES SUBMISSIONS BUT CANNOT BE HELD RESPONSIBLE FOR UNSOLICITED MATERIAL. PRINTED IN JAPAN. REPRINTED IN CANADA AND HONG KONG.

WIDESCREEN: MUSIC, STYLE, PEOPLE, ART　時音トキオンマガジン

HANAJIKAN AUGUST 1999 JAPAN PB: Kadokawa Shoten Publishing Co., Ltd. E: Fumiko Sugamoto AD: Issen Okamoto D: Naoko Onoda / Michiko Kobayashi

花時間

Hanajikan August 1999 Number 95 Contents

総力特集

暑い夏がやってきます。夏を涼しく過ごすための工夫を、「青」をテーマに考えてみました。青い花のあしらい、青い器のカタログ、夏のギフトのラッピングアイデア…など、いろいろな「青」の情報をお届けします。クールで快適、そして美しい夏のための青の世界、お楽しみに。

夏、青と暮らす

表紙 暑い夏を涼しく過ごすために、「青」を生かしたアイデアを集めました。青い花で涼風を感じたり、青い小物でセンスのいい夏を贈ったり…。生活を楽しむコツ、今年は「青」をテーマに考えてみませんか。

悲しみの花を考える

花にはメッセージを伝える力があります。亡くなった人を悼む気持ちをこめて飾る、贈る、悲しみの花について考えてみました。

7 6

COVER

ANNUAL REPORT アニュアルレポート

GILEAD SCIENCES 1997 ANNUAL REPORT 1998 USA
CL: Gilead Sciences CD,AD: Bill Cahan D,I: Lian Ng P: Daniel De Sousa CW: Lana Lauher / Susan Hubbard DF: Cahan & Associates

THE WHEELS ARE IN MOTION 1998 USA
CL: Sound Transit CD,AD,D: Tony Secolo CW: Evelyn Eldridge

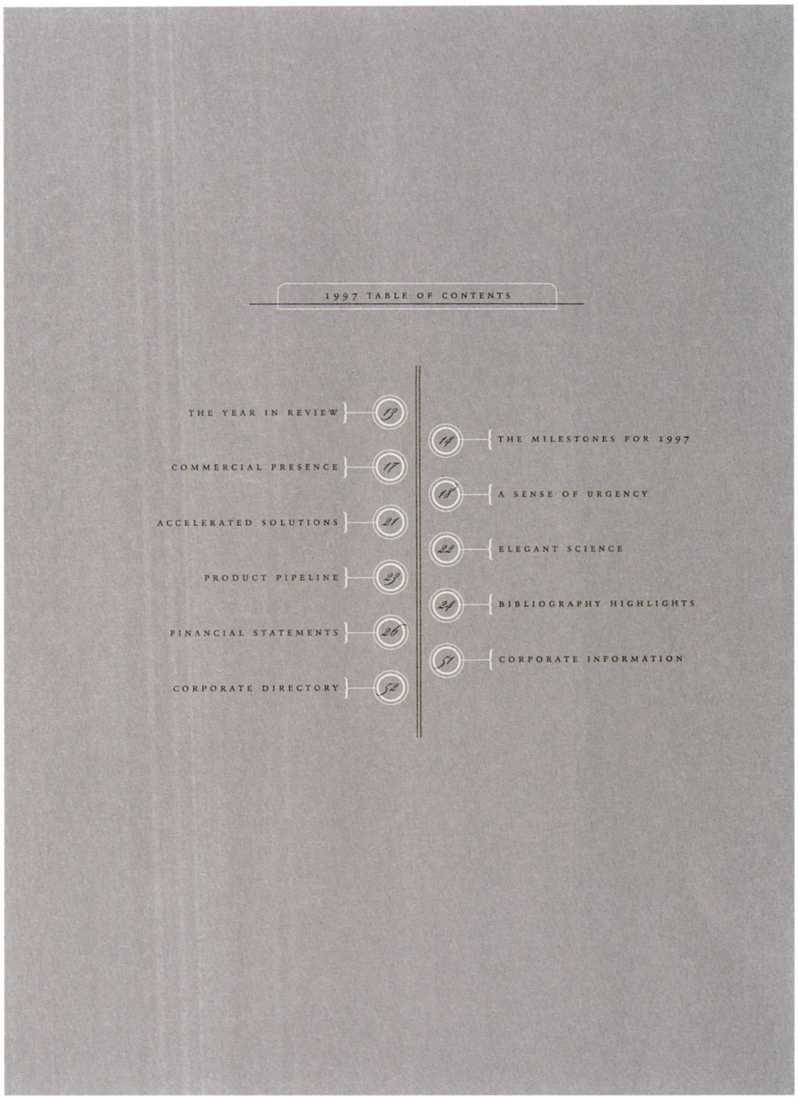

1997 TABLE OF CONTENTS

contents

COVER

COVER

MAGAZINE 雑誌

MERGE NO.0 1998 SWEDEN PB: Merge E: Bo Madestrand / Håkan Nilsson AD: Andreas Karperyd / Lotten Sunna

MERGE NO.3 MARCH 1999 SWEDEN PB: Merge E: Bo Madestrand / Håkan Nilsson AD: Andreas Karperyd / Lotten Sunna

CONTENTS

The editors
Bo Madestrand
bomad@algonet.se
Sina Najafi
sqk0606@is.nyu.edu
Håkan Nilsson
h.nilsson@iname.com
David Serlin
dhs3627@is2.nyu.edu
Charlotte Sunna
charlotte.sunna@expressen.se

Layout
Andreas Karperyd
andreas@freq.se

Advertising
Daggan Stamenkovic
daggan@freq.se

English language consultant
Kristina Riegert
kristina.riegert@statsvet.su.se

Publisher
Håkan Nilsson

Address
Merge
P.O. Box 9223
102 73 Stockholm
Sweden

Phone
+46 8 84 18 94

E-mail
merge@freq.se

Printer
Ekotryck, Stockholm 1998

Illustrations: Page 5: Dennis Rodman – drawing by Dennis Eriksson. Page 11: Olle Borg, courtesy Gallery Andréhn-Schiptjenko. Page 12: Nina Katchadourian, courtesy the artist. Pages 18–19: Rachel Whiteread, photograph by Sue Ormerod, courtesy Artangel. Page 21: Tracey Emin, photograph by Stephen White, courtesy Jay Jopling. Page 26: Spencer Finch – portrait by Mattias Bardå. Pages 31–33: KLF, courtesy Blast First. Page 37: Frank Zappa, photograph by Bo Madestrand. Page 38: Peter Halley, courtesy the artist. Page 39: Tobias Bernstrup, courtesy the artist. Page 43: Will Smith in "Men in Black," courtesy Columbia Pictures.

CONTENTS

Editors-in-Chief
Bo Madestrand
bomad@algonet.se
Sina Najafi
sqk0606@is.nyu.edu
Håkan Nilsson
h.nilsson@iname.com

Co-Editor
David Serlin
dhs3627@is2.nyu.edu

Associate Editors
Patrik Andersson
r_kasak@yahoo.com
Tor Lindstrand
tor.lindstrand@berg-arkitektkontor.com
Charlotte Sunna
charlotte.sunna@expressen.se

Godfather
Daggan Stamenkovic
daggan@freq.se

Graphic Design
Andreas Karperyd
andreas@freq.se

Advertising
Sofie Sweger
+46 8-676 03 21
s.sweger@swipnet.se

Illustrations
Dennis Eriksson

English Language Consultant
Dr. Kristina Riegert
kristina.riegert@statsvet.su.se

Publisher
Håkan Nilsson

Address Europe
Merge
P.O. Box 9223
102 73 Stockholm
Sweden
Tel: +46 8 84 18 94
Fax: +46 8 84 00 18

Address USA
Merge
181 Wyckoff Street
Brooklyn, NY 11217, USA
Tel/Fax: + 1 718 222 8434

Email
info@mergemag.com

WWW
www.mergemag.com

We accept
manuscripts/submissions/query letters via email, fax, or snail mail

Printed in Sweden
by Ekotryck, Stockholm 1998

No.00 COVER

No.03 COVER

CATALOG カタログ

LEATHERMAN 1997 USA CL,CW: Leatherman Tools AD: Jack Anderson AD,D: David Bates D: Lisa Cerveny P: Condit Studio I: Jack Unruh
DF: Hornall Anderson Design Works, Inc.

COVER

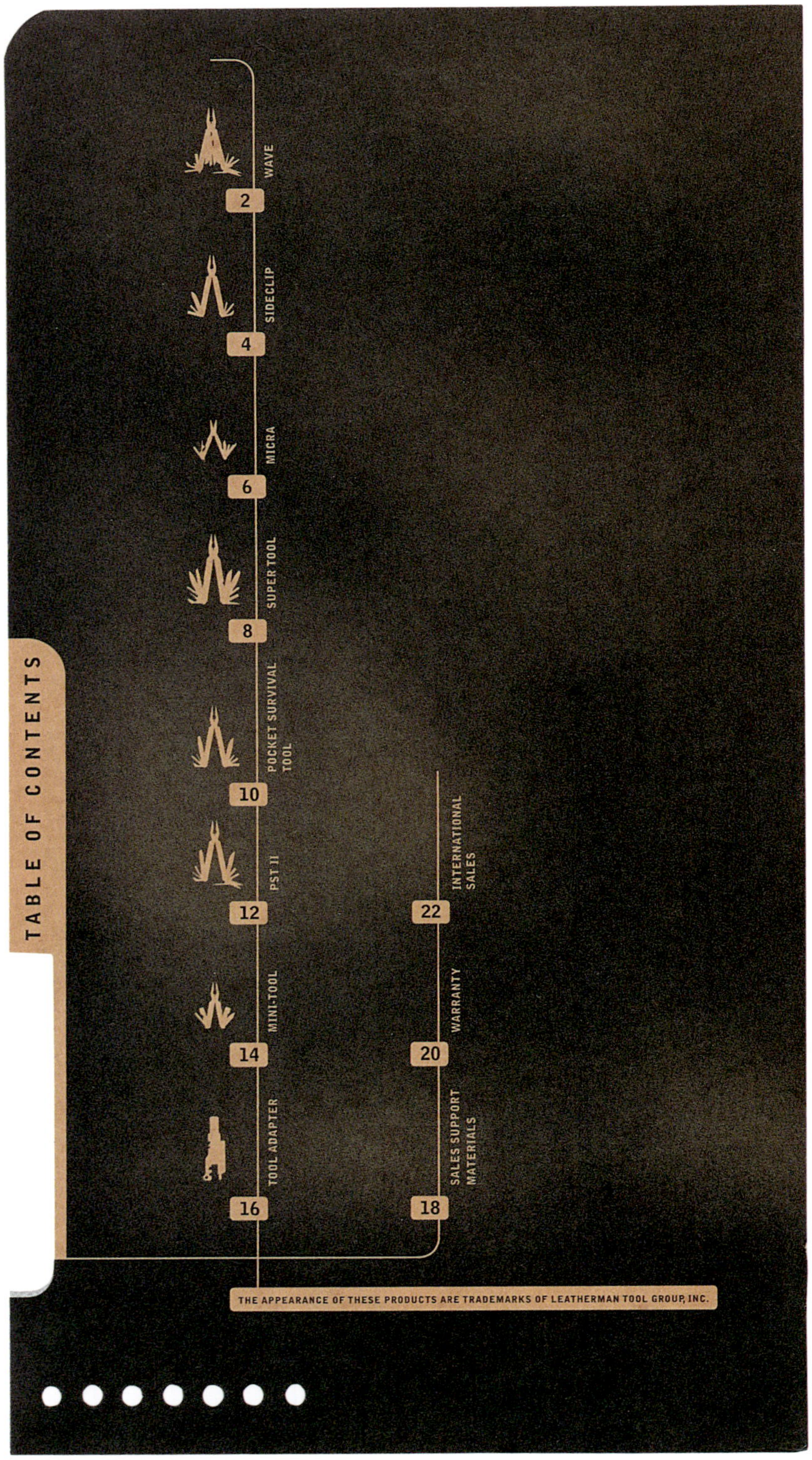

2REBELS TB-101 1997 CANADA CL: 2Rebels / FontShop CD,D,P: Denis Dulude CD,D: Fabrizio Gilardino P: Pol Baril CW: Michel Loslier DF: 2Rebels

COVER

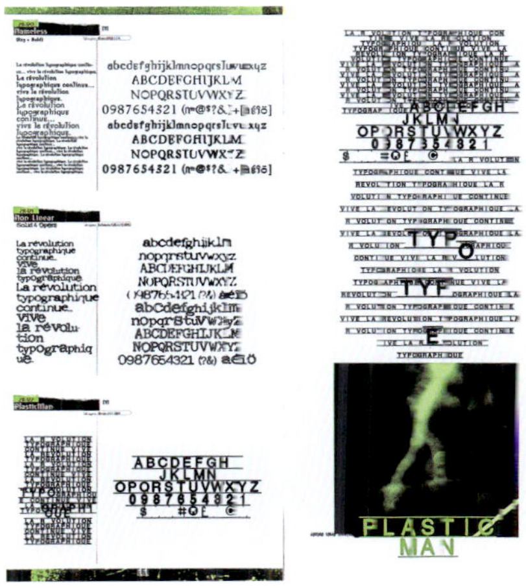

TEXT PAGES

POLYTRADE PAPER CORPORATION LTD. 2000 HONG KONG

CL: Polytrade Paper Corporation Ltd. CD,AD,D: Eric Chan D: Francis Lee D,I: Vivian Chan I: Michael Lau CW: Cat Tyrell / Peter Wong DF: Eric Chan Design Co., Ltd.

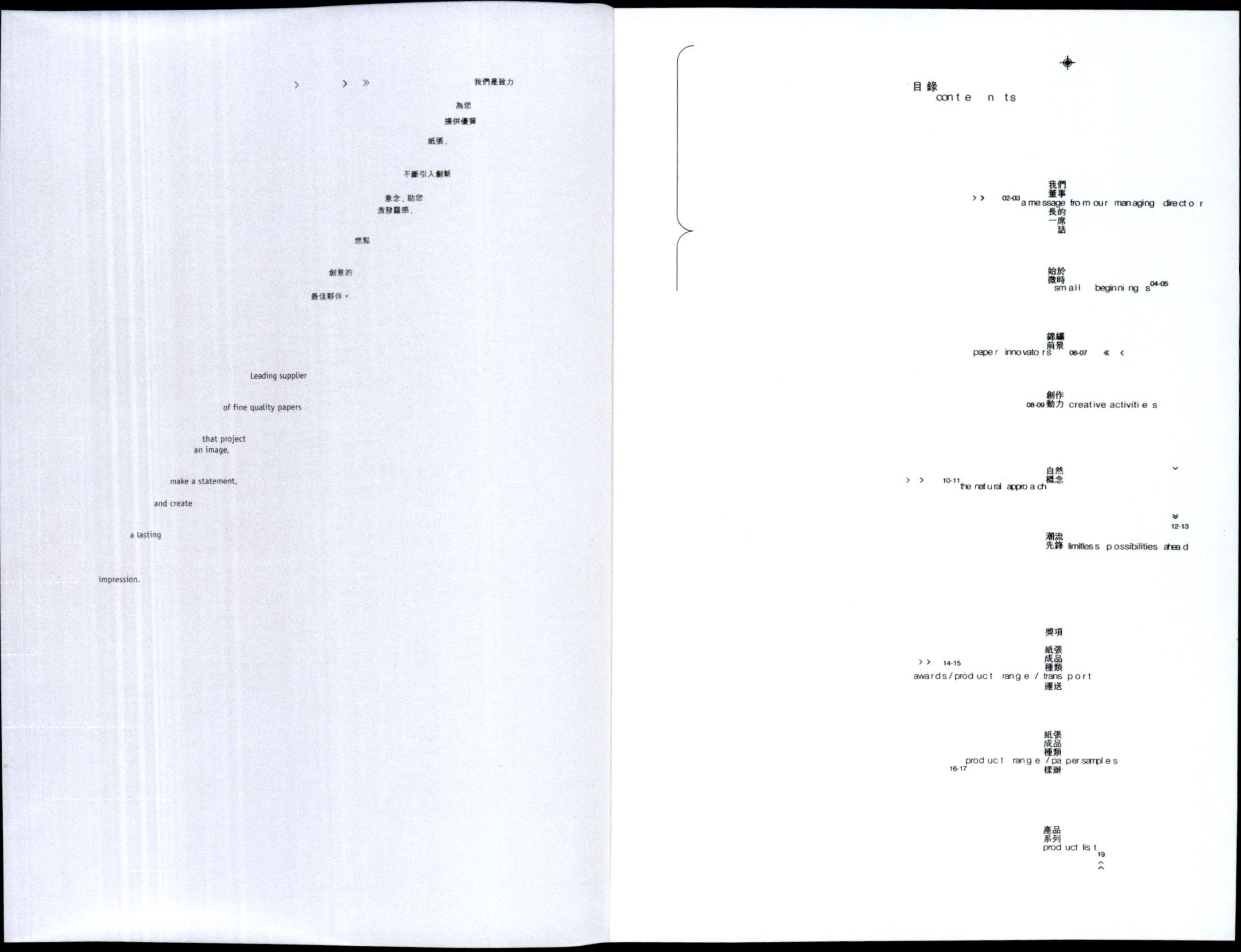

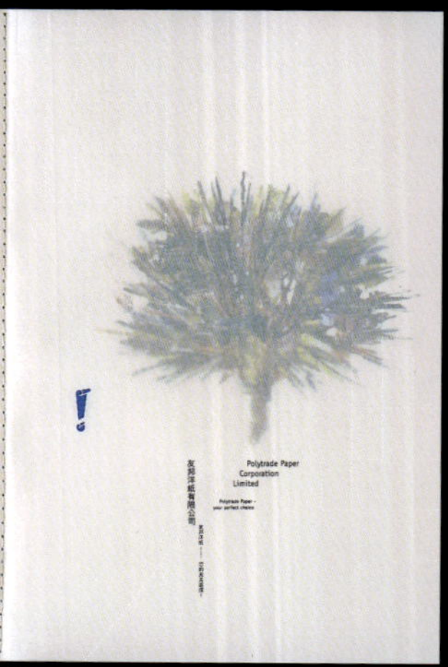

COVER

Contents

この冊子に使用している絵は、フィリップ・フランツ・フォン・シーボルトの旧蔵コレクション「日本植物図譜」から掲載したものです。なお、一部につきましては、デザイン処理を施しております。

見返しの紙はフェルトン 90kgを使用しています。この紙は一年草ケナフを使用して作られた非木材紙です。
本紙はグラフィーエコ100 130kgを使用しています。この紙は古紙配合率100%の再生紙です。
印刷インキは大豆から作られたソイビーンインクを使用しています。

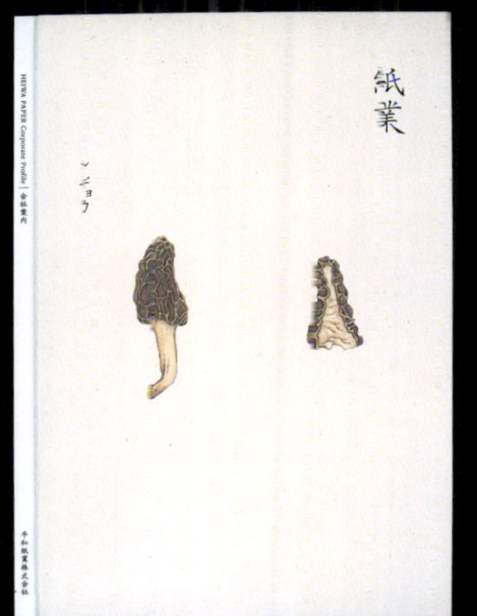

COVER

OLDENBURGISCHES STAATSTHEATER 1998 GERMANY CL: Oldenburgisches Staatstheater AD,D,DF: Fons M. Hickmann / Ulrike Kleine

INHALT

DURCHS HERZ IN DEN KOPF

Geehrtes Publikum,

die Überzeugung, wie eine Aufführung auf Sie wirken soll, hat uns zur Auswahl der Stücke, die wir Ihnen mit diesem Vorschauheft vorstellen wollen, geführt. Theaterarbeit begreifen wir als Versuch, Fragen zu stellen, Antworten zu finden, Impulse zu vermitteln und Sie für einen Abend aus dem Alltag zu entführen. Die Reaktionen auf unsere Aufführungen sind sehr unterschiedlich, weil die Erwartungen jedes Zuschauers an einen Theaterabend sehr verschieden sind. Somit ist es Pflicht und Aufgabe eines hochsubventionierten Dreispartenhauses, mit unterschiedlichen Stücken den Interessen des Publikums entgegenzukommen. Ziel unserer Arbeit wird es sein, Theaterstücke verschiedener Epochen aus dem Bewußtsein unserer Zeit zu interpretieren.

Der 2. Oktober 1998 wird für das Oldenburgische Staatstheater ein besonderer Tag sein: an diesem Abend wird zum ersten Mal auf der Bühne des Kleinen Hauses für Sie gespielt werden. Dieses Theater, das ausschließlich aus Mitteln der KULTURSTIFTUNG NIEDERSACHSEN der ÖFFENTLICHEN VERSICHERUNGEN finanziert wurde, wird in den nächsten Jahren Forum sein für Schauspiel, Tanz, Kammeroper und Musical.

Wir begreifen die Eröffnung als große Chance, durch eine neue Strukturierung unseres Spielplanes mehr Zuschauer - vornehmlich junge - für unsere Arbeit zu interessieren. So können im Großen Haus jetzt vermehrt Stücke aufgeführt werden, die von einem Großteil des Publikums in Stadt und Region gewünscht werden, während im Kleinen Haus am selben Abend Stücke gespielt werden, deren Themen erfahrungsgemäß einen begrenzten Kreis des Publikums ansprechen.

Die Arbeit von Irina Pauls, der neuen Ballettdirektorin in Oldenburg, erwarten wir mit Offenheit, Spannung und Neugierde.

Wir hoffen, Sie in unseren Aufführungen begrüßen zu können und freuen uns auf Ihren Besuch.

COVER

RECRUITMENT BROCHURE 入社案内

THE ENCYCLOPEDIA OF "MISSION" AND "THE FORCE TO CHANGE" AT MC　1999　JAPAN

CL: Mitsubishi Corporation　CD: Masao Tsuji　AD: Ichiro Higashiizumi
P: Risaku Suzuki　I: Keiji Ito　Planning: Wilson Learning Worldwide Inc.

TABLE OF CONTENTS

目次

三菱商事の『仕事』『チカラ』図鑑。

The Encyclopedia of "Mission" and "The Force to Change" at MC.

3　　2

COVER

PAPER KNIFE VOL.6 2000 JAPAN PB: Paper Knife Rocks E,CD: Yusuke Shono D: Namaiki (COVER)

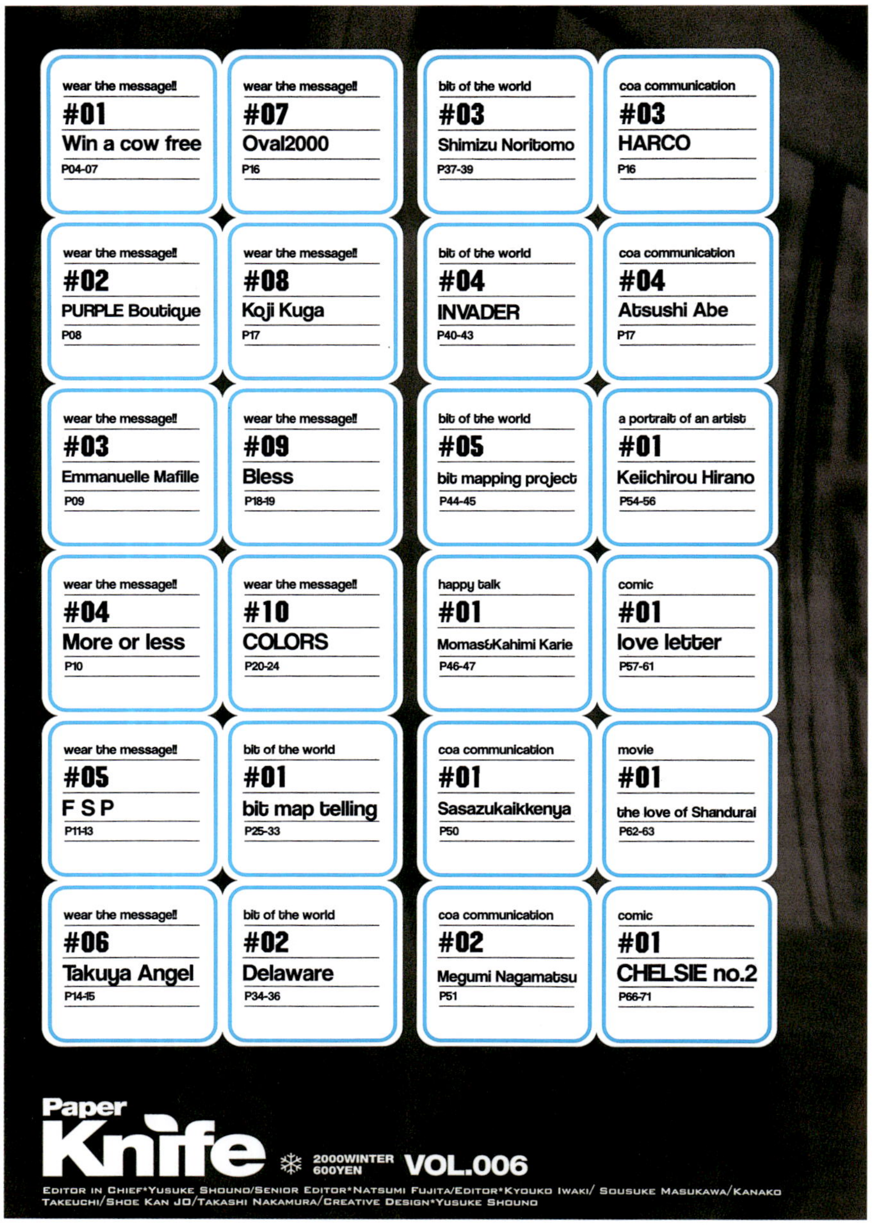

Paper Knife

SPACE MARCH 2000 SWEDEN

PB: SPACE MAGAZINE E: Jonas Lindberg CD,AD,D,TY: Simina Astilean P: Tobias Sjodin I: Alvaro Tapia CW: Sonia Hedstrand DF: Anima Design Ltd. Contributor: Okko Oinonen / Dorinel Marc / Mauro Rongione / Mickadelica / Milou Allerholm / Peter Cornell / Terese Cedervret / Maiken Håverstein / Samuel Dahlberg

…prungliga paviljongen som revs 1930. Den är extremt raffinerad …d sina väggar som varierar speglingar, transparens och opacitet, …isontellt utbredd mellan två grunda bassänger; den ena zenbuddtisk meditativ, den andra med en klassicistisk skulptur mot mar…rfond och fascistisk rysning. I dag har den inte längre något prak…t bruk, ungefär som en övergiven filmstudio. Att en så strikt funk…nalism kan rymma en så teatral dramaturgi!

… övrigt är Barcelona en god stad: varje övergångsställe är avfasat … rullstolar, en kulturell nivå Stockholm bara kan drömma om.

text och foto: Peter Cornell

microbots 75.

Tankar som "vad är det för mening med att få barn när världen ser ut som den gör?" fick Håkan Kåreby att vilja lysa upp lite i vardagen. Leksaker görs för barn och barn är väl fortfarande förknippade med hopp och framtidstro, tänkte Håkan och valde att som sitt examensprojekt designa en leksak, eftersom han ville arbeta med någonting som kändes optimistiskt, något som uttryckte att han trodde på framtiden.

Det var också en önskan om att komma bort lite ifrån det förnuftiga, anpassade och präktiga, som enligt Håkan genomsyrar en stor del av industridesignen idag. Resultatet blev Microbots, en serie elektroniska leksaksfigurer som vänder sig till både pojkar och flickor. Figurerna är tolv centimeter höga och materialen är lätt, gjuten metall, plast och textil. Formen och utseendet är influerat av grafisk design och mangakonst, men det som skiljer dem från andra actionfigurer är elektroniken innanför höljet. Miocroboten är designad för att sitta på sin ägares axel. När en annan Microbot kommer i närheten känner den av det och påkallar uppmärksamhet via ljud, rörelser och vibrationer. Ägaren kan då välja att utmana de andra Microbotägarna i ett dataspel - Peakmaster - som bygger på en enkel, strategisk bedömning av spelaren. En datoriserad och något mer sofistikerad variant av den välkända leken sten, sax och påse. Duellen illustreras med ljud och en efter en kommer de Microbots som förlorar att falla baklänges tills segraren stårensam kvar.

- Det roliga och sköna med att designa leksaker, förutom att de faktiskt är till för att roa andra, menar Håkan, är också att uttrycket, det vill säga hur den ser ut och hur den känns, utgör den största delen av den totala produkten. På det sättet skiljer sig leksaksdesign från andra produkter, där tekniken ofta är mest väsentlig. Leksaker är både konstnärligt och kul, tycker Håkan.

Håkan Kåreby jobbar för tillfället som designer och konceptutvecklare på leksaksföretaget Lego i Danmark.

Terese Cedervret

foto: Peter Orev

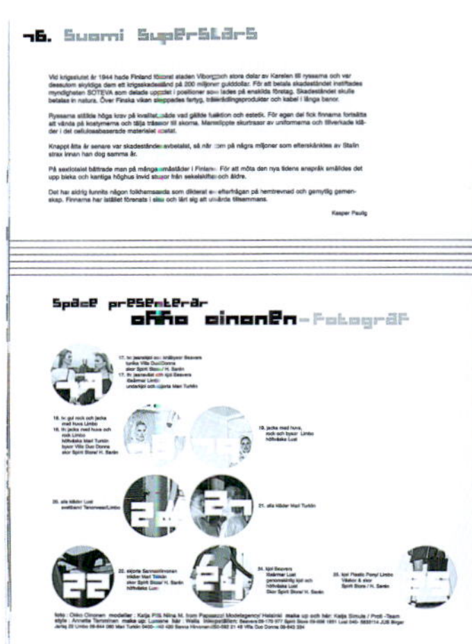

COVER

YOU LOOKIN' AT ME? Erik Salholm on Kitano's *Sonatine*.

At the end of a film, the viewer always returns to his/her own actual situation. It is always an innately "self"-revealing experience; partly because you are filled with an outside narrative which in some ways governs you for the duration of the film (if you participate fully) and partly because of the strangeness of the cinematic event. You emerge from a dark theatre where you have been invisible and it is as though you have just woken up, your temporality disjointed, your sense of space forgotten. For the slightest moment, there's just you.

Obviously the chief difference between film and theatre is that while theatre may employ any variety of tricks to convince the audience otherwise, it is essentially meant to be read, whereas film is meant to be felt viscerally. On the other hand, one of the chief criticisms of much contemporary film is that it has never completely escaped from the trickery or textual constraints of the theatre. Takeshi Kitano's 1993 film *Sonatine* breaks away from this completely, into something like abstraction (at times the dialogue is only an action that the characters perform, like any other), exploring the matrixes of human relations from which viewers cannot distance themselves. What actually falls away is the text, and what is left is space, and particularly a space that is felt through the eyes of the protagonists and the audience, in an interplay of gazes.

In watching, we move away from the act of looking. Watching is not aggressive in the same way as looking. Watching is an activity which we reserve for objects, or events at a distance, like a scene on the street. We can only watch in a position of helplessness or utter passivity. We watch when we cannot look, and in watching we are free from an obsessive desire to visually consume, and can simply absorb. Gazing is the third ocular category, falling somewhere between them, lazily sliding on and off subjects. *Sonatine* invites a measure of all three, but avoids any kind of strict taxonomy, and a matrix of space is built between the characters, upon the balance that each character finds with the other as they shift mode.

Sonatine is an architecture of vision. There are a great many significant gazes, looks and stares in *Sonatine*. They punctuate the emotional narrative, emboss the contextual structure, and shift the film's perspective around in such a way that it can be thought of as an allegory of disempowerment and power, as embodied in the various characters' visual relations. In this sense, *Sonatine* could be discussed under the heading of the politics of looking (there is something panoptic about the characters' imprisoned and codified interaction), but Takeshi's is rarely a Baudelairean gaze, it does not present the viewer with a spectacle, but far more complexly, obtains to the truly cinematic.

The premise of the film centers on a senior member of a Tokyo Yakuza clan, Murakawa (Beat Takeshi), who is commanded to settle a dispute between two warring clans in Okinawa. Jaded from years in the syndicate, he knows that his boss is playing him, but can do nothing about it. A guest of the Nakamatsu clan, Murakawa has lost five soldiers in hits by the Anan clan in the space of a few days. He retreats with his closest men to a beach house away

EXT PAGES

Photo: Petra Hayes

TO ME, THE AIRCRAFT ARE CHARGED WITH A NEW SIGNIFICANCE, COMMUNICATING NEW IDEAS THAT I TRANSLATE INTO GARMENTS.

between couturiers and artists, new and innovative positions in fashion are often read in terms of art criticism. But despite Thorogood's fine art background (he received both his BA and MA from St Martin's, the cliché of the singular, isolated romantic artist doesn't adequately reflect the multi-faceted alliances he fuses between technology, music and fashion. Launched in a London art space last year, his acclaimed "White Noise" collection was a tour de force in collaboration with digital art group Spore and electronic musicians Barbed.

THE INSTALLATION FEATURED ROTATING couture garments suspended from the ceiling along with a synchronised light and music production. Forty computer monitors displayed key inspirations behind the collection, ranging from Charles Babbage and early computer graphics to airport architecture and the musical wizardry of Brian Eno. "I see fashion as a site for many infinite variations and permutations. Like a band uses a producer to cut an album, I take different influences and edit them into a single aesthetic," he says.

THE ETHOS THOROGOOD EMPLOYS IN his design cannot be reduced to a set of precepts or even a formula that applies to the collection as a whole. He explains: "In the 1970s Brian Eno came up with a method for solving problems when he was making *Before and After Science*. In Eno's system of oblique strategies he had these 'oracle cards' that related to a series of conceptual dilemmas. Whenever he reached a problem, he chose a card at random and followed whatever path it indicated, and got some wonderful results. It's like this with my work, I try to solve design problems through unexpected methods and different media."

Throughout the 1990s the value of couture has been questioned by many cynics who dismiss it as an archaic institution without a future. The brilliance of designers like Thorogood, with such a vested interest and dependence on couture, is a strong indication that the creative and magical elements of fashion will continue to thrive through this artistic genre, sustaining a philosophy that is lived rather than consumed.

FORTHCOMING EXHIBITIONS:

London's Victoria & Albert Museum, 14th October–16th January, *The New Millennium: A Forecast of Visual Culture* in the *A Grand Design* exhibition. New York's Fashion Institute of Technology is planning a *Retrospective of British Fashion: The 1960's–Now* for Autumn 2000.

Photo: Petra Hayes

THE LEFT HAND OF GOD

IS THE TRAGEDY OF THE BALKANS A RESULT OF TENSIONS, OR COULD IT BE UNDERSTOOD IN A LARGER AND MORE CONTEMPORARY CONTEXT? SLAVOJ ZIZEK POINTS OUT THE PROBLEMS WITH THE MOST COMMON ARGUMENTS AND OFFERS A NEW PERSPECTIVE.

Design and illustration:
Charlotte Sunna

THE IMPASSE OF THE LEFT The top winner in the contest for the greatest blunder of 1998 was a Latin-American patriotic terrorist who sent a letter bomb to the US consulate to protest against American interference with local politics. Being a conscientious citizen, he wrote his return address on the envelope; but since he did not use enough stamps, the letter was returned to him. Forgetting what he put in it, he opened it and blew himself to death – a perfect example of how a letter ultimately always arrives at its destination.

One could say that something quite similar is happening to the Milosevic regime with the recent NATO bombing. For years, Milosevic sent letter bombs to his neighbors, to Albania, Croatia and Bosnia, igniting fire all around Serbia but keeping himself out of conflict – until finally, his last letter was returned to him.

And there is a kind of poetic justice in the fact that the West finally intervened on behalf of Kosovo. Let us not forget that it was there it all began with Milosevic's ascent to power, legitimized by the promise to amend the underprivileged situation of Serbia within the Yugoslav federation, especially with regard to Albanian "separatism." The Albanians were Milosevic's first target; afterwards, he shifted his wrath onto other Yugoslav republics (Slovenia, Croatia, Bosnia), until, finally, the focus returned to Kosovo – as in a closed loop of Destiny, the arrow returned to the one who shot it. For Yugoslavia did not start to disintegrate when the Slovene "secession" triggered the Domino effect (first Croatia, then Bosnia, Macedonia...); the fragile balance on which Yugoslavia rested was irretrievably disturbed in 1987 when Milosevic's constitutional reforms deprived Kosovo and Vojvodina of their limited autonomy. From Milosevic's seizure of power onwards, the only chance for Yugoslavia's survival was to reinvent its formula: either Yugoslavia under Serb domination or some form of radical decentralization, from a loose confederacy to the full sovereignty of its units. Ignoring this key fact is the problem with Tariq Ali's otherwise admirable essay on the NATO intervention in Yugoslavia:

"The claim that it is all Milosevic's fault is one-sided and erroneous, indulging those Slovenian, Croatian and Western politicians who allowed him to succeed. It could be argued, for instance, that it was Slovene egoism, throwing the Bosnians and Albanians, as well as non-nationalist Serbs and Croats, to the wolves, that was a decisive factor in triggering the whole disaster of disintegration."*

It is true that the main responsibility for Milosevic's success resides in the way others have "allowed him to succeed," in their readiness to accept him as a "factor of stability" and in tolerating his "excesses" with the hope of striking a deal with him. This stance was clearly discernible among Slovene, Croat and Western politicians. But this argument asserts that the responsibility of others is of a fundamentally different nature than that of Milosevic: i.e. the point is not that "they were all equally guilty, participating in nationalist madness," but rather that others were guilty of not being harsh enough towards Milosevic. Furthermore, it

MAGAZINE 雑誌

MERGE NO.8 JUNE 2000 SWEDEN PB: Merge E: Bo Madestrand / Håkan Nilsson AD: Andreas Karperyd / Lotten Sunna

MERGE NO.4 JUNE 1999 SWEDEN PB: Merge E: Bo Madestrand / Håkan Nilsson AD: Andreas Karperyd / Lotten Sunna

No.08 COVER

No.04 COVER

MAGAZINE 雑誌

MERGE NO.0 1998 SWEDEN PB: Merge E: Bo Madestrand / Håkan Nilsson AD: Andreas Karperyd / Lotten Sunna

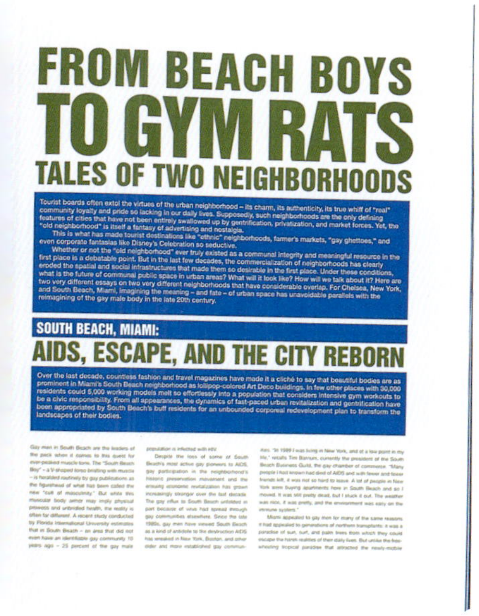

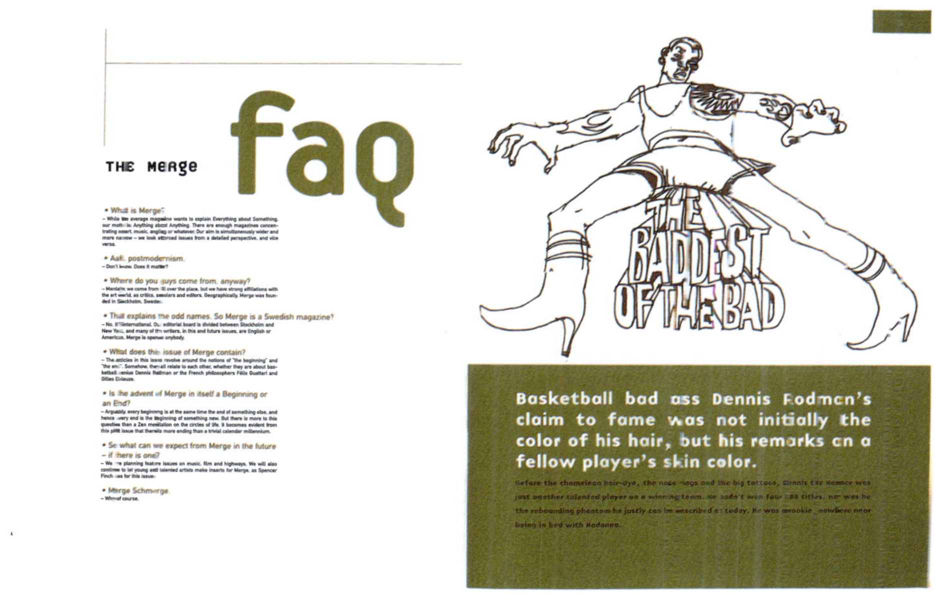

No.00 COVER

MAGAZINE 雑誌

CON:TRAST WISHFUL THINKING 1998 CANADA PB: Domtar E: Liz Chase CD: Theresa Zacharko

(COVER) CD,D,I,TY: Terrance Zacharko P: James Labounty DF: Zacharko Design Partnership
(SPREAD 1 / PAGE 3) CD,D,TY: Terrance Zacharko DF: Zacharko Design Partnership
(PAGE 2 / SPREAD 4) CD: Terrance Zacharko D,CW,I,TY: Francis Baca D,P,I,CW,TY: John Malcolmson P: NASA Archives DF: Rhode Island School of Design Mentor: Hans Van Dijk
(SPREAD 5) CD: Terrance Zacharko D,TY: Sunil Bhandari / Laurie Plater P: Colin Faulkner CW,Research: Helen Battersby DF: Bhandari And Co.

SPREAD 1

COVER

PAGE 2

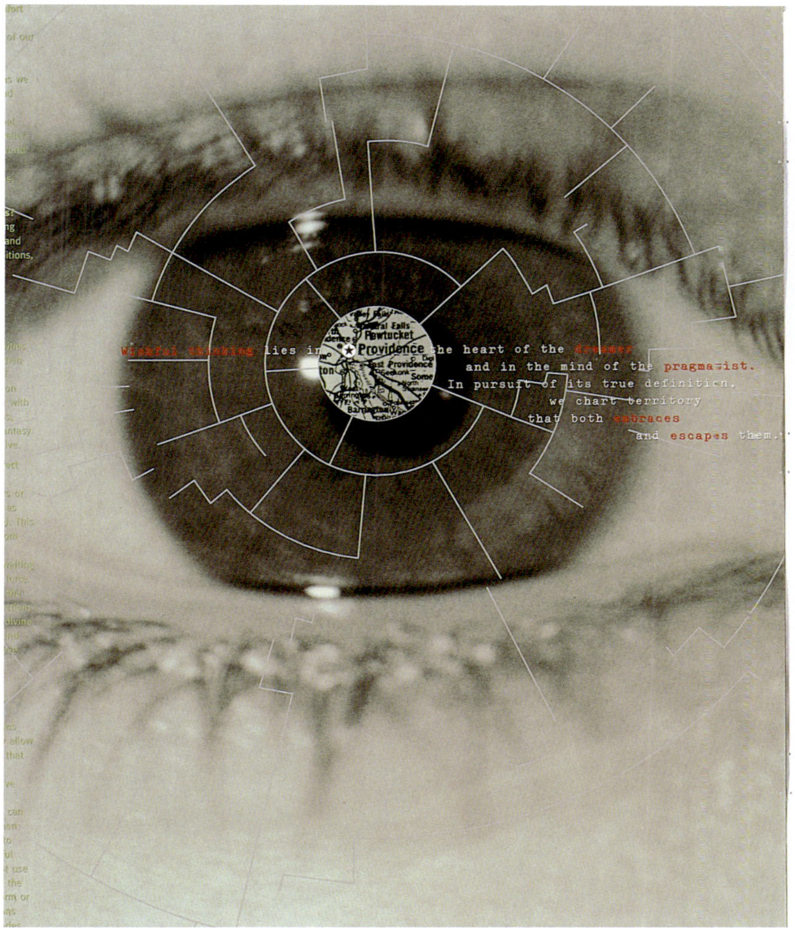

PAGE 3

Chermayeff & Geismar

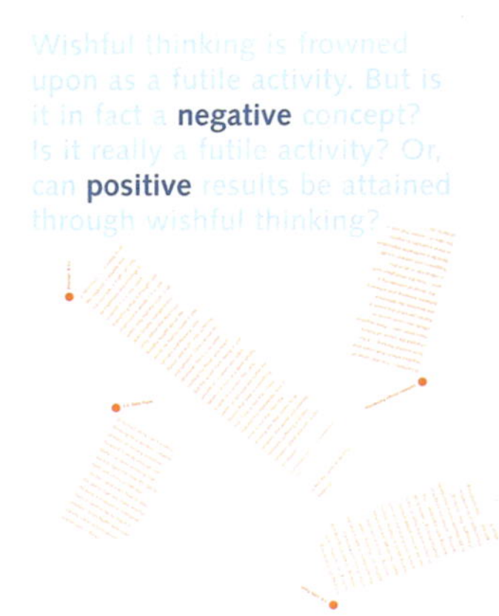

SPREAD 4

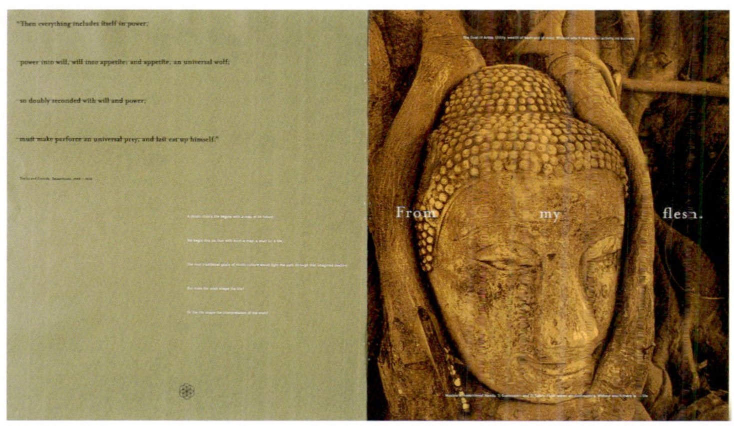

SPREAD 5

EMIGRE NO.50 SPRING 1999 USA PB,DF: Emigre E,AD,D,P,TY: Rudy Vanderlans

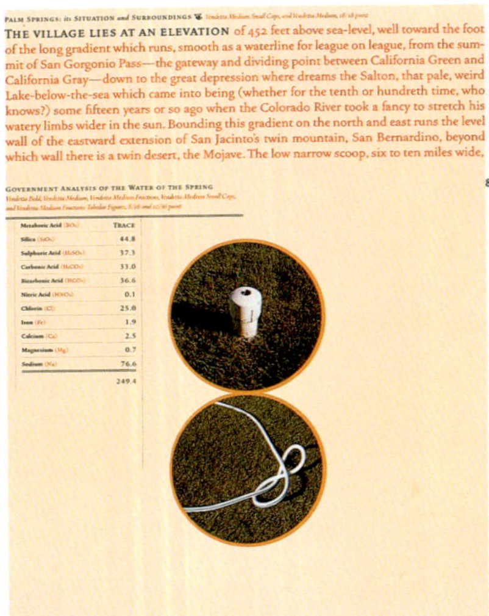

THE VILLAGE LIES AT AN ELEVATION of 452 feet above sea-level, well toward the foot of the long gradient which runs, smooth as a waterline for league on league, from the summit of San Gorgonio Pass—the gateway and dividing point between California Green and California Gray—down to the great depression where dreams the Salton, that pale, weird Lake-below-the-sea which came into being (whether for the tenth or hundredth time, who knows?) some fifteen years or so ago when the Colorado River took a fancy to stretch his watery limbs wider in the sun. Bounding this gradient on the north and east runs the level wall of the eastward extension of San Jacinto's twin mountain, San Bernardino, beyond which wall there is a twin desert, the Mojave. The low narrow scoop, six to ten miles wide,

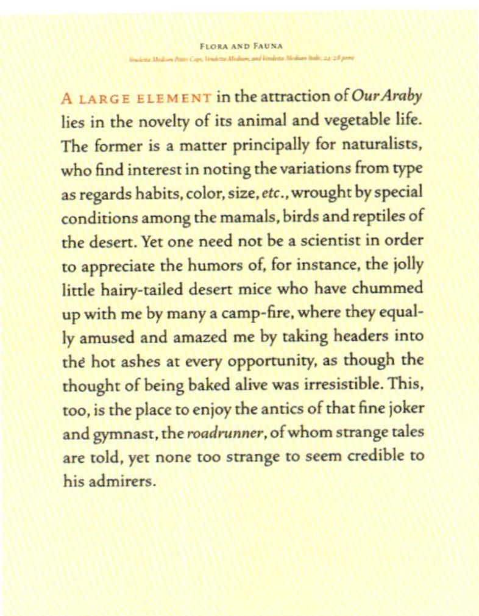

FLORA AND FAUNA

A LARGE ELEMENT in the attraction of *Our Araby* lies in the novelty of its animal and vegetable life. The former is a matter principally for naturalists, who find interest in noting the variations from type as regards habits, color, size, *etc.*, wrought by special conditions among the mamals, birds and reptiles of the desert. Yet one need not be a scientist in order to appreciate the humors of, for instance, the jolly little hairy-tailed desert mice who have chummed up with me by many a camp-fire, where they equally amused and amazed me by taking headers into the hot ashes at every opportunity, as though the thought of being baked alive was irresistible. This, too, is the place to enjoy the antics of that fine joker and gymnast, the *roadrunner*, of whom strange tales are told, yet none too strange to seem credible to his admirers.

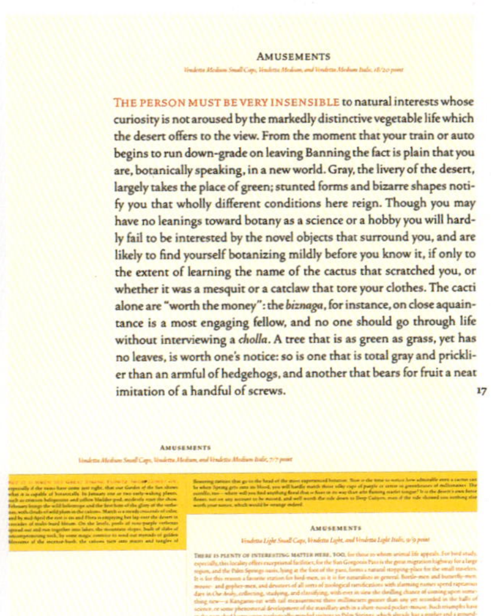

AMUSEMENTS

THE PERSON MUST BE VERY INSENSIBLE to natural interests whose curiosity is not aroused by the markedly distinctive vegetable life which the desert offers to the view. From the moment that your train or auto begins to run down-grade on leaving Banning the fact is plain that you are, botanically speaking, in a new world. Gray, the livery of the desert, largely takes the place of green; stunted forms and bizarre shapes notify you that wholly different conditions here reign. Though you may have no leanings toward botany as a science or a hobby you will hardly fail to be interested by the novel objects that surround you, and are likely to find yourself botanizing mildly before you know it, if only to the extent of learning the name of the cactus that scratched you, or whether it was a mesquit or a catclaw that tore your clothes. The cacti alone are "worth the money": the *bisnaga*, for instance, on close acquaintance is a most engaging fellow, and no one should go through life without interviewing a *cholla*. A tree that is as green as grass, yet has no leaves, is worth one's notice: so is one that is total gray and pricklier than an armful of hedgehogs, and another that bears for fruit a neat imitation of a handful of screws.

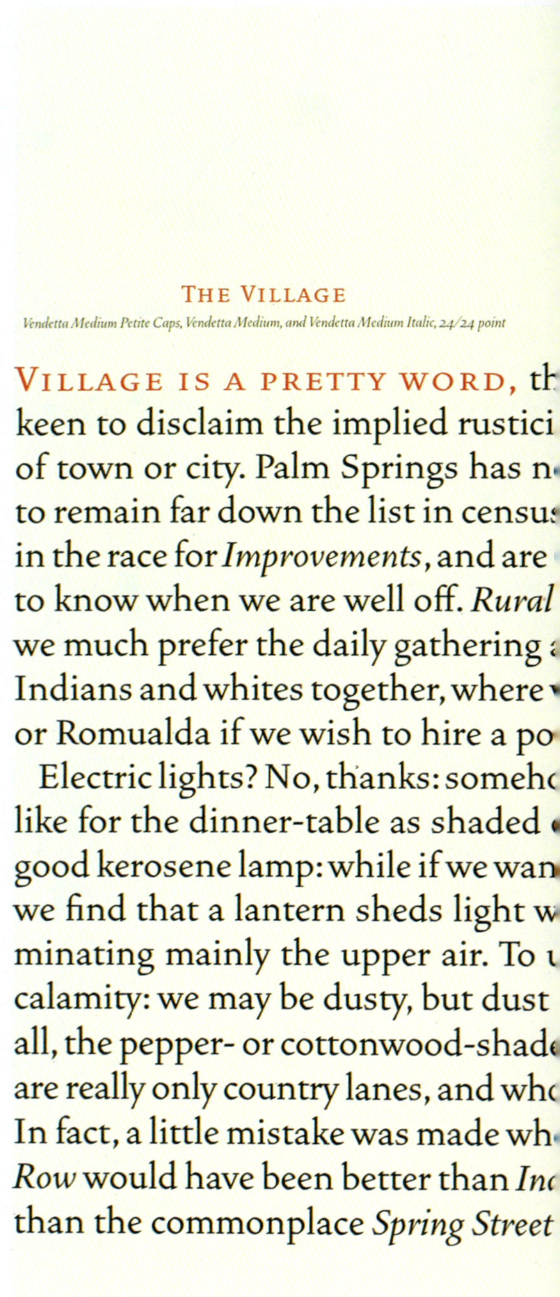

THE VILLAGE

Vendetta Medium Petite Caps, Vendetta Medium, and Vendetta Medium Italic, 24/24 point

VILLAGE IS A PRETTY WORD, th
keen to disclaim the implied rustici
of town or city. Palm Springs has n
to remain far down the list in census
in the race for *Improvements*, and are
to know when we are well off. *Rural*
we much prefer the daily gathering
Indians and whites together, where
or Romualda if we wish to hire a po
Electric lights? No, thanks: someh
like for the dinner-table as shaded
good kerosene lamp: while if we wan
we find that a lantern sheds light w
minating mainly the upper air. To u
calamity: we may be dusty, but dust
all, the pepper- or cottonwood-shade
are really only country lanes, and wh
In fact, a little mistake was made wh
Row would have been better than *In*
than the commonplace *Spring Street*

ambitious settlements are
. to graduate into the rank
aims, and is well content
ns. We decline to take part
feel, anyway) wise enough
)elivery does not entice us:
general store at mail-time,
count on catching Miguel
get the washing done. 13
hing seems to us so home-
s, or for fireside reading a
ll on a neighbor after dark,
ou need it instead of illu-
ent sidewalks would be a
ıral and we prefer it. After
ets of our *Garden of the Sun*
s a country lane cemented?
y were named. *Cottonwood*
venue, and *Hot Springs Lane*

AVERAGE MONTHLY TEMPERATURES AT PALM SPRINGS STATION,
YEARS 1907 TO 1915 INCLUSIVE *Vendetta Medium Small Caps, Vendetta Medium Fractions Tabular Figures, 10/14 point*

	JAN	FEB	MAR	APR	MAY	JUN	JUL	AUG	SEP	OCT	NOV	DEC
HIGHEST	77	80	90	96	104	112	113	112	107	98	87	76
LOWEST	31	37	45	52	66	64	73	73	67	55	42	33
MEAN	53	55	63	69	73	84	90	90	84	73	62	52

AMUSEMENTS

19

Vendetta Medium Small Caps, Vendetta Medium, and Vendetta Medium Italic, 9/9 point

FOR THOSE WHO DELIGHT in cloud-form and sky-scenery, no area of sky that I know approaches in interest that which stretches from the southern extension of San Jacinto Mountain eastward to Santa Rosa Peak. In the rainy season this tract of air forms the very frontier of the opposing meteorological forces, where day after day one may watch the battle between Rain and Drought fought in fashion more spectacular than one sees it elsewhere. Some particular interplay of air-currents, combined with and perhaps arising from the configuration of the land below, give rise to a remarkable diversity of cloud conditions. Above Santa Rosa there will hang for days a vast banner of vapor like the plume that curls from the lip of a volcano, while in the upper air beyond and above it, cirrus, stratus, and cumulus merge and evolve in ceaseless manoeuvres. I know of no other such "cloud-compelling peak" as this, on which another admirer and I have ventured to confer the title or degree of *Santa Rosa de las Nubes* (Santa Rosa of the Clouds).

BOOK 書籍

DAVID BYRNE BOOK 1998 USA CL,CD,P,CW: David Byrne CD,AD,D,I: Stefan Sagmeister D,I: Hjalti Karlsson DF: Sagmeister Inc.

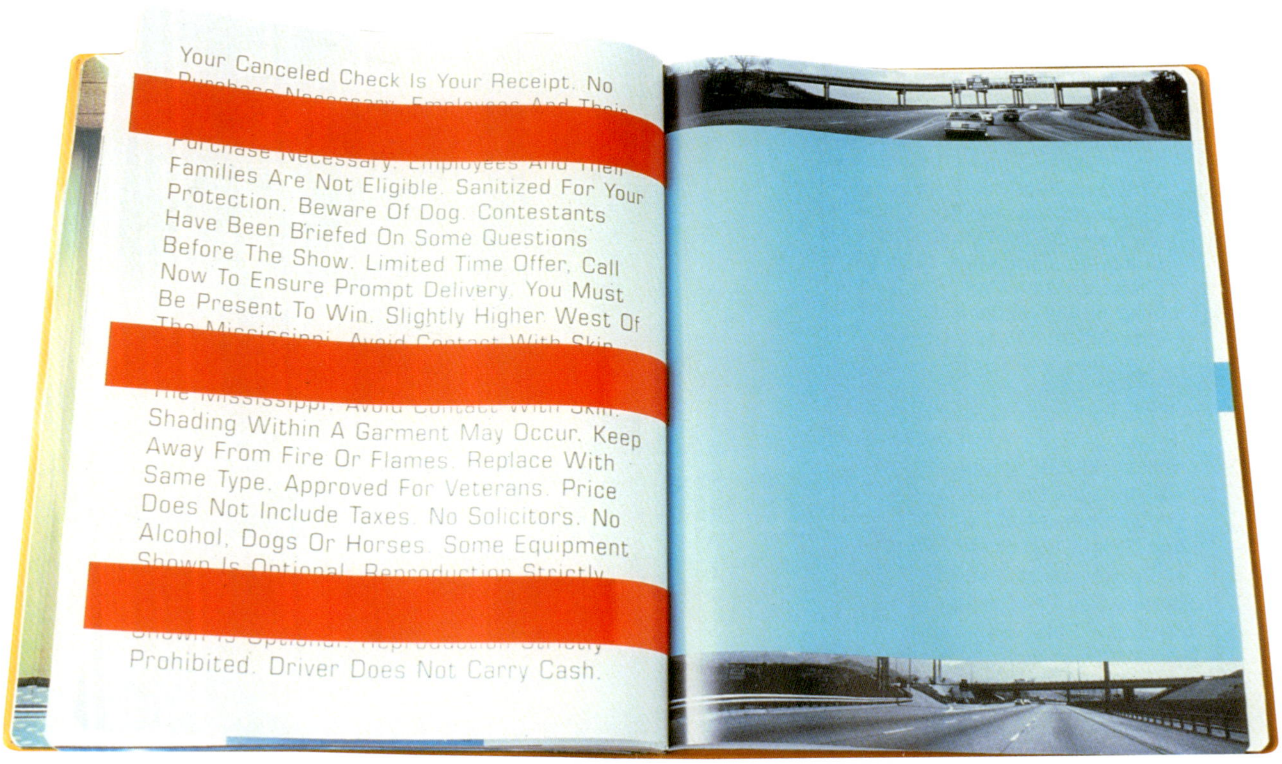

A man on an airplane confesses to you that he has commited a truly horrible crime.
Do you:
A. ☐ Leave justice in the hands of God.
B. ☐ Surreptitiously turn the guilty party in.
C. ☐ Ask to change seats.
You discover that through a bureaucratic error you are getting free phone, gas and electric service.
Do you:
A. ☐ Correct the error.
B. ☐ Feign ignorance.
C. ☐ Thank your lucky stars.
You are given one year to live and have the key to the office safe, and there are millions of untraceable dollars in there.
Do you:
A. ☐ Take the money and run.
B. ☐ Let the rest of your life take its natural course.
C. ☐ Take the money, but give it to an orphanage.
You are accosted in a dark alley by 3 armed youths who demand your wallet, but you are, unbeknown to them, carrying a powerful semi-automatic weapon.
Do you:
A. ☐ Administer justice. Shoot first and ask questions later, it's self defense.
B. ☐ Pull your weapon but leave the scene peacefully.
C. ☐ Give up your wallet and avoid the risk of violent confrontation.

YOUR
DAVID BYRNE

COVER

NEST SPRING 2000 USA PB: Nest LLC E,AD,D: Joseph Holtzman Graphics Director: Tom Beckham TY: Eugene Kuo Production Manager: Della Mancuso
P (COVER): Yoshiko Seino / Tina Barney / Peter de Lory Text: Emily White (SPREAD 1) Printer: Amilcare Pizzi in Milan

FUTURAMA

In the back row of the class a boy brainiac drew pictures with his friends: Roman soldiers fighting dinosaurs, battleships at war with planes, drawings of the teacher looking like an animal or an idiot. When the lessons became truly monotonous he drew elaborate dream houses: a combination of the Bat Cave and the *Playboy* mansion, a garage full of super-duper fast cars, a bed which revolved, maybe a waterbed, maybe a slide going down from the bed into the hot tub, always an endless supply of comic books.

This boy was *The Simpsons* creator Matt Groening, whose most recent animated TV series is the sci-fi satire *Futurama*. Back then he was a smart aleck with a healthy chip on his shoulder, getting into trouble at Ainsworth Elementary in Portland, Oregon.

64 Ainsworth is located in the rich neighborhood of Portland Heights, where most of the kids have brand-new school clothes and plenty of lunch money. The school is shrill, overwhelming, forbidding, even though it advertises itself as one of the Rose City's Finest Educational Institutions. Like Portland itself, Ainsworth is a place where bad dreams flourish. I know this because I went there, too, ten years after Groening did. When I'm in Portland visiting my family, I drive past the brick buildings, the playground with its hopscotch diagrams and jungle gyms, and my brain is wiped out by depressed-girl flashbacks.

Within the boundaries of that school it was possible to witness every type of humiliation: running around the back field during PE even though you were too fat while the kids in the art studio watched you over their potter's wheels and laughed; the sadistic teacher in fourth grade who divided the class into "privileged children" and "bad children"; the walk up to the annex where kids got pantsed or beaten up. There was a cabal of teachers who had been at Ainsworth since before Christ was born, and each new group of students learned the rumors: Mrs. F. lives in an elevator shaft; Mr. A. goes to porno places at night; the gym teacher makes the boys line up naked and he measures all their dicks. Groening remembers Ainsworth this way: "There was this teacher, she had a paddle ready if you misbehaved, and if you cried she made you stand in a garbage can, a full-size garbage can. The shop teacher had an electric generator and he would shock the kids as punishment."

I tell Groening about a first-grade teacher who threatened to strangle a guy we called Freddy the Frog. She wrapped her hands around his neck and said something like "I'm gonna wring your neck!" As I recount this Ainsworth horror story, I'm immediately reminded of Bart Simpson—some pissed-off adult chokes the daylights out of him, his eyes bug out, and he pleads *OK, OK, I surrender*. Certain memories are like cartoons. Certain cartoons are like memories.

Groening is excited and vindicated by the choking story. He says, "Yeah, that's Ainsworth all right. I remember back then vowing that I would never forget what it was like to be a kid. I can't really talk about Portland without talking about this dark side." The black humor of the past drives his imagination. Portland's particular darkness shows itself throughout Groening's work in the gloomy, claustrophobic padded cell of *Life in Hell*; in the contaminated world of *The Simpsons* Springfield (a Portland street map can show you where Reverend Lovejoy, Ned Flanders, and others got their names); in the New New York of *Futurama*, built upon the ashes of the Old New York in the year 3000, where people can buy tickets at the suicide booth,

TEXT Emily White ILLUSTRATION Matt Groening

Reader, you must have noticed the twitchings of Bender as you gave this issue a first flip-through. Bender, hapless alcoholic automaton and a regular on Matt Groening's weekly animated television series *Futurama*, lights up only for **nest**. We also commissioned Groening to design an original *Futurama* interior, and the result, shown on the following pages, is none other than the Dream House of ominously addled Professor Farnsworth. You can only see it here.

SPREAD 1

COVER

NEST SPRING 2000 USA PB: Nest LLC E,AD: Joseph Holtzman Graphics Director: Tom Beckham TY: Eugene Kuo Production Manager: Della Marcusc Text: Kiera Coffee
P: Richard Barnes Printer: Amilcare Pizzi in Milan
Flip Coner Animation: Futurama & TM Twentieth Century Fox Film Company, © 1999 The Curiosity Company, All Rights Reserved

PENCIL CASE

text KIERA COFFEE photographs RICHARD BARNES

He never imagined he'd have to deal with so many pencils. Or erasers. He has one electric pencil sharpener that necessitates holding the pencil at just the right angle in order for it to work. He scouts constantly for used pencils at the local scrap/recycling centers. He buys new pencils too, and receives pencil donations in the mail. A collection of tiny one-inch-long pencils arrives in a baggie with a note reading: "These were my father's pencils." He uses them all. He always needs more. Please send pencils.

Mosaic artist Jason Mecier is working as a commissioned artist, to layer a residential hallway with pencils. The hallway winds along three floors of a staircase in a modest San Francisco home. Various other rooms in the house would have been better to work in, simpler—but other commissioned works were already assigned to those rooms. Though it's as yet unfinished, the pencil work is already wed so completely with the hallway space that it's hard to imagine it elsewhere. It is hard to imagine too, how the homeowner could not be swayed from her bias against pencils. (She's always preferred pens.)

In the past, Jason Mecier has created detailed celebrity portraits using beans and noodles, matches and lighters, yarn, fake fingernails and, sometimes, food. With obsessive attention and devotion, he explores each material until its physical and visceral limitations lead him onward. The earth tones dictated by the bean-and-noodle palette inspired a move to yarn. This time pencils sounded nice. He had never worked with them before. Eileen's Extra Tacky glue and a blow dryer seem to work remarkably well. He applies the glue with his fingers and he must use a hammer if there are changes to be made after the glue has dried. It is staggering to think of how many pencils have been used so far in transforming the hallway's walls, shelves, ceiling—thousands, maybe tens of thousands. It is difficult not to ask Jason what the count is. (He doesn't know.)

In his own home Jason Mecier cannot seem to keep himself in pencils. They inevitably find their way to the pencil hallway. Or, more specifically, to the garage beside the house, where he stores them in various yellow cardboard boxes (the kind new pencils come in), sorted by size, color, and type. After investing two-and-a-half years of work, Jason has decided that this project is halfway done. He will most likely not work with pencils again.

145

Opposite page: Looking across the hall and into the second-floor bedroom of Jaina Davis's Victorian farm cottage (1896) in the Potrero Hill district of San Francisco. The children's portrait, from the mid-1960s, is by West Coast-based artist Margaret Keane. A hallway dado has been created from three-foot-long white pens alternating with yellow and red pencils and surrounded by so-called "brain erasers."

MAGAZINE 雑誌

STUDIO VOICE VOL.283 JULY 1999 JAPAN PB: Infas Co., Ltd. E: Haruyuki Kato AD: Yasushi Fujimoto (cap) Chief D: Hiroyuki Aoki D: Hirofumi Nakajima P: Ken Hayafune (SPREAD 2) DF: Cap

SPREAD 1

SPREAD 2

SPREAD 3

MAGAZINE 雑誌

+81 VOL.6 WINTER 2000 JAPAN PB: D.D. Wave Co., Ltd. E: Toru Hachiga CD: Satoru Yamashita AD,D: Hideki Inaba P: Kohei Higuchi

+81 VOL.7 SPRING 2000 JAPAN PB: D.D. Wave Co., Ltd. E: Toru Hachiga CD: Satoru Yamashita AD,D: Hideki Inaba

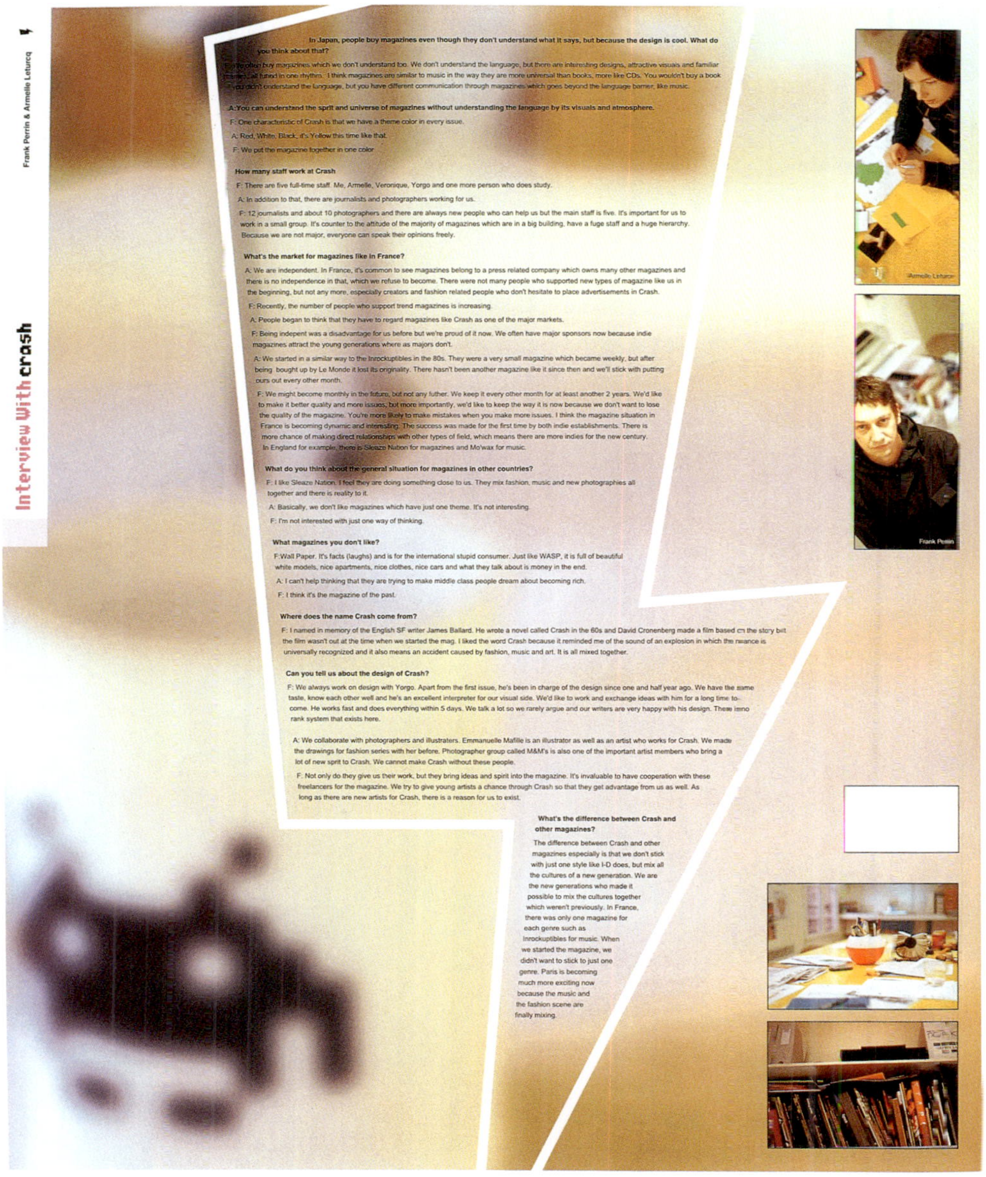

Interview with crash

Frank Perrin & Armelle Leturcq

In Japan, people buy magazines even though they don't understand what it says, but because the design is cool. What do you think about that?

F: We often buy magazines which we don't understand too. We don't understand the language, but there are interesting designs, attractive visuals and familiar [illegible] all tuned in one rhythm. I think magazines are similar to music in the way they are more universal than books, more like CDs. You wouldn't buy a book if you didn't understand the language, but you have different communication through magazines which goes beyond the language barrier, like music.

A: You can understand the sprit and universe of magazines without understanding the language by its visuals and atmosphere.

F: One characteristic of Crash is that we have a theme color in every issue.

A: Red, White, Black, it's Yellow this time like that.

F: We put the magazine together in one color

How many staff work at Crash

F: There are five full-time staff. Me, Armelle, Veronique, Yorgo and one more person who does study.

A: In addition to that, there are journalists and photographers working for us.

F: 12 journalists and about 10 photographers and there are always new people who can help us but the main staff is five. It's important for us to work in a small group. It's counter to the attitude of the majority of magazines which are in a big building, have a fuge staff and a huge hierarchy. Because we are not major, everyone can speak their opinions freely.

What's the market for magazines like in France?

A: We are independent. In France, it's common to see magazines belong to a press related company which owns many other magazines and there is no independence in that, which we refuse to become. There were not many people who supported new types of magazine like us in the beginning, but not any more, especially creators and fashion related people who don't hesitate to place advertisements in Crash.

F: Recently, the number of people who support trend magazines is increasing.

A: People began to think that they have to regard magazines like Crash as one of the major markets.

F: Being indepent was a disadvantage for us before but we're proud of it now. We often have major sponsors now because indie magazines attract the young generations where as majors don't.

A: We started in a similar way to the Inrockuptibles in the 80s. They were a very small magazine which became weekly, but after being bought up by Le Monde it lost its originality. There hasn't been another magazine like it since then and we'll stick with putting ours out every other month.

F: We might become monthly in the future, but not any futher. We keep it every other month for at least another 2 years. We'd like to make it better quality and more issues, but more importantly, we'd like to keep the way it is now because we don't want to lose the quality of the magazine. You're more likely to make mistakes when you make more issues. I think the magazine situation in France is becoming dynamic and interesting. The success was made for the first time by both indie establishments. There is more chance of making direct relationships with other types of field, which means there are more indies for the new century. In England for example, there is Sleaze Nation for magazines and Mo'wax for music.

What do you think about the general situation for magazines in other countries?

F: I like Sleaze Nation. I feel they are doing something close to us. They mix fashion, music and new photographies all together and there is reality to it.

A: Basically, we don't like magazines which have just one theme. It's not interesting.

F: I'm not interested with just one way of thinking.

What magazines you don't like?

F: Wall Paper. It's facts (laughs) and is for the international stupid consumer. Just like WASP, it is full of beautiful white models, nice apartments, nice clothes, nice cars and what they talk about is money in the end.

A: I can't help thinking that they are trying to make middle class people dream about becoming rich.

F: I think it's the magazine of the past.

Where does the name Crash come from?

F: I named in memory of the English SF writer James Ballard. He wrote a novel called Crash in the 60s and David Cronenberg made a film based on the story but the film wasn't out at the time when we started the mag. I liked the word Crash because it reminded me of the sound of an explosion in which the nuance is universally recognized and it also means an accident caused by fashion, music and art. It is all mixed together.

Can you tell us about the design of Crash?

F: We always work on design with Yorgo. Apart from the first issue, he's been in charge of the design since one and half year ago. We have the same taste, know each other well and he's an excellent interpreter for our visual side. We'd like to work and exchange ideas with him for a long time to come. He works fast and does everything within 5 days. We talk a lot so we rarely argue and our writers are very happy with his design. There is no rank system that exists here.

A: We collaborate with photographers and illustraters. Emmanuelle Mafille is an illustrator as well as an artist who works for Crash. We made the drawings for fashion series with her before. Photographer group called M&M's is also one of the important artist members who bring a lot of new sprit to Crash. We cannot make Crash without these people.

F: Not only do they give us their work, but they bring ideas and spirit into the magazine. It's invaluable to have cooperation with these freelancers for the magazine. We try to give young artists a chance through Crash so that they get advantage from us as well. As long as there are new artists for Crash, there is a reason for us to exist.

What's the difference between Crash and other magazines?

The difference between Crash and other magazines especially is that we don't stick with just one style like I-D does, but mix all the cultures of a new generation. We are the new generations who made it possible to mix the cultures together which weren't previously. In France, there was only one magazine for each genre such as Inrockuptibles for music. When we started the magazine, we didn't want to stick to just one genre. Paris is becoming much more exciting now because the music and the fashion scene are finally mixing.

Armelle Leturcq

Frank Perrin

COVER

+81 VOL.5 SPRING 1999 JAPAN PB: D.D. Wave Co., Ltd. E: Toru Hachiga CD: Satoru Yamashita AD,D: Hideki Inaba P: Max & Douglas

(SPREAD 1 / 2) +81 VOL.4 WINTER 1998 JAPAN PB: D.D. Wave Co., Ltd. E: Toru Hachiga CD: Satoru Yamashita AD,D: Hideki Inaba P: Jens Preusse (SPREAD 1)

(SPREAD 3) +81 VOL.3 SUMMER 1998 JAPAN PB: D.D. Wave Co., Ltd. E: Toru Hachiga CD: Satoru Yamashita AD,D: Hideki Inaba P: Anuschka Blommers / Niels Schumm

SPREAD 1

SPREAD 2

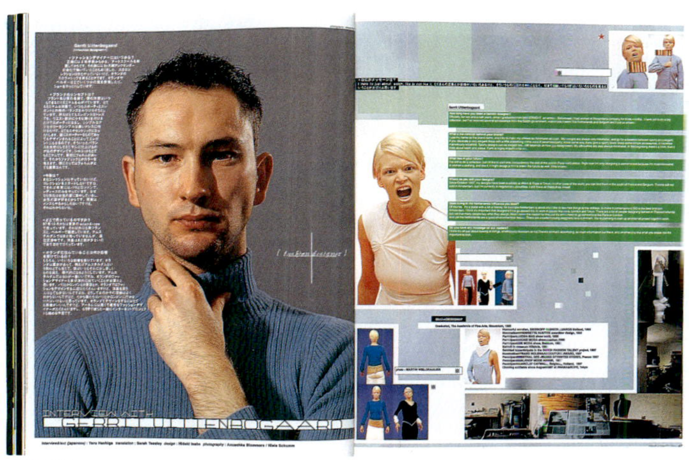

SPREAD 3

MAGAZINE 雑誌

CASA BRUTUS WINTER 1998 JAPAN

PB: Magazine House E: Kazuhiro Saito / Chieko Yoshiie / Yoshikuni Shirai AD: Yasushi Fujimoto (cap) Chief Designer: Kazuyoshi Komatsu D: Rie Matsubara / Yuriko Iwamoto / Noriteru Minezaki P: David Simmonds (COVER) / Ryu Tamagawa / Shinji Doi ST: Hiroaki Kamiyama / Tomomi Nagayama HM: Kenji Akama / Naomi Kubota DF: Cap

WINTER 1998 COVER

UNITY OF COLOR

01

01 UNITY OF COLOR
ミニマムとは色彩の統一です。自然界に存在する乱雑な色をひとつのトーンに統一するのは人間の精神だといえるかもしれません。ル・コルビュジエとその追随者たちは新精神を表現するのに、白を利用しました。色はコンセプトだと言ってもいいでしょう。問われるのは明快さです。モノトーンだけがミニマムではありません。赤も青も虹色も、色彩を統一するシンプルな主張があればいいのです。なぜ白に？　と問われたら、好きだからという答えでいいのです。好きを貫くだけでも色彩のミニマムは見えてきます。

02 REPETITION
ミニマムとは反復です。毎年咲く桜が、繰り返すという行為こそ自然の豊かさの源泉だと教えてくれます。スティーヴ・ライヒのミニマムミュージックが心地よいのは、単純な繰り返しが、知らぬ間に変容する自然の摂理を音楽に写し取っているから。こうした反復を効果的に表現するには、無駄な要素を削ぎ落とす必要があります。反復は眩暈を呼び起こし、無限をシンボライズします。無限に連なる[illegible]海波や市松模様、アラベスク模様やウィリアム・モリスの植物模様に、無限を見、同時に無を見ることもできます。非装飾がミニマムとは限りません。

03 SIMPLICITY
ミニマムとはもちろんシンプルであるということです。「最大の単純の中に最大の芸術がある」60年前、桂離宮の美に心動かされたドイツ人建築家ブルーノ・タウトは画帖の中にそう記しました。著書「日本文化私観」では「日本文化が芸術および人間生活において常に簡素を好む傾向をもっているのなら、これは実に、欧米の教養ある人々が、良い意味で"現代的（モダーン）"と呼んでいるものに他ならない」と述べています。シンプルだからこそ、素材のよさ、仕上げのよさが伝わります。作る側の姿勢もシビアに問われてきます。シンプルな美しさは永遠の難問です。

04 CONTRAST
ミニマムの奥義は対比の美です。光と闇、白と黒、剛と柔、和と洋、伝統とアバンギャルド――こうした対比を楽しむにはちょっとした技と経験が必要です。コンセプトを明快にして、無駄を極限まで削ぎ落とす。まず手始めは、間接照明で光と影を表現するのもいいでしょう。ミースのカンティレバーチェアを和の空間で使ってみるのもいいかもしれません。素材の違いを際立たせるだけの服選びも素敵です。[illegible]を礼讃し、傍ら「もっと光を」とつぶやいてみる。陰の究極が陽を孕み、陽の究極が陰を孕む、そうしたタオ（道）的な対立から美しい調和が生まれます。

05 DIVERSITY
ミニマムとは多様性です。岡倉天心が茶道を通し日本文化を西洋に紹介した「茶の本」という書物があります。そこで茶室に触れています。「数寄屋」（茶室）の原義は好き家であり、空き家とも数奇家とも当てられる、と。詩趣を宿すための仮の住み家だから「好き家」、ある美的必要を満たすために置くもののほかは一切の装飾を欠くから「空き家」、そして不完全崇拝に捧げられ、故意に何かを仕上げずにおいて、想像の働きにこれを完成させるから「数奇屋」だと天心は語っています。つまりミニマムの答えはひとつではありません。人の数だけ答えが存在するのです。

087 Casa DECEMBER 1998　　DECEMBER 1998 Casa 086

DIVERSITY

CLEAN
無菌室の清潔感にモダーンの美を感じます。白さが非日常的な空間の広がりを象徴します。

NATURAL

RECYCLE
最小限の資源を最大限活用するという意味で、リサイクルは、すてきなミニマリズムです。

2-WAY
机と椅子の機能を持った無駄のない形、さらに2-WAYという遊び心も詰めてます。

METALIC

05

NON DESIGN

NO BRAND
ノーブランドも社会的記号です。最小限のデザインだから、この知的な逆説を楽しめます。

FUNCTIONAL
アノニマス（無名性）が、究極の機能的製品を生みます。実用本位で虚飾がないからです。

MICRO COSMOS
最小空間で世界を表現する。盆栽も庭園も茶室も抽象的にデザインされた小宇宙なのです。

NATURAL／檜すのこ3,300円、ヒバ湯桶8,800円（共に東急ハンズ渋谷店）。CLEAN／病院ベッド120,000円（フランスベッド メディカルサービス）、ロス・ラブグローブのチェア56,000円、プランタホルダー《エルバーレ》12,000円（ダ・ドリアデ青山）、Double Row Cordデュベカバー S12,000円、ピローケース3,200円（Calvin Klein home／泰道リビング）。2-WAY／《AZUMI'S》のアームチェア＝テーブル各38,000円（E&Y）。RECYCLE／リサイクルペーパーの封筒各170円（文具スター）。METALIC／トラックチェスト64,000円（BETTER BUILD／東急ハンズ渋谷店）、ダイヤモンドチェア180,000円（マイスター）、スタルクのライト《アラ》75,000円（FLOS／カッシーナ・インターデコール青山本店）。NON DESIGN／英国製のアラジン・ブルーフレームヒーター34,800円（日本エー・アイ・シー）。NO BRAND／エジプト綿のワイドスプレッド・ブロードシャツ3,900円（無印良品青山3丁目店）。MICRO COSMOS／セラミックベース16,000円（ザ・コンランショップ）、草盆栽は参考商品（風庵）。FUNCTIONAL／卸し金大5,500円、小2,000円（共に有次）

093 Casa DECEMBER 1998

最近海外ではZEN STYLEが流行っているそうです。禅を欧米に紹介した鈴木大拙は「ゼロはすなわち無限」と説きました。最小限のデザインを追求しても、答えは無限に存在します。それがデザインの豊かさなのです。禁欲的になる必要はありません。自分なりのミニマルを見つけて、気軽に楽しむことができればいいのです。

CONTRAST

04

MAGAZINE 雑誌

CASA BRUTUS JAPAN — PB: Magazine House E: Kazuhiro Saito / Chieko Yoshiie AD: Yasushi Fujimoto (cap) Chief D: Kazuyoshi Komatsu DF: Cap

(COVER) — P: David Simmonds (WINTER '98) I: Jean-Philippe Delhome (SUMMER '99) / groovisions (AUTUMN '99) / IRMA (Taiko & Associates) (WINTER '99)

(SPREAD 1 / 2) SUMMER 1999 — D: Emu Tsunematsu / Yusuke Nagumo / Mitsuko Watanabe P (SPREAD 1): M.Hasui / Teruyuki Yoshimura / Yukio Futagawa P (SPREAD 2): Matteo Ferrari / Marco Bertoli

(SPREAD 3) WINTER 1998 — D: Rie Matsubara / Yuriko Iwamoto / Noriteru Minezaki P: Takahiro Imashimizu

(SPREAD 4) AUTUMN 1999 — E: Zenta Nishida D: Emu Tsunematsu / Yusuke Nagumo / Mitsuko Watanabe P: Aya Tokunaga / Kenji Yamamoto ST: Tomoko Ogawa Coordination: Mika Nakasho

(SPREAD 5) WINTER 1999 — E: Yoshikuni Shirai D: Yusuke Nagumo / Mitsuko Watanabe P: Manabu Matsunaga

SPREAD 1

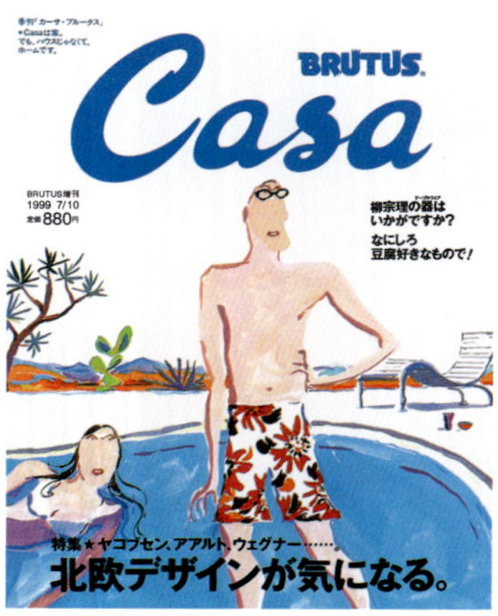

SUMMER 1999 COVER

SPREAD 2

WINTER 1998 COVER

SPREAD 3

AUTUMN 1999 COVER

SPREAD 4

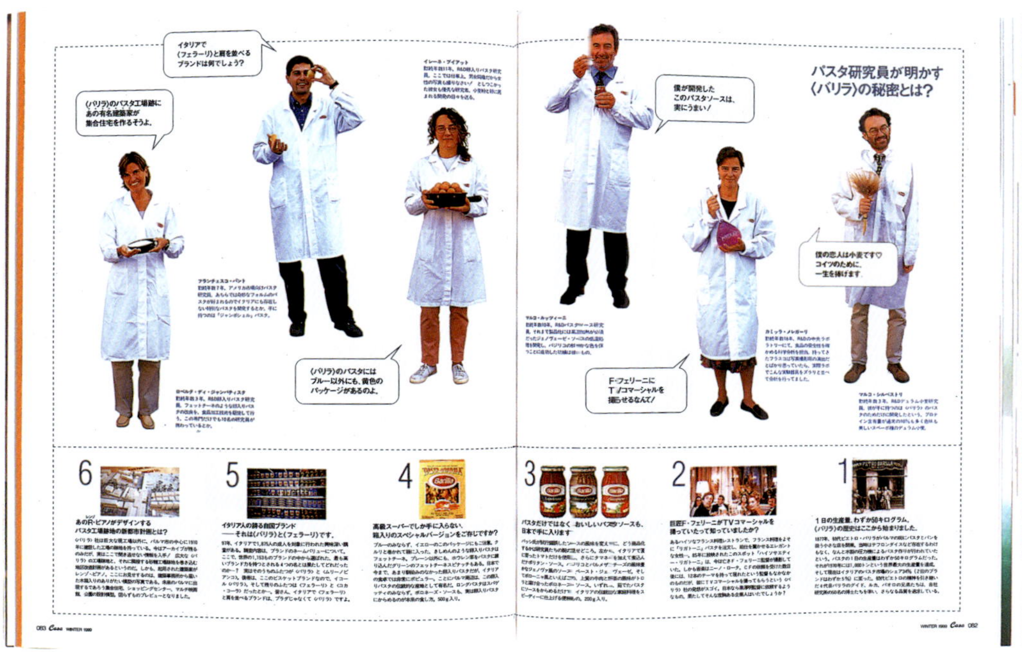

WINTER 1999 COVER

SPREAD 5

MAGAZINE 雑誌

SYNOPSIS NO.6 SPRING 2000 FRANCE

PB,CW: Synopsis Sarl E: Hervé Lavergne CD,AD,D,TY: Stéphane Vrielinck AD,D,TY: Thierry Chapuy / Jean-Patrice Wattinne P: Di Marco (COVER) / J. Nassif (SPREAD 2) CD,DF: L'Éclaireur

SYNOPSIS NO.7 MAY-JUNE 2000 FRANCE

PB,CW: Synopsis Sarl E: Hervé Lavergne CD,AD,D,TY: Stéphane Vrielinck AD,D,TY: Thierry Chapuy / Jean-Patrice Wattinne P: Roger Arpajou (COVER) / Coll. Les Cahiers Du Cinéma (SPREAD 4) CD,DF: L'Éclaireur

SPREAD 1

SPREAD 3

SPREAD 2

SPREAD 4

No.06 COVER

No.07 COVER

SYNOPSIS NO.4 AUTUMN 1999 FRANCE

PB,CW: Synopsis Sarl E: Hervé Lavergne CD,AD,D,TY: Stéphane Vrielinck AD,D,TY: Thierry Chapuy / Jean-Patrice Wattinne P: Lucas Film Ltd. & TM (COVER) CD,DF: L'Éclaireur

No.04 COVER

(SPREAD 1 / 2) BLACK + WHITE NO.38 AUGUST 1999 AUSTRALIA PB: Studio Magazine E,CD: Marcello Grand E: Karen-Jane Eyre AD,D,P (SPREAD 2): Andrew Godfrey P: Adrian Brown (SPREAD 1) I: Nicole Moffat (SPREAD 2: Elephant)

(SPREAD 3) BLACK + WHITE NO.41 FEBRUARY 2000 AUSTRALIA PB: Studio Magazine E,CD: Marcello Grand E: Karen-Jane Eyre AD,D: Andrew Godfrey P: Stephen Oxenbury

SPREAD 1

Junior High Recordings is a record label whose office lies in the black heart of the city of angels: Sunset Boulevard, Los Angeles. The latest offering from this little independent is straight out of the theatre of misanthropy. Gore splatter type on the cd cover spells out the words: DJ TRON – *Chrome Padded Cell*. Underneath, a severed hand, maintaining even in its dismemberment the satanic salute of raised forefinger and pinkie, the gestural representation of mammon, the horned beast. In the hand is an object that could be either a glow stick or a crack vial. The track listing reads like a list of titles Alice Cooper might have rejected on the grounds that they were just too scary: "I'm Going To Hell", "Cerebral Bore", "Asylum Turned Nursery School", "The Fear", "Murder The World", "Cannibal DJ", "House Of Hurt", "Torment The Tortured Souls", "Blood Pressure". It's nasty stuff.

What to make of such a product? If I were more adult, more prone to the familiar nostalgia of the reasonable cultural columnist, the critical response would be easy, almost preprogrammed. There would be an initial tone of shock and an unwillingness to understand: the editorial line that makes an Other of youth. Then a questioning of the inability to inculcate proper civilised values: a strained parental tone wondering where it all went wrong. Then a general sense of resignation about the way the postmodern world is beyond our understanding: an agony about the loss of the familiar and the world the next generation will make.

Not being that particular kind of cultural critic however, my first response is something more like: "Cool!" If nothing else, DJ TRON is a new and interesting permutation in the ever-changing symbolic game of youth culture. It marks a dramatic reinvention of that ancient cult, the Goth, this time via rave and ultraviolence. Musically, perhaps, it's not that interesting. Lame, too-fast computer drum sequences (in a hardcore style) coloured with distorted horror movie samples. *Chrome Padded Cell* is pure noise, with all the negative connotations of such a description. But stylistically it's Anne Rice on crack meets David Lynch on meth-amphetamine. That is to say: a fascinating meeting of minds.

Meet the new Goth. The outsider is in again and Byronic unhappiness has never looked so good. Youth culture hasn't had such a powerful monster since gangsta rap forced its way into the public consciousness 10 years or so ago. Black remains the colour of fear and loathing. But this time around it's an adopted rather than a genetic black; black as a sign. Black worn as kohl, black worn as a trenchcoat.

With Marilyn Manson Goth is big again, but it's gonna get a whole lot bigger. In a country like America, founded by puritans, it makes sense that the most dangerous form of stylistic rebellion would be the inversion of the rich load of biblical imagery that Goth embraces. Manson is the tip of this iceberg, the guy whose managed to forge a consumer product from the frustrations that come from being different, who turned the kid who couldn't quite fit in into the anti-hero whose refusal to do so put them just a cut above the mass.

The moral right in the United States were already up in arms over Manson and his satanic theatrics. In the wake of the Columbine High shootings the moral panic around Goth culture can only be expected to intensify. The Columbine killers, Eric Harris and Dylan Klebold, were part of a clique called the Trenchcoat Mafia, and in what passes for analysis in the media since the bloodshed, they have become associated with Goths because of their fashion sense. All other indications of a relationship between Goth culture and Harris and Klebold are in dispute.

Those who hold the fort for the American mainstream attempt to lay the blame for youth violence anywhere other than the Second Amendment's guardianship of the right to bear arms. *Time* magazine even went as far as comparing Harris and Klebold to the Serbian forces perpetrating the ethnic cleansing in Kosovo. In an essay that linked the teen killers to Serbian soldiers via their taste for overcoats, Roger Rosenblatt wrote "One tries to make sense of the high school killings, and the events in Kosovo may be a way in."

Perhaps, but the killers at Columbine were all-American kids, in Harris' case the son of a decorated Air Force pilot. Why look as far as Serbian troops for a military inspiration for their crimes? When Bill Clinton asked the nation to "reach out to our children and teach them to express their anger and resolve their conflicts with words, not weapons" it had all the credibility that a similar request for greater marital fidelity might have had, coming from the same source. In a nation where war is a frequently employed tool of diplomatic leverage, who could have been surprised that kids would choose guns to settle their differences?

When aberrant children commit evil, the media rolls out the usual suspects: rock music, action films and video games. Rarely does it make connections to the legitimation of violence at the heart of corporate culture. Recently, a business seminar in Sydney was hosted by Stormin' Norman Schwarzkopf and Mikhail Gorbachev. Neither of these men ever so much as ran a corner store. Their qualifications: they presided over the saturated bombing of Iraq and Afghanistan respectively. One has to wonder why the *Daily Telegraph* can only see symptoms of violent behaviour in the fact that Dylan Klebold was "an avid music fan who wore his cap backwards".

When Charlton Heston, head of America's National Rifle Association, runs with the standard line stating "this is not a gun issue, this is a child issue", and recommends that teachers be issued with holstered handguns, one has to wonder how dangerous Goth posturing really is. With such palpable evil all about us, enshrined at the heart of mainstream culture, you don't have to turn to 19th-century *nosferatus* for a kill thrill.

While the DJ TRONs and Marilyn Mansons of the world will generally cop the rap in the aftermath of tragedies like Columbine High, violence is a product on sale everywhere. From revenge films to the best massacre-core shock rock, from mass-market weapons of mass destruction to websites with detailed information on how to increase your kill ratios, from movie icon Charlton Heston's championing of guns to military strategy as the key to better business, this is a bold new age of information capitalism for the terminally paranoid. In the game of media blame, kids and their passions just happen to make a soft target.

SPREAD 2

SPREAD 3

MAGAZINE 雑誌

(SPREAD 1 / 2) BLACK + WHITE NO.38 AUGUST 1999 AUSTRALIA PB: Studio Magazine E,CD: Marcello Grand E: Karen-Jane Eyre AD,D: Andrew Godfrey

(SPREAD 3) BLACK + WHITE NO.41 FEBRUARY 2000 AUSTRALIA PB: Studio Magazine E,CD: Marcello Grand E: Karen-Jane Eyre AD,D: Andrew Godfrey P: Fergus Stothart

SPREAD 1

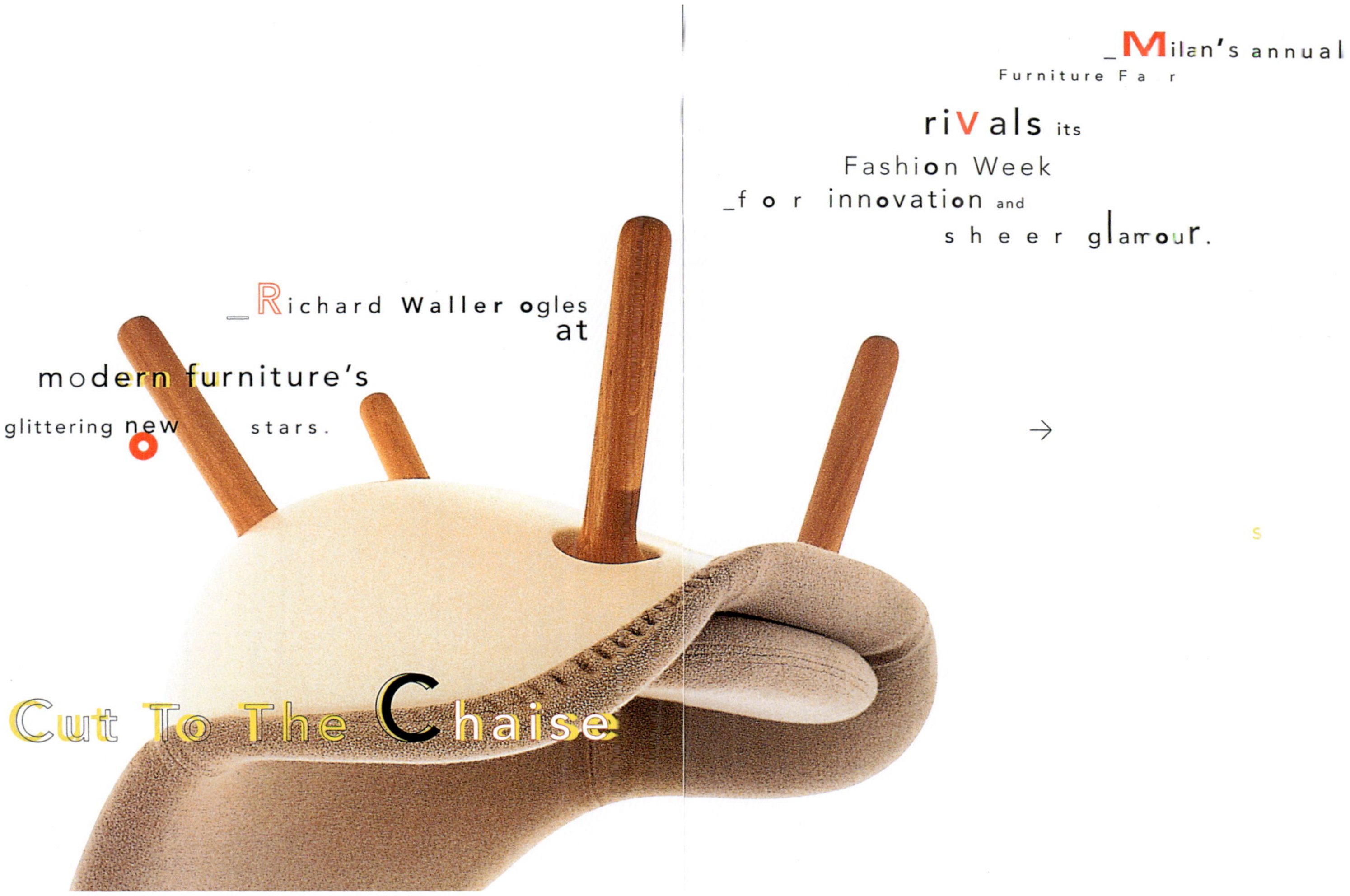

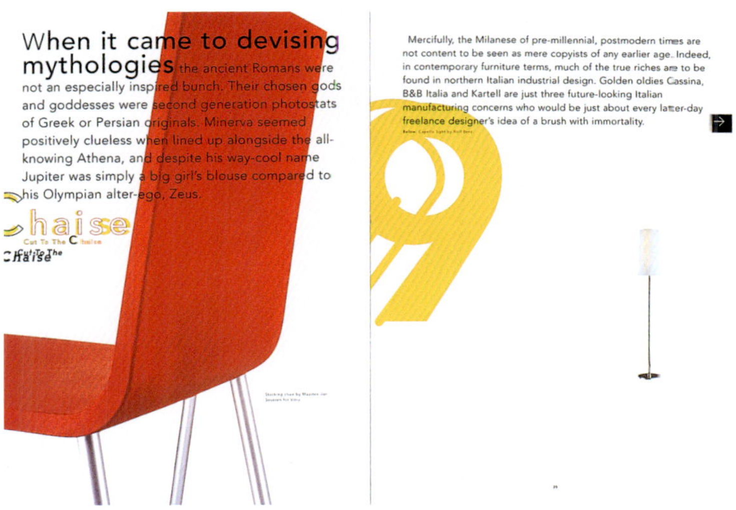

SPREAD 2

SPREAD 3

MAGAZINE 雑誌

BLACK + WHITE NO.28 DECEMBER 1997 AUSTRALIA PB: Studio Magazine E,CD: Marcello Grand E: Karen-Jane Eyre AD,D: Tim McIntyre
P: Daniela Federici (COVER) / Jez Smith

F*#K S**T UP!

THE HISTORY OF POP MUSIC IS PUNCTUATED BY THE STRATEGIC DEPLOYMENT OF NAUGHTY WORDS, BUT HOW DOES ONE CAUSE OFFENCE IN THE 1990S? **text** andrew stafford **photography** jez smith

For about half the population, the new album by techno-rockers the Prodigy gets off to a, well, confrontational start. "Smack My Bitch Up", the opening track from the pithily titled *The Fat Of The Land*, has attracted plenty of heat, much of it from a liberal audience struggling to contain music that it otherwise feels compelled to support.

Triple J loves the song, but considers the title "unnecessary", according to a source at Sony. In America, where the album has been released by Madonna's label Maverick, the song list has been edited to "Smack My ***** Up" and, ludicrously, "Funky ****" ("Funky Shit"). Which is kind of ironic, given Madonna's famous claim that there's nothing like a good spanking.

PERHAPS IT'S BECAUSE THE PRODIGY ARE FOUR WORKING-CLASS YOBS FROM ESSEX THAT "SMACK MY BITCH UP" IS BEING SUBJECTED TO SUCH LITERAL INTERPRETATION.

'Bad' language has a long and distinguished history in pop culture and, particularly, in pop music, where swearing is but one (not always effective) signifier of the rebellion that forms an essential element of the language and iconography of rock'n'roll. Sure, all that talk about a revolution was just that – talk – but revolution these days hardly indicates anything as naive as overthrow of the established order so much as it refers to new ways of seeing the world around us.

Language is the means by which we accomplish this, and when it comes to language, pop culture leads the establishment along by its nose ring. And, as Skunk Anansie would tell us, this process is indeed "fucking political": struggles over the use of sexist versus inclusive (or pc) language is one latter-day example.

In the early days of rock'n'roll, however, it used to be enough simply to drop the offending words. Never mind the context: in 1977 the Sex Pistols achieved instant notoriety not for their music, but for being cajoled into calling William Grundy a "dirty fucker" on BBC television. Yet you won't find a more enduring or compelling example of utter rudeness on record than Johnny Rotten's expostulation "fuck this and fuck that/fuck it all and fuck the fucking brat" on the song "Bodies". Even today, the sheer venom of Lydon's delivery – combined with the fact that he is actually talking about an aborted foetus – is almost thrillingly offensive. (One must admit that in the hands of anyone blessed with less natural charisma than the young John Lydon, the same words would sound pretty silly.)

These days, however, context is everything. Meredith Brooks has just scored a chart-topping hit with her song "Bitch", and maybe if she wasn't so obviously a wind-up Alanis created by American major label machinery, her quasi-feminist appropriation of the term would carry more weight. Pre-Alanis, Liz Phair won an avalanche of critical praise for the graphic sexual content of her debut album *Exile In Guyville*, which contained such lyrical gems as "I want to fuck you like a dog/I'll take you home and make you like it".

Shortly afterwards, Trent Reznor's Nine Inch Nails also had a number one hit with "Closer", featuring the almost identical sentiment "I want to fuck you like an animal". Many men and women consider this to be the ultimate bonking song, yet when black rappers like Snoop Doggy Dogg or Ice T venture into the same territory, they are almost invariably condemned. These days, the words are scarcely as important as who's doing the talking.

Perhaps, then, it's because the Prodigy are four working-class yobs from Essex that "Smack My Bitch Up" is being subjected to such literal interpretation. This is unfortunate. It seems extremely unlikely that the group themselves would individually advocate the maltreatment of women and, surely, the overwhelming majority of their fans realise this.

But it is this contradiction that is the source of the song's power. The group are smart enough to realise that they aren't likely to raise any eyebrows by swearing: "Funky Shit" is hardly meant to be offensive; in fact, it's hilarious. "Smack My Bitch Up", on the other hand, plays on our recognition of a pc pressure point and gleefully stomps all over it. The Prodigy exploit our knowledge that *you can't say things like that any more* – at least, you're not supposed to.

It's often claimed that it's harder to cause offence in the 1990s. It's certainly true that the powers that be haven't kept up with sliding standards of obscenity, at least not if the volume of albums embossed with "Parental Advisory" logos is anything to go by. "Smack My Bitch Up", in the context of a mosh-friendly rave track performed by four electrifried computer abusers with comical hairdos, is a perfect late-'90s example of how pop music reinvents itself; not only with technology, but with language. Lines drawn in the sand will, by definition, be forever shifting. But they are always there to be crossed. ✚

35

No.28 COVER

MAGAZINE 雑誌

MIX! NO.21 JUNE 1998 ARGENTINA CL: MUSIMUNDO AD,D: Andrés Sobrino P: Gustavo Saiegh (COVER) P,CW: Fernando Brenner (SPREAD 1) CW: Marta Dilon (COVER) / Andrea Kowalski (SPREAD 2) Editorial Firm: Editorial Gráfica

SPREAD 1

No.21 COVER

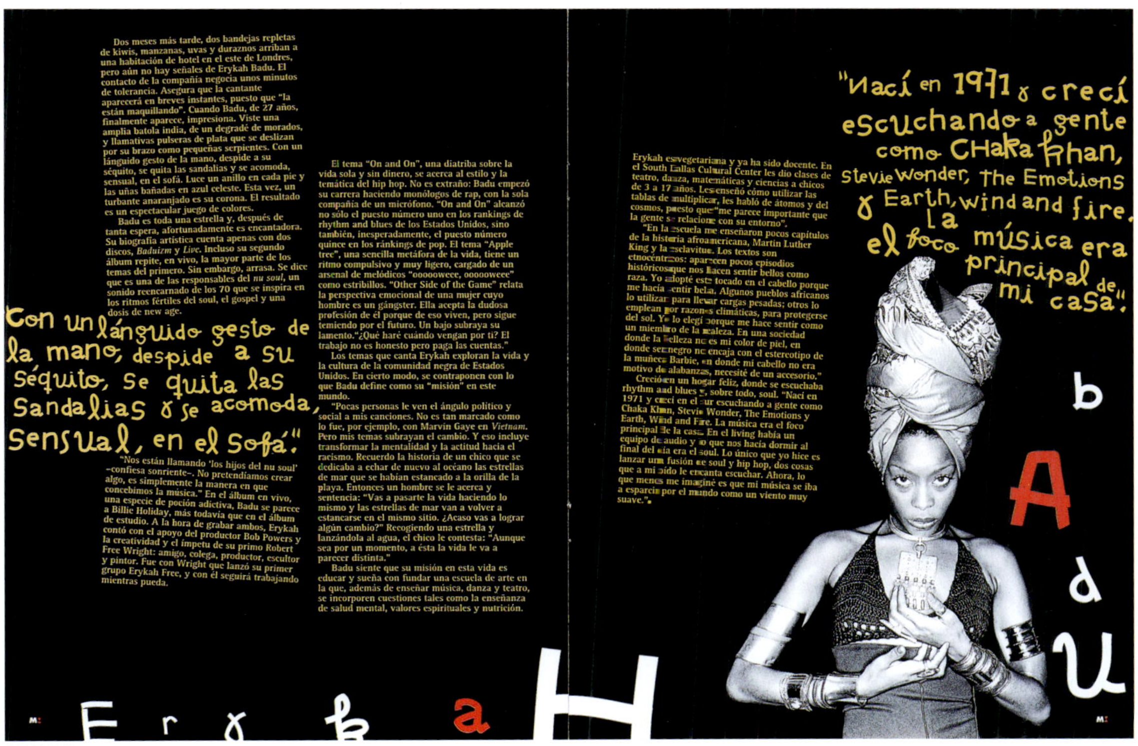

SPREAD 2

BOOK 書籍

DOM PÉRIGNON 1999 AUSTRALIA CL: Swift & Modre Pty Ltd. CD: Sophie Bartho D: Lawrence Hennessy P: Keiichi Tahara DF: Sophie Bartho + Associates

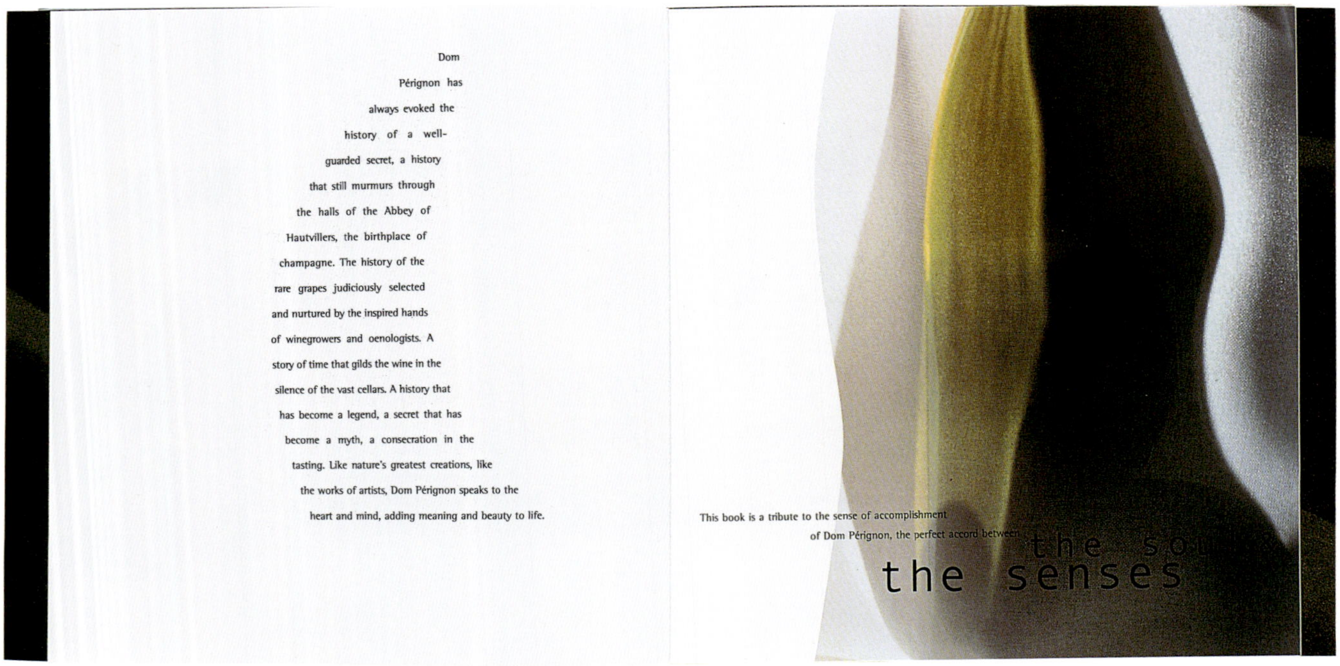
Dom Pérignon has always evoked the history of a well-guarded secret, a history that still murmurs through the halls of the Abbey of Hautvillers, the birthplace of champagne. The history of the rare grapes judiciously selected and nurtured by the inspired hands of winegrowers and oenologists. A story of time that gilds the wine in the silence of the vast cellars. A history that has become a legend, a secret that has become a myth, a consecration in the tasting. Like nature's greatest creations, like the works of artists, Dom Pérignon speaks to the heart and mind, adding meaning and beauty to life.

This book is a tribute to the sense of accomplishment of Dom Pérignon, the perfect accord between

the senses

A Benedictine monk named Dom Pierre Pérignon arrived at the Abbey of St Pierre d'Hautvillers nearly three centuries ago. Seeking out only the best fruit for his top cuvées, he showed an unusual interest in quality.

It may not be unusual by today's standards, but this concept of 'selection' was quit revolutionary for the 17th century.

Dom Pérignon owed his delicacy to his capacity to listen and the good sense to refrain from forcing nature, endeavouring rather to understand it and respect it, the way one respects time...

divine inspiration

COVER

Pinot Noir and Chardonnay compliment each other perfectly as they rise symmetrically

the perfect
balance

Dom Pérignon calls all our senses into play. There is nothing heavy or opulent, simply a sense of perfection; known as assemblage. Pinot Noir and Chardonnay compliment each other perfectly as they rise symmetrically. A subtle, complex interplay, there is nothing further to be added nor subtracted. No one element dominates in the perfect balance known as Dom Pérignon.

The hallmark of every Dom Pérignon cuvée is: ethereal, precise, complex, sensual and silky.

silky

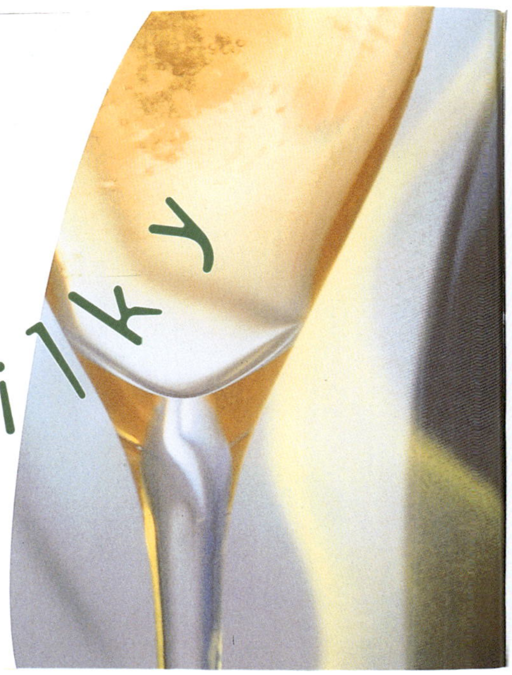

The
ultimate
experience

The wine will offer fantastic sensations – very fine bubbles, a complex bouquet with aromas of white blossom, hazelnut and toasted brioche. The attack is intense, the evolution in the mouth sensual, the finish is endless on the palate. The senses are truly aroused.

MENSWORK MAGAZINE 1998 USA CL: American Crew CD,P: David Raccuglia AD: Marcos Chavez D: Aimee Sealfon CW: Kurt Kueffner / Terry Lane / Craig Hanson DF: Liska + Associates, Inc.

08

on the edge of cut-ting

by Kurt Kueffner

The Menswork effort
is an educationally
driven division of
American Crew.
We are dedicated
to helping professional
stylists obtain the
skills and tools
necessary to develop
and maintain a desir-
able male clientele.

What the Hell
David Raccuglia

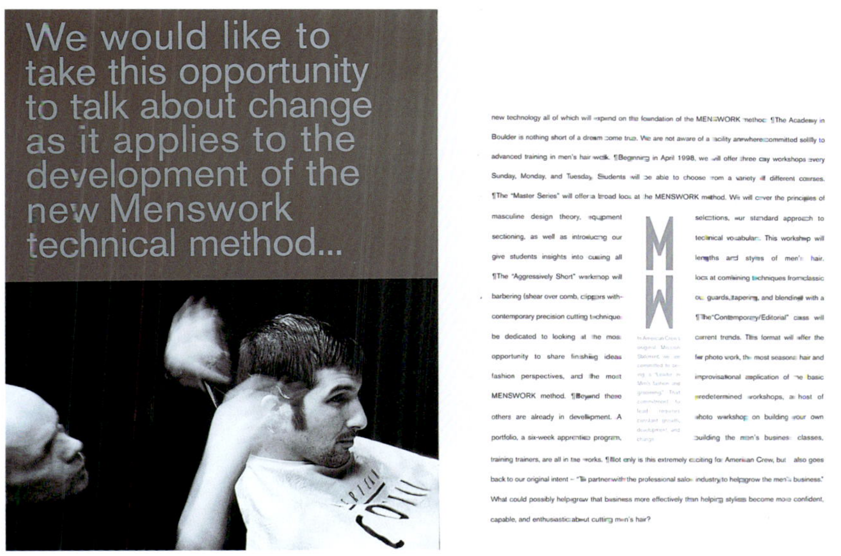
We would like to
take this opportunity
to talk about change
as it applies to the
development of the
new Menswork
technical method...
new technology all of which will expand on the foundation of the MENSWORK method. ¶The Academy in Boulder is nothing short of a dream come true. We are not aware of a facility anywhere committed solely to advanced training in men's hair work. ¶Beginning in April 1998, we will offer three day workshops every Sunday, Monday, and Tuesday. Students will be able to choose from a variety of different courses. ¶The "Master Series" will offer a broad look at the MENSWORK method. We will cover the principles of masculine design theory, equipment selections, our standard approach to sectioning, as well as introducing our technical vocabulary. This workshop will give students insights into cutting all lengths and styles of men's hair. ¶The "Aggressively Short" workshop will look at combining techniques from classic barbering (shear over comb, clippers without guards, tapering, and blending) with a contemporary precision cutting technique. ¶The "Contemporary/Editorial" class will be dedicated to looking at the most current trends. This format will offer the opportunity to share finishing ideas for photo work, the most seasonal hair and fashion perspectives, and the most improvisational application of the basic MENSWORK method. ¶Beyond these predetermined workshops, a host of others are already in development. A photo workshop on building your own portfolio, a six-week apprentice program, building the men's business classes, training trainers, are all in the works. ¶Not only is this extremely exciting for American Crew, but it also goes back to our original intent – "To partner with the professional salon industry to help grow the men's business." What could possibly help grow that business more effectively than helping stylists become more confident, capable, and enthusiastic about cutting men's hair?
MW

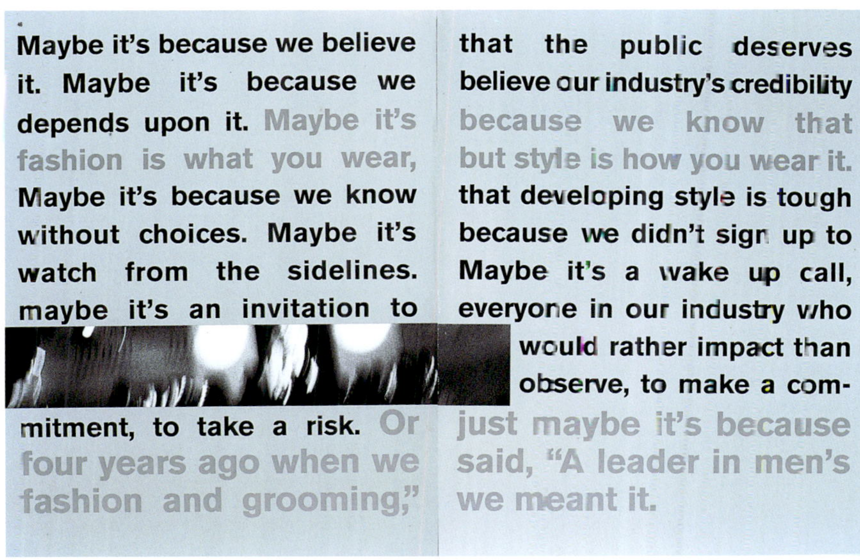
Maybe it's because we believe that the public deserves
it. Maybe it's because we believe our industry's credibility
depends upon it. Maybe it's because we know that
fashion is what you wear, but style is how you wear it.
Maybe it's because we know that developing style is tough
without choices. Maybe it's because we didn't sign up to
watch from the sidelines. Maybe it's a wake up call,
maybe it's an invitation to everyone in our industry who
would rather impact than
observe, to make a com-
mitment, to take a risk. Or just maybe it's because
four years ago when we said, "A leader in men's
fashion and grooming,"
we meant it.

BROCHURE ブローシャー

ERNIE.EY.COM 1999 USA CL: Ernie Online AD,D: Mark Murphy DF: Murphy Design Inc.

how does ernie WORK ?

For an annual membership fee, subscribers gain access to the password-protected Ernie site on the Internet's World Wide Web. This allows them to submit questions directly to Ernst & Young. Subscribers give Ernie their questions, and whatever background information they think is important to provide.

Ernie "Knowledge Providers" sort the questions by subject, and then route them through Ernst & Young's internal knowledge web, or intranet, to the professional who is most knowledgeable about the specific industry and issue at-hand.

Answers are routed directly back to the subscriber on the Ernie web site and are available within two business days. Often an answer can facilitate an ongoing dialogue that may help subscribers to choose an appropriate course of action.

Subscribers can also search the Ernie Previously-Asked Questions database to find similar answers to their business issues. In these cases, responses are immediate, sometimes prompting follow-up questions in the same problem area.

6 | connect to the people of Ernst & Young | http://ernie.ey.com

< Ernie clears your path to success. >

Is there a short-cut to information-gathering and decision-making? Sure. With Ernie on your team, you can avoid getting bogged down with fact-finding task forces and feasibility studies. Best of all, you aren't forced to burden your top people by asking them to evaluate issues that they don't have time for or that may not fit their area of expertise. <> Instead, let your people focus on where they have the most impact — and ask Ernie for the rest! In only two business days, or even sooner, when you consult the PAQ database, Ernie gives you the knowledge you need to seize opportunities as they arise. <>

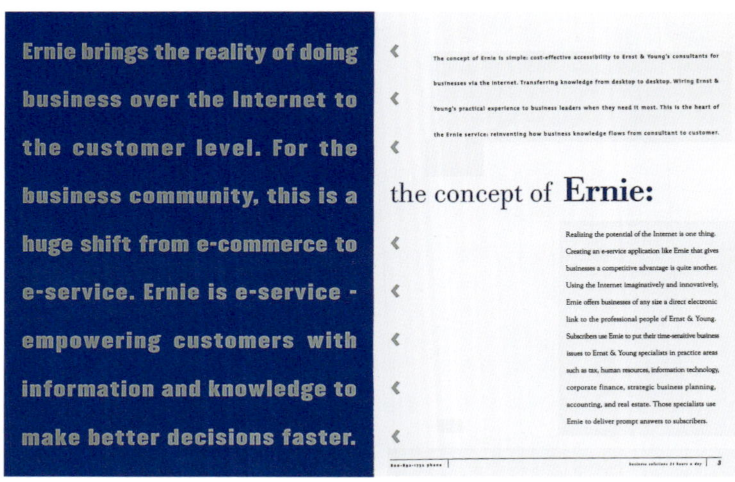

Ernie brings the reality of doing business over the Internet to the customer level. For the business community, this is a huge shift from e-commerce to e-service. Ernie is e-service - empowering customers with information and knowledge to make better decisions faster.

The concept of Ernie is simple: cost-effective accessibility to Ernst & Young's consultants for businesses via the Internet. Transferring knowledge from desktop to desktop. Wiring Ernst & Young's practical experience to business leaders when they need it most. This is the heart of the Ernie service: reinventing how business knowledge flows from consultant to customer.

the concept of Ernie:

Realizing the potential of the Internet is one thing. Creating an e-service application like Ernie that gives businesses a competitive advantage is quite another. Using the Internet imaginatively and innovatively, Ernie offers businesses of any size a direct electronic link to the professional people of Ernst & Young. Subscribers use Ernie to put their time-sensitive business issues to Ernst & Young specialists in practice areas such as tax, human resources, information technology, corporate finance, strategic business planning, accounting, and real estate. Those specialists use Ernie to deliver prompt answers to subscribers.

business solutions 24 hours a day | 3

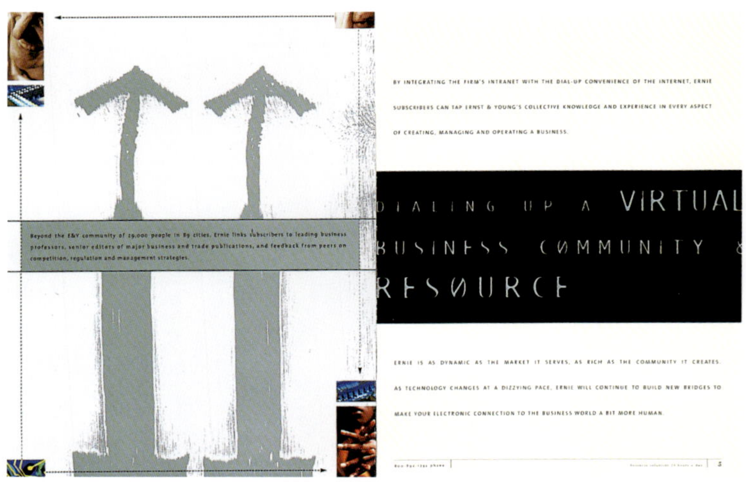

Beyond the E&Y community of 29,000 people in 89 cities, Ernie links subscribers to leading business professors, senior editors of major business and trade publications, and feedback from peers on competition, regulation and management strategies.

BY INTEGRATING THE FIRM'S INTRANET WITH THE DIAL-UP CONVENIENCE OF THE INTERNET, ERNIE SUBSCRIBERS CAN TAP ERNST & YOUNG'S COLLECTIVE KNOWLEDGE AND EXPERIENCE IN EVERY ASPECT OF CREATING, MANAGING AND OPERATING A BUSINESS.

DIALING UP A VIRTUAL BUSINESS COMMUNITY & RESOURCE

ERNIE IS AS DYNAMIC AS THE MARKET IT SERVES, AS RICH AS THE COMMUNITY IT CREATES. AS TECHNOLOGY CHANGES AT A DIZZYING PACE, ERNIE WILL CONTINUE TO BUILD NEW BRIDGES TO MAKE YOUR ELECTRONIC CONNECTION TO THE BUSINESS WORLD A BIT MORE HUMAN.

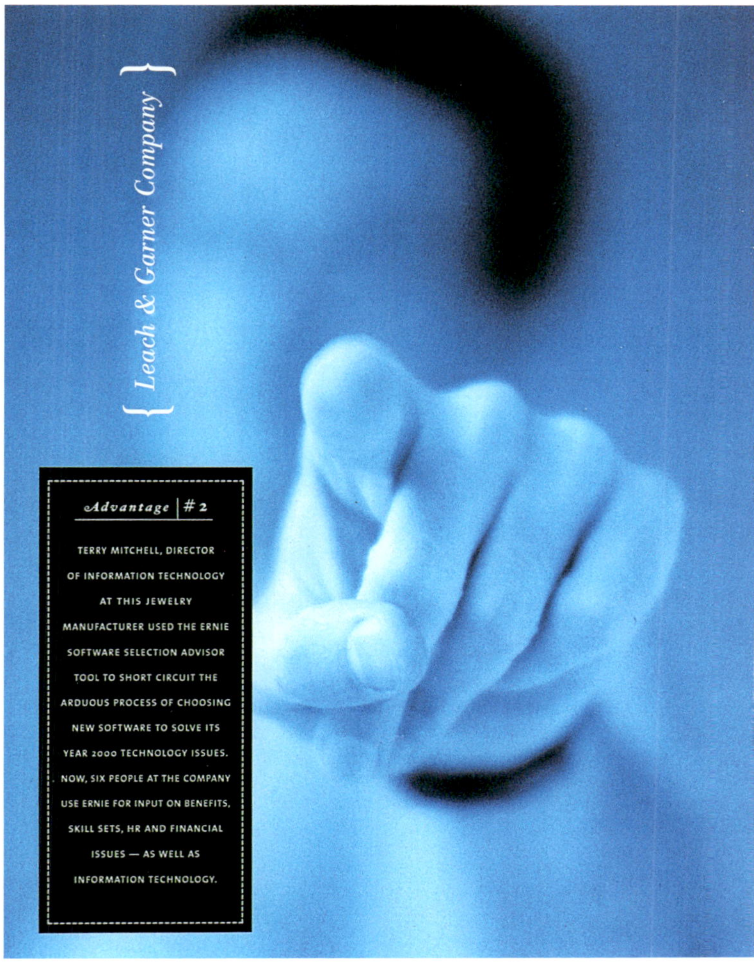

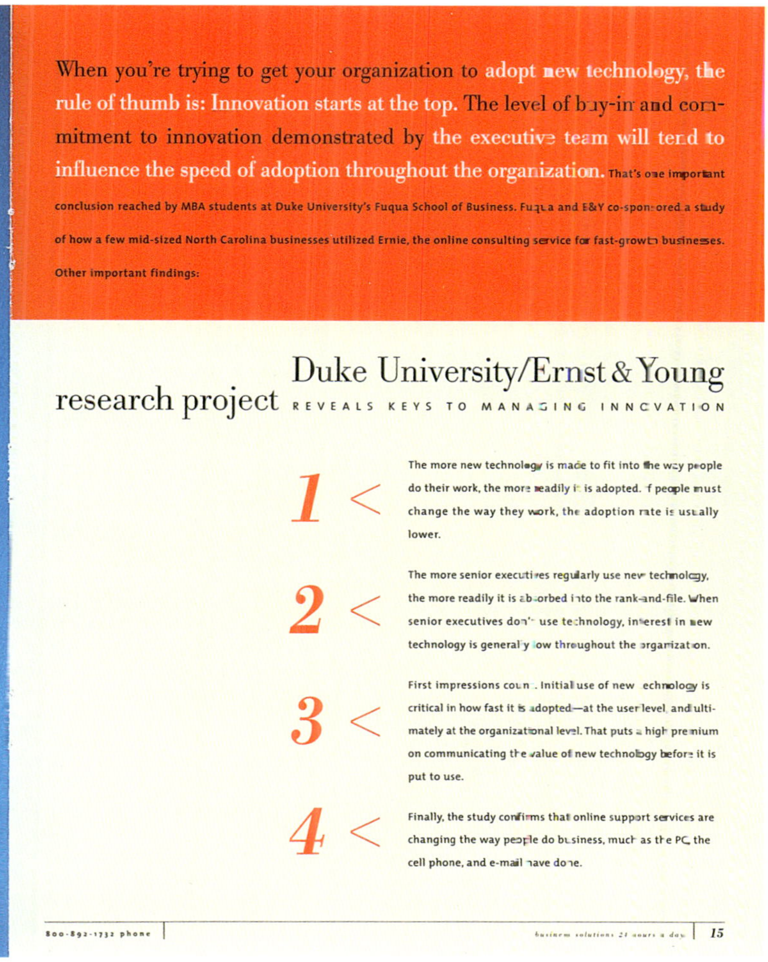

When you're trying to get your organization to adopt new technology, the rule of thumb is: Innovation starts at the top. The level of buy-in and commitment to innovation demonstrated by the executive team will tend to influence the speed of adoption throughout the organization. That's one important conclusion reached by MBA students at Duke University's Fuqua School of Business. Fuqua and E&Y co-sponsored a study of how a few mid-sized North Carolina businesses utilized Ernie, the online consulting service for fast-growth businesses. Other important findings:

Duke University/Ernst & Young research project REVEALS KEYS TO MANAGING INNOVATION

1 < The more new technology is made to fit into the way people do their work, the more readily it is adopted. If people must change the way they work, the adoption rate is usually lower.

2 < The more senior executives regularly use new technology, the more readily it is absorbed into the rank-and-file. When senior executives don't use technology, interest in new technology is generally low throughout the organization.

3 < First impressions count. Initial use of new technology is critical in how fast it is adopted—at the user level, and ultimately at the organizational level. That puts a high premium on communicating the value of new technology before it is put to use.

4 < Finally, the study confirms that online support services are changing the way people do business, much as the PC, the cell phone, and e-mail have done.

800-892-1732 phone | business solutions 24 hours a day | 15

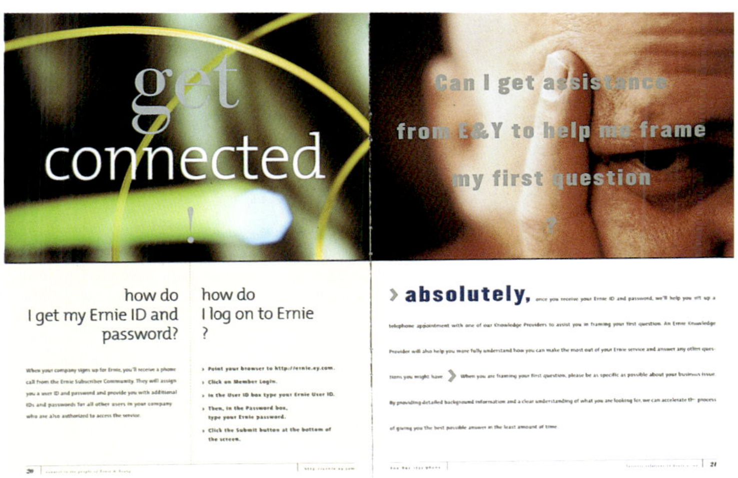

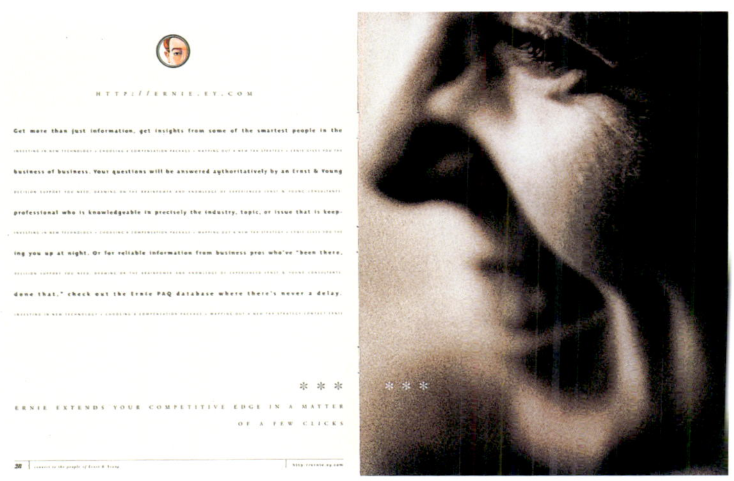

DR. SINGH, THE ER DOCTOR, ELABORATES: "WITH CARDIAC PATIENTS YOU LOOK AT THE EKG. YOU KNOW YOU ARE DEALING WITH AN MI IF THERE ARE ST ELEVATIONS IN AT LEAST TWO CONTIGUOUS LEADS WITH RECIPROCAL CHANGES, BUT SOMETIMES THE EKG ISN'T SO CLEARCUT..."

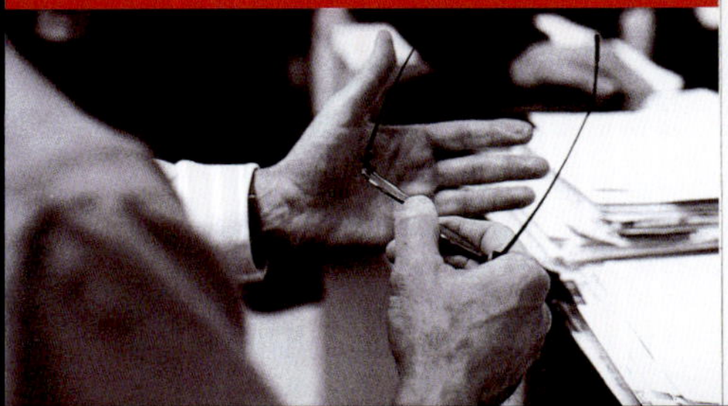

DR. SINGH,
ER DOCTOR

A myocardial infarction, or MI, results from death of cardiac tissue caused by abrupt reduction in coronary blood flow, and subsequent lack of oxygen supplied to the heart (also called ischemia). In more than 90% of patients with acute MI, a thrombus, or blood clot, blocks a coronary artery, often after the rupture of atherosclerotic plaque. The most severe type of heart attack, the transmural MI, involves the whole thickness of the heart muscle, and is often associated with abnormal Q waves on an EKG. The non-Q-wave MI is usually associated with less heart damage and generally results from a thrombus that does not totally block a coronary artery. However, patients with a non-Q-wave MI are more prone to reinfarction, another MI, resulting in further ischemic damage. As any damage to the myocardium can affect the heart's ability to pump, patients with a non-Q-wave MI or unstable angina (another ischemic condition caused by intermittent coronary blockage) carry a much higher long-term risk for death or a subsequent and often more severe MI.

Dr. Singh continues, "Here at this institution we find that about 65% of patients with unstable angina come into the ER complaining of chest pain and/or shortness of breath. They're usually seen within 10 minutes. You have to act fast, because the patient can really lose a lot of heart muscle if insufficient blood flow persists. I call the attending cardiologist STAT if a patient has an MI, and we start pain control, give aspirin to thin the blood and nitroglycerin to dilate the arteries. If the patient is short of breath we give pulsed oxygen. If it's a Q-wave MI, the cardiologist may order a thrombolytic agent or perform direct PTCA." (Thrombolytic agents are used to break up the fibrin mesh surrounding the blood clot that is obstructing blood flow in the arteries supplying the heart muscle.)

As Dr. Singh pauses, Charlotte speaks up. "If the patient has subacute pain, pain that's not too terrible or is being controlled, we can evaluate the situation a bit further. I send a blood sample to the lab to get information on cardiac enzyme levels: CK levels, troponin levels, MB fractionated isoenzymes. It can take anywhere from 45 to 60 minutes or longer to get results..."

"But we don't always wait for the labs," says Dr. Singh. "If a patient has unstable angina, I begin to treat them with IV heparin, an anticoagulant used to try to prevent blood clots from forming, in addition to their aspirin and nitrates. If their blood pressure is high, I give an IV beta-blocker to reduce their heart rate and bring down the pressure, and call a cardiologist to admit them."

Where the patient goes from the Emergency Department depends on the cardiologist, who includes in the decision the required feedback from the emergency physician. The patients can go either to the cardiac care unit (CCU) or the cardiac telemetry unit (CTU), also often called a "step-down" unit. This determination is generally made on the basis of chest pain severity. If a patient has ongoing pain that doesn't resolve even with medication, or "rules in" for an MI, that patient will go to the CCU. A less severe case will be sent to the CTU to be continuously monitored for EKG changes or progression to heart attack.

Dr. Singh continues, "The ER nurse calls the nurses on the unit to give them a report on the patient, to tell them, for example, if the 'labs' were elevated. If cardiac enzymes are not elevated we can pretty much rule out MI, which means the patient most likely has unstable angina. From there, the patient will either continue to be treated medically or undergo some sort of cardiac procedure."

EKG

ELECTROCARDIOGRAM PRINTOUT

The electrocardiogram (also known as EKG or ECG) is a tracing of the electrical activity of the heart muscle detected at the body surface. Different wave patterns show functional information about different areas of the heart, which is divided into four chambers. The two upper chambers, called atria, receive blood from the veins, while the two lower chambers, called ventricles, pump blood into the arteries to become oxygenated or go out to the entire body. The normal EKG shows deflections caused by atrial and ventricular activity, and also the time intervals involved in the coordination of the heart's pumping mechanics. Nurses can perform EKGs, or specialized EKG technicians may be dispatched to different areas of the hospital (such as the Emergency Department) to perform EKGs. Every EKG that is taken at the hospital must be read and confirmed by a cardiologist. Larger hospitals that are computerized may have an EKG from the ER or CCU downloaded to a central computer, where a hard copy may be dispatched to the Cardiology Service for confirmation. Although the EKG is important, it does not give a definitive diagnosis of MI and must be viewed in context with other information such as blood enzyme levels, echocardiography, or angiography.

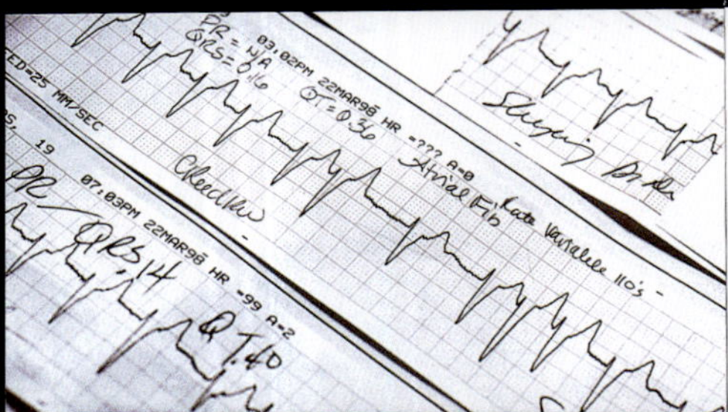

SHAREHOLDER

LETTER

COR THERAPEUTICS IS PLEASED TO PRESENT THE SEVENTH EDITION OF CARDIOVASCULAR CARE—ISSUES AND INSIGHTS, AN EDUCATIONAL REPORT DESIGNED TO ASSIST COR SHAREHOLDERS IN UNDERSTANDING THE CLINICAL ARENA TOWARD WHICH OUR RESEARCH AND DEVELOPMENT PROGRAMS ARE DIRECTED. > THERE ARE MANY CRITICAL THERAPEUTIC CHALLENGES IN IMPROVING SEVERE CARDIOVASCULAR CARE. UNSTABLE ANGINA, ACUTE MYOCARDIAL INFARCTION, DEEP VEIN THROMBOSIS, AND RESTENOSIS ARE REPRESENTATIVE OF CLINICAL SYNDROMES FOR WHICH CURRENT TREATMENT REGIMENS ARE INADEQUATE. ACUTE ISCHEMIC CORONARY SYNDROMES (AICS), CHARACTERIZED BY ACUTE CHEST PAIN CAUSED BY THE PARTIAL OR COMPLETE BLOCKAGE OF THE ARTERIES SUPPLYING OXYGEN TO THE HEART MUSCLE, IS ONE AREA OF NEED FOR WHICH COR PRODUCTS CAN POTENTIALLY

ADDRESS THE NECESSITY FOR IMPROVED THERAPEUTIC REGIMENS, PROVIDING BENEFIT OVER CONVENTIONAL TREATMENTS WHICH MAY BE ASSOCIATED WITH AN UNACCEPTABLY HIGH INCIDENCE OF HEART ATTACK OR DEATH. > AICS REPRESENTS A LARGE AND GROWING SPECTRUM OF DISEASES THAT AFFECTS OVER TWO MILLION PEOPLE ANNUALLY IN THE UNITED STATES ALONE. BECAUSE OF THE IMPORTANCE OF AICS, THIS YEAR'S ISSUE OF CARDIOVASCULAR CARE—ISSUES AND INSIGHTS WILL FOCUS ON THE CLINICAL SETTING FOR THESE DISEASES FROM THE PERSPECTIVE OF SOME OF THE CAREGIVERS WHO GUIDE THE PATIENT WITH ACUTE CHEST PAIN (INDICATIVE OF AICS) ALONG THE TREATMENT PATHWAY. PLEASE JOIN US AS WE EXAMINE THE ROLES OF THESE SPECIAL PEOPLE, WHO ARE AN INTEGRAL PART OF THE PATIENT'S HEALTH CARE EXPERIENCE.

COR THERAPEUTICS, INC.
1997 Annual Report

COVER

AR SHAREHOLDER:

I write this, COR has just received an approvable tter for our first product, INTEGRILIN™ (eptifi- tide), for use in the United States for the treat- ent of patients with acute coronary syndromes and patients undergoing coronary angioplasty. This portant event is a major milestone for us all.

Clinical and regulatory events concerning TEGRILIN™ have occupied center stage throughout ost of 1997 and are continuing to do so in 1998. veral programs in research and development oved forward in 1997, including our second oduct candidate, an oral platelet inhibitor, which in the beginning stages of clinical testing. As we ntinue in our growth plans toward our next stage development, the commercialization of novel ents that will help cardiovascular patients, we el ready to meet the challenges in front of us.

EVELOPMENT OF INTEGRILIN™

TEGRILIN™ is a small synthetic peptide drug ndidate that prevents platelet aggregation. It is tended to be given by injection in hospitals to atients with certain acute cardiovascular diseases.

Clinical development and testing of INTEGRILIN™ as been extensive. More than 15,000 patients ave participated in clinical trials of INTEGRILIN™ ound the world. As part of this clinical testing, two rge Phase III trials have been completed: IMPACT II, 4,010 patient, multi-center trial with patients ndergoing angioplasty, that was completed in 995 and PURSUIT, a 10,948 patient world-wide al in over 700 clinical sites in 28 countries that as completed in 1997. PURSUIT was designed to aluate the safety and efficacy of INTEGRILIN™ in atients with unstable angina or non-Q-wave yocardial infarction ("NQMI"), which are the ajor diseases of acute coronary syndromes.

In August 1997, the results of the PURSUIT trial ere presented by clinical investigators at the uropean Society of Cardiology's annual meeting. he PURSUIT trial was designed to determine the ffect of INTEGRILIN™ as an adjunct to current edical and interventional strategies in the treat- ent of patients with the serious heart conditions of nstable angina or non-Q-wave myocardial infarc- on. INTEGRILIN™ reduced the occurrence of death heart attack in these patients.

Importantly, the population studied represented broad, global distribution of patients and practice trategies, from small primary care hospitals to large tertiary care referral-based institutions. The trial was designed to allow patients to be managed in accordance with the standard medical practice of each clinical site, thereby allowing the study of INTEGRILIN™ in the context of different practice patterns, including the varied administration of concomitant drugs. Patients in the INTEGRILIN™ treated group benefited regardless of the treatment strategy employed by the physician.

COR and Schering-Plough Corporation are worldwide partners for INTEGRILIN™. In connection with Schering-Plough's submission for European marketing approval of INTEGRILIN™, we received an $8 million milestone payment from Schering-Plough in February 1998.

UPCOMING

The next product candidate after INTEGRILIN™ comes from our oral GP IIb-IIIa inhibitor program. Clinical trials began during 1997 and are ongoing. Potential indications for this chronic product candidate may include the prevention of acute coronary syndromes and stroke. Over 32 million people in the United States have evidence of atherosclerosis. Many of these people are at risk of suffering an acute ischemic coronary or cerebrovascular event and are therefore potential candidates for preventive therapies.

COR scientists have also discovered multiple classes of novel small molecule inhibitors of factor Xa/prothrombinase complex as part of our factor Xa program. Specific blockade of this complex may offer safer and more effective approaches to currently available therapies. This program is targeted initially at venous thrombosis, which can lead to the clinical indications of deep vein thrombosis and pulmonary embolism, potentially life threatening events. Research in this area may lead to clinical candidates for both intravenous and oral administration.

BOARD OF DIRECTORS AND MANAGEMENT

In March 1998, we announced the appointment of Charles J. Homcy, M.D. to our Board of Directors. Dr. Homcy will also continue to serve as Executive Vice President, Research and Development at COR, a position he has held since joining COR in 1995.

Also in March, the Board accepted the resignation of William H. Younger, Jr. We would like to take this opportunity to thank Bill for his commitment to COR, which began with its initial funding ten years ago. Bill has given us the benefit of his experience and guidance for all of these years as a friend and

Over 1.5 million people in the U.S. will have heart attacks this year, and 500,000 of them will die.

What you are about to read is a composite look at many of the departments in an academic medical center that deal with patients experiencing acute chest pain diagnosed as AICS. Although no two hospitals are exactly alike, we hope

that at the conclusion of this report you will have a greater appreciation for the compassion and dedication of the medical professionals, the sophistication of technology, and the essential role of clinical research programs.

Called a "step down" unit because the level of monitoring is vigilant but less intense than the CCU, the telemetry unit is for people with unstable angina relieved by nitroglycerin and heparin, or patients who have chest pain, dysrhythmia, or dyspnea (shortness of breath) with MI "ruled out" on the basis of normal cardiac enzyme levels. Many patients on the telemetry unit are being stabilized medically while waiting for diagnostic cardiac catheterization and angioplasty. These patients are monitored by the nurse on the unit, as well as the monitor technician in the CCU. Twenty-four-hour EKGs are stored in the computer and can be retrieved at any time if the patient shows a change in condition or risk.

CTU

STEP DOWN

XILINX 1998 ANNUAL REPORT 1998 USA CL: Xilinx CD,AD: Bill Cahan D,I: Michael Braley CW: Thom Elkjer DF: Cahan & Associates

COVER

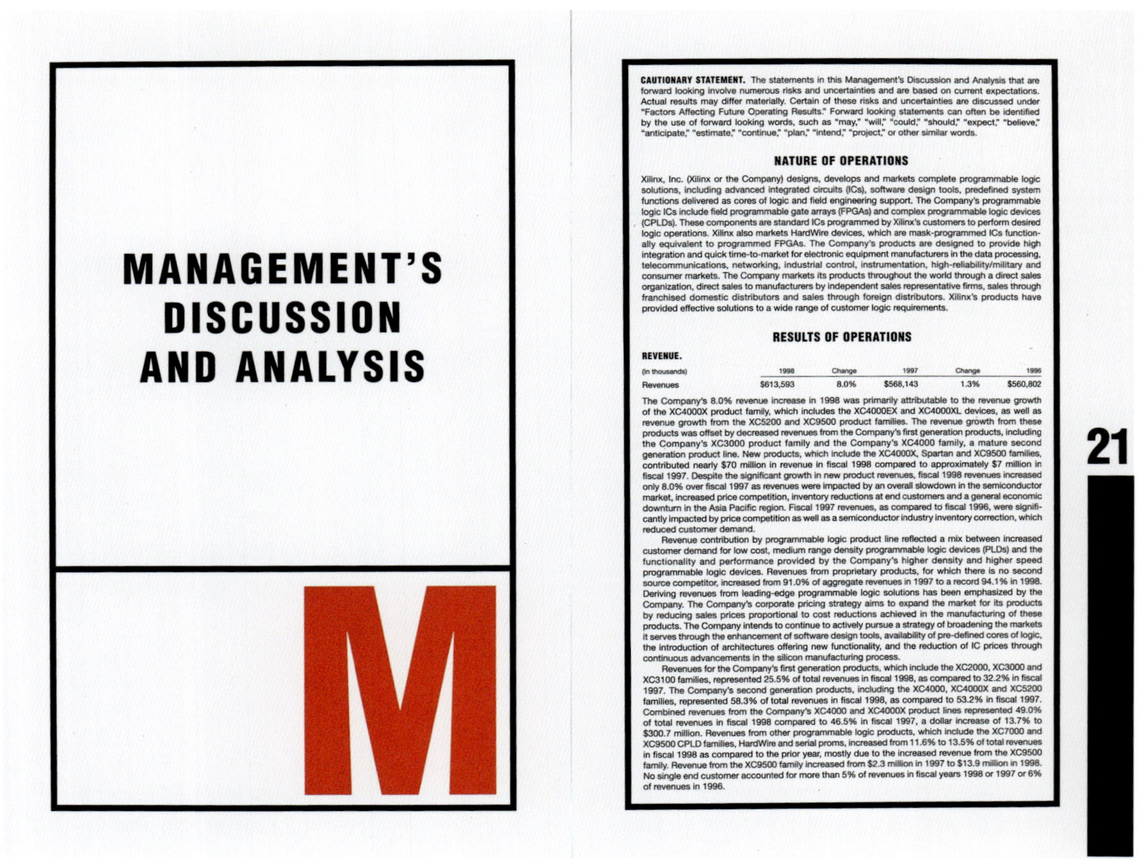

CAUTIONARY STATEMENT. The statements in this Management's Discussion and Analysis that are forward looking involve numerous risks and uncertainties and are based on current expectations. Actual results may differ materially. Certain of these risks and uncertainties are discussed under "Factors Affecting Future Operating Results." Forward looking statements can often be identified by the use of forward looking words, such as "may," "will," "could," "should," "expect," "believe," "anticipate," "estimate," "continue," "plan," "intend," "project," or other similar words.

NATURE OF OPERATIONS

Xilinx, Inc. (Xilinx or the Company) designs, develops and markets complete programmable logic solutions, including advanced integrated circuits (ICs), software design tools, predefined system functions delivered as cores of logic and field engineering support. The Company's programmable logic ICs include field programmable gate arrays (FPGAs) and complex programmable logic devices (CPLDs). These components are standard ICs programmed by Xilinx's customers to perform desired logic operations. Xilinx also markets HardWire devices, which are mask-programmed ICs functionally equivalent to programmed FPGAs. The Company's products are designed to provide high integration and quick time-to-market for electronic equipment manufacturers in the data processing, telecommunications, networking, industrial control, instrumentation, high-reliability/military and consumer markets. The Company markets its products throughout the world through a direct sales organization, direct sales to manufacturers by independent sales representative firms, sales through franchised domestic distributors and sales through foreign distributors. Xilinx's products have provided effective solutions to a wide range of customer logic requirements.

RESULTS OF OPERATIONS

REVENUE.

(In thousands)	1998	Change	1997	Change	1996
Revenues	$613,593	8.0%	$568,143	1.3%	$560,802

The Company's 8.0% revenue increase in 1998 was primarily attributable to the revenue growth of the XC4000X product family, which includes the XC4000EX and XC4000XL devices, as well as revenue growth from the XC5200 and XC9500 product families. The revenue growth from these products was offset by decreased revenues from the Company's first generation products, including the Company's XC3000 product family and the Company's XC4000 family, a mature second generation product line. New products, which include the XC4000X, Spartan and XC9500 families, contributed nearly $70 million in revenue in fiscal 1998 compared to approximately $7 million in fiscal 1997. Despite the significant growth in new product revenues, fiscal 1998 revenues increased only 8.0% over fiscal 1997 as revenues were impacted by an overall slowdown in the semiconductor market, increased price competition, inventory reductions at end customers and a general economic downturn in the Asia Pacific region. Fiscal 1997 revenues, as compared to fiscal 1996, were significantly impacted by price competition as well as a semiconductor industry inventory correction, which reduced customer demand.

Revenue contribution by programmable logic product line reflected a mix between increased customer demand for low cost, medium range density programmable logic devices (PLDs) and the functionality and performance provided by the Company's higher density and higher speed programmable logic devices. Revenues from proprietary products, for which there is no second source competitor, increased from 91.0% of aggregate revenues in 1997 to a record 94.1% in 1998. Deriving revenues from leading-edge programmable logic solutions has been emphasized by the Company. The Company's corporate pricing strategy aims to expand the market for its products by reducing sales prices proportional to cost reductions achieved in the manufacturing of these products. The Company intends to continue to actively pursue a strategy of broadening the markets it serves through the enhancement of software design tools, availability of pre-defined cores of logic, the introduction of architectures offering new functionality, and the reduction of IC prices through continuous advancements in the silicon manufacturing process.

Revenues for the Company's first generation products, which include the XC2000, XC3000 and XC3100 families, represented 25.5% of total revenues in fiscal 1998, as compared to 32.2% in fiscal 1997. The Company's second generation products, including the XC4000, XC4000X and XC5200 families, represented 58.3% of total revenues in fiscal 1998, as compared to 53.2% in fiscal 1997. Combined revenues from the Company's XC4000 and XC4000X product lines represented 49.0% of total revenues in fiscal 1998 compared to 46.5% in fiscal 1997, a dollar increase of 13.7% to $300.7 million. Revenues from other programmable logic products, which include the XC7000 and XC9500 CPLD families, HardWire and serial proms, increased from 11.6% to 13.5% of total revenues in fiscal 1998 as compared to the prior year, mostly due to the increased revenue from the XC9500 family. Revenue from the XC9500 family increased from $2.3 million in 1997 to $13.9 million in 1998. No single end customer accounted for more than 5% of revenues in fiscal years 1998 or 1997 or 6% of revenues in 1996.

VIVUS 1997 ANNUAL REPORT 1998 USA CL: Vivus, Inc. CD,AD: Bill Cahan D,I,CW: Kevin Roberson CW: Jennifer Schraeder DF: Cahan & Associates

97
98

In 1997: the launch of MUSE created much interest in the product. VIVUS' total media impressions exceeded 151 million, with audience reaches of more than 70 million from print articles and 81.5 million from radio and television news stories • Office visits to urologists for treatment of erectile dysfunction, or male impotence, increased by 27 percent • MUSE became the therapy prescribed most often by urologists for erectile dysfunction. • VIVUS expanded its sales force from 50 to 74 representatives • VIVUS' sales force made approximately 50,000 visits to physicians' offices and met with a total of about 12,000 physicians • MUSE was used by approximately 475,000 patients in the United States.

In 1998: the launch of the MUSE advertising campaign will create even more awareness. VIVUS' direct-to-physician campaign will target approximately 300,000 health care professionals: 9,000 urologists, 93,000 primary care physicians, 128,000 other physician specialities and 55,000 pharmacists • VIVUS will reach its audiences through print advertisements in publications such as U.S. News & World Report, Newsweek *and* Time *and in newspapers such as* The Wall Street Journal *and* The New York Times *• Television advertisements will run during the year on networks such as CNN, ABC and CBS • VIVUS will expand its sales force to reach a larger physician audience.*

LOCAL
PROBLEM

LOCAL
SOLUTION

In 1997, VIVUS established MUSE® (alprostadil) in the United States as a first line therapy for treatment of erectile dysfunction: MUSE was launched in January of 1997 and by the end of the year, more than 825,000 prescriptions were written and 8 million units sold, thus establishing MUSE in the United States as a leading treatment for erectile dysfunction by urologists and as one of the top 25 most successful first year pharmaceutical products ever.

Local problem, local solution. Experts agree that for many men erectile dysfunction is a local disorder; consequently, the transurethral delivery of treatment provided by MUSE is a novel, local solution to this local problem. MUSE provides the patient, partner and physician a convenient and minimally invasive treatment which explains, in large part, its rapid acceptance and use in 1997.

Alprostadil safety and efficacy. First licensed as a pharmaceutical in 1981, the safety and efficacy of alprostadil as a therapeutic agent is well established. Experimental intracavernosal injection of alprostadil for the treatment of erectile dysfunction began in the late 1980s and culminated with Food and Drug Administration (FDA) clearance of alprostadil for injection therapy of erectile dysfunction in 1995. VIVUS began clinical trials in 1992, and in five short years, successfully demonstrated that alprostadil also can be delivered safely and effectively via the urethra using a small, plastic applicator rather than a needle.

Novel drug delivery. MUSE uses a novel drug delivery system which consists of a single-use, prefilled plastic applicator designed for easy handling, administration and disposal. The small size of the applicator provides both patient and partner with a discreet and easy-to-use treatment option.

Don Pfaff, Torrance, California
"Rejoicing. Elation. These words are part of what describes the feeling you go through. Because you go into it with some degree of hesitancy and when you get a reaction, you say, 'Yeah, I made a touchdown.'"

Carol Pfaff, Torrance, California
"There is help out there. I would encourage people to pursue every avenue that could lead to a much more satisfying life."

"It is not a show of weakness to confront this problem, it's a show of strength to do this. It's a show of strength to your family and, above all, to yourself."

PROGENITOR 1997 ANNUAL REPORT 1998 USA CL: Progenitor CD,AD: Bill Cahan D,I,CW: Bob Dinetz P: Jay Blakesberg CW: Carrie Wick DF: Cahan & Associates

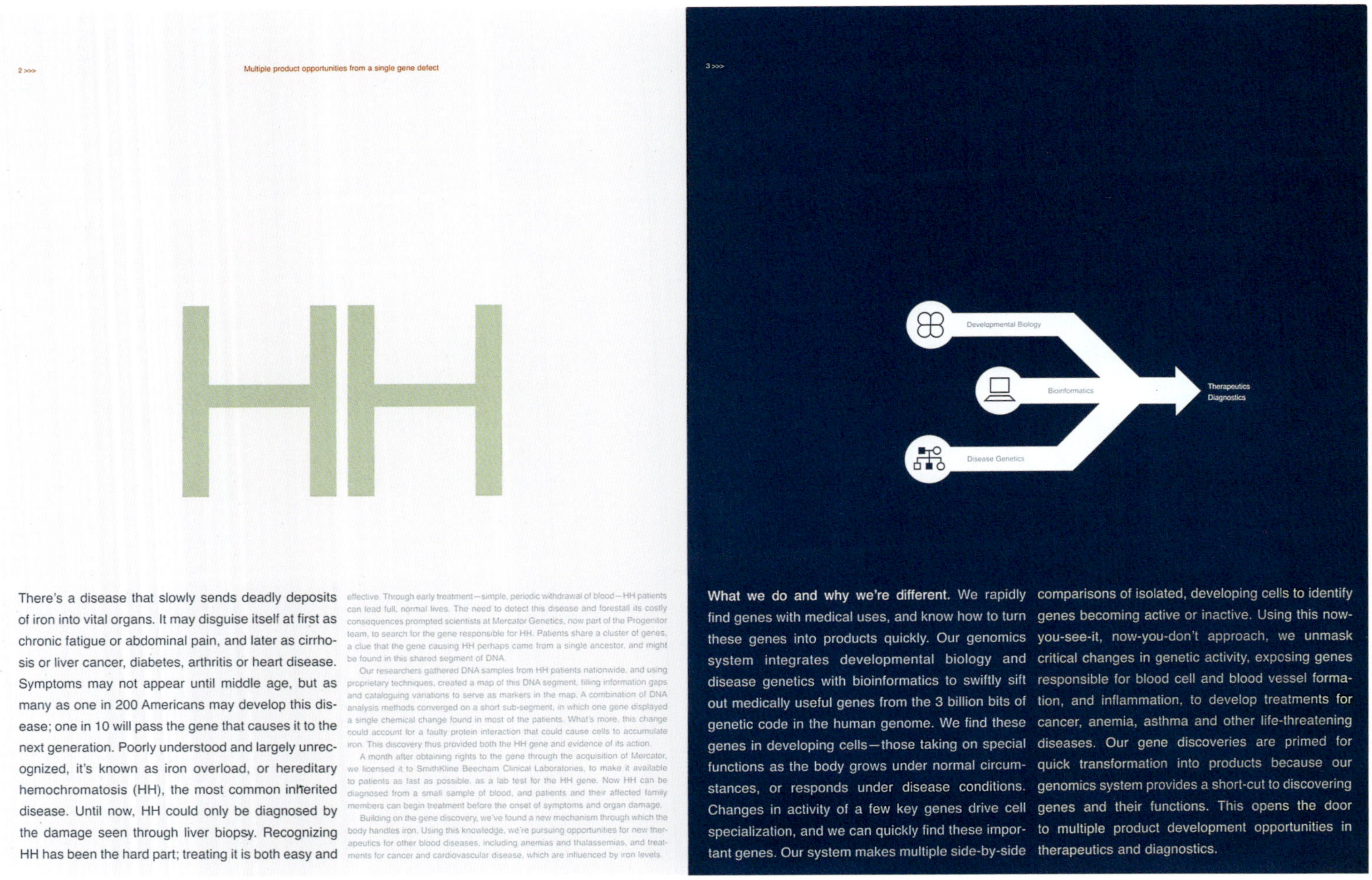

2 >>> Multiple product opportunities from a single gene defect

HH

There's a disease that slowly sends deadly deposits of iron into vital organs. It may disguise itself at first as chronic fatigue or abdominal pain, and later as cirrhosis or liver cancer, diabetes, arthritis or heart disease. Symptoms may not appear until middle age, but as many as one in 200 Americans may develop this disease; one in 10 will pass the gene that causes it to the next generation. Poorly understood and largely unrecognized, it's known as iron overload, or hereditary hemochromatosis (HH), the most common inherited disease. Until now, HH could only be diagnosed by the damage seen through liver biopsy. Recognizing HH has been the hard part; treating it is both easy and effective. Through early treatment—simple, periodic withdrawal of blood—HH patients can lead full, normal lives. The need to detect this disease and forestall its costly consequences prompted scientists at Mercator Genetics, now part of the Progenitor team, to search for the gene responsible for HH. Patients share a cluster of genes, a clue that the gene causing HH perhaps came from a single ancestor, and might be found in this shared segment of DNA.

Our researchers gathered DNA samples from HH patients nationwide, and using proprietary techniques, created a map of this DNA segment, filling information gaps and cataloguing variations to serve as markers in the map. A combination of DNA analysis methods converged on a short sub-segment, in which one gene displayed a single chemical change found in most of the patients. What's more, this change could account for a faulty protein interaction that could cause cells to accumulate iron. This discovery thus provided both the HH gene and evidence of its action.

A month after obtaining rights to the gene through the acquisition of Mercator, we licensed it to SmithKline Beecham Clinical Laboratories, to make it available to patients as fast as possible, as a lab test for the HH gene. Now HH can be diagnosed from a small sample of blood, and patients and their affected family members can begin treatment before the onset of symptoms and organ damage.

Building on the gene discovery, we've found a new mechanism through which the body handles iron. Using this knowledge, we're pursuing opportunities for new therapeutics for other blood diseases, including anemias and thalassemias, and treatments for cancer and cardiovascular disease, which are influenced by iron levels.

3 >>>

What we do and why we're different. We rapidly find genes with medical uses, and know how to turn these genes into products quickly. Our genomics system integrates developmental biology and disease genetics with bioinformatics to swiftly sift out medically useful genes from the 3 billion bits of genetic code in the human genome. We find these genes in developing cells—those taking on special functions as the body grows under normal circumstances, or responds under disease conditions. Changes in activity of a few key genes drive cell specialization, and we can quickly find these important genes. Our system makes multiple side-by-side comparisons of isolated, developing cells to identify genes becoming active or inactive. Using this now-you-see-it, now-you-don't approach, we unmask critical changes in genetic activity, exposing genes responsible for blood cell and blood vessel formation, and inflammation, to develop treatments for cancer, anemia, asthma and other life-threatening diseases. Our gene discoveries are primed for quick transformation into products because our genomics system provides a short-cut to discovering genes and their functions. This opens the door to multiple product development opportunities in therapeutics and diagnostics.

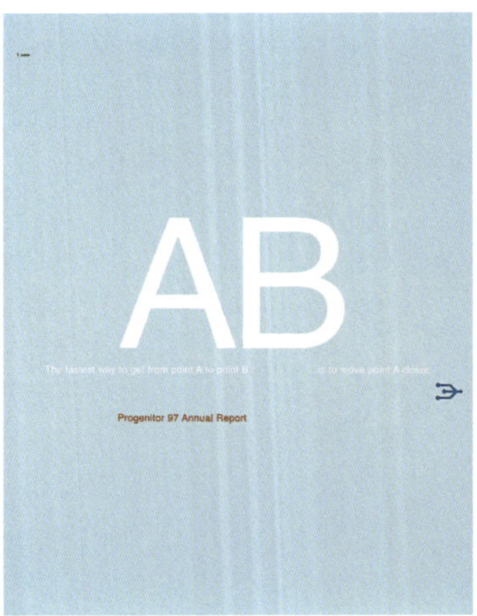

COVER

ESB ENVIRONMENTAL REVIEW 1997 IRELAND CL: Electricity Supply Board CD,AD,D,I: Amanda Brady DF: Creative Inputs

Environmental Performance and Objectives

Air Emissions from Power Stations

Nitrogen Dioxide (NO_x)

Ireland has international obligations regarding the limitation of emissions of NO_x into the atmosphere from large combustion plant.

- Under an EU Directive[5] the annual ceiling for Ireland for emissions from large combustion plant constructed prior to July 1987 is 50,000t.
- Under the Sofia Protocol to the Geneva Convention on Long Range Transboundary Air Pollution, ESB's emissions were, by the year 1994, to be controlled at their 1987 level of 42,000t.

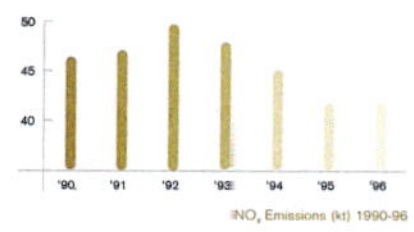

NO_x Emissions (kt) 1990-96

An annual limit of 50,000t thus applied until 1993 and a limit of 42,000t from 1995.

We have met these targets, despite an ongoing increase in the amount of electricity generated. This has been achieved primarily through a substantial investment in technological improvements at our power stations. At Moneypoint an investment of £8M in low-NO_x burners resulted in a 50% reduction in the station's NO_x emissions between 1992 and 1996.

Objective:
Ensure continuous improvement so that NO_x constraint is achieved while meeting load growth.

Sulphur Dioxide (SO_2)

Emissions from our power stations are subject to controls, as follows:

- Under an EU Directive[5] the annual SO_2 emission limit for large combustion plant in Ireland is 124,000t. ESB's allocation is 114,000t.
- The Oslo Protocol to the Geneva Convention on Long Range Transboundary Air Pollution limits Ireland's national emissions by the year 2000 to at least 30% below their 1980 level. Under this protocol ESB will be obliged to limit its SO_2 emissions to a maximum of 82,000t from all plant.

In spite of the need for increased power generation to meet growing electricity sales, ESB has successfully met these obligations. The company achieved this by increasing the use of low sulphur content fuels, albeit at higher cost, and by using natural gas. ESB believes this is the most cost effective option available.

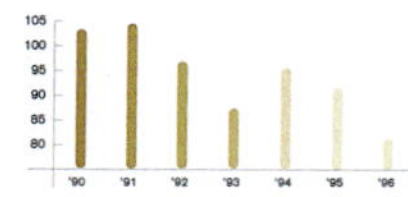

SO_2 Emissions (kt) 1990-96

[5] EU Directive 88/609/EEC

19

COVER

Waste

Our operations inevitably lead to the production of wastes of various types

Power Station Ash

The most significant volume of waste arises at solid fuel power stations in the form of combustion residues or ash removed from stack emissions. This waste arises at our coal fired station at Moneypoint, where we use approximately 2Mt of coal annually, and at our peat burning stations, where we use approximately 3Mt of peat annually. The amount of ash arising annually is typically of the order of 250,000t.

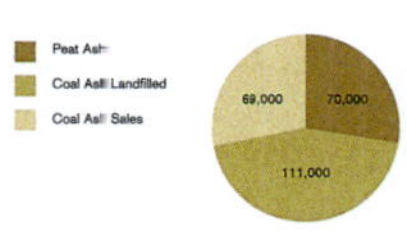

Power Station Ash (t) 1996

It has been ESB policy for some time that ash waste should be used beneficially wherever possible. Annual sales of ash from Moneypoint for use as a raw materials substitute in the cement industry have been of the order of 55,000t - 70,000t over the past few years.

Objective:
Continue beneficial reuse of power station ash and examine new opportunities.

Asbestos

Asbestos insulating material was used in the construction of some ESB power stations. It may become waste material during maintenance operations or during station demolition. Where asbestos insulation has been identified and is accessible, our policy has been that it should be removed and disposed of safely. This is still our policy. Other types of asbestos material in common use in ESB include gaskets, glandpacking, asbestos rope and roofing. These do not pose a threat to health provided normal safety precautions are followed and they are substituted by other materials where suitable replacements are available.

We have adopted procedures to ensure the safe removal of asbestos and we monitor the performance of contractors who carry out this work on our behalf. In 1996 all temporarily stored asbestos was exported and landfilled in Germany by approved hazardous waste contractors. Asbestos removal and demolition commenced at Portarlington Generating Station, which together with Allenwood represent the last major asbestos removal projects for ESB.

Objective:
Continue to deal appropriately with asbestos waste.

23

MAGAZINE 雑誌
BANG DECEMBER 1999 SWEDEN PB: bang E: Ulrika Lorentzi D: Paul Kühlhorn / Eva Liljefors P: Abigail Lane DF: Fellow Designers

Ap-politik

Har chimpanser och andra världskriget något gemensamt? Charlotte Holgersson riktar kritik mot den amerikanske forskaren Francis Fukuyama som finner bevis för mäns genetiskt betingade våldsamhet genom att studera apor.

Visst är det skönt när man i en diskussion kan klämma till med argumentet "men det är ju naturligt, se bara på djuren"? Det går ju inte att säga emot det som är naturgivet, eller hur?

Så måste nog Francis Fukuyama ha resonerat när han skrev sin essä "Women and the Evolution of World Politics" som han fick publicerad i den amerikanska tidskriften *Foreign Affairs* . Fukuyama, som är professor i statsvetenskap, politisk kommentator och rådgivare åt amerikanska staten, har tidigare skrivit bästsäljaren *The End of History and the Last Man* där han för fram den liberala demokratins och marknadsekonomins fördelar. Detta gör han även i sin essä, men istället för att utgå från Kant, Hegel och kritiska läsningar av Marx, så tar han denna gång sin utgångspunkt i chimpansstudier.

Man kan undra vad chimpanser har med kvinnor, världspolitiken och marknadsekonomin att göra. Låt oss gå igenom Fukuyamas argumentation. Det är krigen som utspelas världen över, från Bosnien till Rwanda, som för hans tankar till de aggressiva och stridslystna chimpanserna. Han hävdar att chimpanser och människor inte bara är genetiskt utan även beteendemässigt mycket lika – båda lever i hierarkiska, patriarkala samhällen, där grupper av hanar rutinmässigt angriper och mördar medlemmar av den egna arten, i kampen om att höja sin status i hierarkin.

Krig beror enligt Fukuyama på mäns genetiskt betingade våldsamma gruppbeteende. Kvinnor, däremot, är av naturen mindre våldsbenägna och vi kan därför hoppas på en fredligare värld nu när kvinnor är på frammarsch inom politiken. Men det finns gränser för hur mycket förändring som är möjlig. Eftersom män är mer konkurrensinriktade och aggressiva, så kommer deras makt att bestå. Det kommer alltid att finnas stater som leds av aggressiva och våldsamma män.

Men Fukuyama är optimistisk trots allt. Även om vi inte kan ändra den mänskliga naturen, så kan vi försöka dämpa de skadliga effekterna av männens natur. Detta gör vi genom att främja den liberala demokratin och den moderna kapitalismen. För till skillnad från socialismen och feminismen söker de liberala marknadsekonomierna inte förändra männen, utan erbjuder istället en mängd olika och dessutom mer

39

"Vi vill vara män och medmänniskor"

"Mäns maktutövning ska inte subventioneras"

Mansjourerna har varken den kunskap eller det engagemang som krävs för att motverka kvinnomisshandel. Därför ska de inte heller få statliga medel för det, hävdar Fredrik Bondestam och Stefan Villkatt i sin slutreplik.

kvinna+karl+kvinna+korv

Det är inte synd om männen – inte om kvinnorna heller

001
In dienst van het milieu: Milieudienst

001/A
Iedereen is gebaat bij een schoon milieu. In een stad als Amsterdam gaat dat echter niet vanzelf. Daarom werd in 1990 de 001/A-01 Amsterdam opgericht. Alle kennis over het milieu werd daarmee gebundeld in één dienst, dat als belangrijkste doel heeft om de kwaliteit van het milieu in Amsterdam te verbeteren. Zij doet dit in de eerste plaats door het vergaren van nog meer kennis over het milieu en door het uitvoeren van allerlei milieuwetten (zoals de Wet Milieubeheer en de Wet Geluidhinder) en milieuverordeningen. Daarnaast houdt de het milieu in Amsterdam in de gaten en denkt ze actief mee over oplossingen die het milieu kunnen verbeteren. Verder geeft de dienst gevraagd en ongevraagd adviezen over de meest uiteenlopende milieuzaken. En tenslotte kan iedereen met vragen of klachten over het milieu de 001/A-03 bellen. De 001/A-04 is dus hét centrale aanspreekpunt voor bewoners, bedrijven en bestuurders als het gaat om het milieu in Amsterdam.

002
Een leefbare en duurzame stad

002/A
De 002/A-01 streeft naar een leefbare en duurzame stad. Met leefbaar wordt bedoeld: een stad waar het prettig is om te verblijven, met voldoende groen, waar zaken als geluidshinder, lucht-, water en bodemvervuiling tot een aanvaardbaar minimum zijn teruggebracht en waar op korte afstand van elkaar zonder problemen gewoond, gewerkt en gerecreëerd kan worden.
Dat moet echter ook in de toekomst zo blijven: in die zin moet Amsterdam ook een duurzame stad worden.

002/B
Duurzaam wil zeggen, dat de stad ook meehelpt om 'wereldse' milieuproblemen (verzuring, broeikaseffect, gebruik schaarse grondstoffen) aan te pakken. Amsterdam kan dit doen door bijvoorbeeld meer afval te scheiden, te besparen op energie- en watergebruik, het gebruik van duurzame energiebronnen (zon, wind) te stimuleren of de uitstoot van giftige gassen die het broeikaseffect veroorzaken (zoals autoverkeer) tegen te gaan.

002/C
Duurzaamheid en leefbaarheid gaan vaak samen, maar niet altijd: in dat geval zoekt de 002/C-01 naar het beste evenwicht, of anders gezegd: een oplossing met het hoogste milieurendement.

September 1998 / Tekst: Arnold Korporaal / Ontwerp: Richard Niessen, OK / Druk: Drukkerij Mart.Spruijt / Samenstelling: Voorlichting Milieudienst Amsterdam

Milieudienst Amsterdam Bezoekadres: Weesperplein 4 1018 XA Amsterdam / Postadres: Postbus 922 / 1000 AX / Amsterdam / Telefoon: 020 551 38 88 / Fax: 020 624 06 36 / Telefoon Voorlichting: 020 551 38 38 Milieuklachtentelefoon: 020 620 79 76 / Bereikbaar met het openbaar vervoer: Tram 6,7 en 10 en metro (Halte Weesperplein)

BOOK 書籍

GRAPHIC DESIGN SCRAP BOOK 1996 SLOVENIA (FORMER YUGOSLAVIA)

CL: Group of Authors CD,AD: Eduard Čehovin AD: Boštjan Kenda / Tanja Radež / Darko Miladinović / Slavimir Stojanović / Lena Pislak-Balant / Boris Balant / Dalida Hadžihalilović / Bojan Hadžihalilović

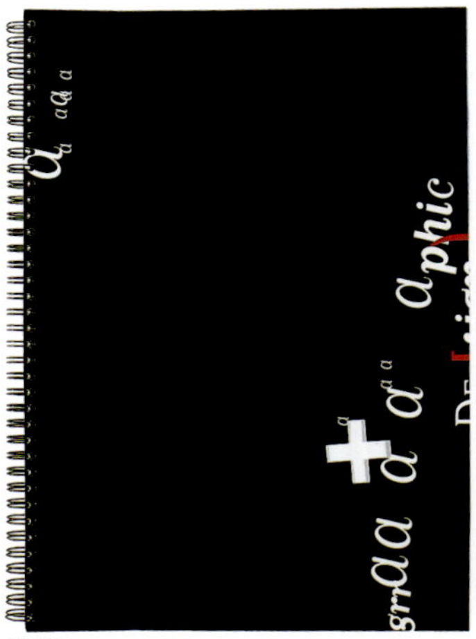

COVER

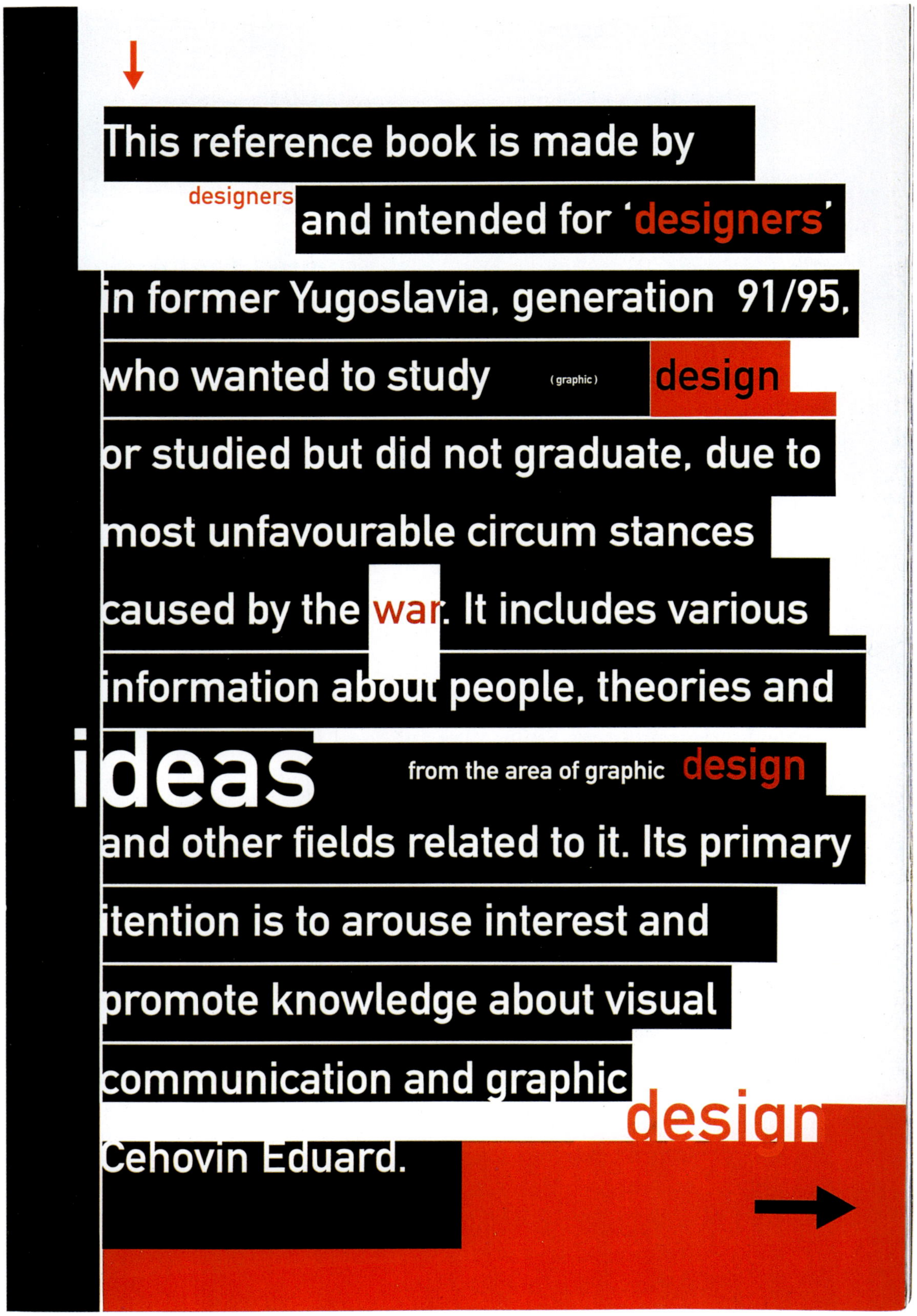

ANNUAL REPORT アニュアルレポート

MILIEUDIENST AMSTERDAM 1997 NETHERLANDS CL: Milieudienst Amsterdam D: Richard Niessen CW: H. van Bergen

COVER

BOOK 書籍
SINGUHR KLANGKUNST 1999 GERMANY CL: Singuhr Hörgalerie D,CW,DF: Cyan P: Roman März

COVER

18.09.–18.10.1998 Glockenraum Treppenhaus

kosmos + turm – bausatz.noto.∞

Carsten Nicolai – bekannter vielleicht in den Kreisen ‹bildnerischer› Objekt- und Installationskunst – experimentiert bereits seit 1993 mit akustischem Material. Der Anlaß damals – eine CD für den Katalog einer Ausstellung. Er selbst äußert,[1] daß von da an ein Großteil seiner Arbeiten von musikalischen Interessen geleitet ist. Dieses Interesse artikuliert sich v.a. im Generieren von abstrakten Material- und Strukturmetamorphosen. Aus Telefonsignalen, Faxgeräten, Modem oder Oszillographen gewinnt Carsten Nicolai seine Datenpools. Doch diese Proben aus dem Klangreservoir des Informationszeitalters verweisen nicht auf ihre Herkunft. Sie bleiben quasi rein, ganz wie die Sounds von Oval, die sich den traditionellen Instrumentarien semantischer Interpretation entziehen, ~~weil keine analytischen Gedanken oder gar das Gedächtnis selbst sich zwischen Musik und Nervensystem schieben~~[2] können. Solche elementarisierten Klänge leben v.a. von ihrer Syntax, von dem, was auf der Basis binärer Strukturen in komplizierte Koexistenzen getrieben wird. Die so entwickelten Kerne, loops und spins bilden bei Carsten Nicolai die Struktureinheiten. Sie tauchen nicht nur in den akustischen, sondern als Prinzipien in den meisten seiner Arbeiten (Tafelbild, Graphiken, Objekte, botanische Welten, Installationen, Logos, Editionen) auf. Auf den vier Plattentellern des Objekttisches drehten sich selbstgefertigte Vinyle, deren Rillen mit akustischen Ressourcen belegt waren, die Carsten Nicolai u.a. im Zusammenhang mit seiner Arbeit zur documenta X entwickelt hatte. Im Unterschied zu den Räumen (Galerie für Zeitgenössische Kunst Leipzig, Galerie in Salzau), in denen der Objekttisch zuvor ausgestellt war, stand er nun völlig frei und allein inmitten der hœrgalerie. Unter Kopfhörern konnten die Besucher ihren eigenen akustischen Kosmos per Tonarm ertasten, scratchen, kombinieren und mischen. Am Fuße der Turmschnecke waren zudem zwei Lautsprecher aufgehängt, die die durch die Besucher erspielten Sounds freigaben. Susanne Binas, 1998

Carsten Nicolai

Biographie geb. 1965 in Karl-Marx-Stadt. 1984 Gärtner. 1985-90 Studium der Landschaftsarchitektur in Dresden. 1992 Mitbegründer des Projektes voxxx.kultur- und kommunikationszentrum in Chemnitz. 1994 Gründung von noton.archiv für ton und nichtton (discographie noton/rastermusic: 1996 noto.spin; ø+noto.mikro makro. 1997 noto.ƒ. 1998 noto.kerne, plate lanch; noto.polyfoto). 1998-99 Atelier im International Studio Program New York. Lebt in Chemnitz und Berlin.

Ausstellungen: 1986 Galerie Eigen+Art, Leipzig. 1991 Lichtinstallation, Kunstwerke Berlin. 1992 Galerie Springer, Berlin; Galerie Condé, Goethe-Institut, Paris. 1993 Galerie Eigen+Art, Berlin; Städtische Kunstsammlungen, Chemnitz; Museum Schloss Morsbroich, Leverkusen. 1994 Espace des Arts, Chalon-sur-Salône; Kunstverein Ulm; Neue Nationalgalerie, Berlin; Städtisches Kunstmuseum, Spendhaus Reutlingen. 1995 Galerie Eigen+Art, Berlin; Galerie Springer, Berlin; Galerie Margrit Gass, Basel; Kunstverein Konstanz. 1996 Leonhardi-Museum, Dresden; Galerie Carol Johnsson, München. 1997 Galerie Eigen+Art, Leipzig und Berlin. 1998 [polyfoto]. Galerie für zeitgenössische Kunst, Leipzig und div. Beteiligungen u.a. documenta X, Kassel; p.s.1 reopening, New York...

Bildtafel m

auschnitte aus dem text zur edition von carsten nicolai: ~~#3 ƒ : turm +kosmos bezieht seine idee auf die welt des robert garcet,~~[3] ~~der seinen kosmos aus existierenden und kombinierbaren elementen gestaltet hat. individuelle ansichten und aus erfahrung gewonnene haltungen sind die bestimmenden prinzipien dessen ordnung. als grundlage dient ƒ : turm +kosmos eine reihe eigens geschaffener zeichnungen und tonmodulationen. die zeichnungen zeigen teile eines ganzen in verschiedenen figurationen – gleich einem bauplan. die ton modulationen, in 48 endlosschleifen (loops) auf zwei schallplatten geschnitten, sind gleichwertige elemente, die sich zu einem eigenen kosmos eigener vorstellung zusammensetzen lassen.~~

~~#4 alle endlosschleifen haben die gleiche anzahl von schlaegen pro minute (133,3333 bpm). bei verwendung von mehreren schallplattenspielern lassen sie sich nahtlos kombinieren + mischen. durch veraenderung der umdrehungen pro minute (pitching) koennen zusaetzlich einzelne loops manipuliert werden. eine weitere moeglichkeit bietet die exzentrische anordnung der platten durch die verwendung der aussermittigen drehpunkte.~~

1 DE:BUG. 14.08.98 2 vgl. Martin Büsser OVAL wie rebellisch ist der reine Sound In: testcard Beiträge zur Popgeschichte Nr.2 1996 S.94 3 ~~robert garcet errichtete in den jahren 1952 bis 1963 in der naehe der belgischen stadt liège den turm von eben ezer. mit sieben stockwerken und einer hoehe von 33 m versinnbildlicht der turm in seiner geometrie das neue jerusalem der apokalypse.~~

Klangkunst in der Tradition der umbrechenden Moderne?

Symposium Klang-Kunst-Räume 09.10.1998

Ausschnitte aus der Podiumsdiskussion mit

Helga de la Motte-Haber
Manos Tsangaris
Andreas Oldörp
Volker Straebel
Gesprächsleitung

Straebel: Es reizt natürlich sehr, die 199[illegible] stattgefundene Podiumsdiskussion während des sonambiente-Festivals hier fortzusetzen. Damals ging es v. a. um die Frage, ob Klangkunst nun eine Gattung sei oder nicht. Lassen Sie uns aber zunächst über die Frage der situationsspezifischen Kunst reden. Einige Arbeiten, die in der singuhr-hoergalerie präsentiert worden sind, werden auch in anderen Räumen gezeigt, zum Beispiel die Fadenorgel von Manos Tsangaris. Deshalb die Frage an Manos Tsangaris: Was sind das für Produktionsbedingungen, wenn man eine Arbeit für den Raum in der Parochialkirche schafft in dem Wissen, daß sie noch einmal in einem anderen Raum präsentiert wird?

Tsangaris: Diese Frage spricht für mich ein grundsätzliches Problem an, weil: Was heißt Situation? In diesem konkreten Fall wußte ich von vornherein, daß die Arbeit an verschiedenen Orten stattfinden wird. Und das hat für mich kompositorische Konsequenzen. Ich versuche stets etwas zu machen, was vielleicht der Situation auch etwas gibt. Niemand reagiert nur. Mir kommt es auf die Balance an zwischen dem, was ich an Räumlichkeit, an zeitlicher Disposition vorfinde und dem, was ich den kompositorischen Input nennen möchte. Wenn das einigermaßen in der Balance ist, sprich, wenn die Arbeit selber auch eine inhaltliche Komponente hat, die für sich erst einmal trägt – das sind sicher alles fragwürdige Begriffe, aber ich nenne das jetzt so –, dann ist es natürlich möglich, sie auch zu transponieren an einen anderen Ort oder auch eventuell für diesen anderen Ort ein wenig zu modifizieren. Die Fadenorgel im Kunstmuseum von [illegible]nder (Dänemark) – das ist ja nicht dieselbe Arbeit. Die Grundelemente, diese kleinen ‹Robots› – also die kleine ‹fliegende Gemeinde› – bleiben erhalten. Aber wonach Sie fragen, das ist für mich die Frage nach dem, was ich gerade den kompositorischen Anspruch genannt habe. Man sagt mir nach, daß ich ein kritisches Verhältnis zur Klangkunst hätte?! Das stimmt so sicher nicht nur: ich finde es sehr wichtig, ein paar auch äußere oder grundsätzliche Voraussetzungen bei der Diskussion um Klangkunst mitzubedenken. Eine Sache ist überhaupt noch nicht genannt worden: Klangkunst in dem Sinne, wie sie hier durch die Arbeit der singuhr-hoergalerie vorgestellt worden ist, ist bis auf die Arbeit von Andreas Oldörp abhängig vom Medium des Lautsprechers. In dem Moment, wo so eine kleine, preiswerte Technologie entwickelt worden ist – preiswert heißt: jeder kann sie erwerben –, da entsteht plötzlich von seiten der Technologie her eine Anregung, Räume mit Lautsprechern zu verwandeln. Ich kenne sehr unterschiedliche Arten zu komponieren, von meiner Geschichte und auch von den unterschiedlichen Diskursen her, aber die Frage: Was verändern Lautsprecher, was passiert in dem Moment, wo Musik reproduzierbar ist, diese Frage ist im tradierten Kontext der ‹Musik-Musik› über weite Strecken auf der akademischen Seite, also in der europäischen Tradition, überhaupt nicht gestellt worden. Im Gegenteil: Es wurde sich dessen bedient: Vervielfältigung – Richard Strauss hat die GEMA quasi zu dem Zwecke erfunden. Ein ‹ordentlicher› Komponist oder eine ‹ordentliche› Komponistin hat sich über Jahrzehnte hinweg diese Frage gar nicht mehr gestellt. Was passiert dann mit dem Klang? Heutzutage ist es doch so: Musik bedeutet, wir drücken auf einen Knopf und dann geht es los – mit anderen Worten: Beschallung. In der Bildenden Kunst ist es so, daß schon der Impressionismus ohne den Reflex auf die Fotokamera, auf die Vervielfältigung, auf die ‹mechanische Reproduktion›, um an Walter Benjamin zu erinnern, gar nicht denkbar gewesen wäre. Das war eine Art natürliche Reaktion von Malern, die ihres Berufsfeldes beraubt worden waren, nämlich Porträt-, Genremalerei und so weiter. Léger hat 1912 das berühmte Bild Die Hochzeit gemalt, in dem er seinen ganz persönlichen, individuellen Blick einer Hochzeit darstellte. Und das war ein eindeutiger Reflex auf die Erfahrungen mit der Fotografie. Um auf die Klangkunst zurückzukommen und ganz konkret auf die Arbeiten für die singuhr-hoergalerie: von zwölf Ausstellungen waren elf lautsprecherabhängig. Und das scheint mir eine ähnliche, durchaus befreiende Reaktion darauf zu sein, daß es eine neue Hardware gibt. Ich erinnere mich an David Tudor. Wenn er in Köln war, ist er erst einmal zu ‹Saturn› gelaufen, weil es da viele kleine billige technische Dinge gab, die er zusammenstecken konnte. Auf diese Weise hat er das Komponieren oder das Arbeiten in Räumen, das situative Arbeiten, für sich unabhängig machen können von der teuren, großen Technologie und auch von dem Erinnerungssystem der Partitur. Bezeichnenderweise ist die Frage des Lautsprechers, also wie ich jedes Beispiel[illegible] herstellen kann und wie ich dann eine konkrete künstlerische Konsequenz daraus ziehe, also die Frage des Materials, von der Hardware her bisher kaum gestellt worden.

63

Wohin zieht es Klangkünstler auf der Suche nach Räumen zur Produktion und Präsentation ihrer Arbeiten?

Symposium Klang-Kunst-Räume 10.10.1998

Jutta Ravenna

Man müßte eine Musique d'ameublement produzieren, genauer gesagt, eine Musik, die an den Geräuschen der Umgebung teilhat und auf diese Rücksicht nimmt. Ich stelle sie mir folgendermaßen vor:
melodiös, die Geräusche der Gabeln
und Messer abschwächend,
sie jedoch nicht dominierend.
Erik Satie, 1920

Warum sollte man Rücksicht auf die Geräusche von Messern und Gabeln nehmen?
Satie behauptet das.
Und er hat Recht.
Andernfalls würde die Musik Mauern errichten müssen, um sich selbst zu verteidigen,
Mauern, die beständig instandgesetzt werden müßten, und über die man sich, selbst um ein Glas Wasser trinken zu können,
die Katastrophe herausfordernd, hinwegsetzen müßte.
Es ist offensichtlich eine Frage,
ob intendierte Handlungen
von jemandem in Relation zu den nichtintendierten der Umgebung gebracht werden.
John Cage, 1961

Kontextbezogenheit

In einigen meiner Arbeiten geht es darum, Musik in einen bestimmten Kontext zu stellen. In der Suche nach Räumen manifestiert sich die Suche nach einem Kontext, d. h. einem realen Bezugssystem, in welches die Arbeit gestellt werden kann. Hierbei unterscheide ich zwischen Räumen mit einem intakten funktionalen Innenleben und funktionsfreien Orten. Mit musikalisch nicht besetzten, funktionsfreien Räumen wie z.B. dem natürlichen Ambiente oder einer zum Großstadtidyll gewordenen Stadtbrache, Baulücken, verwilderten Bahngeländen, stillgelegten Schwimmhallen, leerstehenden Fabrikgebäuden, Bau- und Kriegsruinen bieten sich Spielräume für die ungestörte ästhetische Praxis. Manchmal ist es eine bestimmte akustische Geräuschsphäre, manchmal hingegen die Ruhe, die mich an einen Ort anzieht. Auch ein in regelmäßigen Abständen über einen Ort hereinbrechender Lärm hat mich schon fasziniert. Auf der optischen Ebene sind es andere Merkmale: Die infolge von Witterungseinflüssen entstandene Patina auf der Fassade, das Bröckeln des Gesteins von der architektonischen Form und das mit voranschreitender Zeit zunehmende Verwildern und Überwuchern durch zufällig herbeigeflogene Pflanzensamen, die sich zu Gräsern, Ranken und Büschen an funktionslos gewordenen Orten entwickeln, lösen Erinnerungen aus und wirken zunächst als Inspiration. Später werden sie als räumlicher und akustischer Kontext zum wichtigen Bestandteil bei der Inszenierung einer künstlerischen Idee. (Das ist natürlich nicht zwangsläufig der Fall: Es gibt auch Klangskulpturen, die souverän sind. Diese funktionieren fast überall, egal in welchem Kontext sie präsentiert werden.) Andererseits ermöglichen Klangskulpturen an intakten und belebten Orten wie Brücken, Parks, öffentlichen Plätzen, Bahnhofshallen, in S-Bahnen, Shopping Malls, Universitätsgeländen, Krankenhäusern und Schulen die spannende Integration in Alltagsprozesse. Der alltägliche Lärm der Geräusche vor Ort bildet den akustischen Kontext, zu dem kritisch Stellung bezogen werden kann, in den es einzudringen oder den es zu überlagern gilt. Zunächst erfordert dies eine akustische Bestandsaufnahme, um die Voraussetzung dafür zu schaffen, – im Sinne John Cages – intendierte Handlungen in Relation zu den nichtintendierten der Umgebung zu bringen. Deswegen ist auch der soziale Kontext als außermusikalischer Faktor – wie zum Beispiel die Arbeits-, Bildungs- oder Erholungszusammenhänge in Büros, an Universitäten oder in Parks – für mich von immenser Bedeutung. Dieser wird zum zusätzlichen Steuerelement für die musikalischen Parameter meiner Musik. Bestimmte soziale Vorgänge erfordern beispielsweise leise Klänge, andere das Gegenteil. Manche Situationen erfordern Klangprozesse mit vielen Pausen, um das akustische Umfeld durchscheinen zu lassen, andere andauernde Schallfelder. Darauf werde ich später noch genauer eingehen. Mit dem Einbrechen von Klangkunst in Alltagszusammenhänge verbindet sich ganz konkret die Auseinandersetzung mit der Sozialstruktur des Ortes: Hausmeister, Sicherheitsangestellte für den zivilen Wachschutz, Bibliothekarinnen, Bootsverleiher, Lehrerinnen, Geistliche und Ordnungsbeamte werden zum Dialogpartner oder zu Gegnern des eigenen Engagements. Meine Sensibilität als Klangkünstlerin für die ortsgegebenen Sozial- und Funktionsstrukturen bildet die Voraussetzung dafür, in solchen ungewohnten Zusammenhängen überhaupt arbeiten zu können. Die entscheidende Frage

75

TOD VERSUCHE MICH 1999 GERMANY PB: Cyan Press D,CW,DF: Cyan

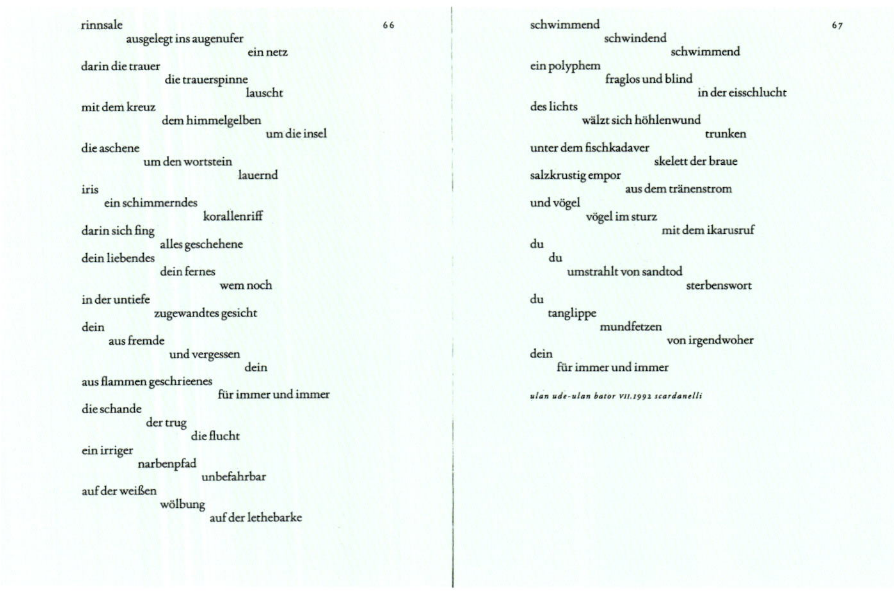

rinnsale
ausgelegt ins augenufer
ein netz
darin die trauer
die trauerspinne
lauscht
mit dem kreuz
dem himmelgelben
um die insel
die aschene
um den wortstein
lauernd
iris
ein schimmerndes
korallenriff
darin sich fing
alles geschehene
dein liebendes
dein fernes
wem noch
in der untiefe
zugewandtes gesicht
dein
aus fremde
und vergessen
dein
aus flammen geschrieenes
für immer und immer
die schande
der trug
die flucht
ein irriger
narbenpfad
unbefahrbar
auf der weißen
wölbung
auf der lethebarke

66

schwimmend
schwindend
schwimmend
ein polyphem
fraglos und blind
in der eisschlucht
des lichts
wälzt sich höhlenwund
trunken
unter dem fischkadaver
skelett der braue
salzkrustig empor
aus dem tränenstrom
und vögel
vögel im sturz
mit dem ikarusruf
du
du
umstrahlt von sandtod
sterbenswort
du
tanglippe
mundfetzen
von irgendwoher
dein
für immer und immer

ulan ude-ulan bator VII.1992 scardanelli

67

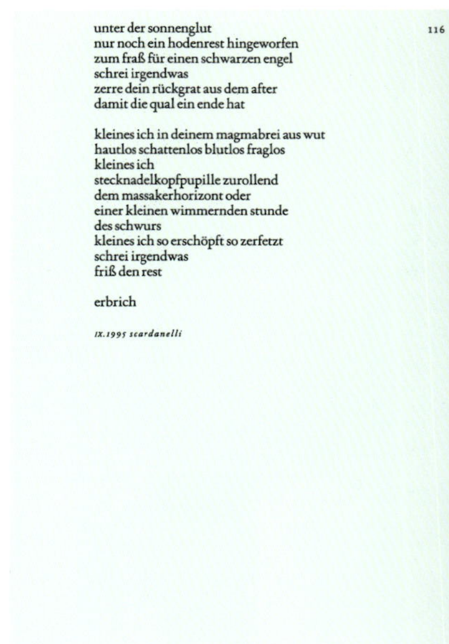

unter der sonnenglut
nur noch ein hodenrest hingeworfen
zum fraß für einen schwarzen engel
schrei irgendwas
zerre dein rückgrat aus dem after
damit die qual ein ende hat

kleines ich in deinem magmabrei aus wut
hautlos schattenlos blutlos fraglos
kleines ich
stecknadelkopfpupille zurollend
dem massakerhorizont oder
einer kleinen wimmernden stunde
des schwurs
kleines ich so erschöpft so zerfetzt
schrei irgendwas
friß den rest

erbrich

IX.1995 scardanelli

116

COVER

aus alten schriften

frag
frag doch
in welch kurzer zeit
in welcher
folge
unendlicher tode
haben wir
die entsetzlichsten namen gefunden
für dies massengrab
in dem wir alle wohnen

sind denn schon alle gestorben
immer ist ein kreis gezogen
unerbittlich um einen hohen stuhl
darauf ein fleisch sich erhebt
das
ich
sagt
ich
und sich
ein wenig regt

trennt aber das reine sehen sich
um ein weniges nur vom begreifen
vom sich fügen ins tägliche
so wird eine truhe im schatten
des altbekannten raums
zum monstrum des entsetzens der fremde

und jene schwärze
die aus offnen schränken wächst
ist wahnsinn hinter deinen augen
die nichts mehr verstehn

fraktale sonnen dann
im firmament
fühl
fühl doch
zwischen dir und nichts
dieser schmale
vorhang fleisch die knochensäule
haut haut
dein dunkelndes pergament
darauf erinnerung
die schmerzensskala
todfrucht
adergeäst
du zwitterwesen
casanova
gottflehender eremit
bleib
bleib doch
im schrecklichen raum
im hohen
der visionen
wer das
geheimnis verletzt
entstellt den mund ins elend seiner
wirklichkeiten

fraktale sonnen
im hirn
firmamenthoch
stürzendes azur
schreib
schreib doch
mit dem
knochensplitter
des ikarus
schreib
auf die wunde der stirn

die feder in händen blutgejagten
wird zum flug nie taugen
dein atem an jahrtausendwänden
war das ende
alles bereits gesagten

fraktale sonnen dann
im firmament
fühl
fühl doch
zwischen dir und nichts
dieser schmale
vorhang fleisch die knochensäule
haut haut
dein dunkelndes pergament

VIII.1995 scardanelli

ARROWS 1997 JAPAN CL: United Arrows CD: Koichiro Yamamoto AD: Kaoru Kasai D: Mayumi Kawahara I: Gianluigi Toccafondo CW: Hiroshi Ichikura
Agency: SUN-AD Co., Ltd.

COVER

Docca icocca?
Solo solo icocca.

オリジナル以外では、様々な商品を海外から買い付けており、なるべく自社輸入することにより、買い易いプライスの実現を目指しています。

服だけでなく、生活の全てを楽しんでいただくための『STYLE FOR LIVING』では、オリジナルのベッド・リネンやシンプルな食器、日本独自の竹を使ったデザインの花器や、中国茶、オーガニック商品などを扱っています。

オーガニックといえばエコ・ソープ『BIO VERSAL』の取扱いも開始する予定です。私達は、オフィスでの廃棄物に対する処理をはじめとして、リサイクルや環境問題に熱心な会社でありたいと願っています。店頭で不要になったプラスティックのハンガーもお客様に差上げています。

楽しく、心地良く暮らすためのヒントのなかには私達人類の友人、犬の存在も忘れてはいけません。都会では、家族同様に暮らしている彼等、犬達のために、まったくスペシャルな犬の服や雑貨も品揃えしています。

そして、もちろん、ヒトの服に関しても、私達とともに年齢を重ねていくお客様方の、新しい世代のために、すこしずつ子供服もスタートしています。

生活を美しく、楽しくしてくれるフレッシュでクリエイティヴなデザイナー達の作品を探して、年に数回、専門のバイヤーが、ヨーロッパやアメリカのコレクションや展示会に足を運んでいます。

良い商品とともに、私達が最も重要視しているのが、良い接客です。販売スタッフは、接客が好きなこと、服を大切に扱ってくれること、を前提として選ばれ、理想像を目指して教育されています。私達の店にはいつも「良い商品、とともに、良いコミュニケーションがあること」を、大切にしたいと考えています。

私達が目指しているのは、沢山売れることや会社が有名になることではなく、お客様に本当に楽しんでいただくこと、一人一人のお客様と末永くおつきあい出来ること、そこにかかわる全ての人々が、より幸せになれるお手伝いをして、社会に貢献することです。

私たちが理想とする会社の姿。それが「束ねた矢」です。

私たちは、ユナイテッドアローズという社名にひとつの目標へ向かって直進する矢（Arrow）を束ねた（United）ものという意味をこめました。共通の理想をめざして突き進む社員一人一人のあり方を「矢」にたとえたのです。社員は歯車のように使われるものではありません。それぞれが十分な個性を持った人間であり、そうした社員の集合体が会社である、という人材に対する考え方を表すものとして、この社名を選んだのです。めざすところへ向かって相互に高め合いながら、どこまでもまっすぐに、ポジティブに突き進んでいくのがユナイテッドアローズ社員の理想像と言うこともできるでしょうか。

その意味で、入社したての新人社員も、本部のスタッフも、役員も、社長も、みんな同じ所へ向かうひとつの矢です。誰でも同じように仕事への提案ができるし、誰もが同じように店へ出てお客さまと接します。一本一本の矢の力を大事に考えるのが、ユナイテッドアローズの基本姿勢です。

Our Commitment Is in Our Name.

At United Arrows, we firmly believe that our employees should be more than mere cogs in the corporate wheel. We recognize that each staff member is a unique individual with unique strengths and experiences, and feel that it is important to foster and encourage these traits in one another as we work toward our goals. We selected "United Arrows" as our company name to reflect this commitment to our employees. The name "United Arrows" signifies a bundle of individual arrows all flying straight toward the same target, with each arrow representing an employee at our company.

We consider all staff at United Arrows to be a valuable contribution to our organization. All employees are invited to share their ideas and suggestions, whether they are new recruits or members of the board. Additionally, staff in all parts of the company have the unique experience of hands-on training at United Arrows stores, giving them a first-hand feel for our approach to products and customer service. By ensuring that each of the "arrows" in our company flies straight and true, we believe that no goal is beyond our reach.

COVER

「しあわせになれる会社ユナイテッドアローズ」栗野宏文

私は働くことが好きだった。15歳くらいから、近所の酒屋の配達を手始めにさまざまなアルバイトをした。自分で働いて、自分で報酬を得ることの充実感とともに、そこにはつねに、家庭や学校では学べない"何か"があったと思う。高校を出るとすぐに、高級婦人注文服のアトリエに入った。いわゆる"お針子さん"である。生地にアイロンをかけたり、裏地をつけたり、裾を始末したり、これらのごく初歩的なワークの中で学んだ服の基本的な構造や、物をていねいにつくりあげるということは、いまも自分の仕事の原点として役に立っている。もうひとつ学んだのは、朝きちんと始業時間前に職場に行くこと。一日のスタートの大切さである。この"お針子修業"は4ヵ月あまり続いたのだが、職人デヴューには18歳は遅すぎたようだ。好奇心旺盛だった私は、先輩職人のすすめもあって大学を受験し、さらに広い視点で物事を学ぶことにした。多くの大学生が遊ぶことに費やす4年間を、私と仲間たちは熱心に学習・研究した。ここで学んだのはさまざまな角度からの"物の見方"である。

大学を卒業した私は再び服に携わることを決心した。今度は日本でも有数の大手婦人衣料チェーン・ストアである。ここで働いた約1年半はその後の私の基礎となった。何事にも積極的に取り組むこと、いい仕事をして上司や同僚に認めてもらうこと、そしてそれが次のステップへと導いてくれること。そうしたことを私は身体で学んだ。しかし、1978年秋、私はこの会社を去ることにした。生意気なようだが、ここで学べることに限界を感じたのも、その理由のひとつであった。そして当時創業2年目の、いわゆるインポートショップに入社した。正直に言うと、はじめはつなぎのアルバイトのつもりであり、もう服の世界とは縁を切る気持も半分あったのだが、仕事が面白く、また素晴らしい仲間にも恵まれたおかげで、いつの間にか、このショップの仕事に夢中になっていた。自分たちの成長にともなって会社もどんどん成長し、自分たちでも予想できなかったくらいの成功をおさめるに至った。この会社には11年関わり、服の仕事が自分にとって一生の仕事になることを強く自覚させられた11年となった。しかし遂にその会社も辞める時がきた。自分たちでひとつのマーケットをつくりあげる面白さも、喜びも味わった。日本の若者のカジュアルファッションを変革することにほんの少しだが影響を与えることができたという自信もできた。

1989年、私たちはユナイテッドアローズをつくった。この会社は人をしあわせにするための組織でありたい。なによりもお客さまに喜んでもらえる商品を提供し続ける場であり、また、そこは自分たちの夢や希望をかなえる場でもあるわけなのだが、その行為・活動を通じて、関わる人、関係者全員がしあわせになれること、そのしあわせを日本のみならず全世界に向けて発し続け、影響し続ける存在にしたいと思っている。私が、はじめて手に針と糸を持たせてもらった日からいままで服を扱うことで学んできたことのすべてと、まだまだ学ばせてくれるであろう幾多の未知なるもの、素敵なもののすべてを、この会社の中でつかみとれるようにしていきたい。

ユナイテッドアローズ常務取締役／販売促進部長

Creating a Company that Brings Happiness

I have always enjoyed working. When I was fifteen, I took a job as a delivery boy at a local liquor shop. In addition to the satisfaction of earning wages for my labor, I also felt that I was acquiring knowledge that I could not gain at home or school. After graduating from high school, I spent four months working at a studio which was producing exclusive custom-tailored women's clothing. It was there that I learned the very basics of the apparel industry as I ironed fabrics, sewed linings, finished hem lines and handled other basic tasks. I also learned the importance of producing things properly and the value of a getting a good start on the day by arriving at work early, lessons which remain with me today. I eventually enrolled in a university, where I not only acquired knowledge about the subjects I was studying, but also learned how to view the world from a wider perspective.

When I graduated from college, I decided to join the apparel industry once again, this time working for a large-scale chain store that sold women's clothing. During my two years there, I discovered that by tackling each job actively and enthusiastically, I would be given even greater challenges and opportunities in the workplace. After leaving that job, I joined a boutique specializing in imported clothing. At the time, I was planning to stay for just a few months, as I could not see myself working in the fashion industry for the rest of my life. However, I was blessed with exciting work and good colleagues, and I soon became immersed in my job. As we grew and matured, so did the company, achieving greater success than we had ever imagined. By the time I left the company eleven years later, I had experienced the pleasure of starting a new trend in the world of casual fashion in Japan. I knew that I would work in the apparel industry for the rest of my life.

In 1989 we founded United Arrows. From the start, it has been my goal to make this a company which brings happiness to everyone involved with our operations. I want to maintain a corporate atmosphere where we can develop new products that bring satisfaction to our customers while providing a forum in which employees can fulfill their dreams and desires. I would like this to be a company where I can utilize the lessons I have learned since first picking up a needle and thread, while continuing to gain new ideas and inspiration from those around me. But above all, I hope that through our activities, United Arrows will be able to add value to people's lives, both in Japan and around the world.

KURINO Hirofumi
Marketing Director, United Arrows

RICHARD LONG: SANGYO SUIGYO 1996 JAPAN PB: Tankosha Publishing Co., Ltd. AD,P: Richard Long D: Tomohiro Itami DF: It Is Design

WIND LINE

A WIND DIRECTION EACH DAY
ALONG A 560 MILE WALK IN 20½ DAYS
FROM THE ATLANTIC COAST TO THE MEDITERRANEAN COAST

PORTUGAL AND SPAIN 1989

風の線

大西洋岸から地中海まで
五六〇マイルを二〇日半かけて歩きながら
日々、風向きをしるした

ポルトガルとスペイン　一九八九年

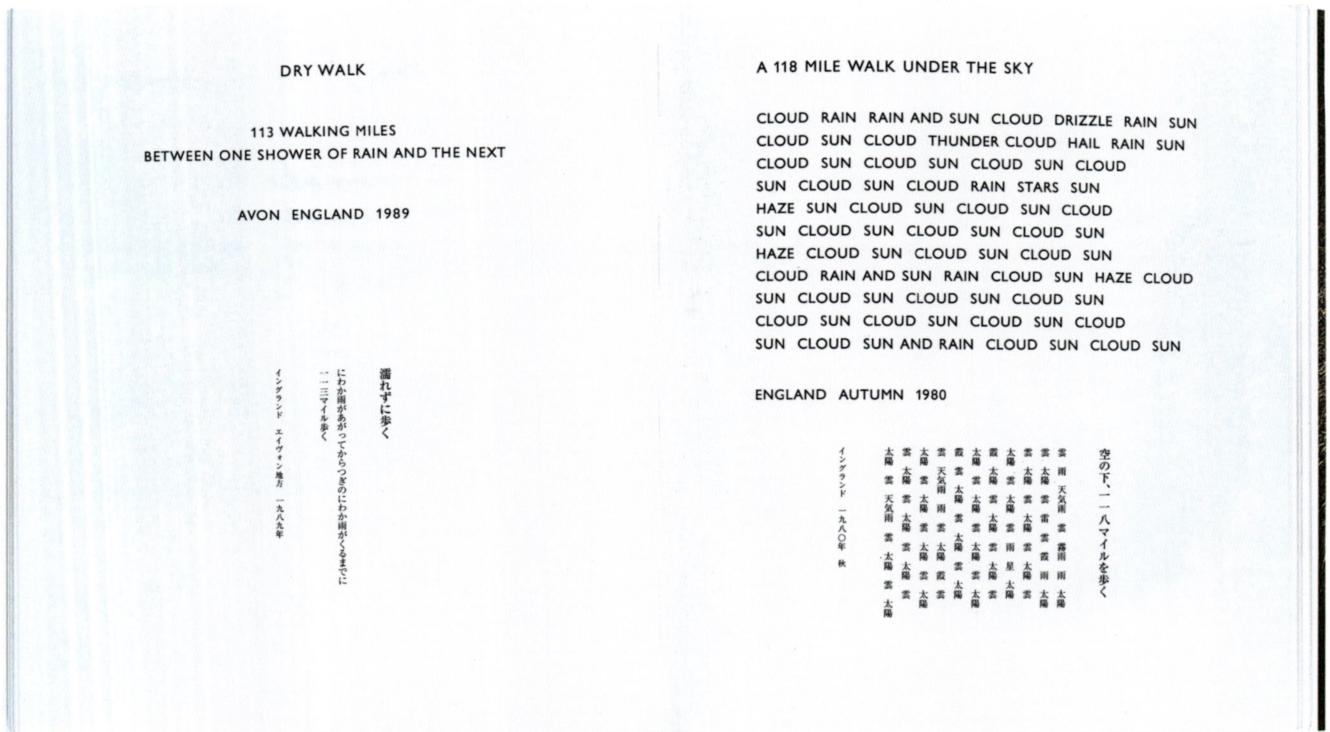

DRY WALK

113 WALKING MILES
BETWEEN ONE SHOWER OF RAIN AND THE NEXT

AVON ENGLAND 1989

濡れずに歩く

にわか雨があがってからつぎのにわか雨がくるまでに
一一三マイル歩く

イングランド　エイヴォン地方　一九八九年

A 118 MILE WALK UNDER THE SKY

CLOUD RAIN RAIN AND SUN CLOUD DRIZZLE RAIN SUN
CLOUD SUN CLOUD THUNDER CLOUD HAIL RAIN SUN
CLOUD SUN CLOUD SUN CLOUD SUN CLOUD
SUN CLOUD SUN CLOUD RAIN STARS SUN
HAZE SUN CLOUD SUN CLOUD SUN CLOUD
SUN CLOUD SUN CLOUD SUN CLOUD SUN
HAZE CLOUD SUN CLOUD SUN CLOUD SUN
CLOUD RAIN AND SUN RAIN CLOUD SUN HAZE CLOUD
SUN CLOUD SUN CLOUD SUN CLOUD SUN
CLOUD SUN CLOUD SUN CLOUD SUN CLOUD
SUN CLOUD SUN AND RAIN CLOUD SUN CLOUD SUN

ENGLAND AUTUMN 1980

空の下、一一八マイルを歩く

雲　雨　天気雨　雲　霧雨　雨　太陽
雲　太陽　雲　雷　雲　霰　雨　太陽
雲　太陽　雲　太陽　雲　太陽　雲
太陽　雲　太陽　雲　雨　星　太陽
霞　太陽　雲　太陽　雲　太陽　雲
太陽　雲　太陽　雲　太陽　雲　太陽
霞　雲　太陽　雲　太陽　雲　太陽
雲　天気雨　雨　雲　太陽　霞　雲
太陽　雲　太陽　雲　太陽　雲　太陽
雲　太陽　雲　太陽　雲　太陽　雲
太陽　雲　天気雨　雲　太陽　雲　太陽

イングランド　一九八〇年　秋

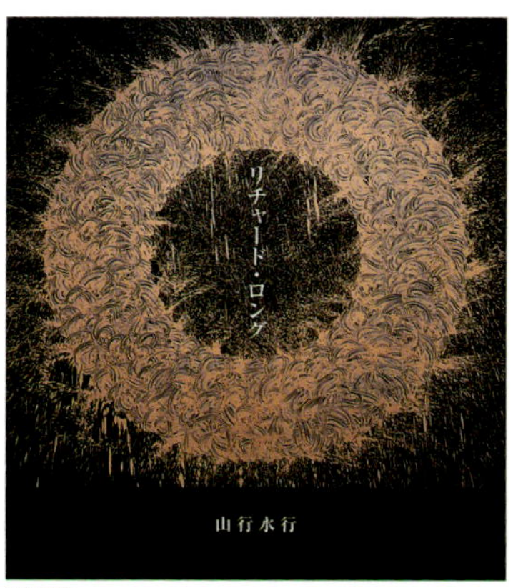

COVER

DUSTLINES

KICKING UP A LINE OF DUST EACH DAY ALONG THE WALKING LINE

A 7 DAY WALK ON THE EAST BANK OF THE RIO GRANDE

EL CAMINO REAL NEW MEXICO 1995

砂埃のすじ

毎日歩く道すじに沿い砂埃のすじを蹴り上げる

リオグランデ川東岸を七日間歩く

エル・カミーノ・レアル　ニューメキシコ州　一九九五年

デス・サークルの旅
リオグランデ川東岸を七日かけて歩く
ニューメキシコ州　一九九五年

62

日本での移動線

拾う　運ぶ　置く
一つの物から　次の物へ
三十五哩の歩行
太平洋の際に沿って

貝から　蟹へ
蟹から　羽へ
羽から　魚へ
魚から　竹へ
竹から　人参へ
人参から　松毬へ
松毬から　炭へ
炭から　海月へ
海月から　枝へ
枝から　貝へ
貝から　貝へ
貝から　海草へ
海草から　小石へ
小石から　犬の骸骨へ
犬の骸骨から　枝へ
枝から　鮫の懸守へ
鮫の懸守から　竹へ
竹から　仙人掌の葉へ
仙人掌の葉から　花へ
花から　丸木へ
丸木から　羽へ
羽から　小石へ
小石から　鴉へ
鴉から　蟹へ
蟹から　小石へ
小石から　歩行の終わりへ

RPORATE PROFILE 会社案内

A PAPER CORPORATE PROFILE 1999 JAPAN CL: Heiwa Paper Co., Ltd. CD,AD: Ken Miki D: Eiji Marui P: Koichi Okuwaki I: Philipp Franz von Siebol
CW: Junichi Hayano Printer: Dai Nippon Printing Co., Ltd.

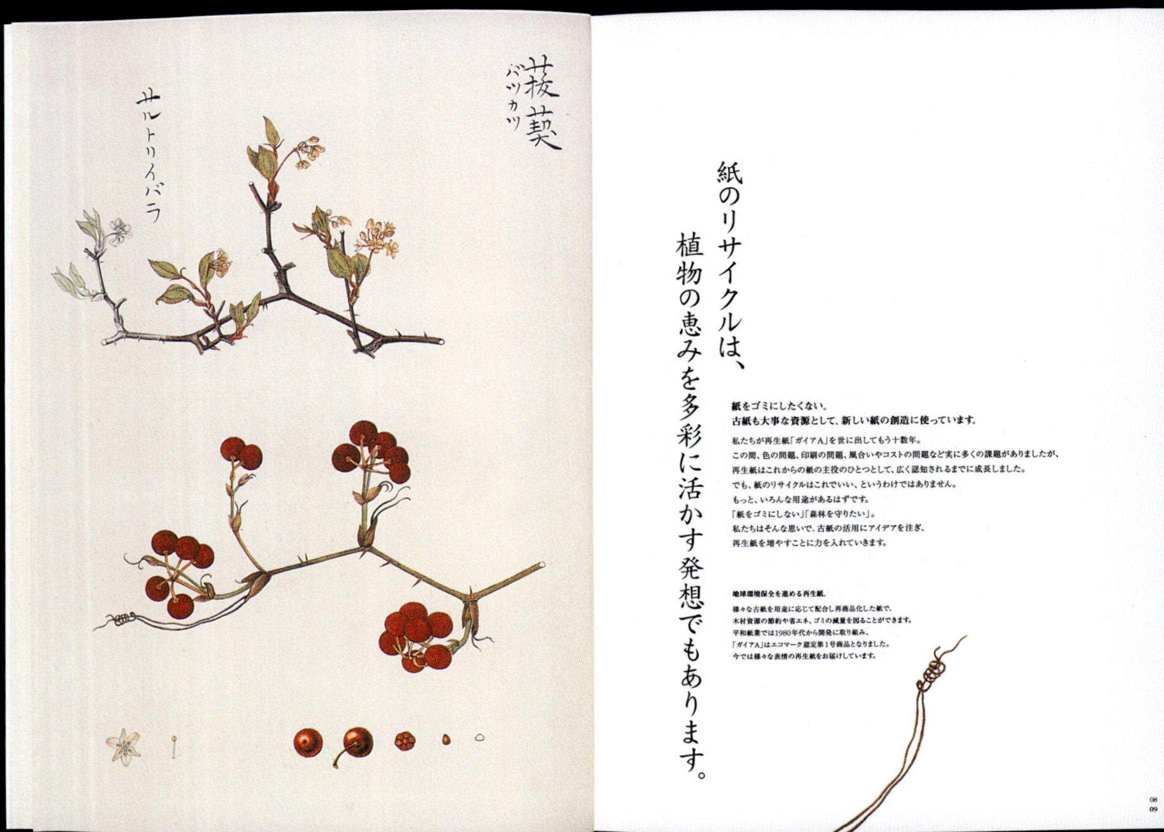

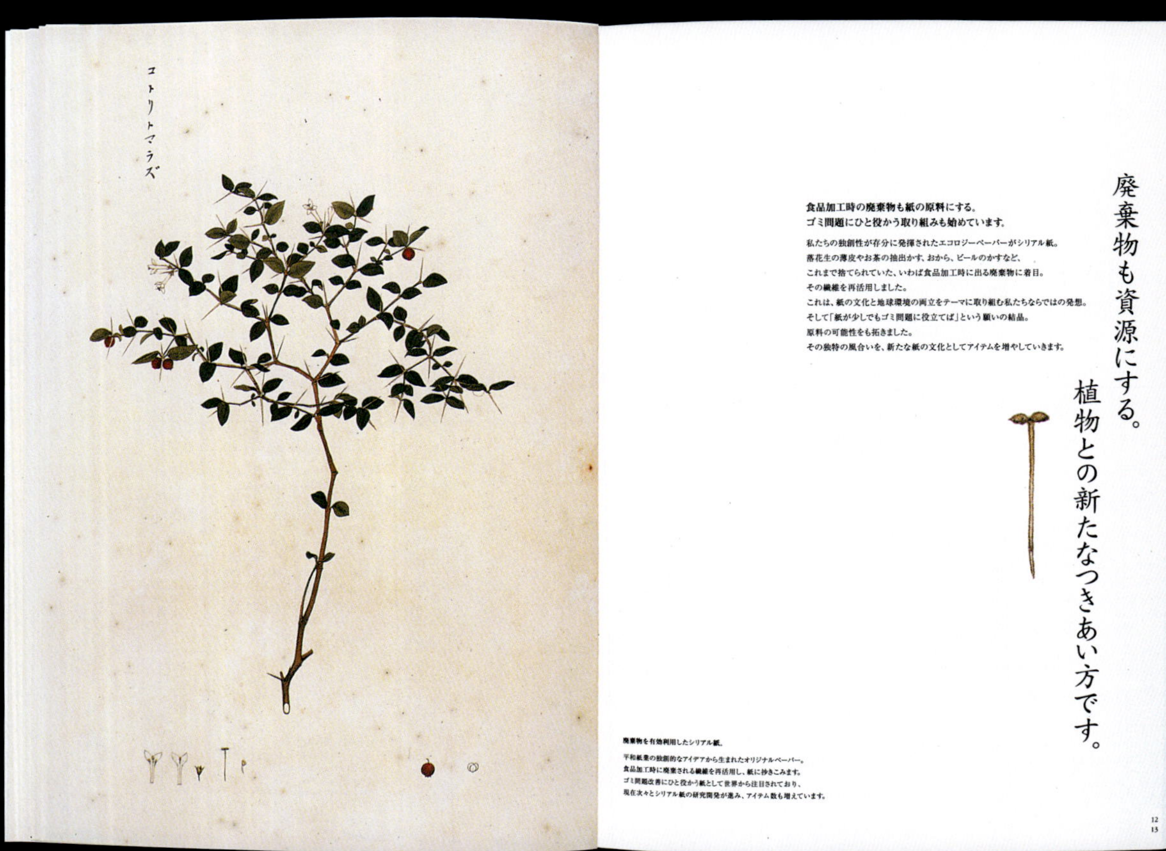

ADE PAPER CORPORATION LTD. 2000 HONG KONG

CL: Polytrade Paper Corporation Ltd. CD,AD,D: Eric Chan D: Francis Lee D,I: Vivian Cha
I: Michael Lau CW: Cat Tyrell / Peter Wong DF: Eric Chan Design Co., Ltd.

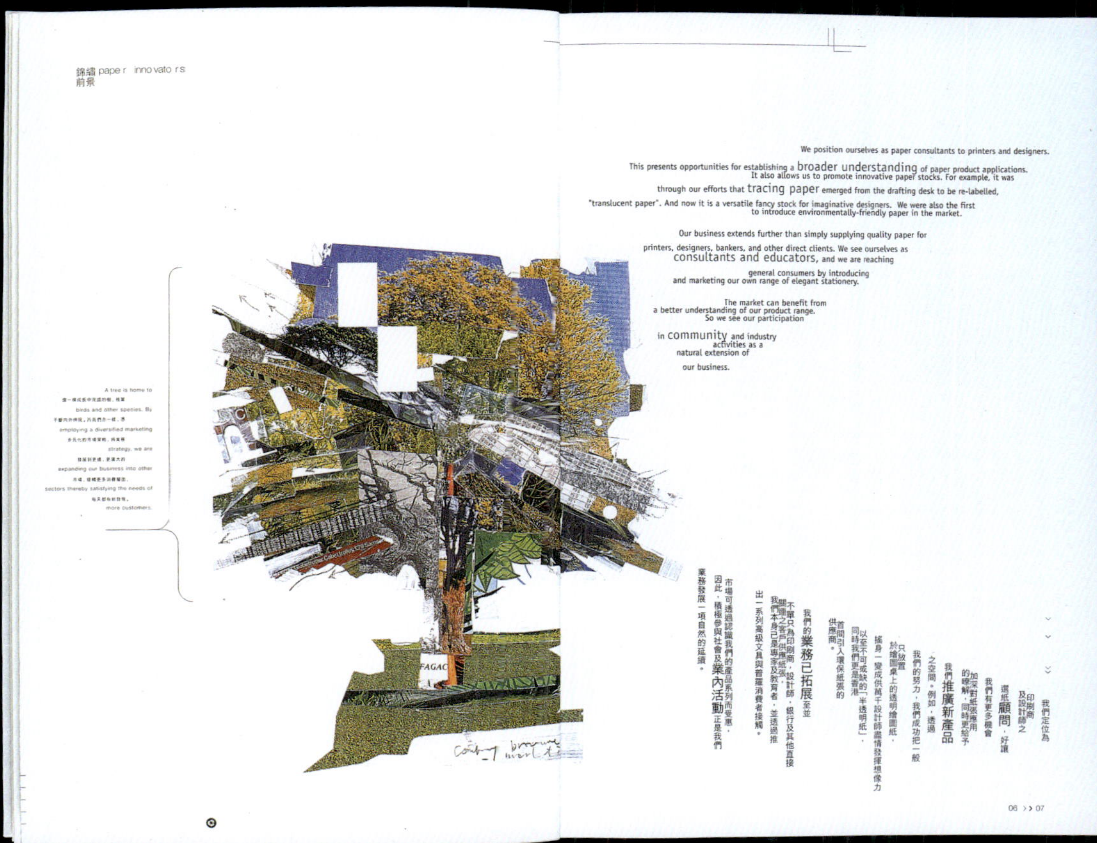

SIGN MAGAZINE 1997 GERMANY CL,DF: SIGN Kommunikation GmbH CD: Karl W. Henschel AD,D,P: Antonia Henschel

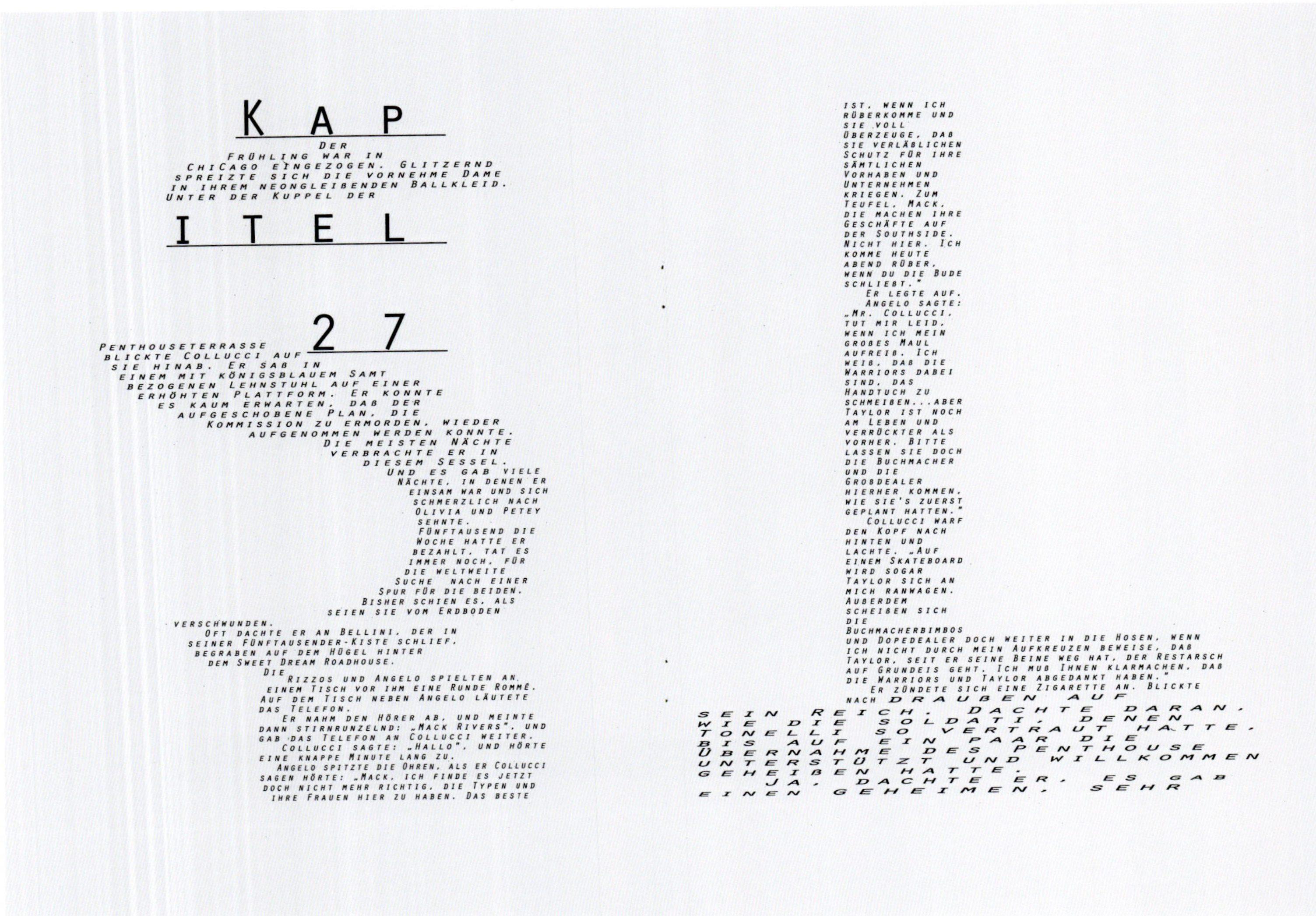

Kap itel 27

Der Frühling war in Chicago eingezogen. Glitzernd spreizte sich die vornehme Dame in ihrem neongleißenden Ballkleid. Unter der Kuppel der Penthouseterrasse blickte Collucci auf sie hinab. Er saß in einem mit königsblauem Samt bezogenen Lehnstuhl auf einer erhöhten Plattform. Er konnte es kaum erwarten, daß der aufgeschobene Plan, die Kommission zu ermorden, wieder aufgenommen werden konnte. Die meisten Nächte verbrachte er in diesem Sessel. Und es gab viele Nächte, in denen er einsam war und sich schmerzlich nach Olivia und Petey sehnte. Fünftausend die Woche hatte er bezahlt, tat es immer noch, für die weltweite Suche nach einer Spur für die beiden. Bisher schien es, als seien sie vom Erdboden verschwunden.

Oft dachte er an Bellini, der in seiner Fünftausender-Kiste schlief, begraben auf dem Hügel hinter dem Sweet Dream Roadhouse.

Die Rizzos und Angelo spielten an einem Tisch vor ihm eine Runde Rommé. Auf dem Tisch neben Angelo läutete das Telefon.

Er nahm den Hörer ab, und meinte dann stirnrunzelnd: „Mack Rivers", und gab das Telefon an Collucci weiter.

Collucci sagte: „Hallo", und hörte eine knappe Minute lang zu.

Angelo spitzte die Ohren, als er Collucci sagen hörte: „Mack, ich finde es jetzt doch nicht mehr richtig, die Typen und ihre Frauen hier zu haben. Das beste ist, wenn ich rüberkomme und sie voll überzeuge, daß sie verläßlichen Schutz für ihre sämtlichen Vorhaben und Unternehmen kriegen. Zum Teufel, Mack, die machen ihre Geschäfte auf der Southside. Nicht hier. Ich komme heute abend rüber, wenn du die Bude schließt."

Er legte auf.

Angelo sagte: „Mr. Collucci, tut mir leid, wenn ich mein großes Maul aufreiß. Ich weiß, daß die Warriors dabei sind, das Handtuch zu schmeißen...aber Taylor ist noch am Leben und verrückter als vorher. Bitte lassen Sie doch die Buchmacher und die Großdealer hierher kommen, wie Sie's zuerst geplant hatten."

Collucci warf den Kopf nach hinten und lachte. „Auf einem Skateboard wird sogar Taylor sich an mich ranwagen. Außerdem scheißen sich die Buchmacherbimbos und Dopedealer doch weiter in die Hosen, wenn ich nicht durch mein Aufkreuzen beweise, daß Taylor, seit er seine Beine weg hat, der Restarsch auf Grundeis geht. Ich muß Ihnen klarmachen, daß die Warriors und Taylor abgedankt haben."

Er zündete sich eine Zigarette an. Blickte nach draußen auf sein Reich. Dachte daran, wie die Soldati, denen Tonelli so vertraut hatte, bis auf ein paar die Übernahme des Penthouse unterstützt und willkommen geheißen hatte.

Ja, dachte er, es gab einen geheimen, sehr

COVER

AUS DEM
STECKTE.
RAUH SAGTE
SMITTY !"
KONGS HAND
SICH AN DIE
SPECIAL IN SEINEM
WIRBELTE HERUM.
ABDRÜCKEN KONNTE,
LÖCHER IN SEINE
DIE EINSCHLÄGE
DEN RÜCKEN. MUND UND
TODESQUAL. TAYLOR
BERÜHRTE FAST KONGS
SANFT SAGTE ER:
LEID, DAß DICH DEINE
EINGEHOLT HAT... WARUM
SMITTY?
WARUM DER HAß? WARUM
ANDER,N SO WEH?...
SMITTY?"
KONG ROLLTE DIE
UND STARRTE
LEUCHTENDEM
HAß INS GESICHT, DAß
ER DEKLAMIERTE
SORGFALT, WIE EIN KIND,

WANDSCHRANK

ER: „ HALT,

SCHLÄNGELTE
ACHTUNDDREIßIGER
HOSENBUND UND ER
BEVOR KONG
PUMPTE TAYLOR ZWEI
BRUST.
LEGTEN KONG FLACH AUF
AUGEN ZUCKTEN IN
BEUGTE SICH VOR UND
GESICHT.
„SMITTY, ES TUT MIR
TEUFLISCHE VERLOGENHEIT
HAST DU ES GETAN,

TUST DU MIR UND DEN
WARUM HAST DU ES GETAN

BRECHENDEN AUGEN HOCH
TAYLOR MIT SOLCH
UND ABGEDREHTEM
TAYLOR ZURÜCKWICH.
MIT GROTESKER
DAS EINEN

DU
BEVOR DU

HALBERINNERTEN, OBSZÖNEN
SCHÜTTELREIM AUFSAGT. „DIR WEHTUN?
ARSCHLOCH...ICH WAR'N TOPNIGGER,
MICH AUS MEINER
SPITZENSTELLUNG BEI DEN
DEVASTATORS RAUSGEBOXT
HAST...SCHEBE...SEITDEM LEG ICH'S DRAUF AN
ZU VERLETZEN UND ZU HASSEN. ICH BIN FROH,
DAß DER ITAKER DIR DIE STELZEN VERSAUT
HAT... ICH HAB IHM GEFLÜSTERT, DAß DU
UNTERWEGS BIST, NIGGER..."

KONG ENTLIEß EINEN FLÜSSIGEN SEUFZER UND STARB. SEIN GESICHT ABSCHEULICH IN KRANKEM TRIUMPH.

TAYLOR KAUERTE STILL UND niedergeschlagen NEBEN KONG UND STARRTE NOCH IMMER IN DAS VERZERRTE GESICHT, ALS BAMA DEN ROLLSTUHL HEREINSCHOB. ER WAR IN BEGLEITUNG VON DEW DROP UND IVORY JONES, TAYLORS PERSÖNLICHEN ORDONNANZEN. SCHWEIGEND FOLGTEN SIE TAYLOR, DER IN SEINEM MOTORGETRIEBENEN ROLLSTUHL ZUM
BUNKER ZURÜCKFUHR

AUS ICEBERG SLIM / TODES FLUCH, ROMAN, MAAS VERLAG, BERLIN, 1995

Axel Wolf
Raus aus der Tretmühle – aber wie?

Vielen Menschen ist ihr Beruf zur Falle geworden. Sie definieren sich fast nur noch über beruflichen Erfolg, Leistung, Geld. So sind sie um so gefährdeter, wenn mit der Karriere etwas schiefläuft. Beruflicher Ehrgeiz macht oft blind für den "Rest des Lebens". Damit die Arbeit nicht allmählich alles auffrißt, empfehlen sich Strategien des Innehaltens, Prüfens – und "Runterschaltens"

Für d[illegible] meisten Menschen ist ihr Beruf der zentrale [illegible] ihrer Identität. Jemand ist nicht einfa[illegible] nur Versicherungs-Bezirksleiter, Oberstudienrätin oder Art Director – sein Ansehen – [illegible] Mensch" häng[illegible] vom beruflichen Erfolg ab. Sicher [illegible] Familienleben, Hobbies, Urlaub etc. sind auch wichti[illegible] aber sie erscheinen [illegible] meisten [illegible] [illegible] wenn es im Beruf nicht klappt. Vor allem anderen [illegible] der berufliche Erfol[illegible] das eigentliche Symbol für gelungene Selbstverwirklichung: Kein Wunder also, daß für diese[illegible] Ziel die besten Ressourcen mobilisiert werden [illegible], über die ein Mensch verfügt: Zeit, Energie, Kreativität. Aber das Leben verengt sic[illegible] allmählich immer mehr auf den Beruf, der verbleibende Rest der Zeit dient nur noch der Regeneration oder dem statusbewußten Konsum.

[illegible] Höhepunkt erreichte diese Entwicklung in den 80er Jahren, und ihre typischen Vertreter waren die karriere-bewußten Yuppies und "Dink"-Paare (double income, no kids – zwei Einkommen, keine Kinder). Der workaholic war der heimliche Held des Erfolgs-Kultes, den die Wirtschaft, aber auch Universitäten und Medien sorgsam pflegten. Die Firmen wetteiferten darin, "Firmenkulturen" zu schaffen: Je wohler sich ein Arbeitnehmer in der Firma fühlt, je mehr er sich mit ihr identifiziert, desto eher akzeptiert er sie als Ersatzfamilie – und leistet freudig mehr.

Heute, in Zeiten der wirtschaftlichen Flaute, breitet sich Ernüchterung aus. Selbst für früher hochangesehene "Zukunfts"berufe wird der Stellenmarkt eng, sogar Ärzte sind in ungeahnter Zahl arbeitslos, hochqualifizierte Manager finden sich plötzlich auf der Straße wieder. Die Firmen werden "lean", die Hierarchien "flach" – was geringere Aufstiegschancen für heranwachsende Generationen bedeutet. Die individuellen Karrierepläne müssen der neuen Situation angepaßt werden.

Gibt es ein Leben jenseits des Schuftens?

Aber auch das psychosoziale Klima der Arbeitswelt hat sich geändert (siehe Daniel Yankelovichs Analyse "Das Ende der fetten Jahre", Heft 3/94). "Erfolg" wird neu definiert und eine Zeit des Umdenkens bricht an: Lohnt es sich wirklich, der beruflichen Lebensplanung alles unterzuordnen? Ist eine Karriere wirklich der die beste Art, sich als Person zu entfalten? Ist der psychische und soziale Preis des beruflichen Erfolges nicht zu hoch? Neue Einsichten wachsen, die schon totgesagten "post-materialistischen Werte" erleben eine Renaissance: es gibt wieder ein Leben jenseits des Schuftens und Scheffelns.

Was aber tun, wenn sich das berufliche Erfolgsstreben schon so verselbständigt hat, daß der Job zur Tretmühle geworden ist? Wenn psychische und physisch[illegible]

26.10.1994 **ich hasse diese tage**
nichts geht voran.
egal, welche lage,
kein gedanke kommt an. k e i n t a g
f ü r I D E E N
nichts bewegt sich alles ist starr
mir klar
kein lüftchen bläst die birne
nichts hat kontur
von sinn keine spur
eingehüllt in wollenem mantel
zugemüllt mit pollenem getantel

Schon packt
mich der
zweifel
mit gier'gem
gekeifel

ICH SCHEIß
AUF DEN
TAG
DER MICH NICHT MAG

ALEXANDER MÄGDEFESSEL

SIGN
SIGN KOMMUNIKATION GMBH
HANAUER LANDSTRAßE 287-289
60314 FRANKFURT
0049-69-9443240
0049-69-94432450 FAX

HTTP://WWW.SIGN.DE/
INFO@SIGN.DE

COMPUSERVE 100013.3716
MAILBOX +49-69-94500259

REDAKTIONELLE MITARBEIT
KARL W. HENSCHEL,
ALEXANDER MÄGDEFESSEL, AXEL WOLF,
DIRK MAXEINER, ICEBERG SLIM,
ERICH MAAS, HEIKO ERNST

GESTALTUNG
ANTONIA HENSCHEL, NICK DUNN,
KARL W. HENSCHEL

TSCHÜSS ADIEU, BYE BYE, SAY GOOD NIGHT GRACIE

TRACE URBAN CULTURE MAGAZINE NO.3 1998 GREECE CL,CD,AD,DF: Altervision D: Tasos Efremidis / Apostolos Rizos / Dimitris Mitsiopoulos / Klimis Mastoridis

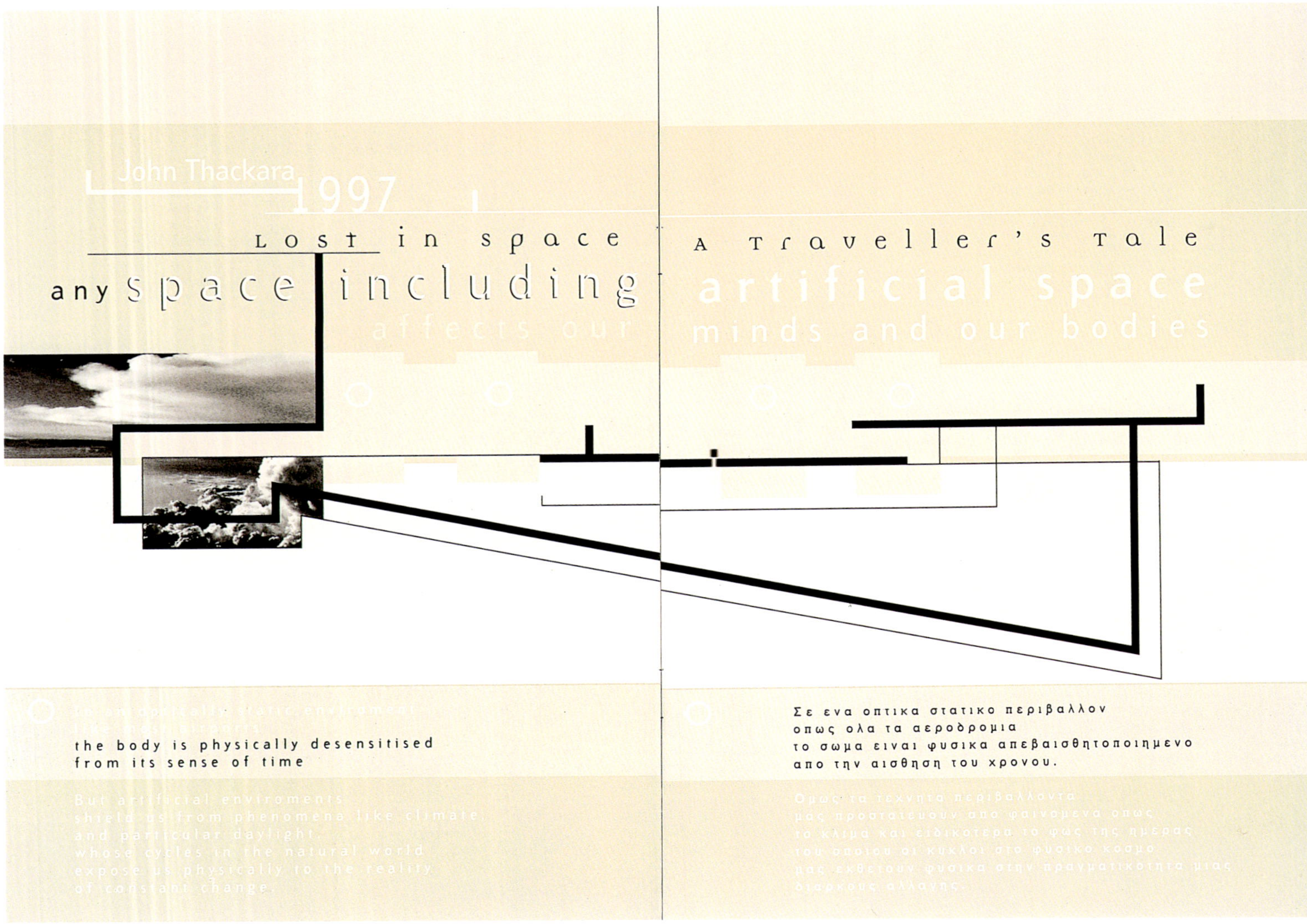

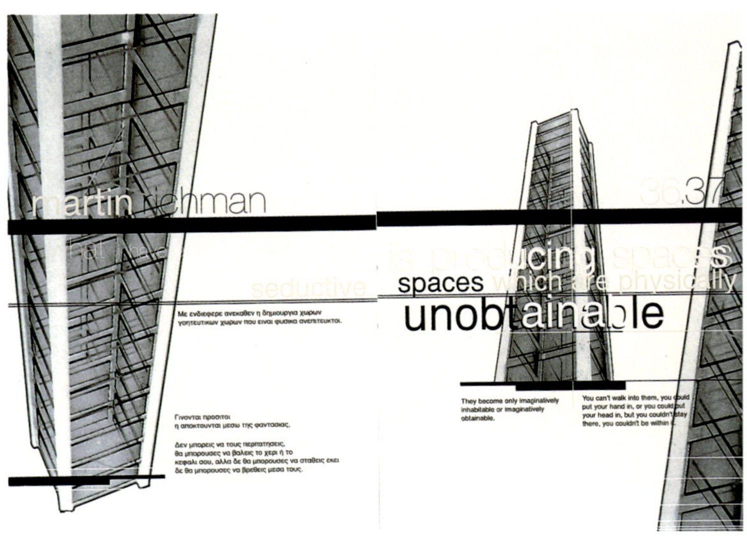

PHOENISSES 1999 GREECE CL: Petros Theodorou CD,AD,DF: Altervision D: Tasos Efremidis / Apostolos Rizos / Dimitris Mitsiopoulos / Klimis Mastoridis

4

ΑΦΡΟΔΙΤΗ ΓΕΩΡΓΙΑΔΟΥ ΠΑΝΑΓΙΩΤΑ ΤΣΕΚΟΥΡΑ

ΕΦΗ ΤΣΟΛΑΚΙΔΟΥ ΕΛΕΝΗ ΛΙΑΠΑ

5

Ιστορικό της μουσικής και της παράστασης

Αφορμή αυτής της δουλειάς ήταν η μουσική μου για τις "Φοίνισσες", που ανέβασε το 1995 η *Τέχνη* του Κιλκίς σε σκηνοθεσία του Δημήτρη Καρέλλη. ...*Πίστευα πάντα ότι τα μοτίβα μιας τραγωδίας ως συναισθήματα, κίνητρα, ανάγκες, συμπεριφορές, συγκρούσεις, κ.λ.π., ανάγονται πεντακάθαρα στα βαθύτερα στρώματα της ανθρώπινης ψυχής, χωρίς πέπλα που πρέπει να ανασηκωθούν για να δούμε τη δυναμική τους. Η θαυμάσια αυτή συνεργασία με τον Δημήτρη Καρέλλη μου έδωσε την ευκαιρία που πάντα επιζητούσα. Να ασχοληθώ με το υλικό μιας τραγωδίας αναζητώντας τον "ήχο" του σαν την κραυγή μιας γυμνής, ακάλυπτης ψυχής, στοχεύοντας απευθείας εκεί όπου οι αντιθέσεις και τα πολλά μας πρόσωπα συνυπάρχουν με μια δική τους αρμονία...*

Τότε, ανακάλυψα ένα σωρό πράγματα που ακόμη επιδρούν καθοριστικότατα στη μουσική μου πορεία. Ιδιότυπες χρήσεις της μουσικής τεχνολογίας, προσεχτική χρήση του τυχαίου, παραδοσιακές αναφορές, στοιχεία νέα και για τους τρόπους μου να συνθέτω αλλά και για ζητήματα εκφραστικών μέσων και τεχνικών.

Εκείνη ακριβώς την περίοδο, έχοντας συγκεντρώσει ένα νέο και ογκώδες ηχητικό υλικό, είχα την ιδέα να δημιουργηθεί με βάση τις ΦΟΙΝΙΣΣΕΣ μία παράσταση βασισμένη μόνο σε ήχο και κίνηση, χωρίς λόγο.

Στις αρχές του 1997, φτιάχνοντας το χοροθεατρικό σχήμα ΕΝΤΡΟΠΙΑ με τη χορεύτρια Έφη Τσολακίδου, η ιδέα της χοροθεατρικής προσέγγισης προχωρεί και δημιουργείται ένα σαφέστατο γενικό πλαίσιο ως προς τη δομή και το ύφος.

Στα τέλη του ίδιου χρόνου, ξαναδουλεύεται η μουσική με βάση αυτό το πλαίσιο.

Αρχές του 1998... Οι ΦΟΙΝΙΣΣΕΣ, ύστερα από πολλές φάσεις επεξεργασίας διαπιστώνω ότι αποτελούν πλέον και ένα ανεξάρτητο από την παράσταση ηχητικό υλικό. Η "Music Kitchen" προτίθεται να εκδόσει τον δίσκο. Ο Γιώργος Ροϊλίδης ως παραγωγός και ο Χαράλαμπος Ιωακειμίδης ως τεχνικός, προσδίδουν μια νέα διάσταση στο υλικό.

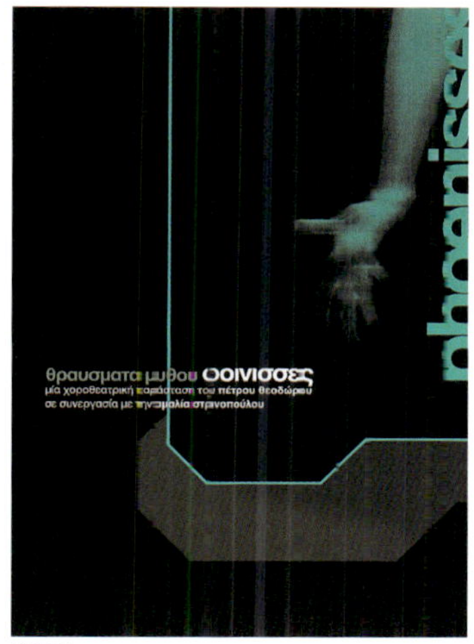

COVER

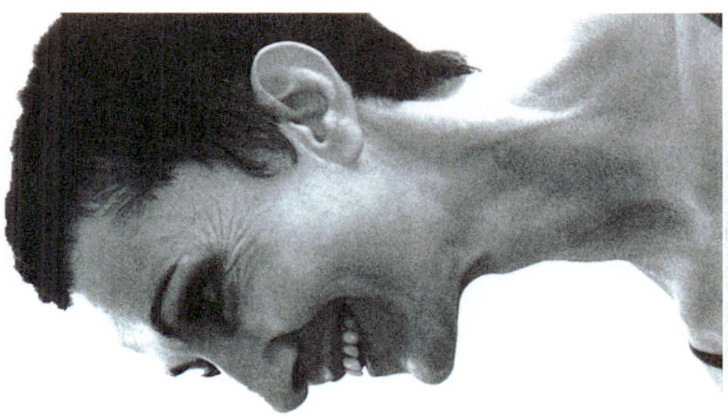

6

ΑΜΑΛΙΑ ΣΤΡΙΝΟΠΟΥΛΟΥ

7

Στα μέσα του 1999 η χοροθεατρική παράσταση περιλαμβάνεται στα "Δημήτρια" και εγκαινιάζεται η τελική φάση της χοροθεατρικής επεξεργασίας.

Η χορεύτρια και χορογράφος Αμαλία Στρινοπούλου αναλαμβάνει τη χορογραφική και κινησιολογική ανάπτυξη του υλικού, επιδρώντας παράλληλα με τη δημιουργική ματιά της στον πυρήνα του. ...*Μπορεί να πέρασαν αρκετά χρόνια για να πάρει σάρκα και οστά αυτή η ιδέα. Όμως μάλλον έτσι έπρεπε να γίνει, αφού η Αμαλία Στρινοπούλου της χαρίζει σήμερα εικόνες και κίνηση λες και τη γνώρισε σε όλα της τα στάδια. Πάρα πολλές φορές βλέπω να υλοποιούνται με εκπληκτική ακρίβεια είτε εικόνες που είχα στο μυαλό μου γράφοντας τη μουσική, είτε εικόνες που θα έχτιζα για αυτή τη δουλειά αν γνώριζα σε τέτοιο βάθος τη γλώσσα του χορού και όλα μοιάζουν να παίρνουν τη σωστή τους θέση. ....*

Το καλοκαίρι του 1999, για τις ανάγκες της παράστασης, συνθέτει συνδετικά κείμενα ο Απόστολος Αποστολίδης. Ολο το πράγμα αποκτά μιάν άλλη λάμψη. "Δένει" ακόμη περισσότερο σεναριακά, διαπνέεται από μιά ιδιόμορφη ποιητικότητα και ένα βαθειά ανθρώπινο θρησκευτικό αίσθημα. Ενας κύκλος που άνοιξε το 1995 θαρρείς και κλείνει, όταν ο Δημήτρης Καρέλλης βρίσκει τον χρόνο να αποδώσει κάποια από αυτά τα κείμενα.

Την ίδια περίοδο προσθέτει και τη δική της πνοή η Ολυμπία Σιδερίδου χτίζοντας το σκηνογραφικό - ενδυματολογικό μέρος με λιτότητα και ευαισθησία. Ο Στράτος Κουτράκης ήδη σκέφτεται τους φωτισμούς και τις ιδιαιτερότητες της δουλειάς αυτής. Παράλληλα, η χορογραφία ολοκληρώνεται και οι χορευτές ζωντανεύουν με τον δικό τους τρόπο την παράσταση. Νέα ερεθίσματα, νέες προοπτικές, νέες αφορμές για περαιτέρω προσθήκες, μεταβολές και επεξεργασίες του ηχητικού υλικού. Ολα γίνονται πλέον ταχύτατα.

Οι συνθήκες συνεργασίας είναι ιδανικές. Μελανό σημείο ένα αλλά καθοριστικότατο: οι σχεδόν ανύπαρκτες οικονομικές δυνατότητες του πλαισίου παραγωγής, το συνεπακόλουθο άγχος και μια διάθεση

ΚΩΣΤΑΣ ΠΕΤΡΙΔΗΣ

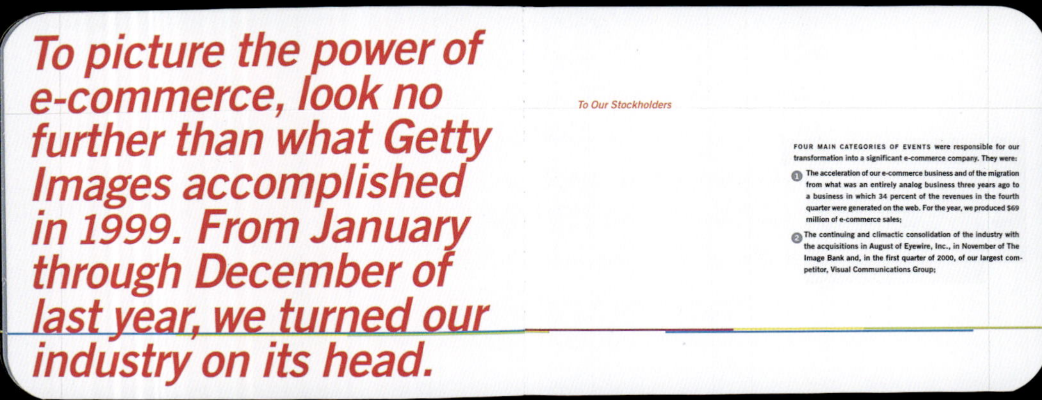

To picture the power of e-commerce, look no further than what Getty Images accomplished in 1999. From January through December of last year, we turned our industry on its head.
To Our Stockholders
FOUR MAIN CATEGORIES OF EVENTS were responsible for our transformation into a significant e-commerce company. They were:
1 The acceleration of our e-commerce business and of the migration from what was an entirely analog business three years ago to a business in which 34 percent of the revenues in the fourth quarter were generated on the web. For the year, we produced $69 million of e-commerce sales;
2 The continuing and climactic consolidation of the industry with the acquisitions in August of Eyewire, Inc., in November of The Image Bank and, in the first quarter of 2000, of our largest competitor, Visual Communications Group;

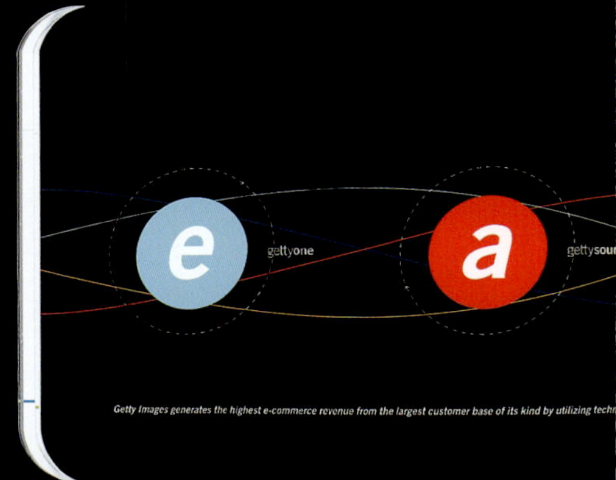

e
gettyone
a
Getty Images generates the highest e-commerce revenue from the largest customer base of its kind by utilizing techn

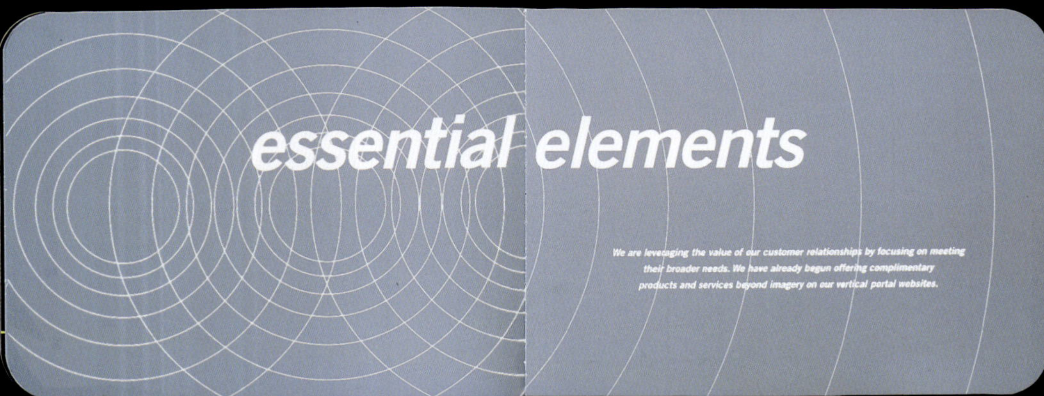

essential elements
We are leveraging the value of our customer relationships by focusing on meeting their broader needs. We have already begun offering complimentary products and services beyond imagery on our vertical portal websites.

TOTAL REVENUE
E-COMMERCE REVENUE
$6.4 Million
$7.4 Million
$2.9 Million

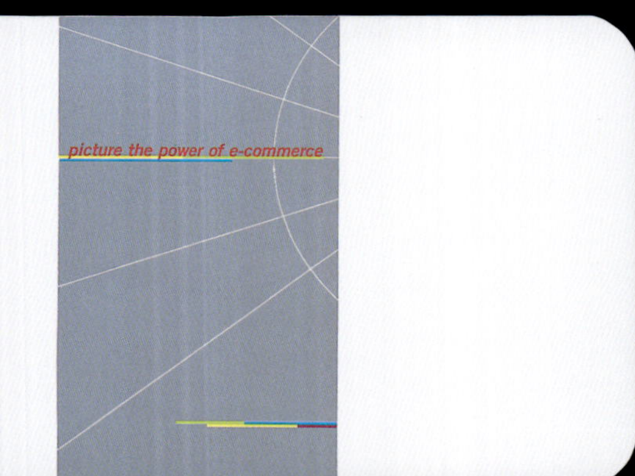

picture the power of e-commerce

COVER

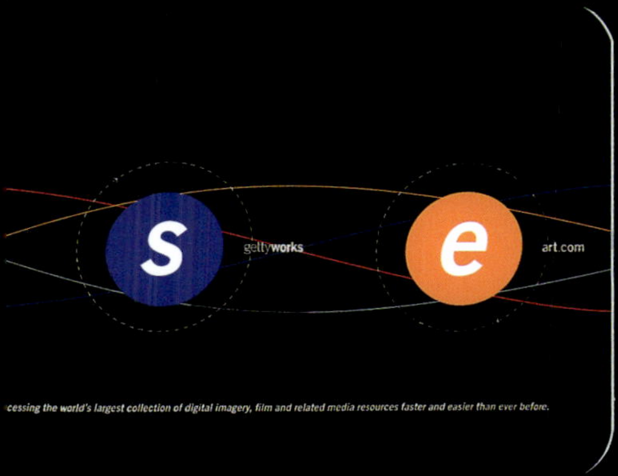
s
gettyworks
e
art.com
cessing the world's largest collection of digital imagery, film and related media resources faster and easier than ever before.

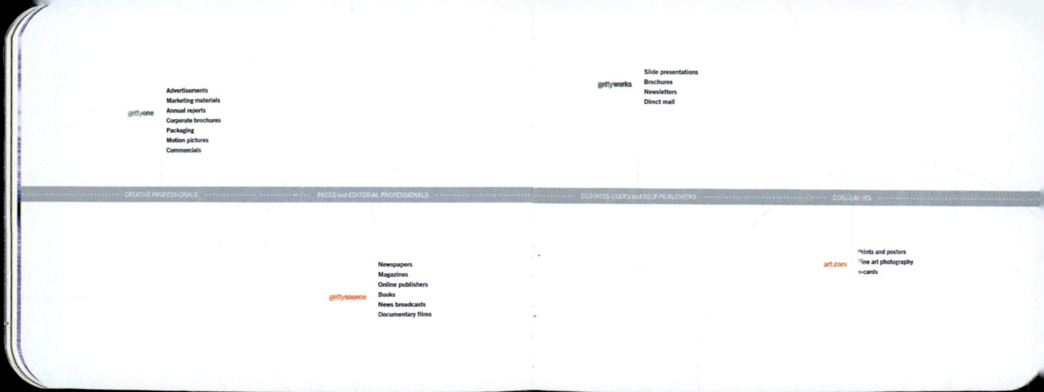
gettyone
Advertisements
Marketing materials
Annual reports
Corporate brochures
Packaging
Motion pictures
Commercials
gettyworks
Slide presentations
Brochures
Newsletters
Direct mail
CREATIVE PROFESSIONALS
PRESS and EDITORIAL PROFESSIONALS
BUSINESS USERS and SELF-PUBLISHERS
CONSUMERS
gettysource
Newspapers
Magazines
Online publishers
Books
News broadcasts
Documentary films
art.com
Prints and posters
Fine art photography
e-cards

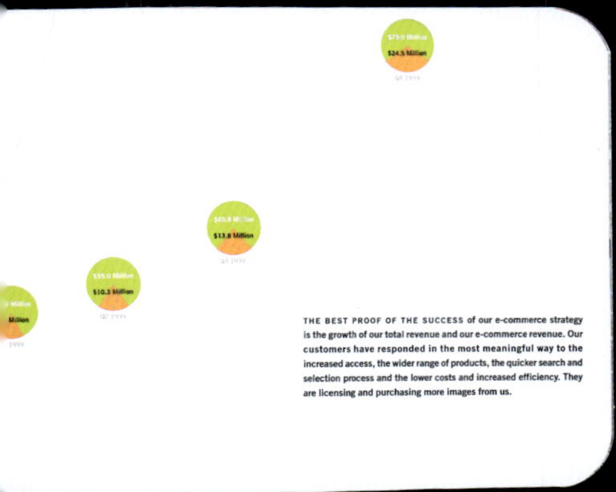
$24.5 Million
$13.8 Million
$10.3 Million
Million
THE BEST PROOF OF THE SUCCESS of our e-commerce strategy is the growth of our total revenue and our e-commerce revenue. Our customers have responded in the most meaningful way to the increased access, the wider range of products, the quicker search and selection process and the lower costs and increased efficiency. They are licensing and purchasing more images from us.

Unlike many other e-commerce companies, we do not have to figure out how to internationalize our business. With offices in more than 20 countries and agents in over 50 countries we have an unrivaled international distribution network.
MUNICH, GERMANY · NEW YORK, USA · PARIS, FRANCE · SÃO
STOCKHOLM, SWEDEN · SYDNEY, AUSTRALIA · TOKYO, JAPAN ·
ZURICH, SWITZERLAND · AMSTERDAM, NETHERLANDS · ATLANTA, USA ·
BELGIUM · BUENOS AIRES, ARGENTINA · CHICAGO, USA · COPENHAGEN,
UNITED ARAB EMIRATES · HAMBURG, GERMANY · HONG KONG, CHINA ·
LONDON, ENGLAND · LOS ANGELAS, USA · MELBOURNE, AUSTRALIA · MILAN,
NEW YORK, USA · PARIS, FRANCE · SÃO PAULO, BRAZIL · SEATTLE, USA ·
AUSTRALIA · TOKYO, JAPAN · TORONTO, CANADA · VIENNA, AUSTRIA · ZURICH,
NETHERLANDS · ATLANTA, USA · BARCELONA, SPAIN · BRUSSELS, BELGIUM ·
USA · COPENHAGEN, DENMARK · DALLAS, USA · DUBAI, UNITED ARAB EMIRATES
KONG, CHINA · LONDON, ENGLAND · LOS ANGELAS, USA · MELBOURNE,
GERMANY · NEW YORK, USA · PARIS, FRANCE · SÃO PAULO, BRAZIL · SEATTLE,
SYDNEY, AUSTRALIA · TOKYO, JAPAN · TORONTO, CANADA · VIENNA, AUSTRIA ·
AMSTERDAM, NETHERLANDS · ATLANTA, USA · BARCELONA, SPAIN ·
ARGENTINA · CHICAGO, USA · COPENHAGEN, DENMARK · DALLAS, USA ·
HAMBURG, GERMANY · HONG KONG, CHINA · LONDON, ENGLAND ·
AUSTRALIA · MILAN, ITALY · MUNICH, GERMANY · NEW YORK, USA ·
SEATTLE, USA · STOCKHOLM, SWEDEN · SYDNEY, AUSTRALIA ·

WE REMAIN COMMITTED TO PROVIDING OUR CUSTOMERS with more complete content and tools, better ways to do their jobs and increasingly innovative solutions.
Our vertical portals will provide in one place all the tools our customers need to do their jobs – including imagery, software, audio, fonts and typefaces, as well as research, industry news and information.
essential impact

RECRUITMENT BROCHURE 入社案内

ARTICLING+SUMMER STUDENT PROGRAMMES 1999 CANADA CL: Fasken Martineau DuMoulin CD: Mikey Richardson / Michael Kelar AD,D: Jason Darbyson P: Janet Bailey CW: Paul Fenn DF: Amoeba Corp.

COVER

ANNUAL REPORT 1999 SWITZERLAND CL: Christoph Merian Stiftung CD,AD,D,DF: Neeser + Müller P: Divers

STÄDTISCHES

«Die CMS bietet uns an, einen attraktiven Steg zu bauen, der die Lücke zwischen dem St. Alban-Rheinweg und der unteren Pfalz schliesst. Wir Baslerinnen und Basler müssten dumm sein, dieses Angebot auszuschlagen ... Der Einwand, der Steg beeinträchtige den Blick auf das Münster und seine Umgebung, wird mit Sicherheit nicht von einer Mehrheit der Bevölkerung geteilt.» (Basler Zeitung, Leserbrief)

Modell des geplanten Rheinuferweges von der Wettsteinbrücke zur Pfalz

Attraktivere Basler Rheinufer

→ VERBESSERTE NUTZUNG DES BEDEUTENDSTEN STÄDTISCHEN ERHOLUNGSRAUMS

Seit 1992 engagiert sich die CMS mit dem Projekt «Attraktivere Basler Rheinufer» für eine verbesserte Nutzung und einen Ausbau der Basler Rheinuferwege. Im Zuge der Sanierung des Rhybadhysli Breiti wurde der damals an vielen Orten sehr schlechte Zustand der Basler Rheinuferwege ins Auge gefasst.
Ziel war es, überall mit möglichst einfachen Veränderungen einen maximalen Nutzen für die Stadtbevölkerung zu bewirken. Nach welchen Kriterien bisher Neuerungen vorgenommen wurden, wie weit das Projekt bis heute gediehen ist und welche Widerstände es bisher auslöste, darüber spricht der Projektleiter Alfred Müller.

Alfred Müller [AM], Projektleiter, im Gespräch

Herr Müller, wo steht heute das 1992 begonnene Projekt «Attraktivere Basler Rheinufer»?

AM: Ende 1998 reichten wir erneut ein Baugesuch ein für den Rheinuferweg von der Wettsteinbrücke zur Pfalz. Es werden allerdings wiederum Einsprachen erhoben. Wir planen diesen Abschnitt nun seit 1992 und ich gehe davon aus, dass er auch 1999 nicht gebaut werden kann. Offen ist auch noch die Renaturierung des Rheinufers am Schaffhauserrheinweg. Wir wurden hier bisher nicht aktiv, weil das Kraftwerk Birsfelden die Austiefung des Rheins plant und die Renaturierung davon abhängt.

Die CMS setzte die Grenze für den Ausbau der Rheinuferwege vor einiger Zeit bei der Dreirosenbrücke fest, obwohl ihr Plan ursprünglich weiterging. Wir wollten eine Verbindung schaffen, auf Grossbasler Seite durch den St. Johannhafen nach Hüningen und auf Kleinbasler Seite durch den Klybeckhafen bis zur Wiese. Die Rheinschifffahrtsdirektion war damals dafür nicht ansprechbar. Nun wurden diese beiden Themen durch die Werkstadt Basel wieder ins Spiel gebracht.

Wenn Sie nun zurückblicken, wie war das ursprüngliche Konzept?

AM: 1992 wurde die CMS angefragt, ob sie die Erhaltung des Rhybadhysli Breiti finanziell unterstützen würde. Ich machte den Vorschlag, das Rhybadhysli am St. Alban-Rheinweg nicht isoliert zu betrachten. An den Basler Rheinufern gab es nur wenige Sonnenplätze, keine Bänke, kaum Duschen für die Rheinschwimmerinnen und -schwimmer. Es gab auch kaum attraktive Beizen oder Bistrots. Der schönste und grösste städtische Erholungsraum wurde vernachlässigt. Die CMS entwickelte zusammen mit den Leuten des Baudepartements ein schlüssiges Konzept. Wir einigten uns darauf, den Fussgängerbereich durchgängig zu überarbeiten. Die gesamten Basler Rheinuferwege sollten verbessert werden. Es ging auch darum zu zeigen, welche Bedeutung diese Verbesserungen in den einzelnen Abschnitten für die angrenzenden Quartiere haben. So wurde beispielsweise der Zugang zur Ueli-Fähre verbessert, denn an dieser Stelle befinden sich auf beiden Seiten des Rheins Alterswohnungen. Sehr viele ältere Menschen gehen dort spazieren. Schliesslich reaktivierten wir zwischen Schwarzwaldbrücke und Kraftwerk Birsfelden die zugewachsenen Fusswege unterhalb der Grenzacherstrasse. Davon profitieren die Leute aus dem Hirzbrunnenquartier.

Unter welchen Gesichtspunkten wurden die Umbauten konkret vorgenommen?

DIE CMS ENGAGIERT SICH FÜR SOZIALE, KULTURELLE UND STÄDTISCHE AUFGABEN IN DER STADT BASEL SOWIE FÜR PROJEKTE IM BEREICH NATUR UND UMWELT.

DIE BASIS FÜR IHRE AKTIVITÄTEN IST DAS STIFTUNGSVERMÖGEN, DAS IHR VON CHRISTOPH MERIAN UND MARGARETHA MERIAN-BURCKHARDT VERERBT WURDE.

VOM REINERTRAG FLIESSEN 10 PROZENT DEM LANDERWERBS- UND BAUFONDS, JE 45 PROZENT DER BÜRGERGEMEINDE UND DER EINWOHNERGEMEINDE DER STADT BASEL ZU.

COVER

ANNUAL REPORT アニュアルレポート

SOUND TRANSIT 1998 ANNUAL REPORT 1999 USA CL: Sound Transit CD,AD,D: Tony Secolo CW: Tim Healy

COVER

SWISSLINE 1997 SWITZERLAND CL: Swissline CD,AD,D: Lucia Frey / Heinz Wild P: Pascal Wüest CW: Kurt Schori DF: Wild & Frey

‹Grüezi, Swissline›. Seit dem 8. Januar 1996 bieten wir Versicherungsprodukte per Telefon an, schnell und unbürokratisch. Als Direktversicherer arbeiten wir ohne Aussendienst, mit modernster Technik und einem kompetenten Beratungsteam am Telefon. Dieses zukunftsweisende Konzept ermöglicht günstige Prämien und erstklassigen Service. Im Mittelpunkt unserer Unternehmensphilosophie stehen unsere Kundinnen und Kunden. Deshalb sind wir nie weiter von ihnen entfernt als das nächste Telefon oder der nächste Briefkasten. Auf der Suche nach Ideen und Visionen setzen wir neue Massstäbe und sind immer einen Schritt voraus. Das ist unsere Verpflichtung, und daran lassen wir uns messen.

Swissline ist eine Tochtergesellschaft der Winterthur, der grössten Versicherungsgruppe im Schweizer Markt.

Swissline hat hochmotivierte Mitarbeiterinnen und Mitarbeiter, die vor und während ihrer Tätigkeit professionell aus- und weitergebildet werden.

Swissline ist im Schadenfall rund um die Uhr für die Kunden da, 365 Tage im Jahr. Ohne lästigen Formularkrieg und ohne lange Entscheidungswege.

3

COVER

Die Kundenorientierung.

Bei der Morgenlektüre fällt Peter M. ein Inserat auf...

Swissline bietet ihre Autopolicen an. Per Telefon kann man direkt und schnell eine Offerte einholen.

Noch am selben Tag telefoniert er Swissline.

Am Tag darauf...

Innert weniger Minuten erhält Peter M. von einer kompetenten Swissline-Verkaufsmitarbeiterin eine persönliche Offerte.

Per Post kommt das schriftliche Angebot mit dem bereits ausgefüllten Antrag.

...die Offerte überzeugt. Peter M. schickt den Antrag zurück.

In aller Ruhe und ohne Kaufdruck vergleicht Peter M. zuhause die Swissline-Offerte mit seiner bestehenden Autoversicherung.

Unterschrift genügt, und schon ist Peter M. Swissline-Kunde...

10

Einige Monate später: ein Autounfall auf dem Weg zur Arbeit.

Sofort nimmt Peter M. mit dem Swissline-Leistungsservice Kontakt auf. Dieser organisiert unverzüglich einen Abschleppwagen samt Ersatzauto.

Eine halbe Stunde später...

Peter M. erhält am Unfallort sein Gratis-Ersatzauto. Der Unfallwagen wird zur Reparatur in das Swissline-Servicecenter gebracht.

Wenige Tage später...

Ende gut, alles gut!

Der Swissline Schadenexperte begutachtet das Auto in der Garage.

Das reparierte Auto wird Peter M. nach Hause gebracht. Natürlich mit der 2jährigen Swissline-Qualitätsgarantie.

Peter M. erhält nach Abschluss des Schadenfalls einen kurzen Fragebogen. Denn Swissline will wissen, ob ihre Kunden zufrieden sind.

11

(SPREAD 1) DAZED & CONFUSED VOL.64 APRIL 2000 UK

PB: Dazed & Confused E: Jefferson Hack Photographic Director: Emma Reeves AD: Martin Bell
P: Eric Johnson

(SPREAD 2 / 3) DAZED & CONFUSED VOL.66 JUNE 2000 UK

PB: Dazed & Confused E: Jefferson Hack Photographic Director: Emma Reeves AD: Martin Bell
P: Alexei Hay (SPREAD 2) / Nadav Kander (SPREAD 3) ST: Jason Farrer (SPREAD 2)

SPREAD 1

DEAD PREZ

TEXT PAUL FLYNN
PHOTOGRAPHY ERIC JOHNSON

THERE'S A MUSICAL MISSILE IN SOMEONE'S POCKET. IT COMES SPELT AS HIP HOP, BUT NOT SINCE THE EARLIEST SIGHTINGS OF PUBLIC ENEMY HAS ANYTHING SOUNDED SO CONSCIOUS.

Dead Prez arrive with no prepackaging; a multi-lateral musical overhaul of established form and something to say for themselves. The duo are M-1 and Stic Man. Allow Stic to explain: "Autographs: bullshit. Stars: bullshit. This is about creating a family. Let's try and build a connection. Let's train together, work together. If you got children let me hold them and hug them and you hold mine. Build a real network, man. A million deep, two, three million deep. Then we don't have to complain about this system. We gonna change it."
The Dead Prez duo are as scholarly in black American history as they are in the intimacies of high-voltage beat-smithery. Their debut album *Let's Get Free* is as exciting as hip hop gets right now. A shoulder holster of machine gun precision, spot perfect rhyming and a collective call to arms that hasn't been heard since the in-fighting and ego of gangsterism started to queer the rapping pitch. *Let's Get Free* owes most to the aforementioned touchstone of PE, but there is a whiff of Arrested Development going on, though obviously looser on the pseud trippy daydream. Dead Prez are concentrating on real Utopias. Knowledge is power. They studied their history. Stic asked to know who Malcolm X was at school in the white dominated Florida suburbs. And now they are ready to spread a message.
They're chilled with the idea of what they've created so far, but the creating will only continue. There's a purpose to it, see. M-1: "We did what our job was. We made it. We can promote it and shit, but people gotta say, 'I love it' or 'this is garbage' or whatever they might say. I'm happy, happy to get it out there. My heart tells me that this record is gonna do what it deserves to do. But I'm already satisfied." Stic is ready for a final word: "Let's not let this shit get popular for popular's sake, or for the sake of my pocket. Let's get it out to resonate. To mean something to me and my ancestors and the next generation."

Let's Get Free *is out March 13 on Epic*

SPREAD 2

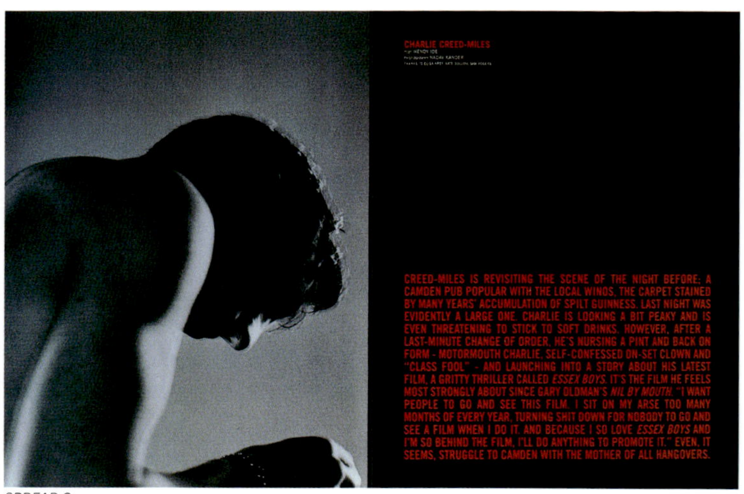

SPREAD 3

MAGAZINE 雑誌

CUT NO.102 MAY 2000 JAPAN PB: Rockin' On Inc. E: Ken Sato AD,D: Hideki Nakajima P: Justin Case (PAGE 3) DF: Nakajima Design

SPREAD 1

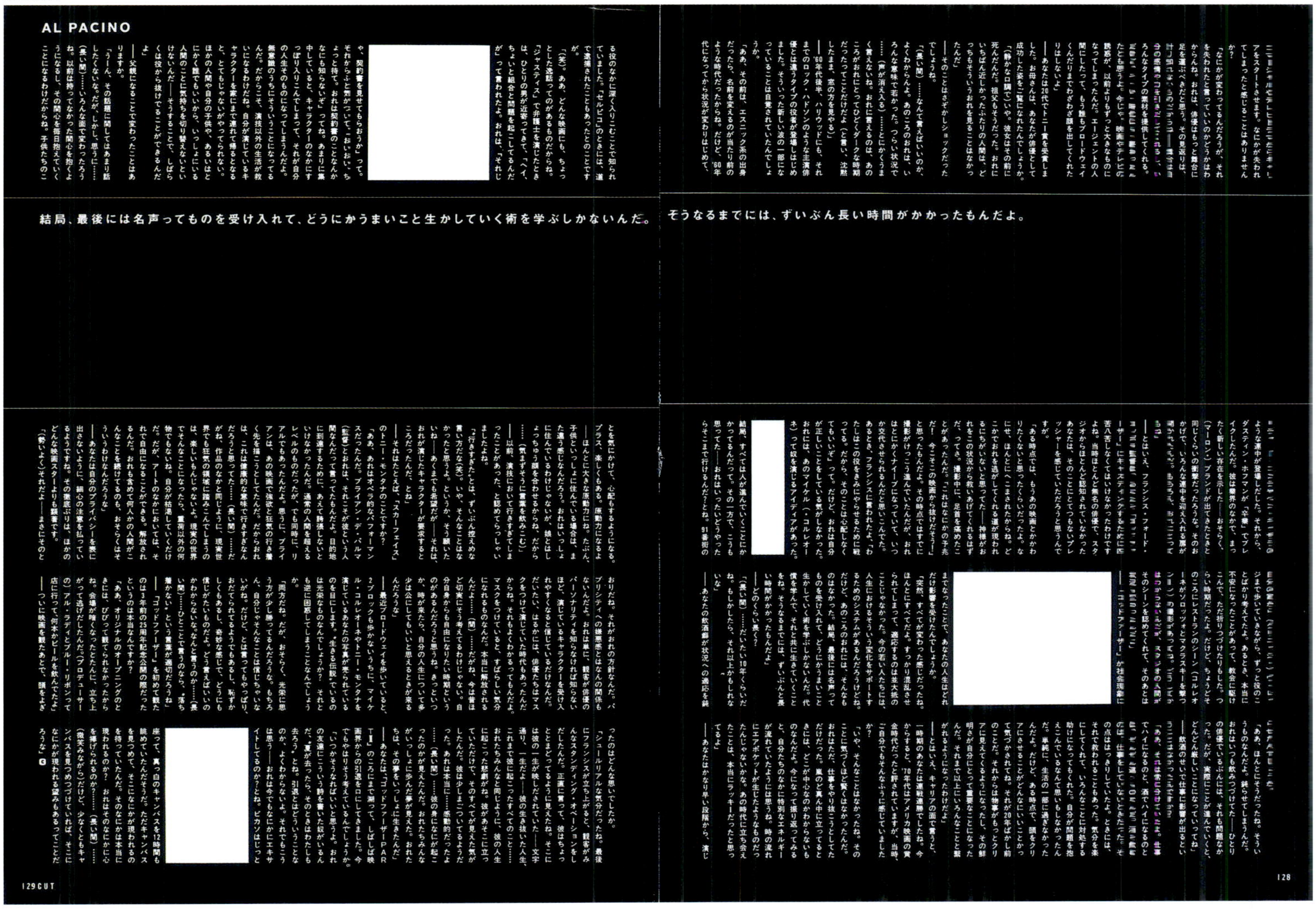

SPREAD 2

PAGE 3

MAGAZINE 雑誌

(SPREAD 1 / 2) RELAX VOL.38 APRIL 2000 JAPAN

PB: Magazine House E: Hitoshi Okamoto AD: Eisaku Ono (NANA) D: Hideyuki Yamano (NANA)
P: Keisuke Naito (SPREAD 1) / Shin Jinushi (SPREAD 2) / Akihiro Nagata (SPREAD 2)

(SPREAD 3~5) RELAX VOL.40 JUNE 2000 JAPAN

PB: Magazine House E: Hitoshi Okamoto AD: Eisaku Ono (NANA) D: Hideyuki Yamano (NANA) / Yoko Komatsu (NANA)
P (SPREAD 3): Takao Maruyama / Keisuke Kurimoto / Shinori Murayama
P (SPREAD 4): Hidetomo Abe / Shinichi Yakoyama / Shinori Murayama

SPREAD 1

SPREAD 2

SPREAD 3

焼之都飲茶家陶茶付移動車、野点、営業場所、時間は不定期にて開催中。問い合わせは℡075-495-8030まで。

モバイルなお茶事。

MOBILE SHOP 001

お客が自分で絵付けをしたら30分ほどでお茶碗が焼けて、その場で自分の茶碗でお茶を飲める移動式カフェがあると聞き、さっそく神戸にGO！ 身長190cm以上ありそうな体格、しかもドラァグクィーンのようなド派手な衣装に身を包んだ大男がリヤカーを持って立っている。彼の名は「きむら としろう じんじん」。旅回りのお茶会ともいえる「野点」を巡回しながら開いている。

「自分が作ったものを見せれるし、お客さんと一緒に作ることもできるし、できたものを見ながら茶飲み話もできる。いろんな喜びがこのリヤカーの中に詰まっているんです。僕にとって、これはかなり贅沢な企画だと思いますね」

最初の頃は公園などでゲリラ的に活動していたが今では日本各地の美術館のイベントに引っぱりダコ状態。数年前にはパリにも招待された。

「作ったり飲んだりしている間に初対面のお客さん同士が仲良くなってたりするんですよね。テーマは「コミュニケーションの誘発」。そのためのリヤカーやお茶碗、衣装ですから」

MOBILE SHOP

モバイルな店

俗に屋台というわけですが、彼らの独自のモバイル哲学を聞いてみましょう。なんともハッピーなオープンマインドですよ。

郊外のカフェ伝道師。

MOBILE SHOP 002

カフェピクニック 栃木県小山市小山9983-9 ℡090-3499-5598 営12〜21時（雨天のときは車庫で営業）、火曜休

栃木県小山市のちょい外れに白壁が映える大きな美容室が1軒だけポツンと建っている。その目の前にクリーム色のかわいらしいTIPEⅡを発見。車の中ではニット帽を被った小柄な男の人がコーヒーカップ片手に美容室を行ったり来たり出前もしている。もしかして、この車はカフェ？「そうなんです。店名はカフェ ピクニックといいます。とりあえず一杯いかがですか！」と、笑顔で迎えてくれた奥澤裕之さんがここんちのオーナーだ。

「これをやる前はフレンチや多国籍レストランのコックを15年間やっていたんです。けど、アルミに囲まれた厨房で仕事する毎日に疑問を感じたというか…。そうこう悩んでいる時に代官山で移動式コーヒー屋台を見ちゃってこれは面白そうだなぁ、って」

店にする車をTIPEⅡに選んだ理由は花が似合いそうだから。もちろん、エンジンなどの内部は徹底的にチェックし、肝心の内装はすべて自分で仕上げた。

「タイルやガラス、アンティークの小物とかを使い温かみのある空間を作ったつもりです。最初はその場その場で移動してやろうと思ったけど、2、3回断られたら根性なくなっちゃいました（笑）。「なんで東京でやらないの？」って、よく言われるんだけど、ここら辺ののんびりした空気のほうが店の雰囲気に合うと思うし。あと、東京ではメジャーかもしれませんがスターバックスの存在を知らない人が結構多いんですね。だから、僕の店がスターバックス代わりにならないといけないじゃないですか（笑）」

雨ニモ風ニモ負ケズ、カフェ伝道！

自由に動く古着屋。

MOBILE SHOP 003

勉族　主な営業場所は渋谷の明治通り沿い。レギュラーものが中心の商品構成で、スヌーピー市スウェットやTシャツ類がおすすめ。営12〜19時、雨天休 ℡090-2336-7804

大きすぎず小さすぎず程よい大きさのトラックを60万円でゲット。壁や床に色を塗り、軽くカスタム。あとは安価でコンディション抜群なウェアさえあれば移動式古着ショップが出来上がったりして。そんなお気楽商売を3月から始めているのが平林保幸さんと水野宏晃さんの同級生コンビ。代表の平林さんに、このおシゴトのイロハを聞いてみた。

「この仕事をやる前は某老舗トラッドショップの販売員でした。そこを辞めた後ロスに語学留学したんですが向こうでは小遣い稼ぎとして古着を売っていまして。だから、商品を仕入れるルートを持っているから、また古着でも売ろうかなーって感じになって。でも、店持つ金もなかったし、もし雑居ビルの家賃が安い部屋を借りたとしても売れる保証なんてどこにもないじゃないですか。客がこなくても店の中でただじっと待つことしかできないしね。だったら、「いっそのこと人がいる場所にこっちから出向いてやろうぜ！」みたいなノリで始めたんです。自由に店を移動できることは、かなり便利だと思う。「次はここら辺に行けば売れるんじゃねぇかなー」という具合に考える面白さもあるしね。今日は明治通りにいるけど、これからは大学の昼休み時間を狙おうかと考えているんだ。で、毎週行く日を決めておけば大学生たちは俺たちの存在を覚えるでしょ。そうだ！ 曜日ごとに行く大学を変えるのもひとつの手だよね」

休日は必ず登場、明治通りの主。

MOBILE SHOP 004

渋谷と原宿の間の明治通りは週末にもなるとケバブ屋からクレープ屋まで、歩いているといろんな屋台系ショップと遭遇する。そんな激戦区でひときわ注目を集めている「ミスターホットドッグ」。たっぷりとチーズが入っているものやピリ辛風味など計4種類のホットドッグを目当てに地方から買いに来るお客さんも多いとか。でも、本当のお目当てはここの御主人、フランキーさんなのでは？「当り前だよ。この通りでは結構な有名人さ。テレビにも出たしね。何でホットドッグ屋かって？ 俺がタコヤキ屋だったら変だろ！」

ミスターホットドック　場所は原宿よりの明治通り沿い。営12時30分〜19時30分、土日のみ

代官山の移動式カフェといえば。

MOBILE SHOP 005

伊藤素樹さんは4年前に脱サラ、移動式カフェの元祖ともいえる「モトヤエクスプレス」を考案した人物。山梨県韮崎で3年間熟成させたコーヒー豆から作られるエスプレッソやカフェラテで、あっという間に常連客を増やし、今では代官山駅前、西郷山公園、ナショナル麻布スーパーマーケットといった具合で店舗を拡大中。仲間も増えたとか。「屋台って普通の店と違い、仕事や人生の悩み事を相談しにくるお客さんが多いんです。けど、僕はそういう話を聞くのが大好き。だからコーヒー屋を始めたようなもんですから」

モトヤエクスプレス　代官山駅前店 営11〜20時、月曜定休／麻布店 営8時30分〜19時、土曜定休／西郷山店 営昼から夕方まで、不定休

SPREAD 4

左／コットンニットパーカ（DUPE）42,000円、蓄肢ポケット付きのナイロンパンツ（SABOTAGE）14,000円、ともにshop33 ℡0422-48-7926　スニーカー（アディダスのZX-900）24,800円 emu / NW ℡03-5458-9089
右／Tシャツ（DUPE）6,900円、ウエストポーチ（airbag）6,800円、ワッペンハット（LOCUST）10,800円、以上shop33　ナイロンパンツ11,800円、リズムシューズ16,800円、ともにdoarat ℡03-3406-1975

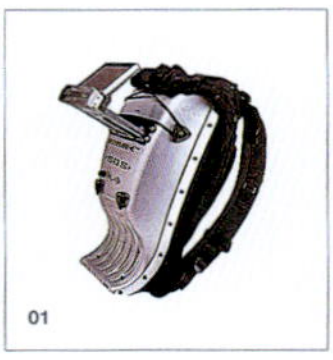

01

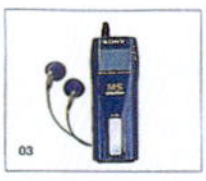

03

07

04

02

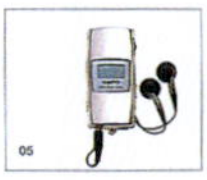

05

06

01 BOBLBE-Eコンセプトモデル DVD おなじみBOBLBE-Eのとんでもないカスタマイズ商品。カーステ用のモニターにDVDプレイヤー付き、しかもバッテリー内蔵　02 BOBLBE-Eコンセプトモデル PS2　お次はプレステ2を搭載。背負ってたらプレイできないって？ どきっ。いえいえ、海で山で所で自然に飽きたらバッグ下ろしてワンプレイ。ともに参考商品 BOBLBE-E Concept Store ℡03-3725-8652　03 MS WALKMAN　海外ヴァージョンで、日本では未発売のカラー。48,000円 スティル シークエンス ℡03-5414-8891　04 リストオーディオプレイヤー　MP3で圧縮、PCからダウンロードして、通常の音質で約66分間メモリー可能。37,000円 カシオ計算機 ℡0570-088901　05 デジタルメモリプレイヤー SSAP 複数の圧縮方式に対応できる画期的な「マルチデコードシステム」搭載のミュージックプレイヤー。37,000円 三洋電機 ℡072-870-4186　06 リストカメラ　今度はデジタルカメラ付き。赤外線ポートでPCにデータの転送も。22,000円 カシオ計算機　07 ポータブルメモリプレイヤー イーミューゼ　ヘッドフォンとプレイヤー一体型のウェアラブルオーディオプレイヤー。カラーリングもスタイルもシャープです。48,000円 シャープお客様サービス ℡0120-078178

THE MOBILER, Dr.TAKASHIRO 002

ドラえフォン＋ERICSSONのキーボード　アジア各国でカスタムされたドラえフォンは、日本と韓国以外なら世界中で使用可能という代物。メール送信も。

ドコモとDDIのPHS内蔵型PCカード　使用するエリアによって感度の良いほうを使うそうで、一体、いくつの会社と契約しているのかは本人にもナゾ。

ERICSSON 1888 WORLD　モデム内蔵型の携帯電話。赤外線ポートでPDAから手軽に通信できる。日本と韓国以外で使用可能という点き。

MOTOROLAのStar TAC　アメリカで購入後、香港で出力アップとスケルトンボディにカスタム。SIMカードをマウントするカードには、エロカード？

Psion revo　イギリス・サイオン社製ハンドヘルドマシンの最新モデル。サイオンは欧州最大のハンドヘルドコンピュータメーカー。「ヨーロッパでは定番。デザインはいいんだけどあんまり使ってない。でも新しく出るものは必ず買って試すから」。幅157mmで69,800円。asxkton ℡03-5772-5172　www.asukton.co.jp

SPREAD 5

What's "HAPPINESS" ?

一見幸せそうに食卓を囲むトリッシュ、ヘレン、ジョイ姉妹と両親のレニーとモナ。しかし、その裏側には…。この5人にミョーなキャラクターの男女がいろいろ絡んで、それぞれの"ハピネス"についての物語が進行してゆく。果たして彼らの"ハピネス"はどこにあるのか。そして誰が"ハピネス"にたどり着けるのか。えっ？ もしかして誰も！？

今、アメリカで最も旬でユニークな役者、P.S.ホフマンが「ハピネス」を語った。

text/ Man Hagihara

とにかく、フィリップ・シーモア・ホフマンには前から一度会ってみたかった。「ブギーナイツ」で彼を気弱なゲイ役に配したP.T.アンダースン監督は、「あれ以降ゲイ役ばっかり。強烈だったんだろうね。ほんとはストレートでいいやつなのに」と笑っていたが、実際あれだけ特徴的な外見で（失礼！）、作品ごとにカメレオンぶりを発揮できるのがスゴい。「ハピネス」ではさらに体重を増やし、汗をダラダラかきながら猥褻なイタ電をかけるというまたまた変態な役柄なのだが、インタビューに現れた本人はずっとスマートで（手は赤ちゃんみたいにプクプクだったが）、不敵な雰囲気さえ漂わせていた。この作品はトッド・ソロンズ監督が長編第1作に失敗し、LAからNYに戻って教師をしていた時の体験もモチーフになっているのだが、それにまず皮肉を一発。

「トッドもNYに戻ってよかったよ。LAは儲かるけど、こういう映画は作れないからさ。ま、僕もたまにつまんない大作で稼いでるけど（笑）」

NYUで演劇を学び、今年2月に始まったオフ・ブロードウェイの舞台「True West」も大評判になっているホフマンは、言論者を武器にするタイプのNY派のようだ。

「「ハピネス」の脚本を初めて読んだ時、センセーショナルだとかショッキングだとかは思わなかった。ただ最高に笑えて、しかも恐ろしくて、ものすごくよく描けてると思ったんだ」

彼がこう語るのは、題材の不穏さ、特にディラン・ベイカー扮するゲイの小児性愛者のエピソードがアメリカで論議を巻き起こしたから。

「でも僕は、この映画のキャラクターはみんな、誰もが投影できる普遍性を持ってると思う。人間ってもののどこかに共感できるし、僕は自分の役にすぐ共感した。それに、これだけ面白いキャラを演らない手はないからね。僕にとってこいつはバッド・ガイじゃない。グッド・ガイなんだ。自分に対するイメージがあまりに強固で大きくて、それが彼のやることを支配してる。他人が入る余裕がまったくなくて、彼は誰とも親密になれないんだ。猥褻なイタ電やテレフォン・セックスが悪いって言うなら、こいつは確かに悪い。でも、逆に言うとそれしかできないっていうか……孤独してるだけなんだよ」

この言葉は「僕はキャラクター全員に深いつながりを感じてる。彼らの中に見いだしたものに心を動かされたんだ」というソロンズの発言に通じる。それにソロンズ自身、その作品や風貌（分厚い黒ぶち眼鏡にカーディガンを羽織りする）で何かとオタクに思われがちなのだが、ホフマンに言わせると「みんなトッドに対して決まりきったイメージを見るんだよね。でも実際の彼はものすごく雄弁だし、社交的だし、あらゆることに関して自分のやり方を持ってて、自信もある。才能があるのは明らかだし……ま、クレイジーなのは確かだけど（笑）」となる。そんな誤解されぶりや、ディラン・ベイカーをして「トッドはああ見えて、すごくセクシーなんだよ」と言わせるところなど、ソロンズ像はなんとなくホフマンにも重なる。「ハピネス」のなんとも言えない"癖になる"持ち味は、このあたりの人々が発している奇妙なセックス・アピールにも多くを負っている気がするのだが。

蛇足ながら、「ハピネス」には使われなかったシーンがいくつかあるらしい。ラストも、ホフマンが三女ジョイに電話をかけるところで終わる予定だったそう。「で、デートの約束をするんだけど、彼女が「あなたの声、聞き覚えがあるわ」って言うんだ（笑）。でも今のラストの方がパワフルだよね」。それはぜひ見て確かめてほしいが、この段階で、しかも愛すべき「ハピネス」ワールドの続きを想像するのは何か怖いような、楽しいような……。ジョイ役のジェーン・アダムスが「とにかく普段とは違う、トッド・ソロンズ・ワールドに引き込まれちゃうの」と言っていたのも、妙にうなずけるのだ。

case 1 TRISH

長姉のトリッシュ（シンシア・スティーヴンソン）は精神科医の夫ビル（ディラン・ベイカー）と2人の子供と幸せな家庭を築いていた。しかしビルには隠れた性癖が。ビルはセラピーを受けたりオナニーしたりしてその性癖を鎮めようとするのだが…。その頃、街では少年レイプ魔が噂になって…。

case 2 HELEN

次女のヘレン（ララ・フリン・ボイル）はエロティックな描写が人気の、美貌の女流作家。そんな彼女をおかずにオナニーに励むのは同じマンションに住むアレン（フィリップ・シーモア・ホフマン）だ。しかしレイプ体験がないことに悩んでいたヘレンはオナニー男のイタ電に「犯しに来てよ！」と…。

case 3 JOY

末妹のジョイ（ジェーン・アダムス）は、30歳を過ぎても独身で、作曲家への夢を捨てられない女。別れた男に罵倒された上に自殺され、心機一転、英語学校の教師になった彼女は、教室でロシア人生徒ヴラッド（ジャレッド・ハリス）に出会う。彼の歌うラブソングにほだされ、つい関係を結ぶが…。

case 4 MONA & LENNY

娘たちも独立し悠々自適な生活を送っていたモナ（ルイーズ・ラッセー）は、夫レニー（ベン・ギャザラ）から突然別居を言い渡される。混乱するモナだったが、自立への道を歩み始める。一方レニーは隣人の熟女ダイアンと情事に及ぶが…。

cinérelax「ハピネス」に70組140名様をご招待！

会場：渋谷シネ・アミューズ
6月22日（木）
20時50分開場、21時00分開演、23時35分終了
第1部：トークショウ　21時00分〜21時20分
出演者／しまおまほ、ミルクマン斉藤（cinérelax座長）
第2部：映画上映　21時20分〜23時35分

ACTUS STYLE BOOK VOL.5 2000 JAPAN CL: ACTUS CD,AD,D: Masanori Araki / Toru Ohshige P: Keiji Ishiuchi / Yoshikazu Watase / Nobuyoshi Mori CW: Yuko Ito / Masumi Yanagisawa

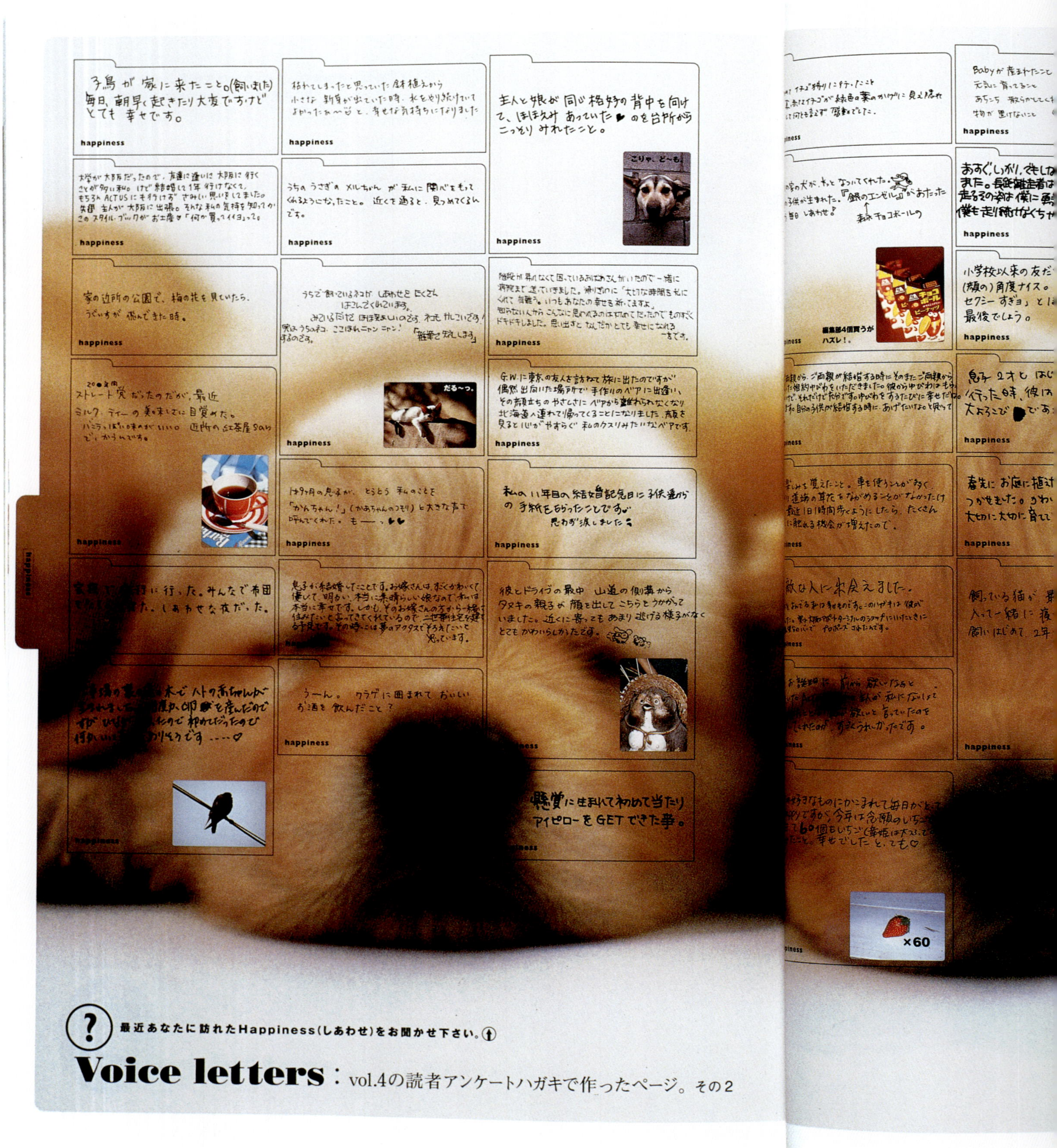

探しもとめていた形のサボテンがみつかったこと。
happiness
夜になると、鈴虫の音が聞こえてくるようになり、その音とともに寝むる事ができる日々にHappinessを感じる。
happiness
happiness
まずは娘が生まれたこと。
happiness
happiness
happiness
happiness
happiness
いろんなところに、いろんなしあわせ。
182/183

インテリアのアイデアいっぱい展。
心優しいクリエーターの皆さんをご紹介します。

バイヤーウーマンのお仕事。
ACTUS MD Planner Interview
MARINHA GRAND
もしもし・・・。
じゃあ、また。

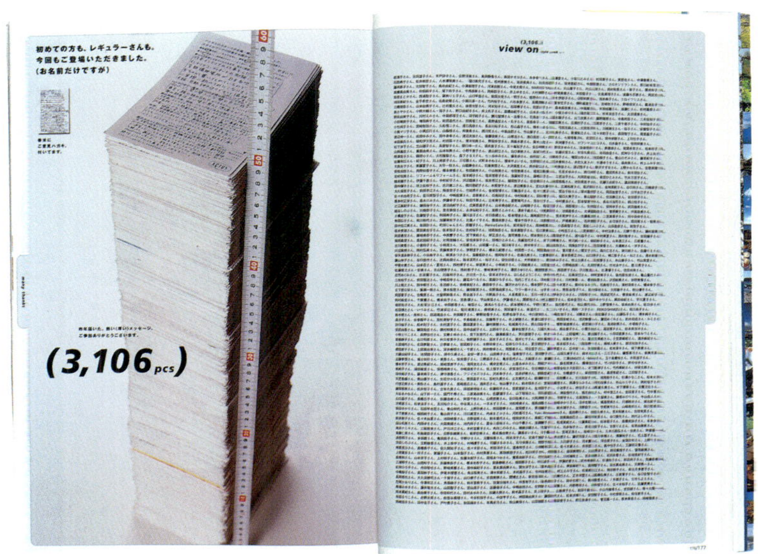

初めての方も、レギュラーさんも、今回もご登場いただきました。(お名前だけですが)
view on
(3,106pcs)

ECÍFFO VOL.35 AUTUMN 1999 JAPAN CL: KOKUYO Co., Ltd. CD: Akihiro Kishimoto AD: Shintaro Abe P: Francesco Radino / Roberto Carra

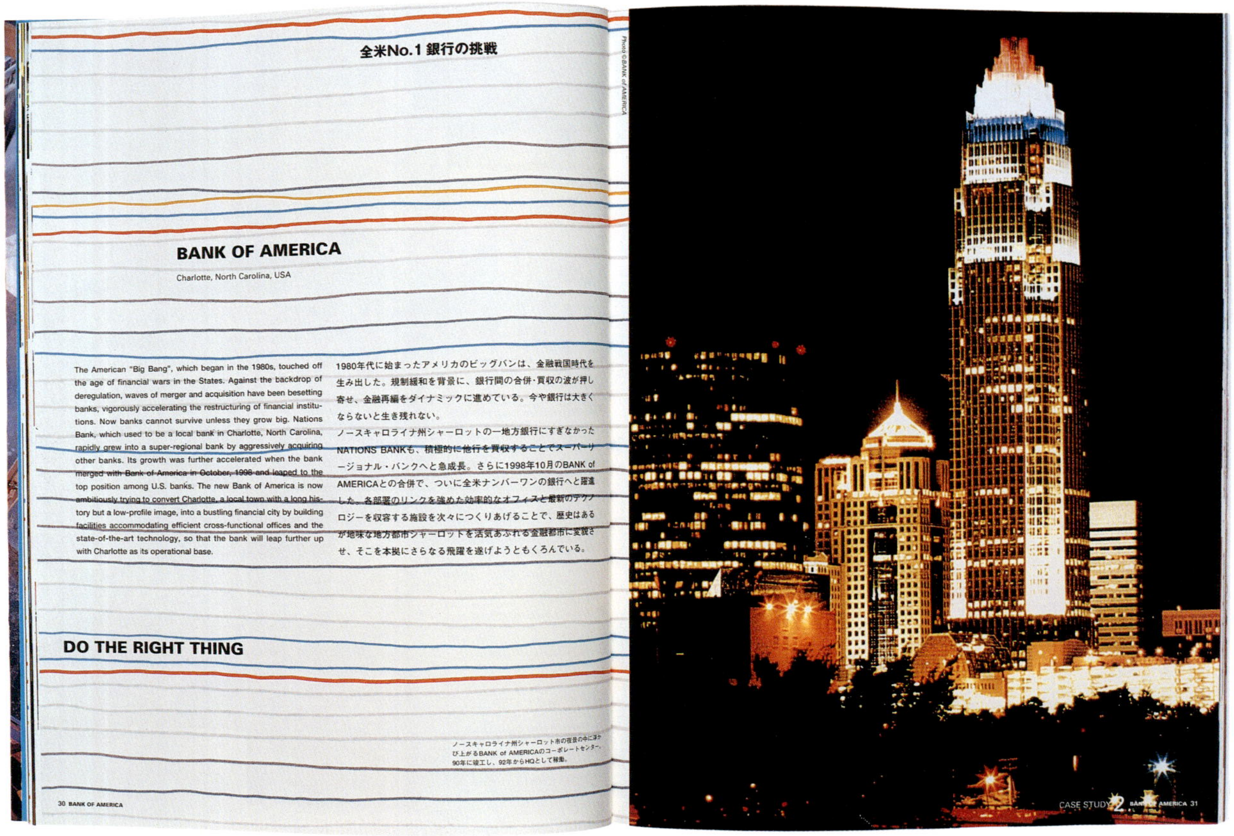

全米No.1 銀行の挑戦

Photo ©BANK of AMERICA

BANK OF AMERICA

Charlotte, North Carolina, USA

The American "Big Bang", which began in the 1980s, touched off the age of financial wars in the States. Against the backdrop of deregulation, waves of merger and acquisition have been besetting banks, vigorously accelerating the restructuring of financial institutions. Now banks cannot survive unless they grow big. Nations Bank, which used to be a local bank in Charlotte, North Carolina, rapidly grew into a super-regional bank by aggressively acquiring other banks. Its growth was further accelerated when the bank merged with Bank of America in October, 1998 and leaped to the top position among U.S. banks. The new Bank of America is now ambitiously trying to convert Charlotte, a local town with a long history but a low-profile image, into a bustling financial city by building facilities accommodating efficient cross-functional offices and the state-of-the-art technology, so that the bank will leap further up with Charlotte as its operational base.

1980年代に始まったアメリカのビッグバンは、金融戦国時代を生み出した。規制緩和を背景に、銀行間の合併・買収の波が押し寄せ、金融再編をダイナミックに進めている。今や銀行は大きくならないと生き残れない。
ノースキャロライナ州シャーロットの一地方銀行にすぎなかったNATIONS BANKも、積極的に他行を買収することでスーパーリージョナル・バンクへと急成長。さらに1998年10月のBANK of AMERICAとの合併で、ついに全米ナンバーワンの銀行へと躍進した。各部署のリンクを強めた効率的なオフィスと最新のテクノロジーを収容する施設を次々につくりあげることで、歴史はあるが地味な地方都市シャーロットを活気あふれる金融都市に変貌させ、そこを本拠にさらなる飛躍を遂げようともくろんでいる。

DO THE RIGHT THING

ノースキャロライナ州シャーロット市の夜景の中に浮かび上がるBANK of AMERICAのコーポレートセンター。90年に竣工し、92年からHQとして稼働。

30 BANK OF AMERICA

CASE STUDY 2 BANK of AMERICA 31

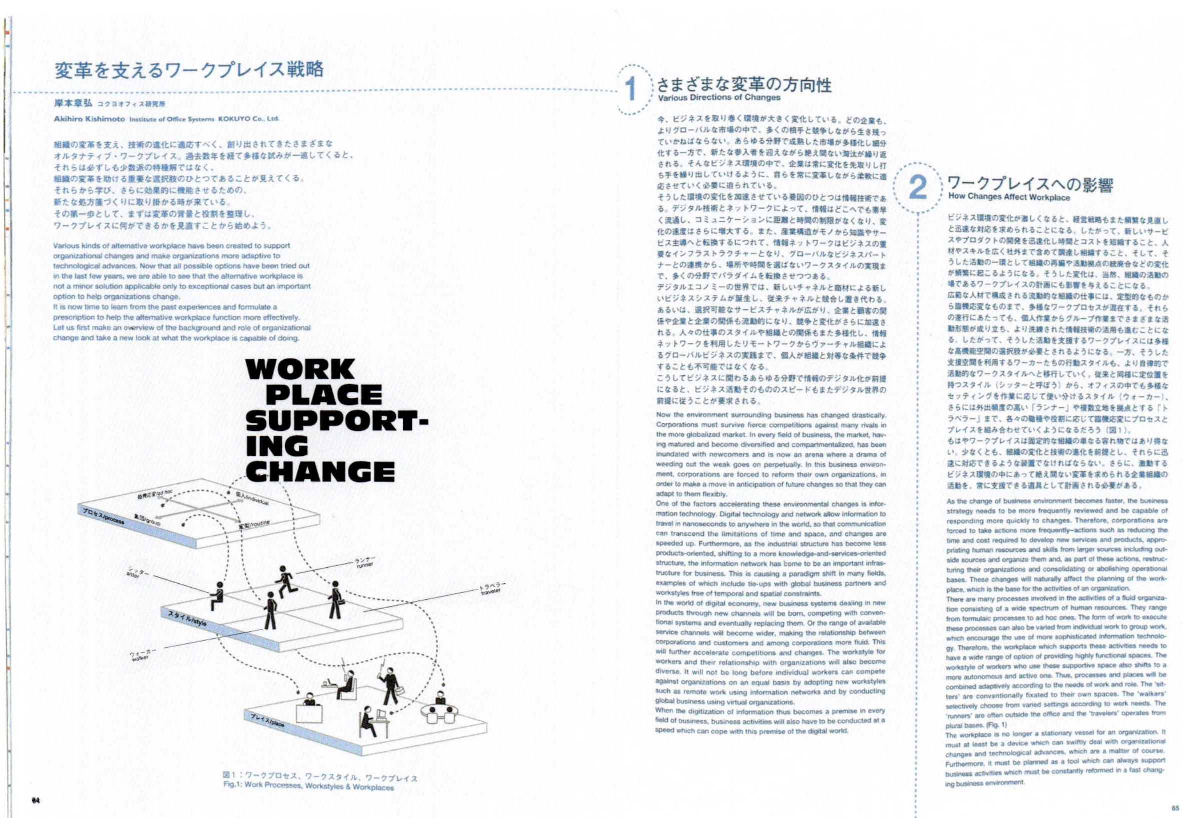

変革を支えるワークプレイス戦略

岸本章弘 コクヨオフィス研究所

Akihiro Kishimoto Institute of Office Systems KOKUYO Co., Ltd.

組織の変革を支え、技術の進化に適応すべく、創り出されてきたさまざまなオルタナティブ・ワークプレイス。過去数年を経て多様な試みが一巡してくると、それらは必ずしも少数派の特種解ではなく、組織の変革を助ける重要な選択肢のひとつであることが見えてくる。それらから学び、さらに効果的に機能させるための、新たな処方箋づくりに取り掛かる時が来ている。その第一歩として、まずは変革の背景と役割を整理し、ワークプレイスに何ができるかを見直すことから始めよう。

Various kinds of alternative workplace have been created to support organizational changes and make organizations more adaptive to technological advances. Now that all possible options have been tried out in the last few years, we are able to see that the alternative workplace is not a minor solution applicable only to exceptional cases but an important option to help organizations change.
It is now time to learn from the past experiences and formulate a prescription to help the alternative workplace function more effectively. Let us first make an overview of the background and role of organizational change and take a new look at what the workplace is capable of doing.

WORK PLACE SUPPORTING CHANGE

図1：ワークプロセス、ワークスタイル、ワークプレイス
Fig.1: Work Processes, Workstyles & Workplaces

64

1 さまざまな変革の方向性
Various Directions of Changes

今、ビジネスを取り巻く環境が大きく変化している。どの企業も、よりグローバルな市場の中で、多くの相手と競争しながら生き残っていかねばならない。あらゆる分野で成熟した市場が多様化し細分化する一方で、新たな参入者を迎えながら絶え間ない淘汰が繰り返される。そんなビジネス環境の中で、企業は常に変化を先取りし打ち手を繰り出していけるように、自らを常に変革しながら柔軟に適応させていく必要に迫られている。
そうした環境の変化を加速させている要因のひとつは情報技術である。デジタル技術とネットワークによって、情報はどこへでも素早く流通し、コミュニケーションに距離と時間の制限がなくなり、変化の速度はさらに増大する。また、産業構造がモノから知識やサービス主導へと転換するにつれて、情報ネットワークはビジネスの重要なインフラストラクチャーとなり、グローバルなビジネスパートナーとの連携から、場所や時間を選ばないワークスタイルの実現まで、多くの分野でパラダイムを転換させつつある。
デジタルエコノミーの世界では、新しいチャネルと商材による新しいビジネスシステムが誕生し、従来チャネルと競合し置き代わる。あるいは、選択可能なサービスチャネルが広がり、企業と顧客の関係や企業と企業の関係も流動的になり、競争と変化がさらに加速される。人々の仕事のスタイルや組織との関係もまた多様化し、情報ネットワークを利用したリモートワークからヴァーチャル組織によるグローバルビジネスの実践まで、個人が組織と対等な条件で競争することも不可能ではなくなる。
こうしてビジネスに関わるあらゆる分野で情報のデジタル化が前提になると、ビジネス活動そのもののスピードもまたデジタル世界の前提に従うことが要求される。

Now the environment surrounding business has changed drastically. Corporations must survive fierce competitions against many rivals in the more globalized market. In every field of business, the market, having matured and become diversified and compartmentalized, has been inundated with newcomers and is now an arena where a drama of weeding out the weak goes on perpetually. In this business environment, corporations are forced to reform their own organizations, in order to make a move in anticipation of future changes so that they can adapt to them flexibly.
One of the factors accelerating these environmental changes is information technology. Digital technology and network allow information to travel in nanoseconds to anywhere in the world, so that communication can transcend the limitations of time and space, and changes are speeded up. Furthermore, as the industrial structure has become less products-oriented, shifting to a more knowledge-and-services-oriented structure, the information network has come to be an important infrastructure for business. This is causing a paradigm shift in many fields, examples of which include tie-ups with global business partners and workstyles free of temporal and spatial constraints.
In the world of digital economy, new business systems dealing in new products through new channels will be born, competing with conventional systems and eventually replacing them. Or the range of available service channels will become wider, making the relationship between corporations and customers and among corporations more fluid. This will further accelerate competitions and changes. The workstyle for workers and their relationship with organizations will also become diverse. It will not be long before individual workers can compete against organizations on an equal basis by adopting new workstyles such as remote work using information networks and by conducting global business using virtual organizations.
When the digitization of information thus becomes a premise in every field of business, business activities will also have to be conducted at a speed which can cope with this premise of the digital world.

2 ワークプレイスへの影響
How Changes Affect Workplace

ビジネス環境の変化が激しくなると、経営戦略もまた頻繁な見直しと迅速な対応を求められることになる。したがって、新しいサービスやプロダクトの開発を迅速化し時間とコストを短縮すること、人材やスキルを広く社外まで含めて調達し組織すること、そして、そうした活動の一環として組織の再編や活動拠点の統廃合などの変化が頻繁に起こるようになる。そうした変化は、当然、組織の活動の場であるワークプレイスの計画にも影響を与えることになる。
広範な人材で構成される流動的な組織の仕事には、定型的なものから臨機応変なものまで、多様なワークプロセスが混在する。それらの遂行にあたっても、個人作業からグループ作業までさまざまな活動形態が成り立ち、より洗練された情報技術の活用も進むことになる。したがって、そうした活動を支援するワークプレイスには多様な高機能空間の選択肢が必要とされるようになる。一方、そうした支援空間を利用するワーカーたちの行動スタイルも、より自律的で活動的なワークスタイルへと移行していく。従来と同様に定位置を持つスタイル（シッターと呼ぼう）から、オフィスの中でも多様なセッティングを作業に応じて使い分けるスタイル（ウォーカー）、さらには外出頻度の高い「ランナー」や複数立地を拠点とする「トラベラー」まで、各々の職種や役割に応じて臨機応変にプロセスとプレイスを組み合わせていくようになるだろう（図1）。
もはやワークプレイスは固定的な組織の単なる容れ物ではあり得ない。少なくとも、組織の変化と技術の進化を前提とし、それらに迅速に対応できるような装置でなければならない。さらに、激動するビジネス環境の中にあって絶え間ない変革を求められる企業組織の活動を、常に支援できる道具として計画される必要がある。

As the change of business environment becomes faster, the business strategy needs to be more frequently reviewed and be capable of responding more quickly to changes. Therefore, corporations are forced to take actions more frequently–actions such as reducing the time and cost required to develop new services and products, appropriating human resources and skills from larger sources including outside sources and organize them and, as part of these actions, restructuring their organizations and consolidating or abolishing operational bases. These changes will naturally affect the planning of the workplace, which is the base for the activities of an organization.
There are many processes involved in the activities of a fluid organization consisting of a wide spectrum of human resources. They range from formulaic processes to ad hoc ones. The form of work to execute these processes can also be varied from individual work to group work, which encourage the use of more sophisticated information technology. Therefore, the workplace which supports these activities needs to have a wide range of option of providing highly functional spaces. The workstyle of workers who use these supportive space also shifts to a more autonomous and active one. Thus, processes and places will be combined adaptively according to the needs of work and role. The 'sitters' are conventionally fixated to their own spaces. The 'walkers' selectively choose from varied settings according to work needs. The 'runners' are often outside the office and the 'travelers' operates from plural bases. (Fig. 1)
The workplace is no longer a stationary vessel for an organization. It must at least be a device which can swiftly deal with organizational changes and technological advances, which are a matter of course. Furthermore, it must be planned as a tool which can always support business activities which must be constantly reformed in a fast changing business environment.

65

ECÍFFO VOL.36 SPRING 2000 JAPAN CL: KOKUYO Co., Ltd. CD: Akihiro Kishimoto AD: Shintaro Abe P: Francesco Radino / Roberto Carra

ゼロタイム・スペース

米国コーネル大学のインターナショナル・ワークプレイス・スタディーズ・プログラムでは、1998年から2年間をかけて「(FM分野での)不確実性のマネジメント」(Managing Uncertainty) というテーマに取り組んできた。本号のテーマ「アジル・ワークプレイス」とも軌を一にするこの研究が一段落した今、同プログラムの責任者であるベッカー教授に、具体的な事例をまじえて解説していただいた。

Zero-Time Space

Franklin Becker, Ph.D.
International Workplace Studies Program
Cornell University

Zero-Time Space

T 先行きの見えないジレンマ
he Uncertainty Dilemma

テクノロジー、企業の合併・買収、労働力人口の変貌、常に変容する企業戦略、新しい仕事のやり方、グローバル規模の企業競争一こうした要因が出揃って慢性的な先行き不透明状態が生み出され、企業はやむなく、ビジネス経営戦略をめぐって、考え方を新たにすることを迫られている。

ワークプレイスにおける不確定要素の種類

チームの規模と構成
組織改革
合併・買収
ビジネスチャンスの立地
ビジネスチャンスのタイムパターン
新しいテクノロジー
労働力人口動態
世界の政治と金融市場

おそらく、われわれを取り囲む数々の新しいテクノロジーほど、先の見えない様相が際立っている分野はないだろう。われわれはこの現象を「最近の出来事」と考えているが、ATM(現金自動預払機)の経験からも分かるように、これは未経験の問題ではない。ATMの当初の目的は銀行の窓口の混雑緩和だった。しかしいったんATMの味をしめると、顧客たちは1日24時間、年中無休のサービスを要求した。しかも場所を問わずにだ。つまり、スーパーマーケットやコンビニ、ガソリンスタンドなどにも設置しろというのだ。その結果何が起こったか?銀行は不動産の膨大なだぶつきを抱え込んで、今なおそこから抜け出そうともがいている。不安定な状況を迅速かつ臨機応変に処理することは、企業がそのオフィススペースの調達、建設、管理のやり方を変革することだ。「統合的ポートフォリオ戦略(IPS)」を推進する上で、コスト削減はいまだに重要な動因だが、第一の原動力は柔軟性、つまり必要とされる時/場所に必要な期間だけ、適切なタイプと広さのオフィススペースを提供できる能力だ。これは「かんばん方式」や無駄を省いた生産工程と同じ考え方を踏まえたもので、必要最小限の資源だけに金を払い活用せよということだ。

ゼロタイム・スペース戦略	Zero-Time Space Strategies
方針	**Policy**
ノンテリトリアル・オフィス	• Non-territorial offices
時間依存の計画VSイベント依存の計画	• Time vs. event-paced planning
外枠骨組み方式と「ダーク(暗い)」スペース	• Shelling and "dark" space
「複製」デザイン	• "Copy exactly" design
テレワーク	• Telework
高度に標準化されたソリューションとカスタム・ソリューションのミックス	• Mix highly standard and customized solutions
建設	**Construction**
ユニット組立て式建造物	• Pre-engineered structures
移動式	Mobile
規格ユニット式	Modular
拡張式	Tensile
調達	**Procurement**
フルサービス型オフィス	• Fully-serviced offices
余剰収容スペース	• Excess capacity space
リソースの共有	• Shared resources
設計立案	**Design**
将来の使用方法の予測;用途転換を考慮した設計	• Anticipate future uses; design for conversion
規格ユニット(パーツキット)による自立構造型システム	• Modular (kit-of-parts) and free-standing systems
揚げ床式フロア	• Raised access floors
組合わせ再編成の容易なモバイル家具	• Mobile and easily reconfigured furniture
ソフトウェアでプログラム可能なHVACシステム	• Software-based programmable HVAC systems
高天井・広スパン構造	• High bay and clear span structures
フレックス(可変)ゾーンと固定ゾーン;引込み幹線ケーブル	• Flexible and fixed zones; services spines

I 統合的ポートフォリオ戦略(IPS)
ntegrated Portfolio Strategy (IPS)

財務ポートフォリオにとって重要な多様性の考え方は、統合的ポートフォリオ戦略(IPS)にとっても同様に重要である。「オーソドックス」タイプのオフィスビルの中に、従来通りオフィススペースを借りたり持ったりすることだけを、適切なソリューションとみなすような不動産・ファシリティ戦略は、フレキシビリティやスピードという観点からいえば、不十分なのである。

IPSの思考は、より広範なソリューションを対象とし、その中には、標準タイプのビルに比べると、30%からほとんど100%まで建設期間を短縮できる、拡張式ビル・規格ユニット式ビル・移動式ビル、あるいは占有面積でなく使用回数で料金が決まるフルサービス型オフィス、そしてさまざまなタイプのテレワークを可能にする情報テクノロジーの活用などが含まれている。

Z ゼロタイム・スペース
ero-Time Space

「ゼロタイム・スペース」という構想は、小回りのきくきびきびとした組織で「ゼロタイム(待ち時間ゼロ)で行動する」という考え方の借用だ。あるスペースを使いたい(あるいは出ていきたい)というニーズが生まれたときから、できるだけ(限りなくゼロに近い)短期間で、調達ができ、また建設、使用開始が可能になるようなスペースが、ゼロタイム・オフィススペースだ。物理的には新しい建設方法によって、組織的には新調達方式で、技術的には遠隔勤務を可能にする情報技術の可能性を活用することで、そして運用的にはオフィススペースの割り振りと活用についての新しい方針を立てることによって、ゼロタイム・オフィススペースが実現するのだ。

44 ZERO-TIME SPACE　ZERO-TIME SPACE 45

縦横に走る街路の上にはケーブルトレイが設けられた。配線は、居住区と居住区をまたぐ黒いポールを伝ってパネルシステムへと下りていく。

6 NORTEL NETWORKS Canada　NORTEL NETWORKS Canada 7

MARTHA STEWART BABY MARCH 2000 USA PB,DF: Martha Stewart Omnimedia E: Alice Gordon AD: Deb Bishop / Barbara deWilde D: Angie Gubler
P: Minh & Wass (SPREAD 1) / Sang An

SPREAD 1

G

irls can wish upon a star—or a planet or two—with a mobile fashioned from spheres into a fantasy constellation.

I

n the middle of the night, low bedside lighting enables you to pore over Dr. Spock or to find your way from crib to changing table.

R

est assured, out of sight but within earshot, by hanging a room-dividing curtain from the ceiling between crib and daybed.

L

ittle ones soon appreciate small cradles of their own to tuck in their new babies.

do you know? An infant's lips and tongue are so sensitive that she can use them to "see" the shape of an object she'll later recognize with her eyes. Mobiles, ubiquitous above babies' cribs, were invented in the 1930s by the sculptor Alexander Calder and became popular as decorations a few decades later. Some babies are born with a surprising amount of hair, even on their shoulders, which disappears after the second or third month. Among babies born in 1880, Martha was the seventh most popular name. By 1890 she had lost out to Ethel and never again has been a top-ten choice. **Parents in the U.S. tend to teach babies language by identifying objects (nouns), while parents in Korea point out actions (verbs).** Mother Goose first appeared in France in 1697. She was the narrator of a collection of tales that included the now famous "Sleeping Beauty" and "Puss in Boots." Swaddling—wrapping a baby in a long cloth—is an ancient method of dressing infants that can help them sleep and actually soothe colic in some.

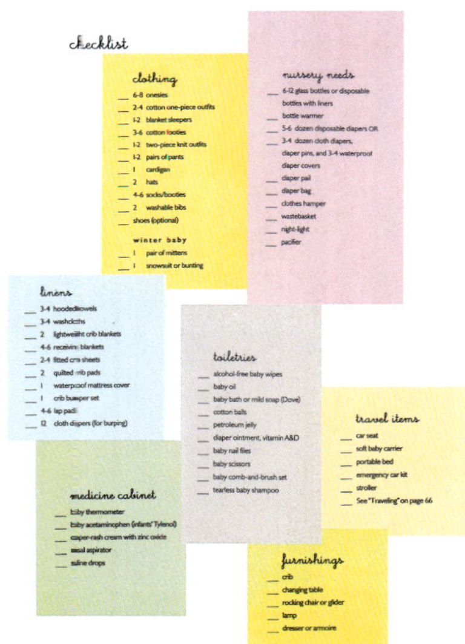

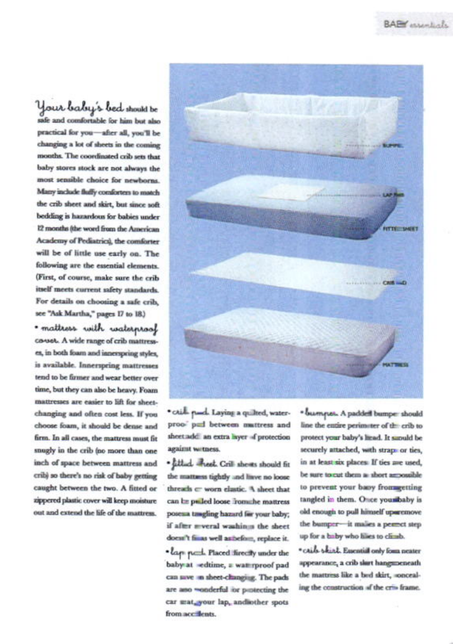

COLORS 36 MONOCULTURE FEBRUARY-MARCH 2000 ITALY PB: Colors Magazine S.r.l. Editorial Director: Oliviero Toscani E: Renzo di Renzo
Creative Editor: Richard Christiansen AD: Tetsuya Tamano D: Anna Maria Stilllone

onecare

pop a pill Americans swallow US$80 billion worth of pills a year. (And it's not always because they're sick: They take pills to grow hair, lose weight and quit smoking.) But adverse reactions to medication send 1.5 million to the hospital and 100,000 to the morgue yearly. The rest of the world is catching up: One in 10 people in the UK swallow painkillers every day, though overuse can damage the liver or kidney. In France, some 200,000 people are addicted to antidepressant pills. The habit is slow to catch on in Africa, but pharmaceutical companies are working to change that. In 1994, US company Eli Lilly donated enough antibiotics to treat a million people in Rwanda (the gift was tax-deductible and the antibiotics were nearing their expiration date anyway). According to French medical relief group Médecins sans Frontières, feeding them to locals would have been inappropriate and dangerous.

get a vaccination shot Humankind is injected with US$3 billion worth of vaccines a year. What convinces everyone to brave the needle? Laws, usually: Until recently, in 42 US states children without hepatitis B shots couldn't go to school. And the United Nations calls cease-fire days in war zones so children can be rounded up and vaccinated. But skin rashes, swelling and fever might not be the only side effects. The Rotashield vaccine, developed to protect against rotavirus, a cause of fatal diarrhea, has been linked to a potentially deadly bowel disease (it's now banned in the USA). And in a 1970s tuberculosis vaccine test in India, more people who had been vaccinated ended up with TB than those who had not. According to Dr. Jayne Donegan, who worked on the UK's measles vaccination campaigns, most "accidents" are never reported. "When people report side effects, they are discounted as not causally related," says Jayne. Soon people may not even know they've been vaccinated: To cut the costs of administering vaccines, Canadian scientists recently developed genetically engineered potatoes that contain hepatitis B and cholera vaccines.

get HIV "Cholera is a huge problem in Bangladesh—in Paris there's nothing to worry about," says Dr. Chris Beyrer, of Johns Hopkins University, USA. Instead, AIDS infects people everywhere (at the rate of about 16,000 people a day). "It's a great equalizer," says Dr. Beyrer. Or is it? When American and European scientists first warned the world about AIDS, they focused their message on drug use and gay sex. And that was the message that spread throughout the world. Instead most AIDS victims in Asia and Africa are heterosexual. (In India, which has the world's largest number of people infected with HIV, simply getting married puts women at the greatest risk.) And the most effective treatment—AZT—costs about US$20,000 per patient per year. In Botswana, where one-third of all sexually active adults are HIV positive, the per capita gross domestic product is just $2,500.

go chemical Treating patients with herbal medicines isn't profitable: Plants can't be patented. (The stinging nettle, a plant used to treat arthritis, grows wild, and anyone can gather it.) But if a drug company invents a new molecule, they own the formula. That's why each year pharmaceutical companies in the UK spend £2 billion (US$3.2 billion) to develop chemical drugs, while over 15 years only £3 million ($4.8 million) has been spent on developing herbal medicine. Yet the UK's alternative medicine practitioners now outnumber conventional practitioners. Vijaya Venkat, a naturopath in Mumbai, India, says: "Allopathy [Western medicine] is the dominant system because it's the pharmaceutical companies that support most medical research."

swallow vitamins Vitamin sales are growing worldwide by about four percent a year—and Americans are leading the way. "There are people that take literally hundreds [of vitamins a day]," says Scott Olschanski, who makes exercise equipment. (He and his wife limit their intake to "between 10 and 20.") According to Roche, a Swiss vitamin maker, good promotion is a key. "Vitamins are a consumer good," says Roche spokesman Peter Wullschleger. Europe tends to follow America's example, he says. And "Asia is doing well. In urban areas [there], it is fashionable to take vitamins when you have the money because the Americans do also." That's not the only reason their use is spreading, says Dr. Oliver Chitalu, of Chelstone, Zambia. Vitamins in Zambia are cheap, widely available, and often considered "an alternative to food."

unamedicación

traga una píldora Los norteamericanos engullen cada año pastillas por un valor de 80.000 millones $US (y no siempre porque están enfermos: toman píldoras para que les crezca el pelo, para perder peso y para dejar de fumar). Pero las reacciones alérgicas a los medicamentos mandan a 1.500.000 consumidores al hospital y a 100.000 a la funeraria cada año. El resto del mundo sigue la tendencia: una de cada 10 personas en el Reino Unido ingiere analgésicos a diario, aunque la utilización prolongada puede dañar el hígado o el riñón. En Francia, unas 200.000 personas son adictas a los antidepresivos. El hábito no termina de echar raíces en África, pero los laboratorios farmacéuticos están trabajando para que eso cambie. En 1994, la empresa estadounidense Eli Lilly donó suficientes antibióticos como para tratar a 1 millón de personas en Ruanda (el donativo era desgravable y, de todas formas, los antibióticos estaban a punto de caducar). Según el grupo de ayuda médica francés Médicos sin Fronteras, suministrarlos a los habitantes de la zona habría sido inadecuado y peligroso.

consigue una vacuna Las vacunas inyectadas anualmente a los humanos representan un valor de 3.000 millones $US. ¿Qué ayuda a afrontar la aguja? Las leyes, por lo general. Hasta hace poco, en 42 Estados de EE UU, los niños no vacunados de la hepatitis B no podían ir al colegio. Y la ONU convoca jornadas de alto el fuego para poder reagrupar a los niños y vacunarlos. Pero las reacciones cutáneas, las hinchazones y la fiebre podrían no ser los únicos efectos secundarios. La vacuna Rotashield, desarrollada para proteger del rotavirus, que provoca una diarrea mortal, ha sido vinculada con una enfermedad intestinal potencialmente fatal (ahora está prohibida en EE UU). Y en un test de la vacuna de la tuberculosis efectuado en los años 70 en la India, enfermaron de tuberculosis más personas vacunadas que las que no lo estaban. Según la doctora Jayne Donegan, que trabajó en las campañas británicas de vacunación contra el sarampión, la mayoría de los *accidentes* no se comunican nunca. "Cuando los pacientes informan de efectos secundarios, no se cuentan como causas relacionadas", dice Jayne. Dentro de poco, la gente ya ni sabrá si ha sido vacunada: para rebajar los costes de la administración de las vacunas, unos científicos canadienses desarrollaron hace poco patatas manipuladas genéticamente que contienen las vacunas de la hepatitis B y el cólera.

pilla el SIDA "El cólera hace estragos en Bangladesh, aunque en París no hay nada que temer", dice el doctor Chris Beyrer, de la universidad John Hopkins de EE UU. El SIDA, en cambio, infecta a todos por igual (al ritmo de unas 16.000 personas diarias). "Es un gran ecualizador", dice el doctor Beyrer. ¿O no? Cuando los científicos norteamericanos y europeos advirtieron por primera vez al mundo del SIDA, centraron su mensaje en la drogadicción y en la homosexualidad. Y ése fue el mensaje que se extendió por todo el mundo. Pero casi todas las víctimas del SIDA de Asia y África son heterosexuales (en la India, el país con el mayor número de personas infectadas por el virus del SIDA, el simple hecho de casarse ya supone un riesgo terrible para las mujeres). Y el tratamiento más eficaz, el AZT, viene a costar unos 20.000 $US anuales por paciente). En Botsuana, donde una tercera parte de la población adulta sexualmente activa es seropositiva, el producto interior bruto per cápita no supera los 2.500 $.

lánzate a lo químico Tratar a los pacientes con medicamentos a base de hierbas no es rentable: las plantas no pueden patentarse (la ortiga, un vegetal utilizado para tratar la artritis, crece libremente y está al alcance de todos). Pero si un laboratorio inventa una nueva molécula, es propietario de la fórmula. Por eso, los laboratorios farmacéuticos del Reino Unido gastan cada año 2.000 millones £ (3.200 millones $US) para desarrollar drogas químicas, mientras que, durante más de 15 años, sólo se han invertido en el desarrollo de la medicina a base de hierbas 3 millones £ (4,8 millones $). Y sin embargo los adeptos a la medicina alternativa sobrepasan ahora a los de la convencional. Vijaya Venkat, una naturópata de Mumbai (India), dice: "La alopatía [medicina occidental] es el sistema dominante porque son las empresas farmacéuticas las que financian la mayoría de las investigaciones médicas".

engulle vitaminas Las ventas de vitaminas crecen a un ritmo anual de un 4% en todo el mundo (y los norteamericanos se llevan la palma). "Hay personas que toman centenares [de vitaminas al día]", dice Scott Olschanski, que fabrica aparatos de gimnasia (él y su mujer se limitan a ingerir "entre 10 y 20"). Según Roche, un fabricante suizo de vitaminas, lo que importa es la promoción. "Las vitaminas son un bien de consumo", dice el portavoz de Roche, Peter Wullschleger. Y añade que Europa sigue la tendencia norteamericana. Y "Asia va avanzando; entre las personas acomodadas de las zonas urbanas está de moda tomar vitaminas, porque lo hacen los americanos". Esa no es la única razón de que su consumo se esté extendiendo, dice el doctor Oliver Chitalu, de Chelstone (Zambia). En Zambia las vitaminas son baratas, fáciles de encontrar y a menudo consideradas como "una alternativa a la comida".

"The idea is a simple one: Diversity is good... Over the years, there's been a lot of talk about the planet becoming "smaller"—that technology, whether it's the jet plane or fax machine or communications satellite, is erasing the differences between cultures and peoples. We don't think this should be the case. The message of this magazine is that your culture (whoever you are) is as important as our culture (whoever we are). We think that the real value of all the electronic stuff that creates links between places otherwise completely removed from each other is that it allows all of us to see further and broaden our ways of thinking. We want to know what you are doing over there (wherever you are), and we're pretty sure that you want to know what we're doing here (wherever we are)... One more thing: While COLORS is being distributed globally, in five bilingual editions, we feel a little funny about being global. It makes us feel like we're McDonald's, and we're not. We don't want to sell our culture to you. We want you to tell us about your culture. We want to know what we left out and what we should include next time. Tell us who your heroes are or what you eat for breakfast or whether there are tribes where you live. Write to us. COLORS, 50 West 17 Street, New York, NY 10011 USA".

COLORS 1, fall/winter 1991

"Nuestra idea es simple: en la variedad está el gusto. A través de los años se ha hablado mucho sobre como el planeta se está haciendo más pequeño, que la tecnología—ya que sea de aviones o de los faxes o de los satélites de comunicaciones—está borrando las diferencias entre las gentes y sus culturas. Nosotros pensamos que no debería ser así. El mensaje de esta revista es que tu cultura (seas quien seas) es tan importante como la nuestra. Creemos que el valor verdadero de los aparatos electrónicos está en los vínculos que crean entre lugares, que de otras formas estarian aislados, y que nos permite ver más allá y conocer otras formas de pensar. Queremos saber lo que estás haciendo allá (estés donde estés) y estamos casi seguros que tú tambien quieres saber lo que estamos haciendo nosotros aquí (estemos donde estemos)... Una cosa más: aunque COLORS se distribuye en todo el mundo, con ediciones en cinco idiomas, nos sentiamos un poco incómodos con la idea de ser globales. Nos hace sentir como si fueramos McDonald's y no lo somos. No queremos venderte nuestra cultura. Queremos que tú nos cuentes más sobre la tuya. Queremos saber qué nos quedó para incluirlo la próxima vez. Dinos quiénes son tus héroes o qué te gusta desayunar o si hay tribus donde tu vives. ¡Escríbenos! COLORS, 50 West 17 Street, New York, NY 10011 USA".

COLORS n° 1, otoño/invierno 1991

COLORS 01 REWIND

COLORS 36 FAST FORWARD

Nine years have passed since we wrote this in the first issue of our (and your) magazine. In the meantime new technologies have appeared—the Internet above all—and COLORS has moved many times, here and there in the world. We now publish eight editions and more will follow. But we still haven't changed our idea. By celebrating Monoculture we really want to celebrate once again the value of diversity. Ideally, this should be our last will and testament, our unconditional surrender to our sworn enemy. Monoculture kills or—what's even worse—it captures us with a radiant toothpaste smile. It erases differences in the name of a mistaken sense of cleanliness and progress. Its passwords are imperatives, clumsily presented as "advice to consumers," and shopping malls all over the world are the new concentration camps. There's a war out there, even though we weren't aware of it. And in this war we are at the same time victims and executioners. It's a "precooked and warmed-over" war, where we and our secret need for approval are the enemy. But we're pleased to discover that some pockets of resistance to overpowering Monoculture are still out there—a silent, concealed guerrilla force made up of disorganized differences. Just like COLORS.

COLORS 36, february/march 2000

Han pasado nueve años desde que escribimos esta palabra en el primer número de nuestra (y tu) revista. Entretanto, han aparecido nuevas tecnologías (sobre todo Internet) y COLORS se ha mudado un montón de veces a diferentes lugares del mundo. Ahora publicamos ocho ediciones, y vendrán otras más. Pero seguimos con la misma idea. Al celebrar la Monocultura lo que en realidad celebramos es la diversidad. Idealmente, ésta debería ser nuestra última voluntad y testamento, nuestra rendición sin condiciones ante nuestro enemigo jurado. La Monocultura nos mata o, todavía peor, nos captura con una radiante sonrisa de dentífrico. Borra las diferencias en nombre de un erróneo sentido de la pulcritud y del progreso. Sus contraseñas son imperativas, torpemente presentadas como *servicio al consumidor*. Y los centros comerciales de todo el mundo son los nuevos campos de concentración. Aunque no lo sepamos, se está librando una guerra. Y en esa guerra somos al mismo tiempo las víctimas y los verdugos. Es una guerra *precocinada y recalentada*, donde nosotros y nuestro secreto necesitamos la aprobación del enemigo. Pero nos alegra descubrir que algunas bolsas de resistencia a la tiránica Monocultura siguen ahí (unas fuerzas guerrilleras silenciosas y ocultas, formadas de diferencias organizadas). COLORS quiere seguir siendo su voz y su mirada por mucho tiempo.

COLORS n° 36, febrero/marzo 2000

No.36 COVER

BROCHURE ブローシャー

ACT AGAINST AIDS 2000 JAPAN CL: Amuse Inc. CD: Hiroshi Naito / Yukako Fujiwara AD: Kenji Nakao / Takeshi Sato D: Yoshiyuki Akagawa DF: Victor Design Center

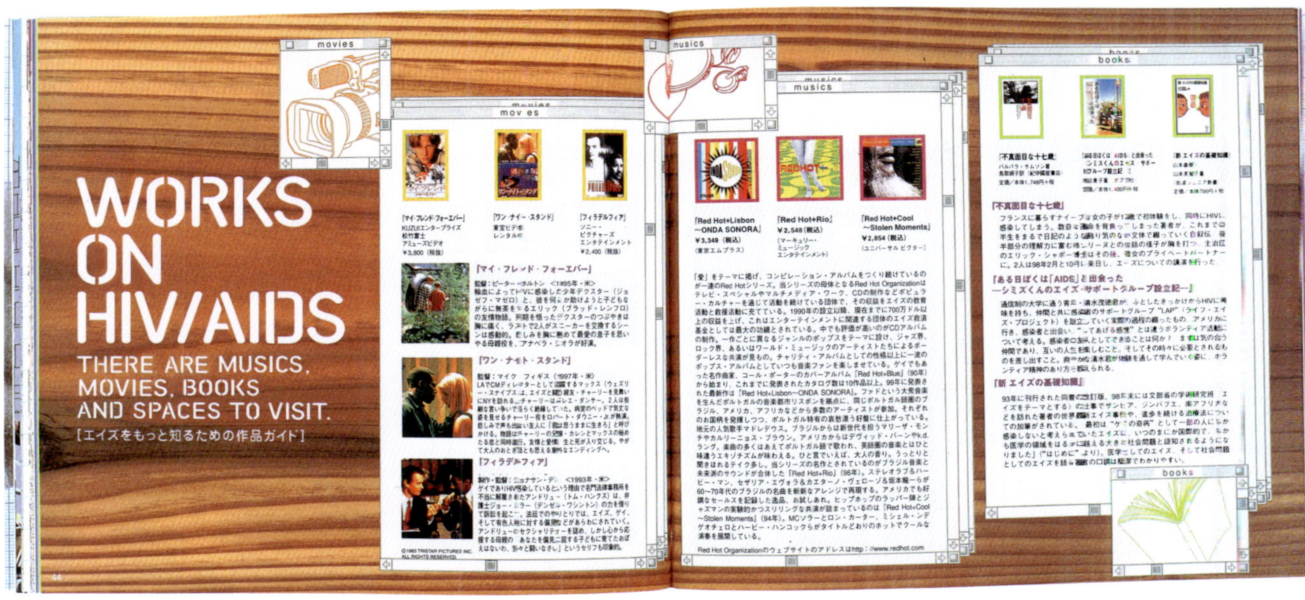

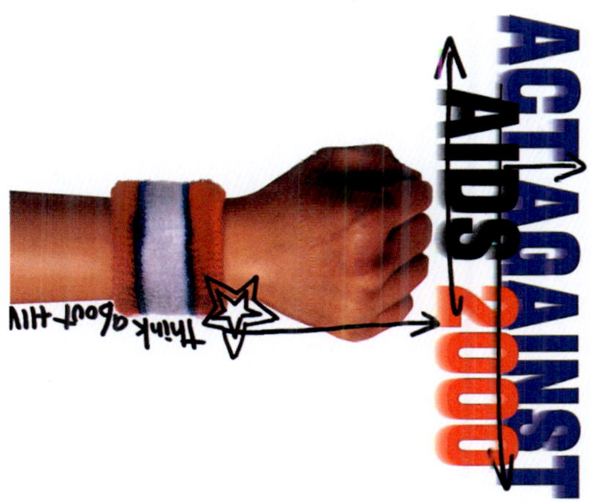

COVER

TEXT PAGES

BOOK 書籍

GASBOOK 6 1999 JAPAN PB: DesignEXchange Co., Ltd. CD,AD: Akira Natsume D: Hideki Inaba

COVER

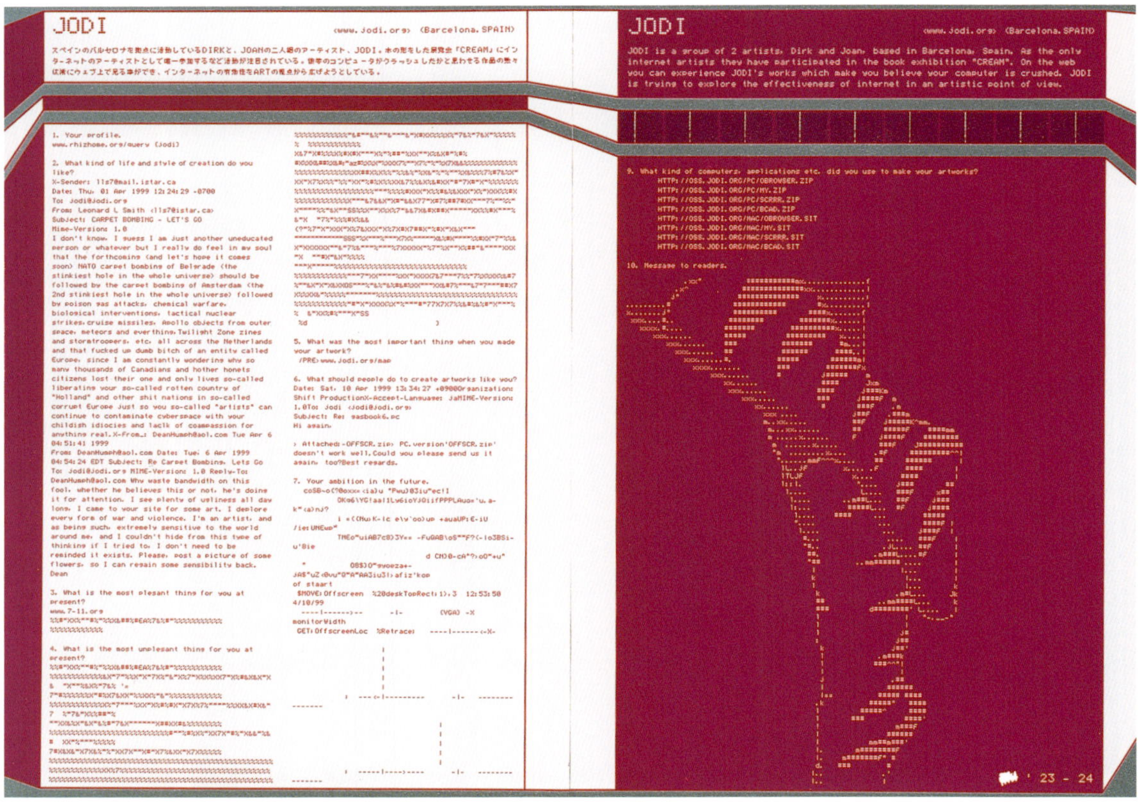

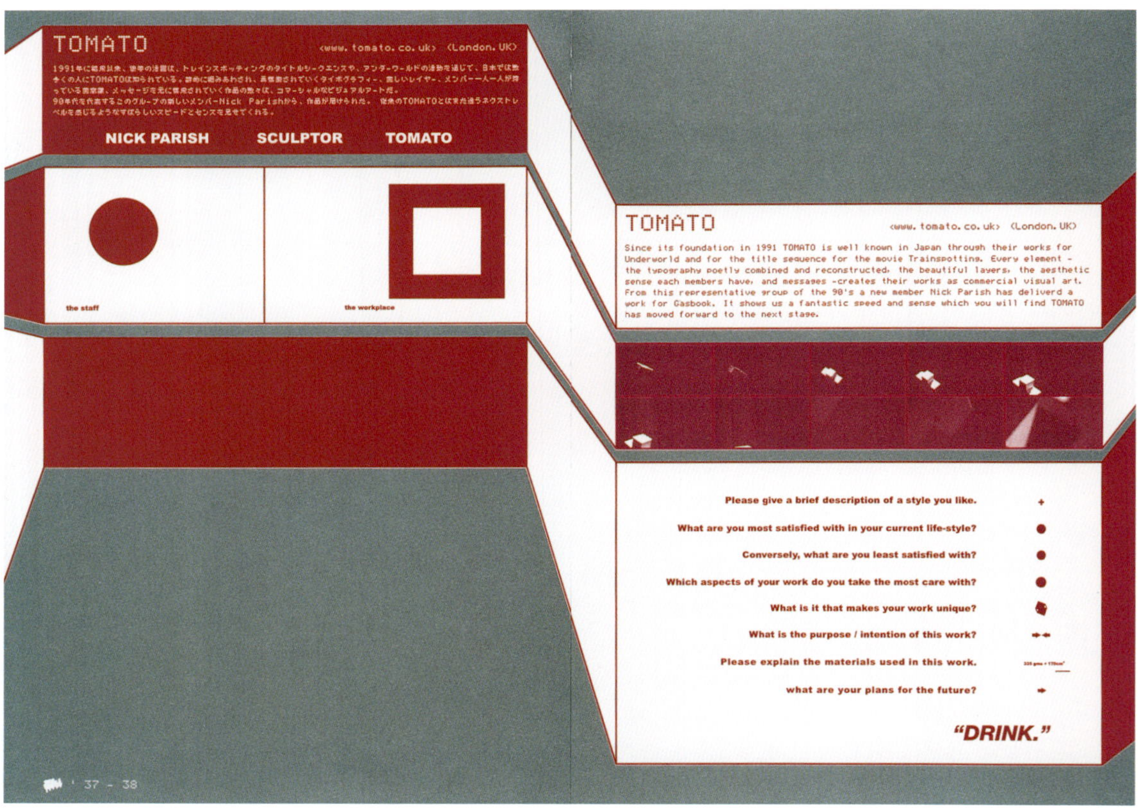

MAGAZINE 雑誌

PAPER KNIFE VOL.6 2000 JAPAN PB: Paper Knife Rocks E,CD: Yusuke Shono

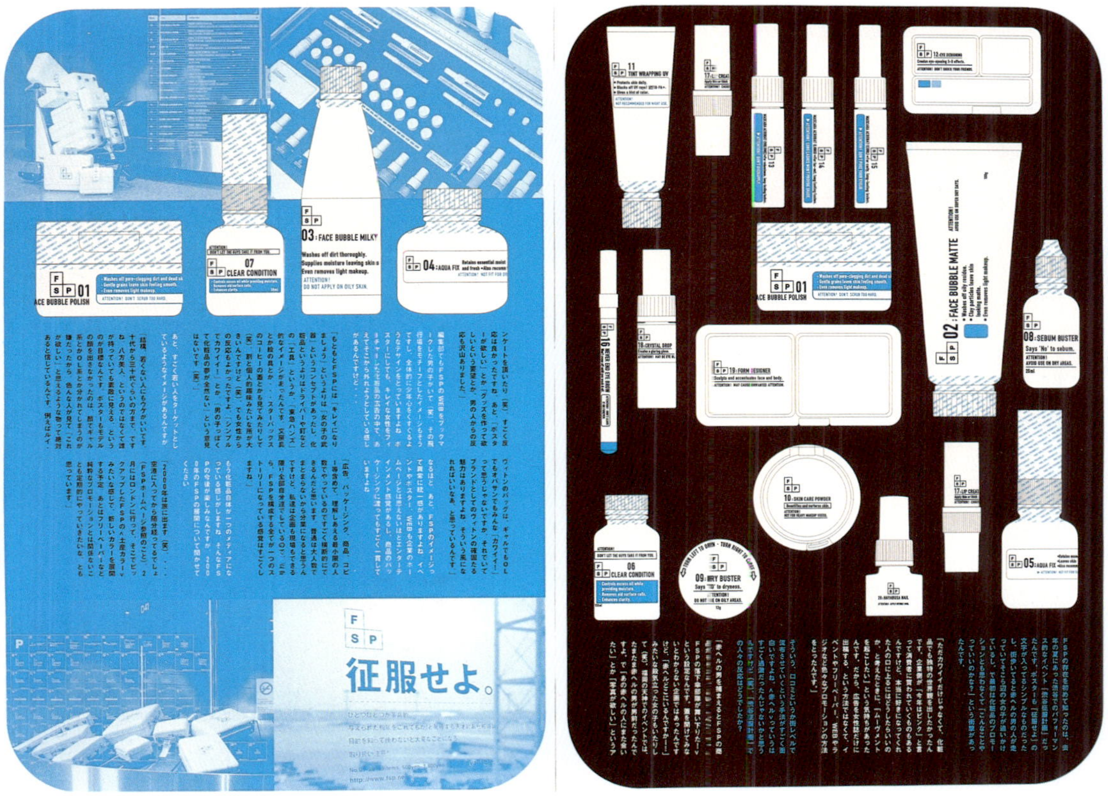

COVER

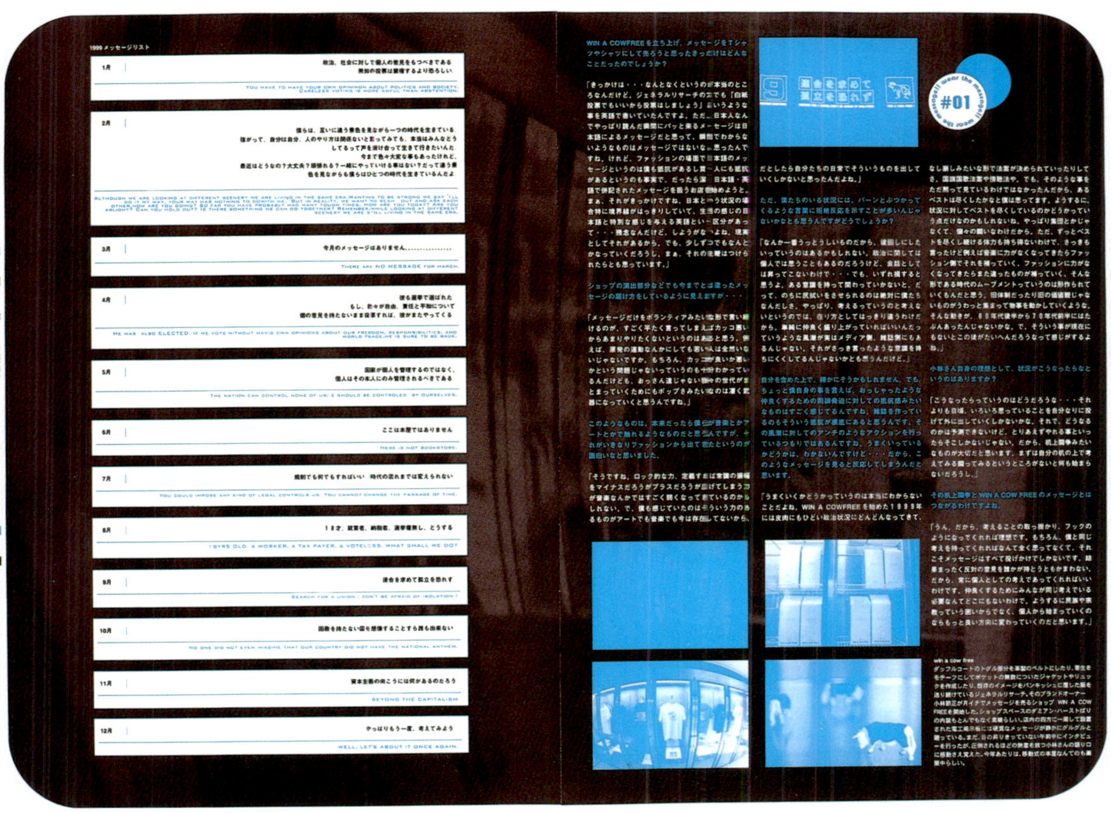

TEXT PAGES

THE ENCYCLOPEDIA OF "MISSION" AND "THE FORCE TO CHANGE" AT MC 1999 JAPAN CL: Mitsubishi Corporation CD: Masao Tsuji AD: Ichiro Higashiizumi P: Risaku Suzuki I: Keiji Ito Planning: Wilson Learning Worldwide Inc.

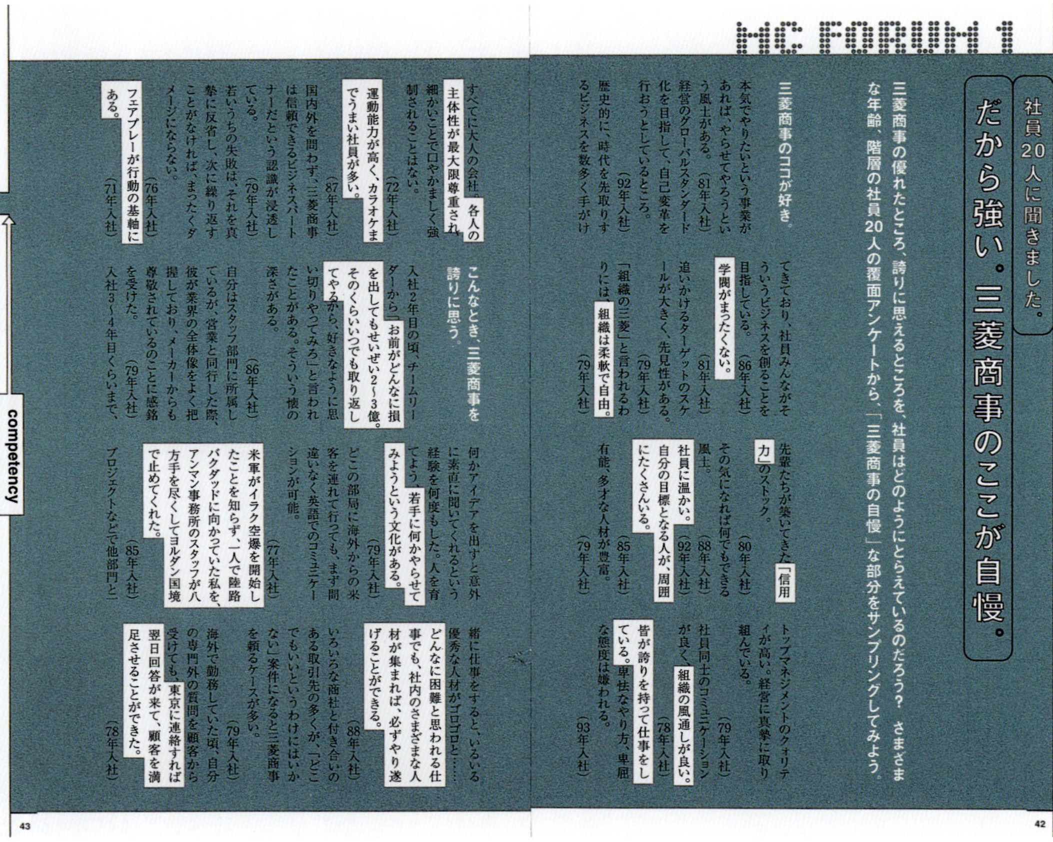

MC FORUM 1

社員20人に聞きました。

だから強い。三菱商事のここが自慢。

三菱商事の優れたところ、誇りに思えるところを、社員はどのようにとらえているのだろう？ さまざまな年齢、階層の社員20人の覆面アンケートから、「三菱商事の自慢」な部分をサンプリングしてみよう。

三菱商事のココが好き。

本気でやりたいという事業があれば、やらせてやろうという風土がある。（81年入社）

経営のグローバルスタンダード化を目指して、自己変革を行おうとしているところ。（92年入社）

歴史的に、時代を先取りするビジネスを数多く手がけてきており、社員みんながそういうビジネスを創ることを目指している。（86年入社）

学閥がまったくない。（81年入社）

追いかけるターゲットのスケールが大きく、先見性がある。（79年入社）

「組織の三菱」と言われるわりには、組織は柔軟で自由。（79年入社）

先輩たちが築いてきた「信用力」のストック。（80年入社）

その気になれば何でもできる風土。（88年入社）

社員に温かい。（92年入社）

自分の目標となる人が、周囲にたくさんいる。（85年入社）

有能、多才な人材が豊富。（79年入社）

トップマネジメントのクォリティが高い。経営に真摯に取り組んでいる。（79年入社）

社員同士のコミュニケーションが良く、組織の風通しが良い。（78年入社）

皆が誇りを持って仕事をしている。卑怯なやり方、卑屈な態度は嫌われる。（93年入社）

すべてに大人の会社。各人の主体性が最大限尊重され、細かいことで口やかましく強制されることはない。（72年入社）

運動能力が高く、カラオケまでうまい社員が多い。（87年入社）

国内外を問わず、三菱商事は信頼できるビジネスパートナーだという認識が浸透している。（79年入社）

若いうちの失敗は、それを真摯に反省し、次に繰り返すことがなければ、まったくダメージにならない。（76年入社）

フェアプレーが行動の基軸にある。（71年入社）

こんなとき、三菱商事を誇りに思う。

入社2年目の頃、チームリーダーから「お前がどんなに損を出してもせいぜい2〜3億。そのくらいいつでも取り返してやるから、好きなように思い切りやってみろ」と言われたことがある。そういう懐の深さがある。（86年入社）

自分はスタッフ部門に所属しているが、営業と同行した際、彼が業界の全体像をよく把握しており、メーカーからも尊敬されていることに感銘を受けた。（79年入社）

入社3〜4年目くらいまで、何かアイデアを出すと意外に素直に聞いてくれるという経験を何度もした。人を育てよう、若手に何かやらせてみようという文化がある。（79年入社）

どこの部局に海外からの来客を連れて行っても、まず間違いなく英語でのコミュニケーションが可能。（77年入社）

米軍がイラク空爆を開始したことを知らず、一人で陸路バクダッドに向かっていた私を、アンマン事務所のスタッフが八方手を尽くしてヨルダン国境で止めてくれた。（85年入社）

プロジェクトなどで他部門と一緒に仕事をすると、いるいる優秀な人材がゴロゴロと……。どんなに困難と思われる仕事でも、社内のさまざまな人材が集まれば、必ずやり遂げることができる。（88年入社）

いろいろな商社と付き合いのある取引先の多くが、「どこでもいいというわけにはいかない」案件になると三菱商事を頼るケースが多い。（79年入社）

海外で勤務していた頃、自分の専門外の質問を顧客から受けても、東京に連絡すれば翌日回答が来て、顧客を満足させることができた。（78年入社）

competency

43 42

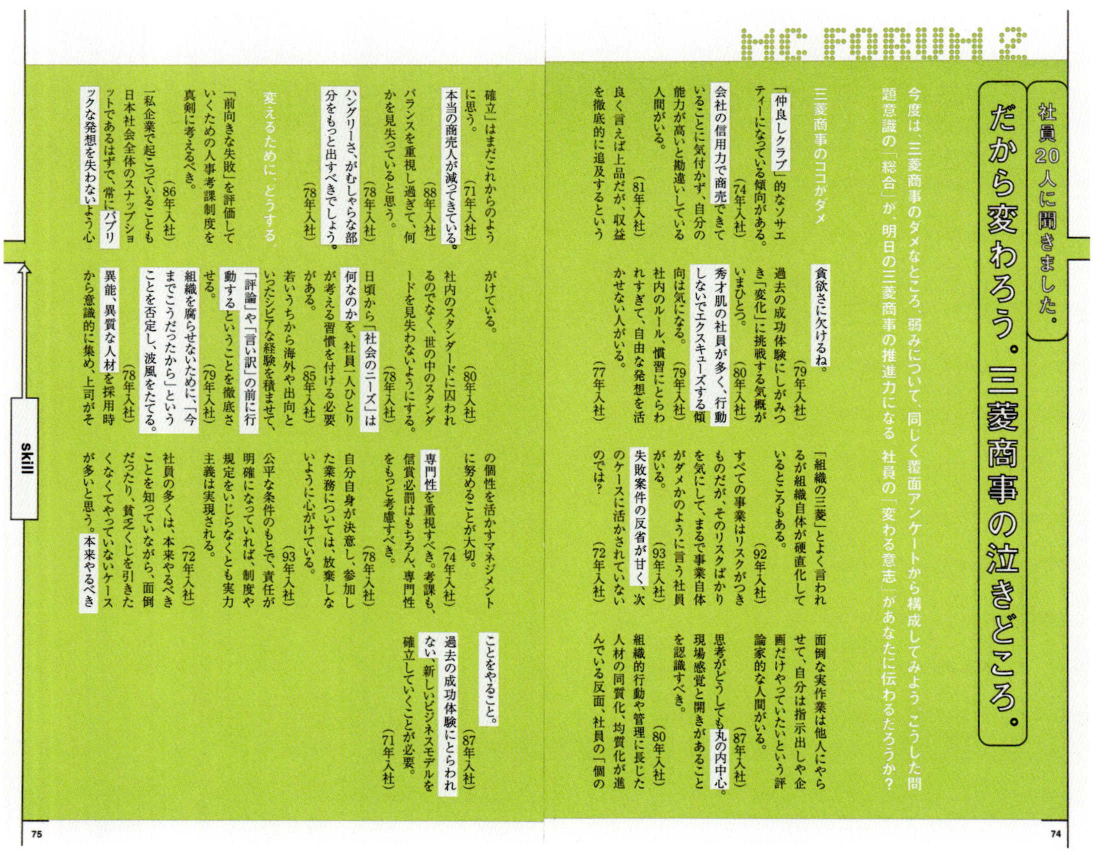

MC FORUM 2

社員20人に聞きました。

だから変わろう。三菱商事の泣きどころ。

今度は、三菱商事のダメなところ、弱みについて、同じく覆面アンケートから構成してみよう。こうした問題意識の「総合」が、明日の三菱商事の推進力になる 社員の「変わる意志」があなたに伝わるだろうか？

三菱商事のココがダメ

「仲良しクラブ」的なソサエティーになっている傾向がある。（74年入社）

会社の信用力で商売できていることに気付かず、自分の能力が高いと勘違いしている人間がいる。（81年入社）

良く言えば上品だが、収益を徹底的に追及するという貪欲さに欠けるね。（79年入社）

過去の成功体験にしがみつき「変化」に挑戦する気概がいまひとつ。（80年入社）

秀才肌の社員が多く、行動しないでエクスキューズする傾向は気になる。（79年入社）

社内のルール、慣習にとらわれすぎて、自由な発想を活かせない人がいる。（77年入社）

「組織の三菱」とよく言われるが組織自体が硬直化しているところもある。（92年入社）

すべての事業はリスクがつきものだが、そのリスクばかりを気にして、まるで事業自体がダメかのように言う社員がいる。（93年入社）

失敗案件の反省が甘く、次のケースに活かされていないのでは？（72年入社）

面倒な実作業は他人にやらせて、自分は指示出しや企画だけやっていたいという評論家的な人間がいる。（87年入社）

思考がどうしても丸の内中心。現場感覚と開きがあることを認識すべき。（80年入社）

組織的行動や管理に長じた人材の同質化、均質化が進んでいる反面、社員の「個の確立」はまだこれからのように思う。（71年入社）

本当の商売人が減ってきている。（88年入社）

バランスを重視し過ぎて、何かを見失っていると思う。（78年入社）

ハングリーさ、がむしゃらな部分をもっと出すべきでしょう。（78年入社）

変えるために、どうする。

「前向きな失敗」を評価していくための人事考課制度を真剣に考えるべき。（86年入社）

一私企業で起こっていることも日本社会全体のスナップショットであるはずで、常にパブリックな発想を失わないよう心がけている。（80年入社）

社内のスタンダードに囚われるのでなく、世の中のスタンダードを見失わないようにする。（78年入社）

日頃から「社会のニーズ」は何なのかを、社員一人ひとりが考える習慣を付ける必要がある。（85年入社）

若いうちから海外や出向といったシビアな経験を積ませて、「評論」や「言い訳」の前に行動するということを徹底させる。（79年入社）

組織を腐らせないために、「今までこうだったから」ということを否定し、波風をたてる。（78年入社）

異能、異質な人材を採用時から意識的に集め、上司がその個性を活かすマネジメントに努めることが大切。（74年入社）

専門性を重視すべき。考課も、信賞必罰はもちろん、専門性をもっと考慮すべき。（78年入社）

自分自身が決意し、参加した業務については、放棄しないように心がけている。（93年入社）

公平な条件のもとで、責任が明確になっていれば、制度や規定をいじらなくとも実力主義は実現される。（72年入社）

社員の多くは、本来やるべきことを知っていながら、面倒だったり、貧乏くじを引きたくなくてやっていないケースが多いと思う。本来やるべきことをやること。（87年入社）

過去の成功体験にとらわれない、新しいビジネスモデルを確立していくことが必要。（71年入社）

skill

75 74

SAMSUNG ANNUAL REPORT 1998 CANADA CL: Samsung CD: Mary Scott AD,D Vanessa Eckstein CW: Eric La Brecque DF: Maddocks & Company / Blok Design

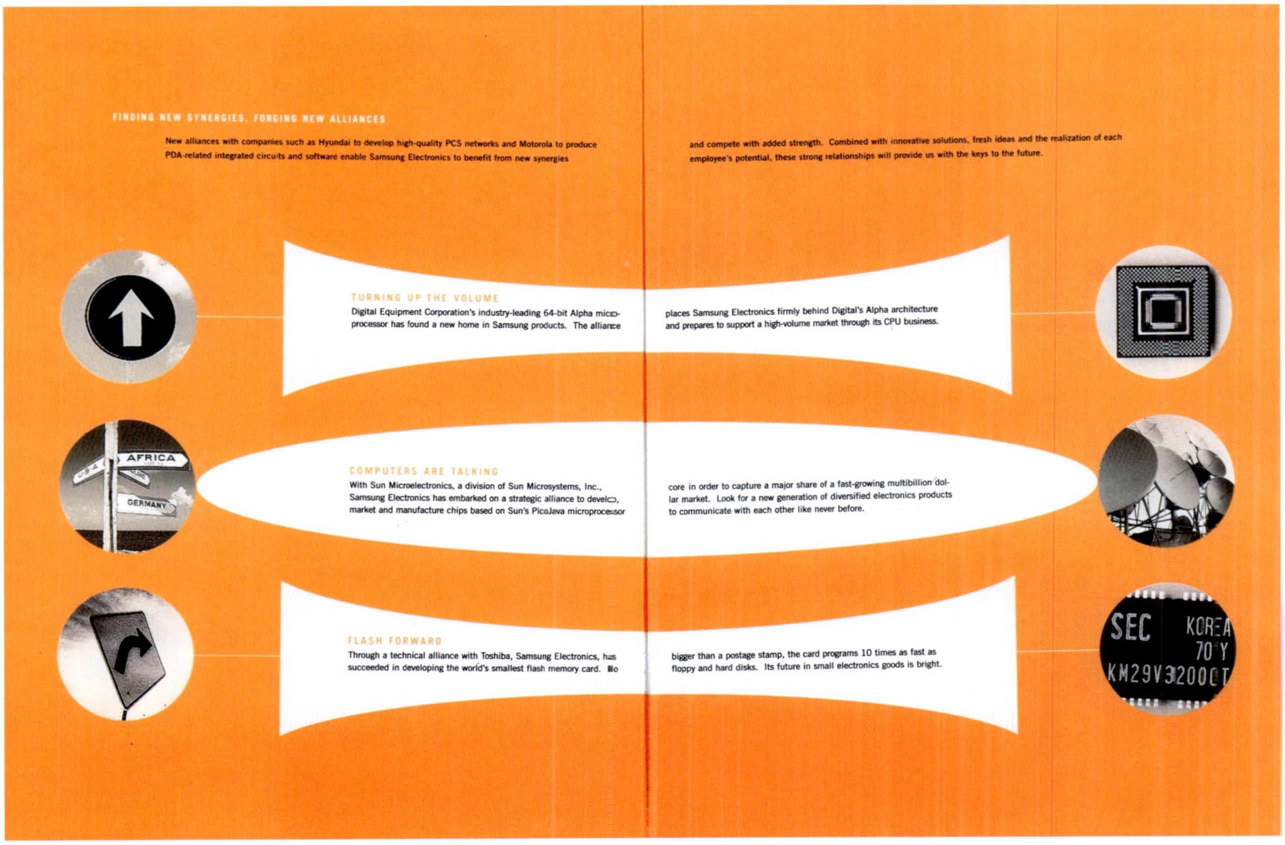

FINDING NEW SYNERGIES, FORGING NEW ALLIANCES

New alliances with companies such as Hyundai to develop high-quality PCS networks and Motorola to produce PDA-related integrated circuits and software enable Samsung Electronics to benefit from new synergies and compete with added strength. Combined with innovative solutions, fresh ideas and the realization of each employee's potential, these strong relationships will provide us with the keys to the future.

TURNING UP THE VOLUME

Digital Equipment Corporation's industry-leading 64-bit Alpha microprocessor has found a new home in Samsung products. The alliance places Samsung Electronics firmly behind Digital's Alpha architecture and prepares to support a high-volume market through its CPU business.

COMPUTERS ARE TALKING

With Sun Microelectronics, a division of Sun Microsystems, Inc., Samsung Electronics has embarked on a strategic alliance to develop, market and manufacture chips based on Sun's PicoJava microprocessor core in order to capture a major share of a fast-growing multibillion dollar market. Look for a new generation of diversified electronics products to communicate with each other like never before.

FLASH FORWARD

Through a technical alliance with Toshiba, Samsung Electronics, has succeeded in developing the world's smallest flash memory card. No bigger than a postage stamp, the card programs 10 times as fast as floppy and hard disks. Its future in small electronics goods is bright.

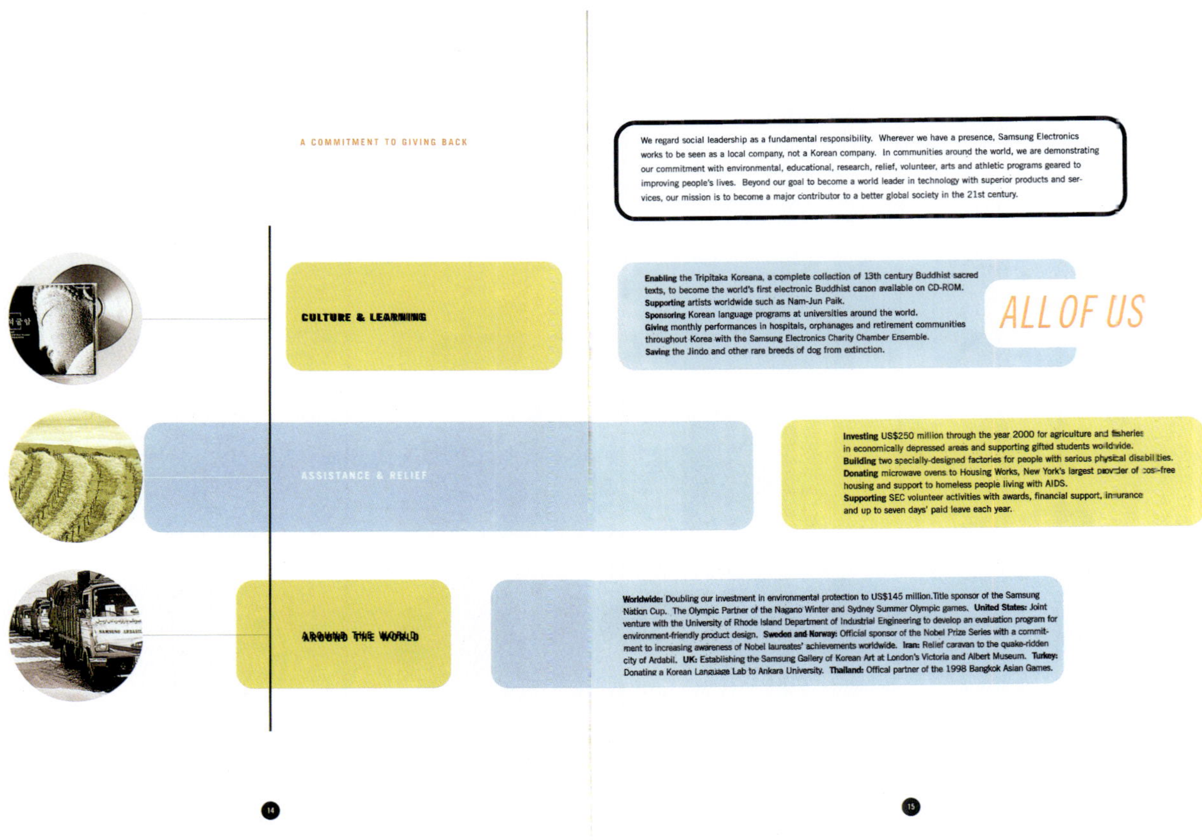

A COMMITMENT TO GIVING BACK

We regard social leadership as a fundamental responsibility. Wherever we have a presence, Samsung Electronics works to be seen as a local company, not a Korean company. In communities around the world, we are demonstrating our commitment with environmental, educational, research, relief, volunteer, arts and athletic programs geared to improving people's lives. Beyond our goal to become a world leader in technology with superior products and services, our mission is to become a major contributor to a better global society in the 21st century.

CULTURE & LEARNING

Enabling the Tripitaka Koreana, a complete collection of 13th century Buddhist sacred texts, to become the world's first electronic Buddhist canon available on CD-ROM.
Supporting artists worldwide such as Nam-Jun Paik.
Sponsoring Korean language programs at universities around the world.
Giving monthly performances in hospitals, orphanages and retirement communities throughout Korea with the Samsung Electronics Charity Chamber Ensemble.
Saving the Jindo and other rare breeds of dog from extinction.

ALL OF US

ASSISTANCE & RELIEF

Investing US$250 million through the year 2000 for agriculture and fisheries in economically depressed areas and supporting gifted students worldwide.
Building two specially-designed factories for people with serious physical disabilities.
Donating microwave ovens to Housing Works, New York's largest provider of cost-free housing and support to homeless people living with AIDS.
Supporting SEC volunteer activities with awards, financial support, insurance and up to seven days' paid leave each year.

AROUND THE WORLD

Worldwide: Doubling our investment in environmental protection to US$145 million.Title sponsor of the Samsung Nation Cup. The Olympic Partner of the Nagano Winter and Sydney Summer Olympic games. **United States:** Joint venture with the University of Rhode Island Department of Industrial Engineering to develop an evaluation program for environment-friendly product design. **Sweden and Norway:** Official sponsor of the Nobel Prize Series with a commitment to increasing awareness of Nobel laureates' achievements worldwide. **Iran:** Relief caravan to the quake-ridden city of Ardabil. **UK:** Establishing the Samsung Gallery of Korean Art at London's Victoria and Albert Museum. **Turkey:** Donating a Korean Language Lab to Ankara University. **Thailand:** Offical partner of the 1998 Bangkok Asian Games.

14 15

COMMUNICATE SASKFILMS ACTIVITIES FOR 1997 1998 CANADA CL,CW: SaskFILM CD,AD,D: Catharine Bradbury DF: Bradbury Design Inc.

EDITORIALS

DEBUT DIRECTOR PROGRAM MAKES DIRTY MONEY

8

DIRTY MONEY

The second project to be produced in 1997 under the auspices of the Debut Director program, *Dirty Money* is an action comedy, a genre relatively new to Saskatchewan. When well-meaning Hal Norbert (Iain McLean) applies for work as a "driver," he gets more than he bargained for as his erstwhile employers turn out to be small-time bank robbers, eager to set him up for the crime. The story follows a number of twists as Hal tries to turn himself in and clear his name.

In keeping with the objectives of the Debut Director program, the crew, cast and principals behind this half hour television program were all from Saskatchewan, many receiving their first dramatic credit.

Dirty Money was produced in association with STV, a member of the Global system. Major financial support was received from SaskFILM and Telefilm Canada, and from the Saskatchewan Motion Picture Association (SMPIA). Corporate sponsors included Kodak, Panavision Canada, Studio Post and Transfer and Royal Bank.

The director of *Dirty Money* was Dean Evans; the screenplay was written by Donna-Lynn McGregor. The project was produced by Regina-based Partners in Motion; producer was Chris Triffo and Production Manager was Joan Spiers.

Matt Holdesried, spokesperson for Moose Jaw's younger generation.

Photo: Jeff Beesley

HAVING THE LAST WORD FROM MOOSE JAW

It's summer in Moose Jaw, Saskatchewan, a quiet town in the middle of the Canadian prairie.

Or was that the middle of nowhere?

When you're young, that's how summer in Moose Jaw can feel. It's a nice town to retire to, but how many 20-year-olds are thinking of retiring?

Enter Murray Brace and Gary Hyland, two men with different ideas on what this town needs. Murray's a brash, young promoter who's trying to keep a struggling pro-baseball team on the field. Gary's an outspoken poet who's organizing a first-class literary festival. Two different projects. Two different motives. But one common goal: to give those who live in Moose Jaw something to believe in.

For one man, there will be a last-minute success. For the other, bitter disappointment...

This documentary was a labour of love for 24 year old director Jeff Beesley, who lives in Moose Jaw. Jeff's previous work includes the award-winning documentary *Percy, Me and Bobby McGee*, and he is currently in pre-production on the low budget feature *Rust*, a co-production with Toronto-based Deborah Day Film Productions Inc. Regina-based co-writer Devin Keefe worked closely with Jeff throughout production, and videographer Todd Irving realized the unique look of the film.

The Last Word From Moose Jaw was produced by Gordon McLennan of Regina-based Reel Eye Media. Gordon's skills as a director and producer have been applied to a number of recent productions including the TV movie *Paris or Somewhere*, low budget feature *Risk*, and documentaries including *The Play's the Thing* and *The Trickster*. Gordon is currently in pre-production on the low budget feature *Bad Money* and is developing his own screenplay entitled *Standard Deviation*.

The Last Word From Moose Jaw was broadcast on CBC Newsworld's Rough Cuts series on November 29, 1997. The producer is currently in discussions regarding international distribution.

SERIES MADE OF TOUGH STUFF

Tough Stuff explores the lives of individuals who suffer, cope and survive, day by day. Their courage and tenacity are almost unimaginable. These unsung heroes live with life-threatening illnesses and serious disabilities, they bravely accept their fates whether it be life, death or merely another day on this earth surrounded by the people they love.

The three one-hour documentary episodes document the fighting spirit of these individuals and show how their illnesses or disabilities challenge the people nearest them. Produced by Anthony Towstego of Tri-Media Productions in Saskatoon, the project brings together the directorial skills of Bonnie Andrukaitis (*DES: An Uncertain Legacy, After Tianimen Square*) and Anthony Towstego, and is researched by Dr. Colleen Fitzgerald and Bonnie Andrukaitis. Writer and Production Manager for the series is Jeff Martel.

Tough Stuff will be broadcast in 1998 on Vision-TV and Saskatchewan Communications Network (SCN). The series was developed with assistance from the National Film Board, SCN and SaskFILM, and is produced with the participation of the Canada Television and Cable Production Fund and SaskFILM. Facilities were provided by the Edge Productions.

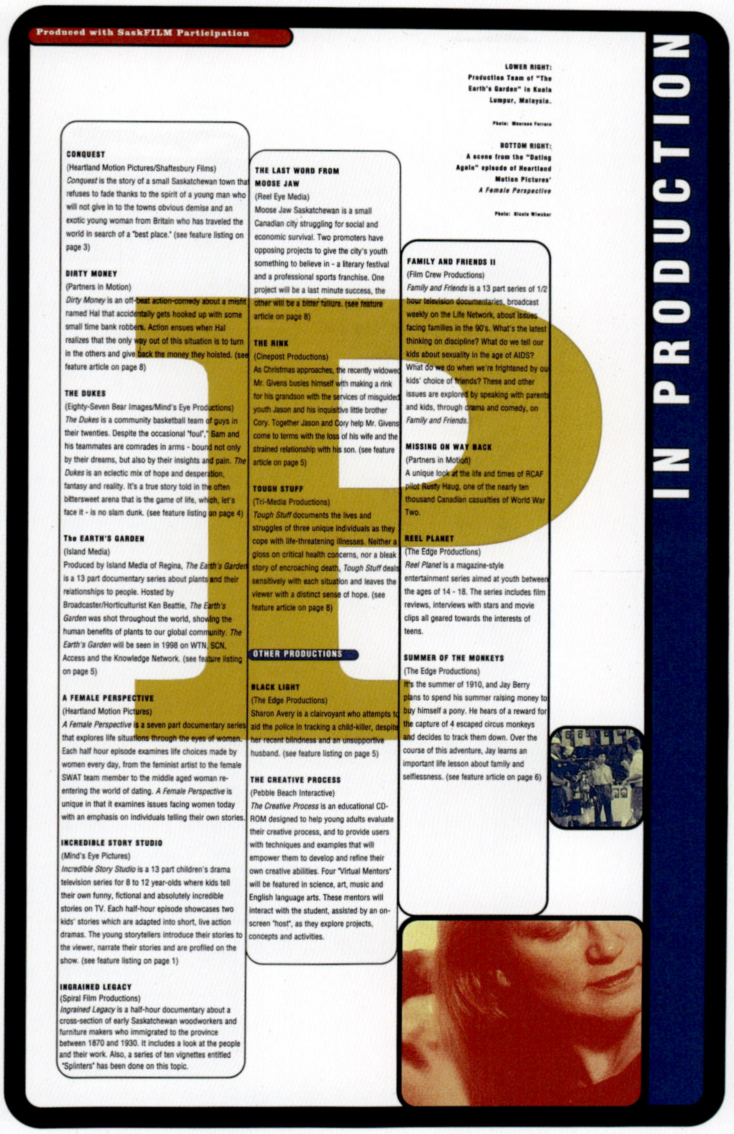

Produced with SaskFILM Participation

IN PRODUCTION

CONQUEST
(Heartland Motion Pictures/Shaftesbury Films)
Conquest is the story of a small Saskatchewan town that refuses to fade thanks to the spirit of a young man who will not give in to the towns obvious demise and an exotic young woman from Britain who has traveled the world in search of a "best place." (see feature listing on page 3)

DIRTY MONEY
(Partners in Motion)
Dirty Money is an off-beat action-comedy about a misfit named Hal that accidentally gets hooked up with some small time bank robbers. Action ensues when Hal realizes that the only way out of this situation is to turn in the others and give back the money they hoisted. (see feature article on page 8)

THE DUKES
(Eighty-Seven Bear Images/Mind's Eye Productions)
The Dukes is a community basketball team of guys in their twenties. Despite the occasional "foul"," Sam and his teammates are comrades in arms - bound not only by their dreams, but also by their insights and pain. *The Dukes* is an eclectic mix of hope and desperation, fantasy and reality. It's a true story told in the often bittersweet arena that is the game of life, which, let's face it - is no slam dunk. (see feature listing on page 4)

The EARTH'S GARDEN
(Island Media)
Produced by Island Media of Regina, *The Earth's Garden* is a 13 part documentary series about plants and their relationships to people. Hosted by Broadcaster/Horticulturist Ken Beattie, *The Earth's Garden* was shot throughout the world, showing the human benefits of plants to our global community. *The Earth's Garden* will be seen in 1998 on WTN, SCN, Access and the Knowledge Network. (see feature listing on page 5)

A FEMALE PERSPECTIVE
(Heartland Motion Pictures)
A Female Perspective is a seven part documentary series that explores life situations through the eyes of women. Each half hour episode examines life choices made by women every day, from the feminist artist to the female SWAT team member to the middle aged woman re-entering the world of dating. *A Female Perspective* is unique in that it examines issues facing women today with an emphasis on individuals telling their own stories.

INCREDIBLE STORY STUDIO
(Mind's Eye Pictures)
Incredible Story Studio is a 13 part children's drama television series for 8 to 12 year-olds where kids tell their own funny, fictional and absolutely incredible stories on TV. Each half-hour episode showcases two kids' stories which are adapted into short, live action dramas. The young storytellers introduce their stories to the viewer, narrate their stories and are profiled on the show. (see feature listing on page 1)

INGRAINED LEGACY
(Spiral Film Productions)
Ingrained Legacy is a half-hour documentary about a cross-section of early Saskatchewan woodworkers and furniture makers who immigrated to the province between 1870 and 1930. It includes a look at the people and their work. Also, a series of ten vignettes entitled "Splinters" has been done on this topic.

THE LAST WORD FROM MOOSE JAW
(Reel Eye Media)
Moose Jaw Saskatchewan is a small Canadian city struggling for social and economic survival. Two promoters have opposing projects to give the city's youth something to believe in - a literary festival and a professional sports franchise. One project will be a last minute success, the other will be a bitter failure. (see feature article on page 8)

THE RINK
(Cinepost Productions)
As Christmas approaches, the recently widowed Mr. Givens busies himself with making a rink for his grandson with the services of misguided youth Jason and his inquisitive little brother Cory. Together Jason and Cory help Mr. Givens come to terms with the loss of his wife and the strained relationship with his son. (see feature article on page 5)

TOUGH STUFF
(Tri-Media Productions)
Tough Stuff documents the lives and struggles of three unique individuals as they cope with life-threatening illnesses. Neither a gloss on critical health concerns, nor a bleak story of encroaching death, *Tough Stuff* deals sensitively with each situation and leaves the viewer with a distinct sense of hope. (see feature article on page 8)

OTHER PRODUCTIONS

BLACK LIGHT
(The Edge Productions)
Sharon Avery is a clairvoyant who attempts to aid the police in tracking a child-killer, despite her recent blindness and an unsupportive husband. (see feature listing on page 5)

THE CREATIVE PROCESS
(Pebble Beach Interactive)
The Creative Process is an educational CD-ROM designed to help young adults evaluate their creative process, and to provide users with techniques and examples that will empower them to develop and refine their own creative abilities. Four "Virtual Mentors" will be featured in science, art, music and English language arts. These mentors will interact with the student, assisted by an on-screen "host", as they explore projects, concepts and activities.

LOWER RIGHT: Production Team of "The Earth's Garden" in Kuala Lumpur, Malaysia.

Photo: Maureen Ferrara

BOTTOM RIGHT: A scene from the "Dating Again" episode of Heartland Motion Pictures' *A Female Perspective*

Photo: Nicole Wiesbar

FAMILY AND FRIENDS II
(Film Crew Productions)
Family and Friends is a 13 part series of 1/2 hour television documentaries, broadcast weekly on the Life Network, about issues facing families in the 90's. What's the latest thinking on discipline? What do we tell our kids about sexuality in the age of AIDS? What do we do when we're frightened by our kids' choice of friends? These and other issues are explored by speaking with parents and kids, through drama and comedy, on *Family and Friends*.

MISSING ON WAY BACK
(Partners in Motion)
A unique look at the life and times of RCAF pilot Rusty Haug, one of the nearly ten thousand Canadian casualties of World War Two.

REEL PLANET
(The Edge Productions)
Reel Planet is a magazine-style entertainment series aimed at youth between the ages of 14 - 18. The series includes film reviews, interviews with stars and movie clips all geared towards the interests of teens.

SUMMER OF THE MONKEYS
(The Edge Productions)
It's the summer of 1910, and Jay Berry plans to spend his summer raising money to buy himself a pony. He hears of a reward for the capture of 4 escaped circus monkeys and decides to track them down. Over the course of this adventure, Jay learns an important life lesson about family and selflessness. (see feature article on page 6)

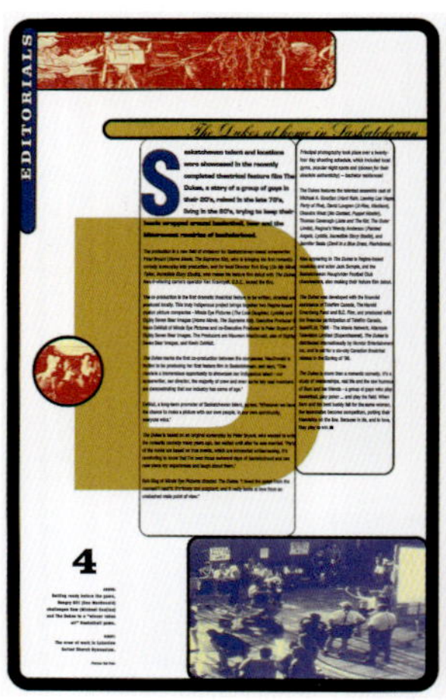

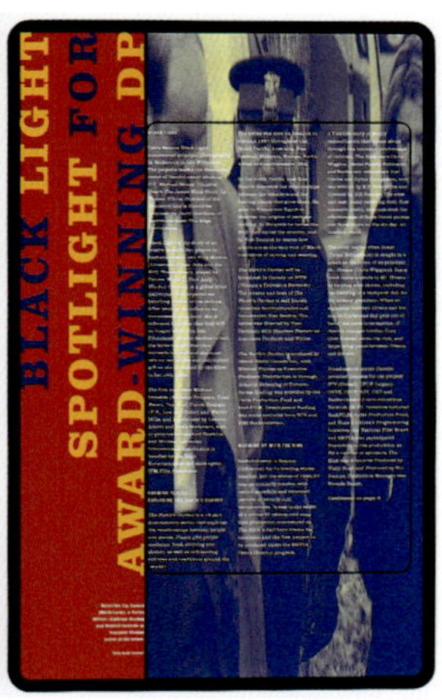

COVER

BROCHURE ブローシャー

FOSTER PEPPER SHEFELMAN CAPABILITIES BROCHURE 1999 USA

CL: Foster Pepper Shefelman AD: John Hornall AD,D: Katha Dalton
D: Mary Hermes / Steffanie Lorig / Alan Copeland / Michael Brugman P: Paul Conrath
CW: Suky Hutton DF: Hornall Anderson Design Works

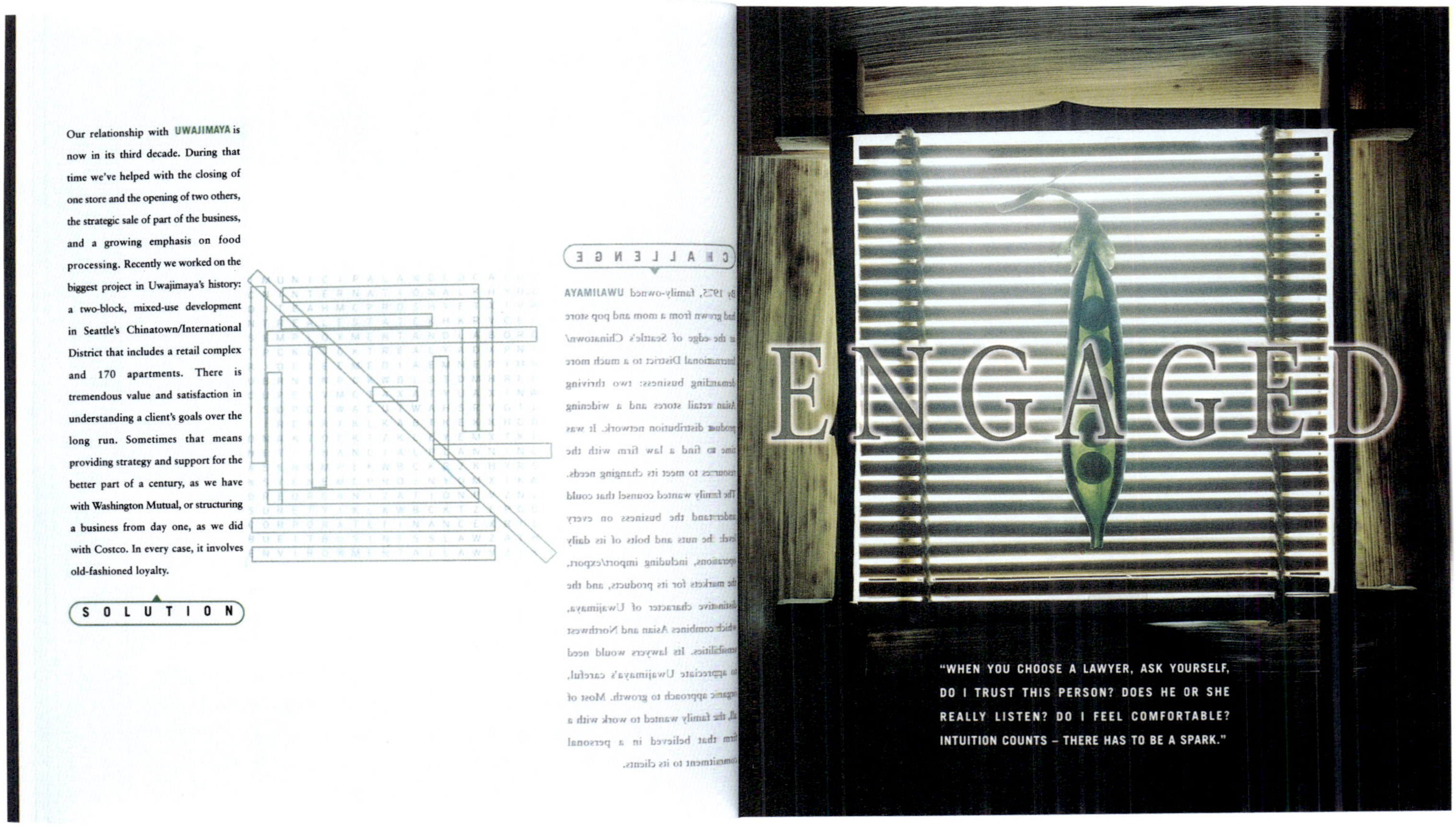

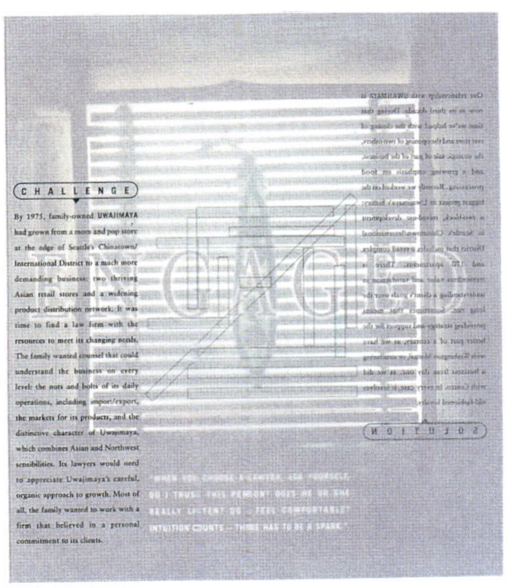

COVER

L'ÂME DU GRUYÈRE 1999 FRANCE/SWITZERLAND CL: Mifroma CD,AD,D: Marc Borgers P: Nicolas Repond CW: Didier Schmutz DF: Borgers Unlimited

A mesure que se prolonge le séjour dans les caves de Mifroma, le goût s'allonge, s'enrichit. Mais un affinage de longue durée ne va pas sans risque. Les meules requièrent un maximum d'attention et de suivi. Il faut constamment surveiller l'évolution; après douze mois d'encavage, il peut arriver que des pièces tournent déjà au goût de poireau ou de vinaigre.

Dans les Halles de Rungis

"Les consommateurs évoluent diablement vite. Depuis deux ans, nous avons enregistré une baisse de 50% sur le Gruyère de 6 mois. La demande s'est reportée sur les produits fruités, qui affichent une nette augmentation. Nous avons une forte demande pour les Gruyères d'alpage."

Les crémiers parisiens qui viennent s'approvisionner ici recherchent des fromages sortant de l'ordinaire. Ils sont servis par des professionnels animés de cette passion du fromage qui inspire la confiance. Dans les Halles de Rungis, il y a commerce bien sûr, mais un commerce à échelle humaine, loin du profit à outrance. On recherche avant tout la qualité du produit et la satisfaction du client.

Exigences de base des grossistes de Rungis: douze mois d'affinage au minimum. Pâte fruitée, longue, grasse. Croûte noire. Les cirons ne dérangent pas. Au contraire, l'œil français apprécie l'aspect rustique.

Festin de vache

Flouve odorante, fétuque noirâtre, pâturin des Alpes, trèfle brun, anthyllis, alchémille, trèfle des Alpes, la vache se régale. Gourmande, elle recherche par-dessus tout le plantain des Alpes, le pissenlit des Alpes et la livèche mutteline – la plante qui donne au fromage d'alpage son goût de noisette. Plus prosaïquement, le pouvoir nutritif de la pelouse alpine est incomparable à d'autres cultures végétales de plaine. Composée de trois espèces végétales (graminées, légumineuses et plantes à fleurs ou dicotylédones), la flore alpine est très variée, tendre, pauvre en cellulose, mais riche en matières azotées; cette herbe favorise la lactation. Une forte évaporation, amplifiée encore par le vent, de grands écarts thermiques et une courte période de végétation sont autant de contraintes qui éliminent les plantes les plus faibles. Seules subsistent les meilleures, pour le plus grand plaisir des ruminants qui, de plus, choisissent en toute liberté les herbages de leur convenance... *"Question de goût personnel. Si tu passes quelques jours avec les bêtes, tu verras bien que les vaches ne mangent pas toutes la même herbe. Comme nous, elles ont leurs préférences!"* Germain et son fils avouent sans honte ne pas connaître le nom de toutes les fleurs qui composent le menu du troupeau. Plus alchimistes que botanistes, ils ont en revanche la maîtrise du lait.

COVER

BOOK 書籍

WALKER EVANS: SIGNS 1998 USA CL: J. Paul Getty Museum D: Jeffrey Cohen P: Charles Passela / Ellen Rosenbery DF: J. Paul Getty Trust Publication Services

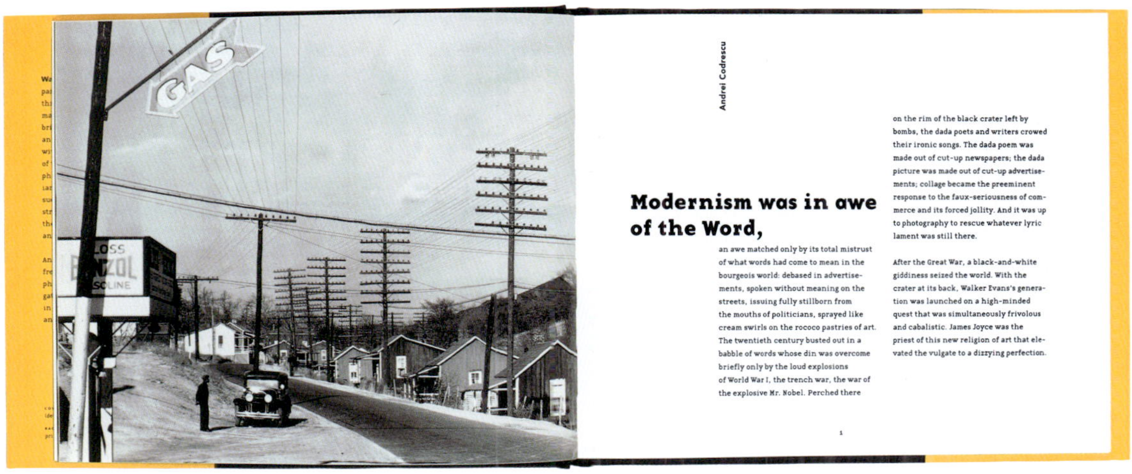

Andrei Codrescu

Modernism was in awe of the Word,

an awe matched only by its total mistrust of what words had come to mean in the bourgeois world: debased in advertisements, spoken without meaning on the streets, issuing fully stillborn from the mouths of politicians, sprayed like cream swirls on the rococo pastries of art. The twentieth century busted out in a babble of words whose din was overcome briefly only by the loud explosions of World War I, the trench war, the war of the explosive Mr. Nobel. Perched there on the rim of the black crater left by bombs, the dada poets and writers crowed their ironic songs. The dada poem was made out of cut-up newspapers; the dada picture was made out of cut-up advertisements; collage became the preeminent response to the faux-seriousness of commerce and its forced jollity. And it was up to photography to rescue whatever lyric lament was still there.

After the Great War, a black-and-white giddiness seized the world. With the crater at its back, Walker Evans's generation was launched on a high-minded quest that was simultaneously frivolous and cabalistic. James Joyce was the priest of this new religion of art that elevated the vulgate to a dizzying perfection.

1

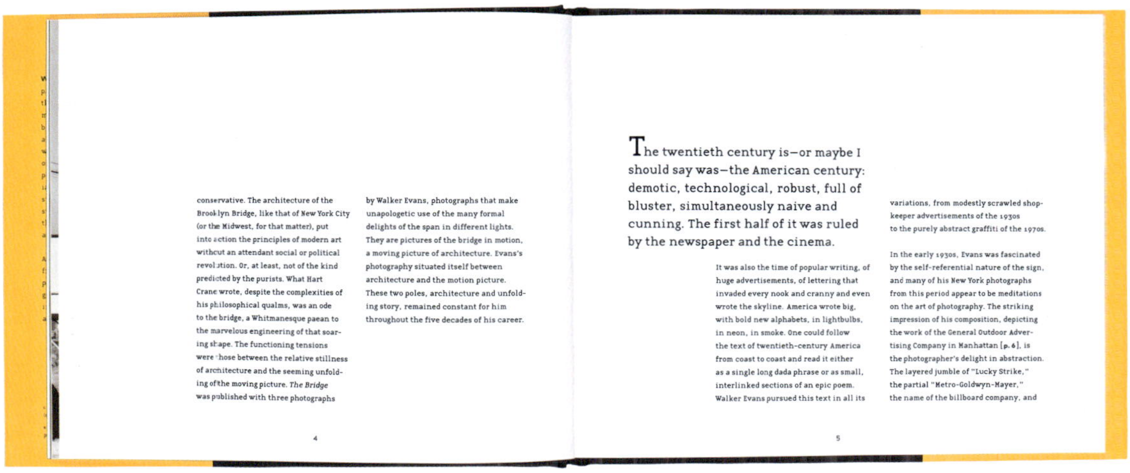

conservative. The architecture of the Brooklyn Bridge, like that of New York City (or the Midwest, for that matter), put into action the principles of modern art without an attendant social or political revolution. Or, at least, not of the kind predicted by the purists. What Hart Crane wrote, despite the complexities of his philosophical qualms, was an ode to the bridge, a Whitmanesque paean to the marvelous engineering of that soaring shape. The functioning tensions were those between the relative stillness of architecture and the seeming unfolding of the moving picture. *The Bridge* was published with three photographs by Walker Evans, photographs that make unapologetic use of the many formal delights of the span in different lights. They are pictures of the bridge in motion, a moving picture of architecture. Evans's photography situated itself between architecture and the motion picture. These two poles, architecture and unfolding story, remained constant for him throughout the five decades of his career.

4

The twentieth century is—or maybe I should say was—the American century: demotic, technological, robust, full of bluster, simultaneously naive and cunning. The first half of it was ruled by the newspaper and the cinema.

It was also the time of popular writing, of huge advertisements, of lettering that invaded every nook and cranny and even wrote the skyline. America wrote big, with bold new alphabets, in lightbulbs, in neon, in smoke. One could follow the text of twentieth-century America from coast to coast and read it either as a single long dada phrase or as small, interlinked sections of an epic poem. Walker Evans pursued this text in all its variations, from modestly scrawled shopkeeper advertisements of the 1930s to the purely abstract graffiti of the 1970s.

In the early 1930s, Evans was fascinated by the self-referential nature of the sign, and many of his New York photographs from this period appear to be meditations on the art of photography. The striking impression of his composition, depicting the work of the General Outdoor Advertising Company in Manhattan [p. 6], is the photographer's delight in abstraction. The layered jumble of "Lucky Strike," the partial "Metro-Goldwyn-Mayer," the name of the billboard company, and

5

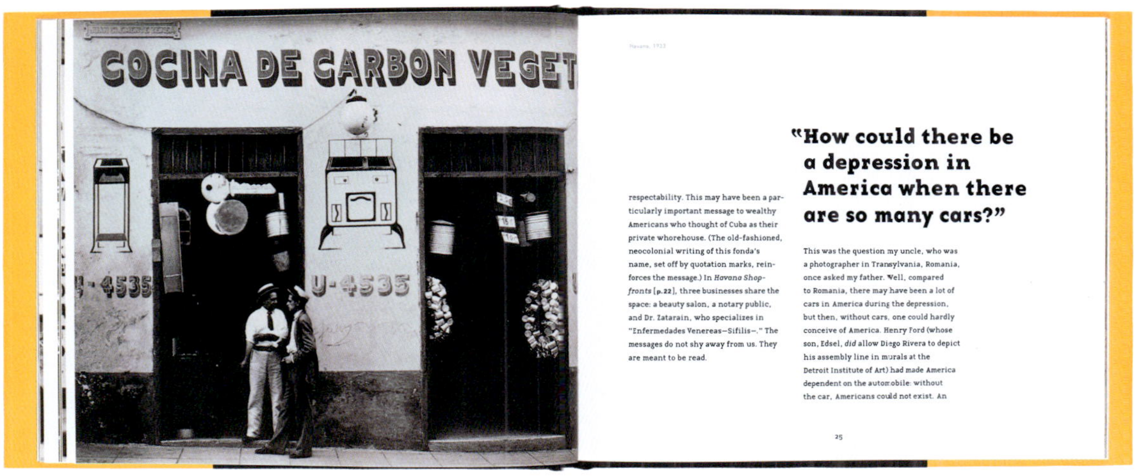

Havana, 1933

respectability. This may have been a particularly important message to wealthy Americans who thought of Cuba as their private whorehouse. (The old-fashioned, neocolonial writing of this fonda's name, set off by quotation marks, reinforces the message.) In *Havana Shopfronts* [p. 22], three businesses share the space: a beauty salon, a notary public, and Dr. Zatarain, who specializes in "Enfermedades Venereas—Sifilis—." The messages do not shy away from us. They are meant to be read.

"How could there be a depression in America when there are so many cars?"

This was the question my uncle, who was a photographer in Transylvania, Romania, once asked my father. Well, compared to Romania, there may have been a lot of cars in America during the depression, but then, without cars, one could hardly conceive of America. Henry Ford (whose son, Edsel, *did* allow Diego Rivera to depict his assembly line in murals at the Detroit Institute of Art) had made America dependent on the automobile: without the car, Americans could not exist. An

25

COVER

BROCHURE ブローシャー

NIESWAND TEASER BROCHURE 1999 GERMANY CL: Nieswand Printers CD,AD,D,I: Johannes Plass P: Olaf Fippinger CW: Georg Butter DF: Mutabor HH

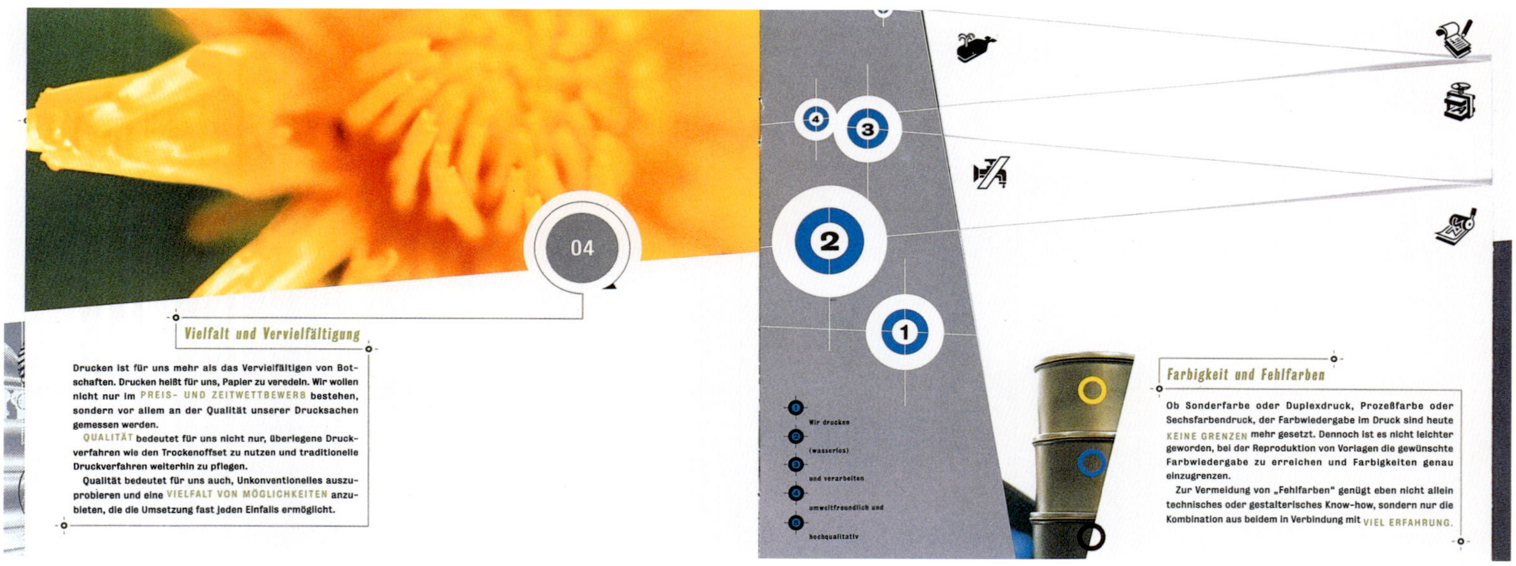

COVER

BROCHURE ブローシャー

VOOT 1999 BELGIUM CL: Ateliers De La Rue Voot CD,AD,D: Frederic Vanhorenbeke CW: Jean Luc Breuer DF: Coast

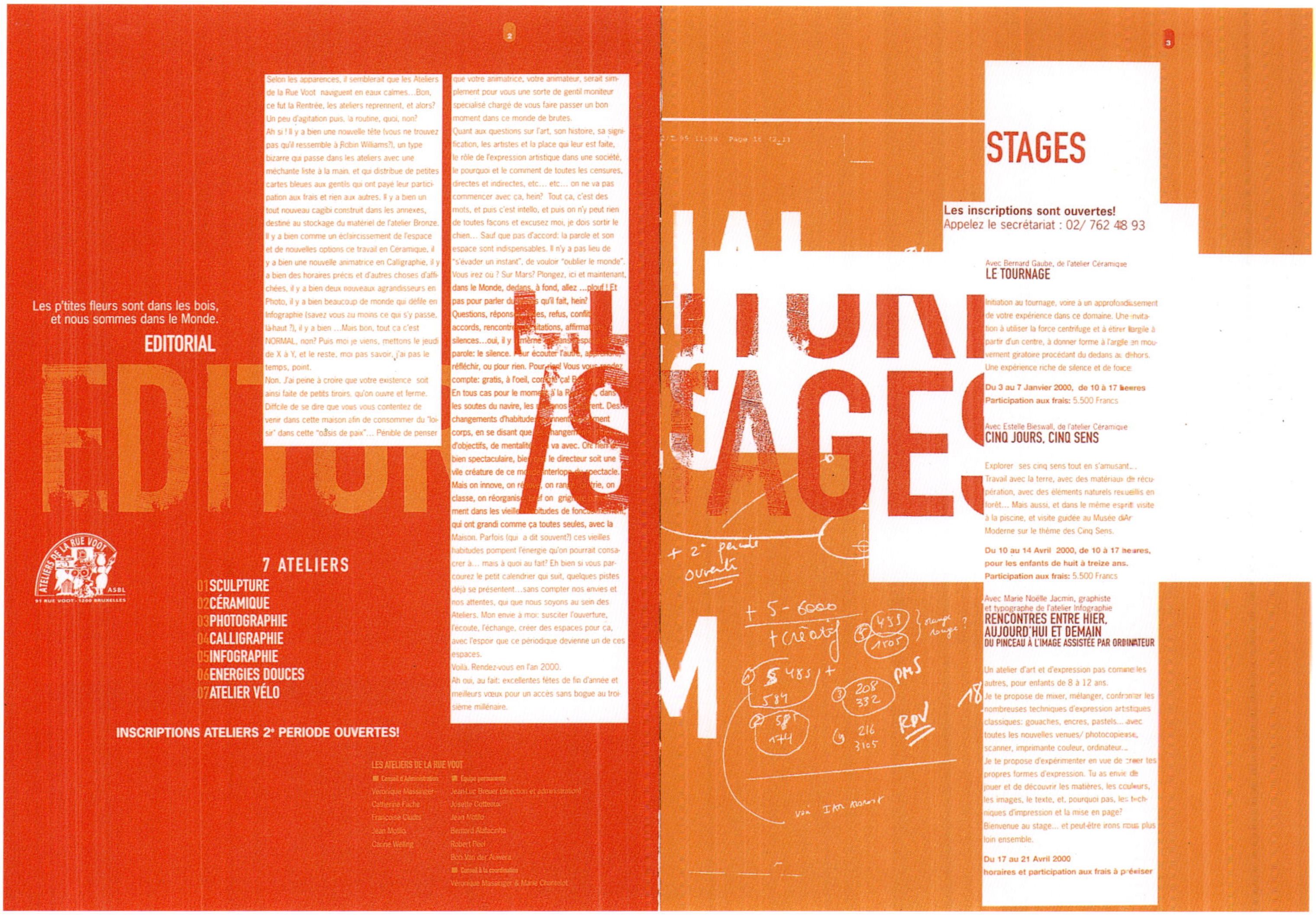

COVER

YUMMY! THE BEST COOKBOOK EVER BY KIDS 1996 NETHERLANDS CL: Oilily D,I: Paul Roeters / Jeroen Hoedjes CW: Eric Alink DF: Studio Kluif

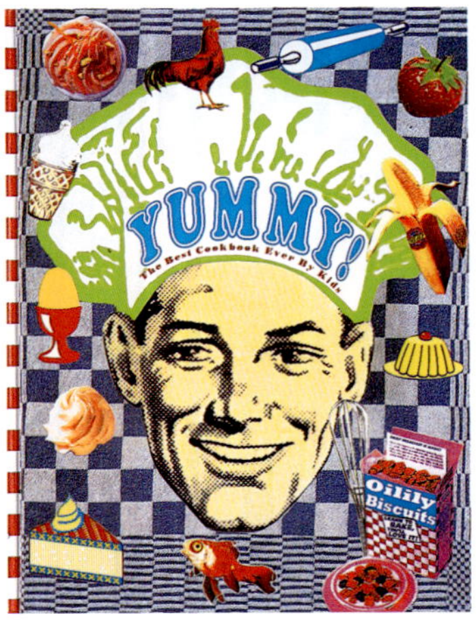

COVER

TAPTOE WINTER BOOK 1999 NETHERLANDS PB: Publisher Malmberg D: Paul Roeters / Jeroen Hoedjes DF: Studio Kluif

COVER

PAMPHLET パンフレット

TOPSTITCH 1997 USA CL: Topstitch CD: Lanny French D: Giorgio Davanzo CW: Peter Stocker DF: Foundation

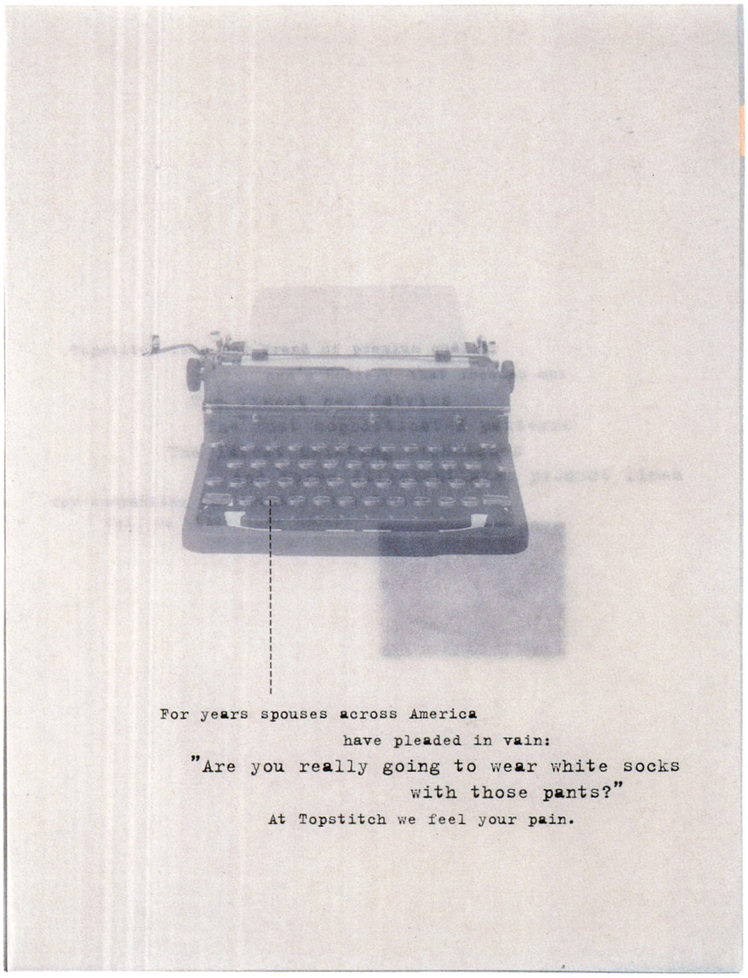

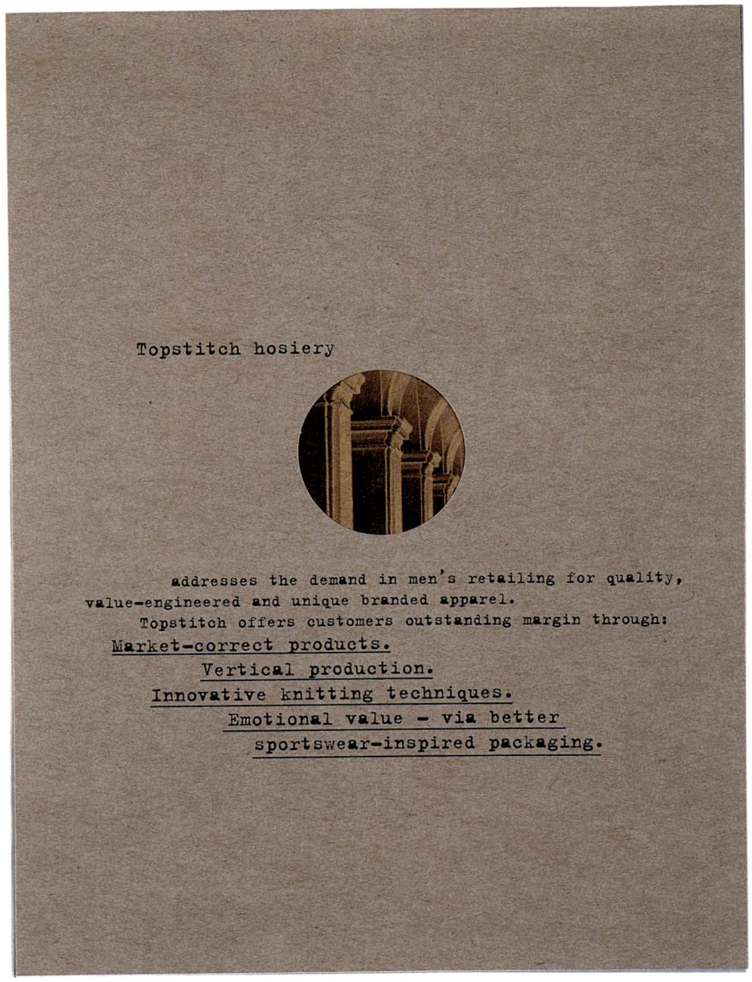

COVER

ACTUALITY 1997 USA

CL: California College of Arts and Crafts, School of Design AD,C: Bob Aufuldish P: Luis Delgado / Various CW: Mark Bartlett / Various
DF: Aufuldish & Warinner

word communication

Katherine Inglis

In today's changing and sometimes alienating world, it becomes increasingly important to remember the rituals that once bound people together. **Traditionally, family dinners served as one of the most effective rituals in this sense. Not only did they physically unite families on a daily basis, but they provided an open forum for discussion allowing children and adults alike to learn from and bond over each other's words. With the family structure and social values changing, the importance of this ritual is being lost.** Using typography in combination with a dinner table setting, I have tried to illustrate both the value in and endangerment of this ritual. The fundamental benefits of dining together are listed on the legs of the table: debating, arguing, sharing, philosophizing, articulating, reflecting. Circling the table are some of the modern circumstances that draw people away from the dinner table: conflicting schedules, dueling careers, the 80 hour work week, fast food, television. **As a result, fewer and fewer families dine together on a regular basis.** On the dinnerware itself, statistics illustrate the extent to which these factors have impaired communication. **In light of these facts, it is no wonder that parents often feel alienated from their children and that children lack the support and attention they once received from their parents. In order to communicate and nurture one another in a consistent and meaningful way we must reevaluate our priorities.** Not until we re-learn how to communicate within the home can we possibly hope to solve the problems our society faces at large.

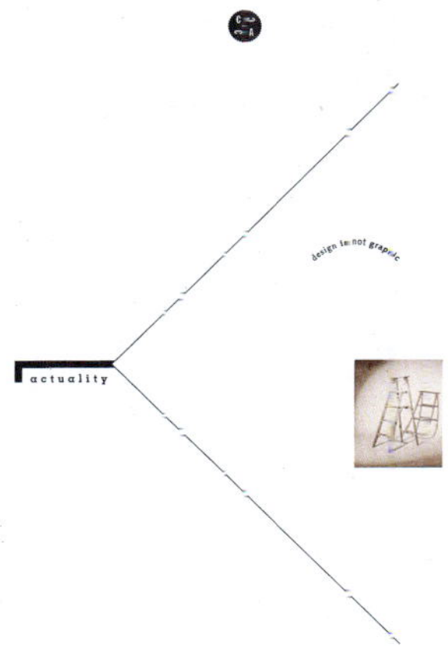

COVER

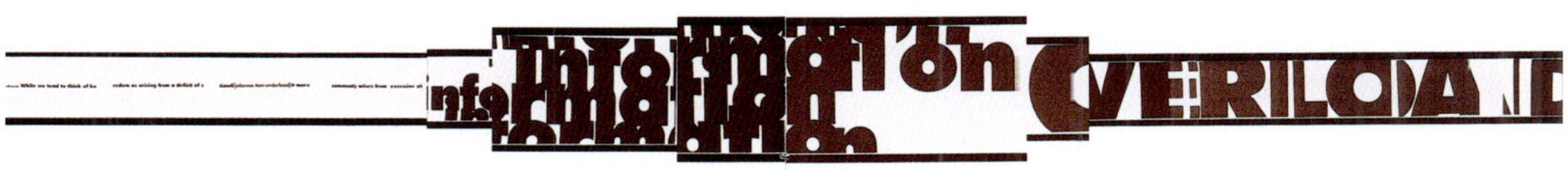

endeavor. While we tend to think of boredom as arising from a deficit of stimulation (information underload)

it more commonly arises from excessive stimulation: information overload.

The art of conversation has been preempted by technology in almost every area of our lives.

The idea that humans are more fallible than machines has caused us to turn towards technology for information and problem solving.

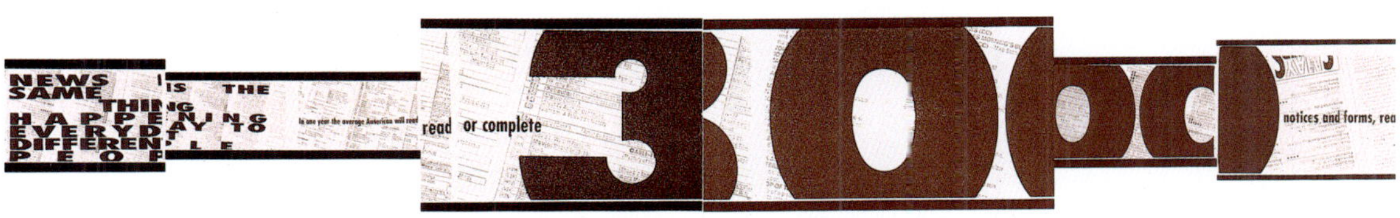

News is the same thing happening every day to different people.

In one year the average American will read or complete 3,000 notices and forms.

The search for technological progress is no longer a means but has become an end in itself,

escaping from human control and thus dominating man, alienating us from ourselves and our environment.

Ein Traum ohne Wirklichkeit bedeutet mir ebensowenig wie eine Wirklichkeit ohne Traum. Und das Theater besteht ja nur aus verwirklichten Träumen.

Max Reinhardt

MUSIK THEATER

Götterdämmerung
Zeitgenössische Oper
La sonnambula
Boris Godunow
Cosi fan tutte
Alcina
Glückliche Reise
Der Wildschütz
Don Pasquale

LA SONNAMBULA

Premiere 29. Januar 99

10

Vincenzo Bellini versuchte Ende der zwanziger Jahre des vorigen Jahrhunderts den belcanto-Stil im Sinne Rossinis zu größerer Dramatik zu führen. Nachdem Rossini 1829 seine letzte Oper geschrieben hatte, befand Bellini sich in heftiger Konkurrenz zu Donizetti. *La Straniera*, *I Puritani* und *Norma* waren, zusammen mit *La Sonnambula* seine größten Opernerfolge, die im 19. Jahrhundert weit verbreitet waren. In diesem Jahrhundert mußten seine Werke für das Musiktheater erst wieder entdeckt werden und erlebten durch Sängerinnen wie Maria Callas eine Renaissance. Man darf es als Kuriosum bezeichnen, daß in Oldenburg - soweit das Theaterarchiv Auskunft gibt - seit 1945 auf keinen Fall, wahrscheinlich sogar noch nie, eine Oper von Vincenzo Bellini aufgeführt wurde, so daß mit der Oldenburger Erstaufführung von *La Sonnambula* erstmals auch der Komponist Bellini vorgestellt wird.

Die Geschichte handelt von der schönen Amina, die dem reichen Elvino angetraut werden soll. Auch die Wirtin Lisa hat ein Auge auf den Gutsbesitzer geworfen und überlegt, wie sie die geplante Hochzeit hintertreiben kann. Unerkannt ist Graf Rodolfo, der Schloßbesitzer, zurückgekehrt. Zunächst nimmt er Quartier im Gasthof, wo einzig Lisa ihn wiedererkennt und versucht, seine Aufmerksamkeit zu erlangen. Bei einem nächtlichen Besuch in seinem Zimmer beobachtet sie, wie die schlafwandelnde Amina durchs Fenster steigt und sich in das Bett des Grafen legt. Graf Rodolfo, der jetzt erst hinzukommt, verläßt taktvollerweise das Zimmer, aber Lisa holt die Dorfbewohner und stellt Amina bloß. Damit ist die Verlobung mit Elvino geplatzt. Keiner glaubt dem Grafen Rodolfo, keiner hat bisher vom Phänomen des Schlafwandelns gehört. Erst am Hochzeitstag von Elvino und Lisa kommt die Wahrheit ans Licht.

Oper von Vincenzo Bellini

Oldenburger Erstaufführung

(in italienischer Sprache)

Musikalische Leitung: Raoul Grüneis

Inszenierung: Michael Beyer

Bühne und Kostüme: Markus Pysall

Großes Haus

BORIS GODUNOW

Premiere 26. März 99

11

Musikalisches Volksdrama nach

Alexander Puschkin und Nikolaj Karamsin

von Modest Mussorgskij (Urfassung)

Musikalische Leitung: Reinhard Seifried

Inszenierung, Bühne und Kostüme:

Joachim Griep

Großes Haus

Ein Vorfall aus der russischen Geschichte inspirierte Mussorgskij zu diesem großen Musikdrama: die Schwester des aus einem tartarischen Geschlecht stammenden Boris Godunow war mit Zar Fjodor I. (einem Sohn Iwan des Schrecklichen) verheiratet. Die Ehe blieb kinderlos. Boris Godunow ließ den Stiefbruder seines Schwagers, Dimitrij, und damit den letzten männlichen Nachkommen der Familie, ermorden, um sich selbst zum neuen Zaren zu krönen.

Die Oper beginnt mit der Krönungsszene des Boris - aus der Sicht des Volkes beschrieben: mit der Knute werden die Menschen gezwungen, die Bittkundgebungen für die Wahl des neuen Zaren nicht zu unterbrechen. Pilger beten, daß Aufruhr und Gottlosigkeit dem Vaterland erspart bleiben mögen. Unter den Huldigungen der Bojaren schreitet Boris zur Krönung in die Kathedrale. Bedroht wird Boris' Herrschaft durch die Nachricht, der ermordet geglaubte Dimitrij stünde an der polnischen Grenze, vom polnischen König und dem Papst unterstützt, bereit, den Zaren zu stürzen. Gewissensqualen und Wahnsinnsvisionen suchen Boris heim. Dimitrij ist in Wirklichkeit ein Mönch, der sich die Unzufriedenheit des geknechteten russischen Volkes zunutze macht. Boris stirbt und setzt seinen Sohn als Nachfolger ein. Draußen, in der Nähe der Stadt Kromy, jubelt das Volk begeistert dem falschen Dimitrij zu. Ein Schwachsinniger beklagt am Ende das tragische Schicksal seiner russischen Heimat.

Ganz bewußt nennt Mussorgskij seine Oper »Volksdrama«, spielt doch das russische Volk, sowohl in den Massenszenen als auch in individuellen Charakteren, die Hauptrolle und bietet somit eine anspruchsvolle Aufgabe für den Opernchor. Der spezifisch »russische« Tonfall der Komposition entsteht u.a. durch die Verwendung von Volksmelodien und die Verarbeitung russischer Kirchenmusik.

WAHLABONNEMENTS

72

Wahl-Abonnement

– 10 Vorstellungen aus den Produktionen des Staatstheaters
– Einteilung nach Platzgruppen
– Gültigkeit für eine Spielzeit

Dieses Abonnement ermöglicht es Ihnen, Kartenreservierungen an der Theaterkasse persönlich oder schriftlich eine Woche vor Beginn des allgemeinen Vorverkaufs vorzunehmen.
Davon ausgenommen sind Sonderveranstaltungen wie Silvester, Gastspiele usw. Der Wahl-Abonnementsausweis berechtigt nicht zum Einlaß.

Jugendwahl-Abonnement

10 Vorstellungen aus dem Gesamtspielplan ohne Anspruch auf einen bestimmten Platz – ab der 2. Platzgruppe –
Einheitspreis: DM 100,-

Für Jugendliche bis 18 Jahren, Schüler, Auszubildende, Studierende bis 35 Jahre, Helferinnen und Helfer im freiwilligen sozialen Jahr, Wehrpflichtige und Ersatzdienstleistende gegen Vorlage des entsprechenden Ausweises.
Das Jugendwahlabonnement kann nur jeweils für zwei Personen pro Vorstellung eingelöst werden.

Abonnementserweiterungen

Zusätzlich zu den Abonnements kann, mit Ausnahme der Wahlabonnements, bei der Buchung ein kleines Wahlabo mit zwei Vorstellungen der entsprechenden Platzgruppe erworben werden.
Diese Gutscheine können für eine beliebige Vorstellung des Oldenburgischen Staatstheaters gegen eine Eintrittskarte eingelöst werden.
Davon ausgenommen sind Sonderveranstaltungen wie Silvester, Gastspiele u.s.w.

Ab DM 130,-

Platzgruppe I	DM 415,-
Platzgruppe II	DM 365,-
Platzgruppe III	DM 290,-
Platzgruppe IV	DM 220,-
Platzgruppe V	DM 170,-
Platzgruppe VI	DM 130,-

Für DM 100,-

Ab DM 26,-

Platzgruppe I	DM 83,-
Platzgruppe II	DM 73,-
Platzgruppe III	DM 58,-
Platzgruppe IV	DM 44,-
Platzgruppe V	DM 34,-
Platzgruppe VI	DM 26,-

KONZERTABONNEMENT

73

Konzert- Abonnement So, Mo und Di

4 Vorstellungen im Großen Haus
4 Vorstellungen in der Weser-Ems-Halle

Kammerkonzert

Im Abonnement 6 Konzerte im Kleinen Haus

Ab DM 124,-

Platzgruppe I	DM 368,-
Platzgruppe II	DM 324,-
Platzgruppe III	DM 280,-
Platzgruppe IV	DM 232,-
Platzgruppe V	DM 168,-
Platzgruppe VI	DM 124,-

Für DM 87,-
unnumerierte Plätze

AUGUST HINRICHS BÜHNE

Bühnenleiter:
Herwig Dust
An den Voßbergen 43,
26133 Oldenburg,
Telefon 0441/42376
Kartenvorverkauf
an der Theaterkasse
Theaterwall 28

Abonnements
1, 2, 3, 4, 5, 6, 8, und Nr. 7, Sonntagnachmittag

3 Vorstellungen im Kleinen Haus

Schauspiel
Foftein
Rose Bernd
Dat Hörrohr

Ab DM 40,-

Platzgruppe I	DM 58,-
Platzgruppe II	DM 52,-
Platzgruppe III	DM 47,-
Platzgruppe IV	DM 40,-

NOTORIETY 1997 USA CL: California College of Arts and Crafts, School of Design AD,D Bob Aufuldish P: Luis Delgado / Various CW: Mark Bartlett CF: Aufuldish & Warinner

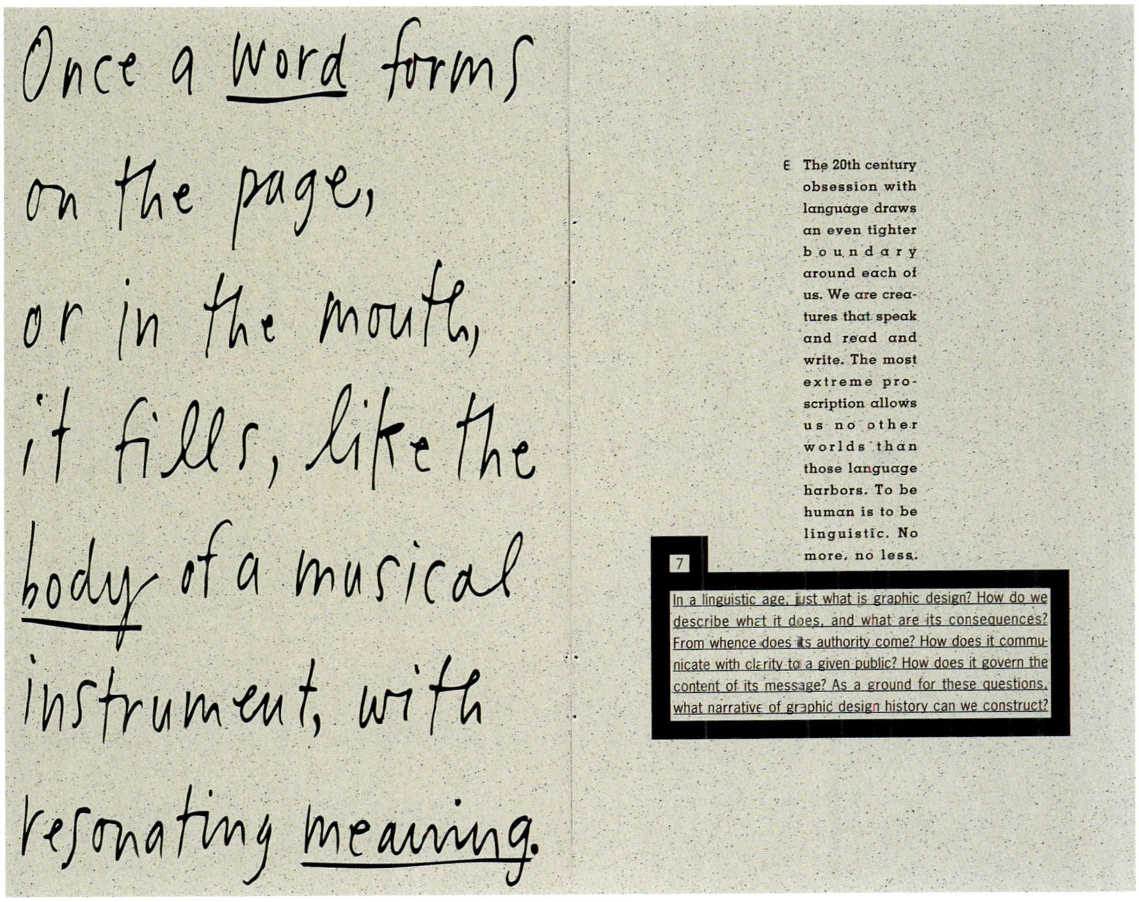

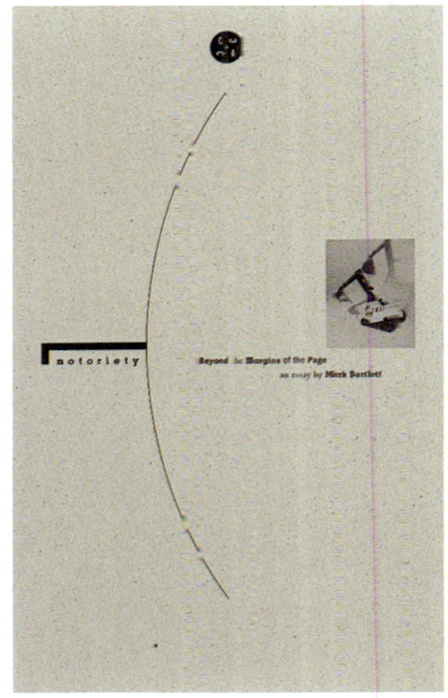

COVER

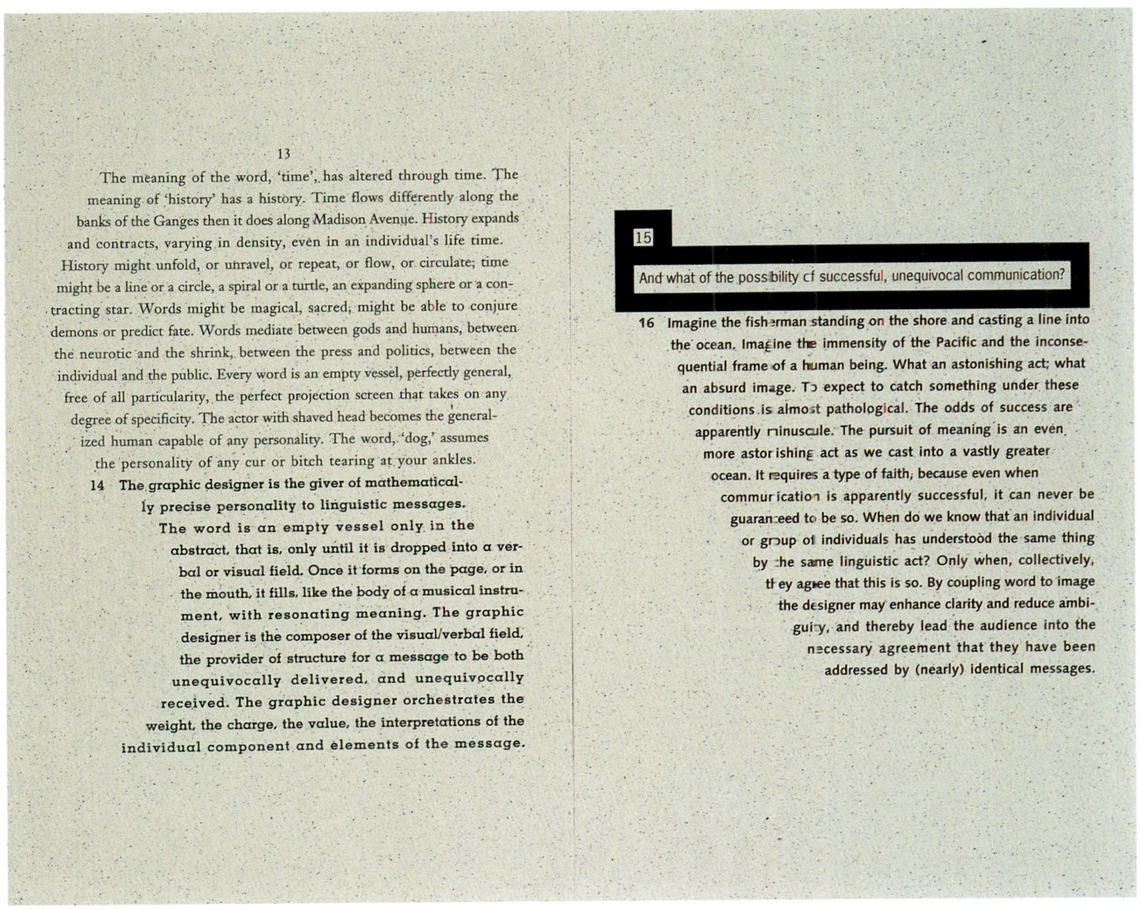

CATALOG カタログ

HARMONIA 4 1999 JAPAN

CL: H+B Lifescience Co., Ltd. CD: Daisuke Nakatsuka AD: Junko Nakatsuka
D: Fumiyo Kitazume / Hiromi Yamada / Mayumi Inoue / Tomoko Kanou P: François Gillet / Goro Arizona / Shozo Nakamura
CW: Tom Nakatsuka / Kenji Inoue / Yoshiyuki Watanabe Title design: Yoshifumi Nakashima DF: Nakatsuka Daisuke Inc.

COVER

サイクレアー ご注文は 0120-810-610まで。

紫外線から肌を守るために皮膚の基底層にあるメラノサイトはメラニン色素を作ります。でもストレス時によるメラニン色素の過剰生成や新陳代謝の遅れがシミソバカスの原因となります。

メラニン
メラノサイト
日焼けした肌のイメージ断面図

天然持続性美肌ビタミンCはブドウ糖を結合したビタミンC。肌の上では熱や空気に強く、体内ではブドウ糖が外れてビタミンCと同様に働きます。AA-2Gはアスコルビン酸2-グルコシドの略称です。

砂漠や荒野に暮らす女性たちは、なぜベールを被っているのでしょう。それは宗教や習慣以前に、つよい日差しから顔や体を守りたいという、女性の意志のあらわれではないでしょうか。考えてみれば、現代日本の生活は、砂漠ほどではないにしても、紫外線を裸の顔にあび、冷暖房のなかで、一年中ストレスにさらされているわけですから、厳重な注意が必要です。

林原は、そんな環境に対して「美肌化粧品」というコンセプトを提出します。美肌とは、シミ・ソバカスのない白い肌、すなわち「美白」と、みずみずしく透明感のある素肌、いいかえれば「保湿」という、化粧品に求められるふたつの要素を同時に満たそうというもの。林原は、この美肌を実現するために、自社が開発したふたつの基本成分を用意。サイクレアーに処方しました。

天然持続性美肌ビタミンC(AA-2G)は、美白効果を期待して処方されています。このビタミンCは、グルコース(ブドウ糖)と結合することで、従来とは違って熱や酸化に強い性質を獲得しました。ですから、皮膚の基底層にあるメラノサイトまで確実に届いて、メラニンの生成を長時間にわたって抑えます。

もうひとつの基本成分トレハロースには、すぐれた保湿効果があることが、確認されています。トレハロースは、自然界にごく普通にみられる糖質ですが、砂漠や荒野で、干からびた生物を甦らせる「復活現象」で知られます。林原は、天然のデンプンから、この糖質の量産化に世界ではじめて成功したのです。いかがですか。サイクレアーは、医薬部外品、無香料、無着色。基本の3ステップを補強し相乗効果が期待できる新製品も次々に登場しています。詳しくは次の頁をどうぞ。

SCiCLAIR
FACE WASH

19

肌は枯れたら、捨てられますか。

林原の安定型ビタミンC、トレハロース配合の美肌化粧品。サイクレアー。

マービー ご注文は 0120-810-610まで。

インシュリンは膵臓が分泌するホルモン。上がりすぎた血糖値を抑える、脂肪を優先的に取り込むなどの働きがあります。そのため糖質と脂肪を一緒に摂れば太る原因につながります。また働きが低下すれば糖尿病の原因となります。

マービーの原料は、還元麦芽糖水飴。トウモロコシなどのデンプンを酵素で分解してできた麦芽糖(分子が二つの糖)を還元することで、消化吸収されにくい分子構造をつくりました。

スリムの大敵は、脂肪と一緒に甘いものを食べることといわれます。それではその原理を考えてみましょう。「砂糖が血糖値を上げると、脂肪を体にためこむインシュリンが分泌されます」と語るのはダンベル体操で有名な、筑波大学の鈴木正成教授。すい臓から分泌されるホルモンであるインシュリンには、上がりすぎた血糖値を抑えて正常に保つ大切な働きと、脂肪を優先的に体に蓄積してしまうダイエット中の人には困った働きがあるのです。

そこで砂糖のように使えるのに、血糖値を上げにくい。またインシュリンの分泌を促しにくい性質のある、低カロリー甘味料マービーをご紹介いたしましょう。

マービーの原料は、トウモロコシなどの天然のデンプンから生まれた、還元麦芽糖水飴。林原の酵素技術が、小腸で吸収されにくい分子構造を実現しました。血糖値の急激な上昇を起こさないため、インシュリンの分泌を促しにくく、脂肪分と一緒に摂っても安心です。また、虫歯の原因となる酸や粘膜質をつくらないのでお子さまのおやつにもおすすめです。

マービーは、熱を加えても苦味が出たり、色が変わることがないので、ふつうのお料理にも堂々とお使いいただけます。ダイエット中の人は家族と別メニューでは寂しいですよね。煮物や料理の甘味料、お菓子づくりなどに、ご家族皆さんでお使いください。

糖尿病、肥満症用の厚生省許可特別用途食品に認定されて、25年以上愛用されてきたマービー。林原の1世紀をこえる研究開発から生まれた、この進化した水飴の長所を最後にもう一つご紹介します。それはなにより美味しいことです。

MARVIE

31

水飴がひとを救う。

自然が生んだ、理想の低カロリー甘味料。マービー。

COMPANY PROFILE 1998 JAPAN CL: Mercedes-Benz Japan Co., Ltd. CD: Kazuhiko Takagi AD: Kenji Inukai D: Kazuo Aono P: Tsuyoshi Ohsawa CW: Hiroshi Satoh
Agency: Magnetic Communications Inc. Planning: Adlay Inc.

Mercedes-Benz
Philosophy
歴史

1928年頃のジンデルフィンゲン工場。当時、ダイムラー・ベンツはすでに乗用車、商用車の大量生産を始めていました

The Sindelfingen Plant ca.1928. Daimler-Benz AG had already begun producing both passenger cars and commercial vehicles.

1844年生まれのカール・ベンツは1882年に2サイクル・エンジンを開発した後、1886年にパテント3輪ガソリン自動車を発表

Born in 1844, Karl Benz completed the two-cycle engine in 1882 and presented the gasoline-powered three-wheeled Patent Motor Car in 1886.

ゴットリープ・ダイムラーは1834年生まれ。1885年にエンジンを搭載した2輪車を考案、翌1886年に4輪ガソリン自動車を発表

Gottlieb Daimler was born in 1834. After devising an engined two-wheeled car in 1885, he premiered the four-wheeled gasoline car in 1886.

自動車の歴史が幕を開けたのは1886年のことでした。それまで独自にエンジンや2輪車の開発を行ってきた2人のドイツ人が時を同じくして画期的な発表を行ったのです。ゴットリープ・ダイムラーが4輪ガソリン自動車を、カール・ベンツが3輪ガソリン自動車を発明。2人は方法論に違いこそあれ、それぞれ同じ夢を抱いていたのです。そしてこの時、メルセデス・ベンツの歴史も輝かしい最初の一歩を記すことになりました。

左◎ダイムラー4輪自動車は馬車を改造し、エンジンを搭載していました
右◎ベンツ3輪自動車は後部に大きなフライホイールを備えていました

Left: Daimler made his four-wheeler by modifying a horse-powered coach and fitting it with an engine.
Right: Benz's three-wheeler is equipped with a large flywheel at the rear.

ダイムラー社はその後も斬新なエンジンの開発を続け、タクシーやトラックの開発にも精力的に取り組みました。1900年代初頭にはダイムラー社の飛行船や航空機用のエンジンが開発されています。一方、ベンツ社もバス、デリバリーバン、ツーリングカーなど用途に応じたさまざまなタイプの自動車を発表、1894年に小型車「ベロ」の量産を小規模ながら始めました。

「メルセデス」は1899年にダイムラー社がニースで開催された自動車レースに出場した際のレース車の名称です。当時、ダイムラーの良きビジネスパートナーであったエミール・イェリネックの11歳になる末娘の名にちなんで名付けられたものです。「メルセデス」はその後も多くのレースで輝かしい戦績を残し、ダイムラーは「メルセデス」をダイムラー車の商標として登録。メルセデス・ベンツの名はこれに由来しているのです。この間、ベンツもヨーロッパで盛んに行われるようになった自動車レースに積極的に参加していました。ダイムラーとベンツはここでも良きライバルとなり、2人が送り出した自動車は常に上位に入賞、その技術は絶大な信頼を集めることになったのです。

The history of automobiles opened its first chapter in 1886 when two Germans who had independently developed engines and motor bikes made epoch-making announcements. Gottlieb Daimler invented a gasoline-engined four-wheeled car, and Karl Benz a three-wheeler. Although their methods differed, they both had the same dream. That is when Mercedes-Benz took its first step in history.

When Daimler's company took part in a motor race in Nice in 1899, the company named its racing car "Mercedes" after the eleven-year-old youngest daughter of Emil Jellinek, one of the company's good business partners. Mercedes won victories in many races later on, and Daimler registered the name as the trademark of its cars. The name Mercedes-Benz comes from this. In the meantime, Benz's company was also an active player in many car races organized in Europe. Here too, Daimler and Benz were good rivals. Their cars always won top prizes, building great public trust in their technical standards.

メルセデス・ベンツの歴史は自動車の歴史だと言われています。それはメルセデス・ベンツ車がいつの時代にも最先端の技術と最高の品質を誇る自動車であることを意味しているのです。

The history of Mercedes-Benz is often referred to as the history of the automobile, meaning that Mercedes cars have formed the pinnacle of quality and the state-of-the-art over time.

History

20 21

COVER

Mercedes-Benz
Philosophy
デザイン

「ガルウィング(カモメの羽)」と呼ばれるドアを備えた300SL。美しいシルエットの中に、当時のメルセデス・ベンツの最新技術が秘められています

Beneath its beautifully shaped body, the 300SL Gull-wing conceals state-of-the-art Mercedes technology of its time.

新時代のコンパクトセダンとして高い評価を集めるCクラス

The C-class has found great favor with motorists as the compact sedan of the new generation.

1959年から1971年まで生産されたW111シリーズ。気品にあふれたフロントマスクと優雅なボディーラインで、「タテ目」の愛称とともに現在も多くのファンに親しまれています

The W111 was produced from 1959 to 1971. The graceful front design and elegant flow of lines of the "vertical eyes" still attract many enthusiasts.

デザインとは、高機能を実現するための性能そのものである。メルセデス・ベンツは常にそう考えてきました。100年以上にわたるメルセデス・ベンツの歴史は、そのまま自動車の歴史であると同時に、自動車という工業製品のデザイン変遷の足跡でもあります。長い年月を通じて、メルセデス・ベンツは常に時代の最先端を行く技術を生み出し、それらにふさわしい形を与え続けてきました。

たとえばメルセデス・ベンツ300SL。1954年に発表されたこのモデルは、跳ね上げ式のガルウィング・ドアを備えた斬新なデザインで、当時の人々に大きな衝撃を与えました。その精悍なスタイルは40年以上を経てなお新鮮な輝きを放ち続け、歴史に残る名車として世界の自動車愛好家たちの憧れを集めています。

しかし300SLが、今日まで名車と呼ばれてきた真の理由は、革新的なデザインだけにあるのではありません。この車には、当時メルセデス・ベンツが開発したばかりの鋼管製スペースフレームが採用されていました。ガルウィング・ドアは軽量かつ高剛性を実現した画期的なフレーム構造を、座席のサイド部分で断ち切ることなく、しかもスムーズな乗降を可能にするために生まれたアイディアだったのです。機能追求の極限から生まれた新しいデザインという点で、300SLはまさにメルセデスらしいメルセデスとして、長くその名を歴史にとどめてきました。

「それは応用未来学にほかならない」。車のデザインとは何かとの問いに、メルセデス・ベンツ社デザイン部門統括本部長 ブルーノ・サッコはそう答えています。約30年にわたってメルセデス・ベンツのデザインを手がけてきたサッコは、さらに「エンジニアリングと同じ水準の革新性を確保すること」、「車の持つ高度な機能性を反映すること」、「常に伝統というフィルターを通して見ること」の3つを、メルセデス・ベンツのデザイン哲学の柱として挙げています。

言うまでもなくこの哲学は、現在のメルセデス・ベンツ車にも忠実に受け継がれています。1993年にデビューし、新時代のコンパクトセダンとして高い評価を集めているCクラスの発表に際して、「この車のスタイルに、流行を追うデザインを探しても見当たらない。あるのは、メルセデス・ベンツ独自の機能性の追求から生まれた現代性だけだ」と語ったサッコの言葉が、そのことを如実に示しています。メルセデス・ベンツにとってデザインとは、常にその時代の最高の機能を創り出すための、いわば必然的な手段であり、そこから生まれた美しく合理性に満ちたシルエットは、長い時を超えて生き続ける自動車の生命そのものなのです。

Mercedes-Benz has always considered design to be the "performance" element that underpins a car's functionality. Over one hundred years of Mercedes-Benz history, synonymous with the hundred-year history of the automobile, represents over one hundred years of the evolution of the form at the industrial product called the automobile.
The legendary Mercedes-Benz 300SL of 1954 is a good example. The striking gull-wing design made a great impression on many drivers. After forty years, the Spartan styling remains refreshing. The 300SL is a real classic, attracting car enthusiasts throughout the world.

"It's nothing more than applied futurology." This was the answer of Bruno Sacco, Head of Design at Mercedes-Benz, when he was asked what designing cars is really about. And when the C-class was premiered in 1993, Sacco who for thirty years has been the driving spirit behind Mercedes design, commented, "You can find no trend-chasing design elements in the styling of this car. All you find is the modernity created through the typical Mercedes pursuit of functionality."
For Mercedes-Benz, design is a necessary means of creating the highest functionality of the time. The beautiful and logical form is itself the life of the car, transcending the passage of time.

たった一本の線にも重要な意味と必然がある。メルセデス・ベンツは車のデザインを通じて、技術の可能性と未来像を探り続けてきました。

Every single line is significant and necessary. Through car design, Mercedes has always inquired into the potential and future of technology.

Design

30 31

COVER

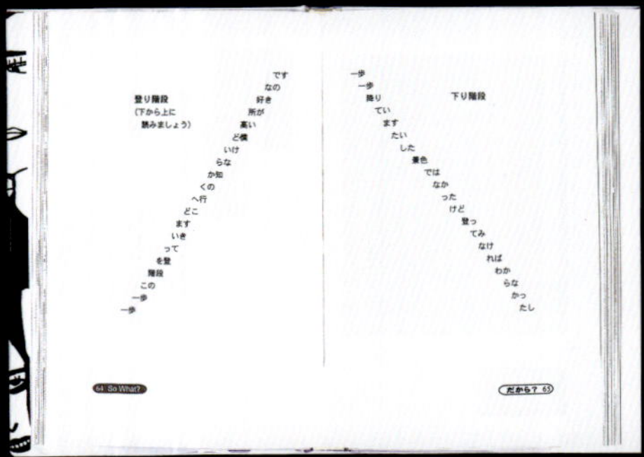

登り階段
(下から上に
読みましょう)

です
なの
好き
所が
高い
ど僕
いけ
らな
か知
くの
へ行
どこ
ます
いき
って
を登
階段
この
一歩
一歩

64 So What?

一歩
一歩
降り
てい
ます
たい
した
景色
では
なか
った
けど
登っ
てみ
なけ
れば
わか
らな
かっ
たし

下り階段

だから? 65

山手線の全駅名を順番に間違わずにスラスラと言える青年

山手線の全駅名を順番に間違わずにスラスラと言える
青年は
今、中央線も言える
高尾まではもちろん
大月までも言える
そのうち甲府までも言えるようになる
山手線の駅名も忘れないように復習してる
新宿、代々木、原宿、渋谷、恵比寿、目黒、
五反田、大崎、品川、田町、浜松町、新橋、
有楽町、東京、神田、秋葉原、御徒町、上野、鶯谷、
日暮里、西日暮里、田端、駒込、巣鴨、大塚、池袋、
目白、高田馬場、新大久保、新宿
ようし!
外回りでもやってみよう
新宿、新大久保、高田馬場、目白、池袋、大塚、巣鴨、
駒込、田端、西日暮里、日暮里、鶯谷、上野、御徒町、
秋葉原、神田、東京、有楽町、新橋、浜松町、田町、
品川、大崎、五反田、目黒、恵比寿、渋谷、原宿、
代々木、新宿
ようし!

118 So What?

一番きれいな雪の破片を見つけ
そしてそれを食べようと考えている青年

一番　きれいな
雪の　破片を
彼は　食べようと　考えて　いる
一度しかない　人生　後悔は
したく　ない　じっくりと　見定めて
最良のものを　食べる
結構きれいな　雪の　破片が
降りて　きても　彼は　食べない
そのうちに　もっときれいな　雪の
破片が　降りてくるのだと　信じている
そして　そのまま
雪は　雨に　変わる
一番きれいな　雪の　破片はおろか
二番目も
三番目も
口にしないまま

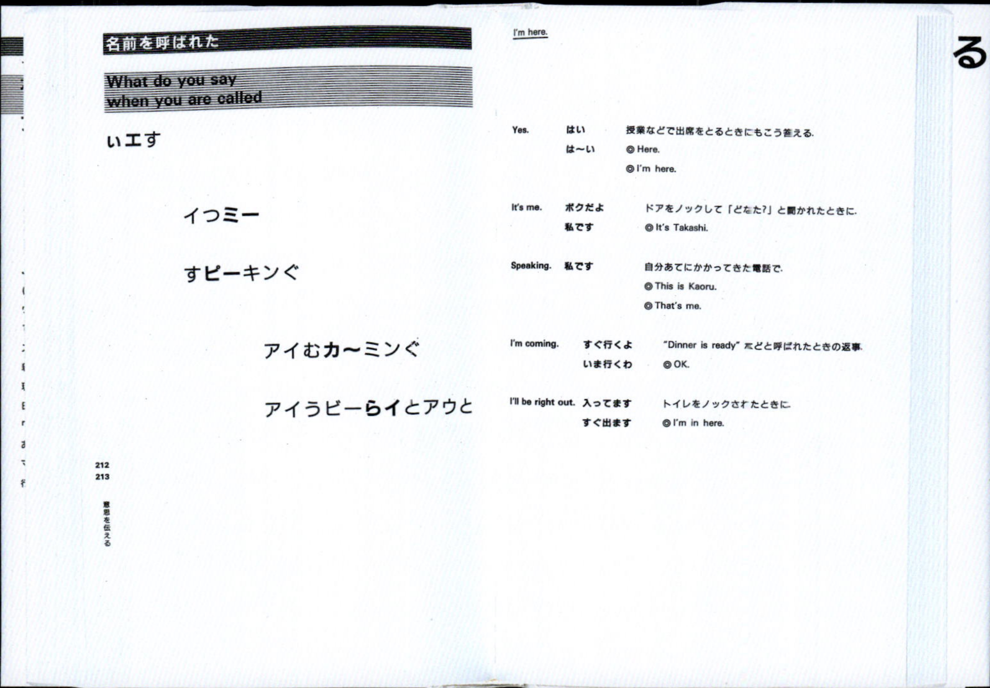

名前を呼ばれた
What do you say
when you are called
ぃエす
イつミー
すピーキンぐ
アイむカ〜ミンぐ
アイうビーらイとアウと
I'm here.
Yes. はい は〜い 授業などで出席をとるときにもこう答える。 Here. I'm here.
It's me. ボクだよ 私です ドアをノックして「どなた?」と聞かれたときに。 It's Takashi.
Speaking. 私です 自分あてにかかってきた電話で。 This is Kaoru. That's me.
I'm coming. すぐ行くよ いま行くわ "Dinner is ready" などと呼ばれたときの返事。 OK.
I'll be right out. 入ってます すぐ出ます トイレをノックされたときに。 I'm in here.
212
213
意思を伝える
る

ちょっとした
話し方
アメリカ口語

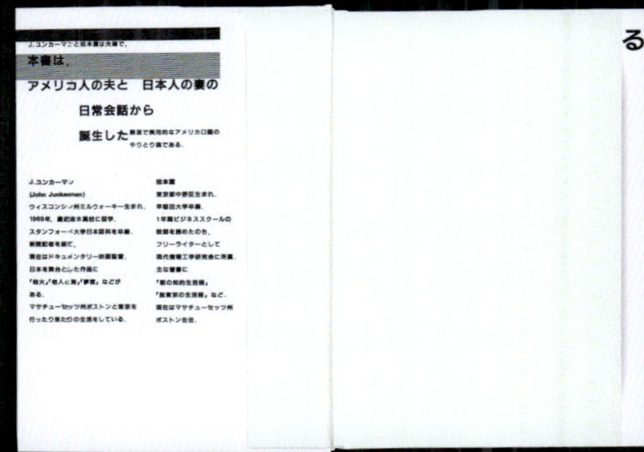

本書は、
アメリカ人の夫と　日本人の妻の
日常会話から
誕生した
る

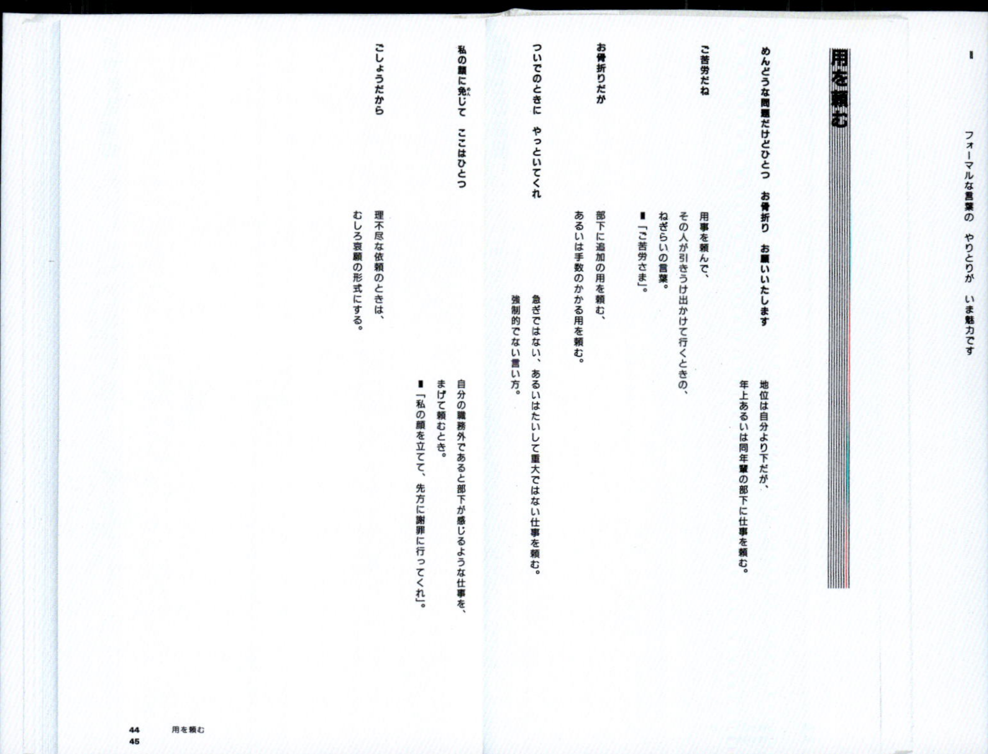

I
フォーマルな言葉の　やりとりが　いま魅力です
用を頼む
めんどうな用事だけどひとつ　お骨折り　お願いいたします
地位は自分より下だが、年上あるいは同年輩の部下に仕事を頼む。
ご苦労だね
用事を頼んで、その人が引きうけ出かけて行くときの、ねぎらいの言葉。■「ご苦労さま」。
お骨折りだが
部下に追加の用を頼む、あるいは手数のかかる用を頼む。
ついでのときに　やっといてくれ
急ぎではない、あるいはたいして重大ではない仕事を頼む。強制的でない言い方。
私の顔に免じて　ここはひとつ
自分の職務外であると部下が感じるような仕事を、まげて頼むとき。■「私の顔を立てて、先方に謝罪に行ってくれ」。
ごしょうだから
理不尽な依頼のときは、むしろ哀願の形式にする。
44
45
用を頼む

ちょっとした
ものの言い方

1 礼儀正しさ
2 聡明さ
3 自分がある

WEB 1995 JAPAN CL, P: Laforet Harajuku CD: Katsuhisa Sato AD: Kei Nagashima D: Akihiko Tsukamoto CW: Mitsuru Yoshida DF: WEB Plannning Room

MAGAZINE 雑誌

DAZED & CONFUSED VOL.64 APRIL 2000 UK

PB: Dazed & Confused E: Jefferson Hack Photographic Director: Emma Reeves AD: Martin Bell P: Mike Thomas TY: Neil Emery / Adam Thorpe Coordination: Sasha Hirschfeld

MAGAZINE 雑誌

ESQUIRE JAPAN VOL.14 NO.5 MAY 2000 JAPAN PB: Esquire Magazine Japan E: Kiyoshi Hayashi AD: Hisashi Sakurai
P: Yoshiaki Tsutsui (SPREAD 1) / Michele Biancucci (SPREAD 2) / Davide Dainelli (SPREAD 2)

SPREAD 1

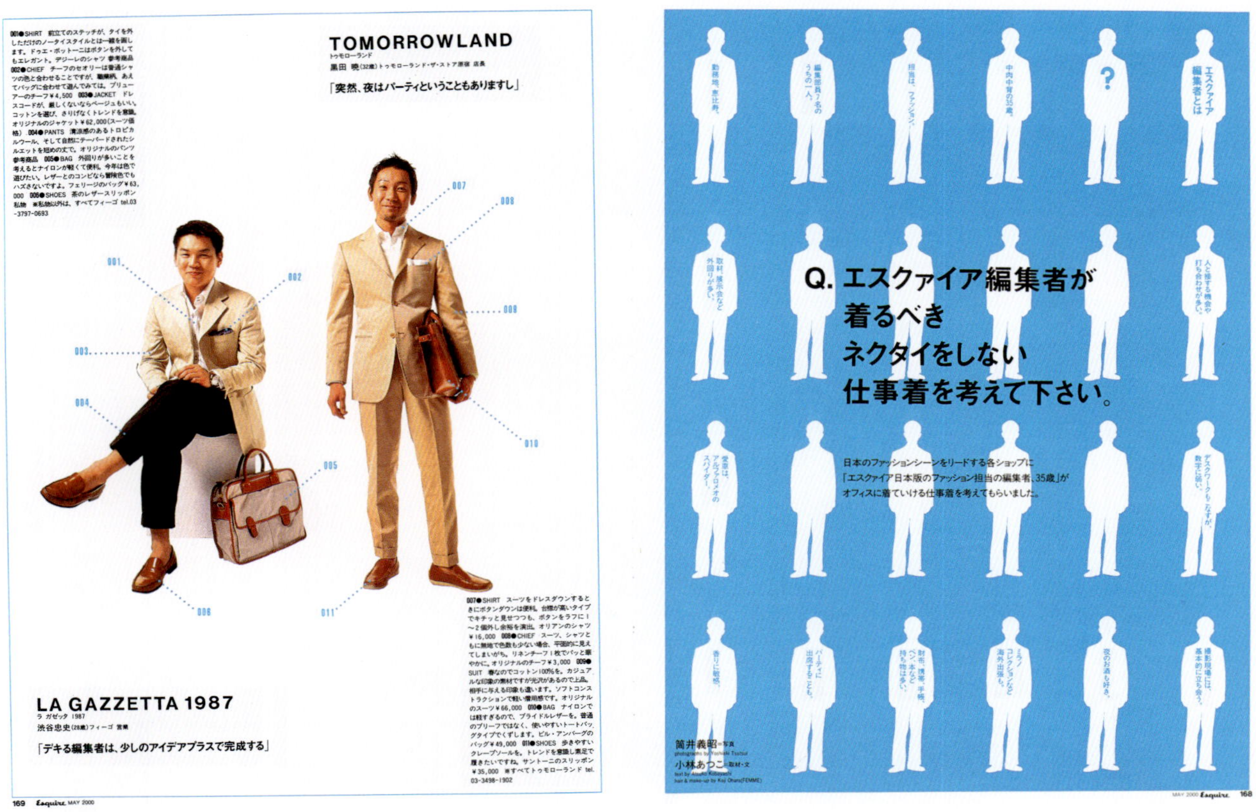

SPREAD 2

MAGAZINE 雑誌

CASA BRUTUS WINTER 1999 JAPAN

PB: Magazine House E: Kazuhiro Saito / Chieko Yoshiie / Yoshikuni Shirai (SPREAD 2) AD: Yasushi Fujimoto (cap) Chief D: Kazuyoshi Komatsu D: Yusuke Nagumo / Mitsuko Watanabe P: Toshitaka Niwa HM: Yasuyoshi Kato (SPREAD 2) ST: Tomomi Nagayama / Reé Ogura (SPREAD 2) Coordination: Chinatsu Kambayashi (SPREAD 1) DF: Cap

SPREAD 1

SPREAD 2

MAGAZINE 雑誌

CASA BRUTUS AUTUMN 1999 JAPAN

PB: Magazine House E: Kazuhiro Saito / Chieko Yoshiie AD: Yasushi Fujimoto (cap) Chief D: Kazuyoshi Komatsu D: Emu Tsunematsu / Yusuke Nagumo / Mitsuko Watanabe P: Toshitaka Niwa ST: Tomomi Nagayama Coordination: Chinatsu Kambayashi DF: Cap

MAGAZINE 雑誌

(PAGE 1) CASA BRUTUS AUTUMN 1999 JAPAN
PB: Magazine House E: Kazuhiro Saito / Chieko Yoshiie / Kazumi Yamamoto AD: Yasushi Fujimoto (cap)
Chief D: Kazuyoshi Komatsu D: Emu Tsunematsu / Yusuke Nagumo / Mitsuko Watanabe
P: Tadataka Saigo / Tomoko Taketugu ST: Akiko Saito DF: Cap

(PAGE 2) CASA BRUTUS WINTER 1998 JAPAN
PB: Magazine House E: Kazuhiro Saito / Chieko Yoshiie / Yoshikuni Shirai AD: Yasushi Fujimoto (cap)
Chief D: Kazuyoshi Komatsu D: Rie Matsubara / Yuriko Iwamoto / Noriteru Minezaki P: Yasuo Terusawa DF: Cap

PAGE 1

PAGE 2

MARTHA STEWART BABY MARCH 2000 USA

PB, DF: Martha Stewart Omnimedia E: Alice Gordon AD: Deb Bishop / Barbara deWilde D: Angie Gubler
P: Maria Robledo (SPREAD 1) / Gentle & Hyers (SPREAD 2) / John Dolan (SPREAD 3)

homemade molasses-wheat bread is toasted and slicked with butter and marmalade for a snack. The recipe involves no yeast, so two loaves are quick and easy to make. Freeze one; use the other for sandwiches and nibbling for up to one week.

sandwiches needn't be a production: Three versions on toasted whole-wheat English muffins—peanut butter, banana, and raisin; strawberries and yogurt drizzled with honey; and mashed avocado and chickpea with carrots and greens—balance fat and protein. And they're portable.

seasoned salt adds texture and the flavors of dill, fennel, and black pepper to two high-protein snacks: hard-boiled eggs and edamame, the young pods of soybeans. Hard boil several eggs at a time and keep refrigerated. Edamame are found in the freezer section of grocery stores.

avocados seem indulgent, but they are protein-rich. Sprinkled with lime juice and filled with tuna and sunflower seeds, they make an excellent snack. Use them as a base for salad, citrus, or beans drizzled with vinaigrette. A glass of pink-grapefruit juice is a tart complement.

snacks are meals and meals are snacks when you're in the harried world of infant care or pregnancy. Foods with a long shelf life, foods with mild flavors, and foods with portability are what you're looking for. Whatever food you crave, make or buy extra, and freeze half to warm up for nighttime feedings.

hot baked potatoes are hard to beat when you want food that tastes good and sticks to your ribs. Trusty Idaho baking potatoes and slightly caramelized sweet potatoes, cooked in a high-heat oven for an hour, are even better dressed with delicious, healthy toppings.

sweet potatoes are actually a member of the morning glory family, but they and real potatoes are full of potassium, iron, calcium, and vitamins A and C. Be sure to eat the skin: It retains about 80 percent of the vitamins' value after cooking.

rethink your need for four pats of butter and all that sour cream. Potatoes themselves aren't fattening; it's the heavy toppings that can do you in. Make each potato an entire little meal in itself. Enjoy the flavor of fat, but remember a little goes a long way.

good combinations (top to bottom): Low-fat sour cream or yogurt with black-olive tapenade; steamed asparagus and green peas, lemon, and extra-virgin olive oil; sea salt, cracked black pepper, and a bit of butter; lentils, feta cheese, and extra-virgin olive oil; and tofu with scallions, sesame seeds, and low-sodium soy sauce.

119

SPREAD 1

whole grain

Doctors usually recommend starting babies on some type of dry rice cereal as their first solid food. Mixed with breast milk, formula, or boiled water, its mild flavor is a good transition from nursing or formula. Only buy sugar-free, organic baby cereals, fortified with minerals and iron, found in health-food and large grocery stores. These cereals are delicious and more nutritious than non-organic white-rice cereals.

applesauce

Wash and core 4 pounds of apples (skins on), and cut into 1-inch pieces. Simmer apples, covered, in a large saucepan with ⅓ cup water until tender, about 10 minutes. Transfer mixture to a blender. Working in small batches, blend until smooth. Pass through a fine sieve. For coarser texture, pass apples through a food mill or pulse in a food processor. Fill ¼-cup plastic containers or ice-cube trays. Makes 4¼ cups or about 48 cubes.

pear

Wash, peel, and core 3 pounds of ripe pears. Cut into 1-inch pieces. Simmer, covered, in a large saucepan with ⅓ cup water until tender, 5 to 10 minutes. Drain; reserve cooking liquid. Transfer pears to a blender. Working in small batches, blend until smooth. Add reserved liquid if needed. Pass through a fine sieve for a smooth texture. For a coarser texture, mash with a fork. Fill ¼-cup plastic containers or ice-cube trays with purée. Makes 2½ cups or about 28 cubes.

plum

Wash and quarter 2 pounds of ripe plums. Discard pits. Simmer plums, covered, in a large saucepan with ¼ cup water until tender, about 10 minutes. Transfer plums to a blender. Working in small batches, blend until smooth. Add up to ⅓ cup boiled and cooled water if needed. Pass mixture through a fine sieve for the smoothest texture. Fill ¼-cup plastic containers or ice-cube trays with purée. Makes 3 cups or about 30 cubes. Use same method for peaches, apricots, and other stone fruits.

sweet potato

Wash 2½ pounds of sweet potatoes (skins on), and cut into 2-inch pieces. Arrange pieces on a steamer rack in a large pan over 1 inch of water. Cover and bring to a boil. Reduce heat. Steam until tender, about 12 minutes. Pulse in a food processor or pass through a food mill fitted with the smallest disk. Add formula, breast milk, or boiled and cooled water as needed. Fill ¼-cup plastic containers or ice-cube trays with purée. Makes 3 cups or about 30 cubes. Use same method for new or baking potatoes and any winter squash.

green bean

Wash and trim the stem ends of 2 pounds of green beans. Arrange beans on a steamer rack in a large pan over 1 inch of water. Cover and bring to a boil. Reduce heat. Steam until tender, about 8 minutes. Plunge beans into cold water to stop the cooking. Pulse in a food processor or pass through a food mill fitted with the medium disk. Add formula, breast milk, or boiled and cooled water as needed. Fill ¼-cup plastic containers or ice-cube trays with purée. Makes 2⅔ cups or about 24 cubes. Use same method for green peas.

carrot

Scrub 1½ pounds organic carrots (peel if not organic), and cut into 1-inch pieces. Arrange carrots on a steamer rack in a large pan over 1 inch of water. Cover and bring to a boil. Reduce heat. Steam until tender, about 12 minutes. Plunge carrots into cold water to stop the cooking. Pulse in a food processor or pass through a food mill fitted with the medium disk. Add formula, breast milk, or boiled and cooled water as needed. Fill ¼-cup plastic containers or ice-cube trays with purée. Makes 3 cups or about 30 cubes.

apple slice

Your baby has eaten her way from loose, liquid purées to chunky, thick ones. Now you may introduce pieces of food. This makes life much easier. Try giving her pieces of your own food, and see what she likes. Be careful to avoid anything too small, such as nuts, grapes, raisins, or other dried fruit. They are difficult for a baby to chew and could cause choking. In addition to fruits, vegetables, and meat, try pieces of toast and bagels.

SPREAD 2

For a **sponge bath,** fold a bath towel to make an absorbent cushion for the baby to lie on. For babies who do not like to lie flat, use a folded hand towel as a pillow under the shoulders and head.

1. Ready your supplies: a waist-high sturdy table, a basin of warm water for a sponge bath (a plastic tub for the tub bath), two washcloths, two to three towels, cotton balls, a cup, alcohol wipes, unscented mild soap such as Dove Soap or pure castile soap, and baby shampoo.

2. Lay the baby on the towel. With a clean corner of a washcloth or moistened cotton ball, wash each eye, moving from inner to outer eye. Use only warm water. Wash the nose with another clean corner of the washcloth and the mouth with another.

3. To wash the hair, use a pea-size amount of castile soap or baby shampoo. Wash with a massaging motion, going gently over the soft spot. To rinse, wet a second washcloth, leaving some water in it, and squeeze it over the baby's scalp.

7. Wash the hip area, legs, and feet. These are very ticklish parts of the body for some babies. Use big gentle motions for both washing and drying.

8. To do a leg massage, take the baby's left foot or ankle in your right hand, and hold the top of the thigh in your left hand. With your left hand, stroke the leg from buttock to heel, squeezing in a milking motion. Reverse the motion, and repeat.

9. To wash the back and buttocks, use your dominant hand to push the baby onto her side. Leaving your hand there for support, wash the back and buttock area with your free hand, then dry.

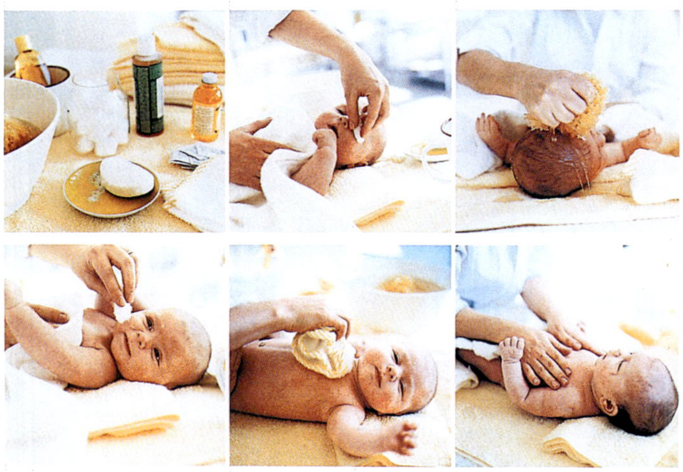

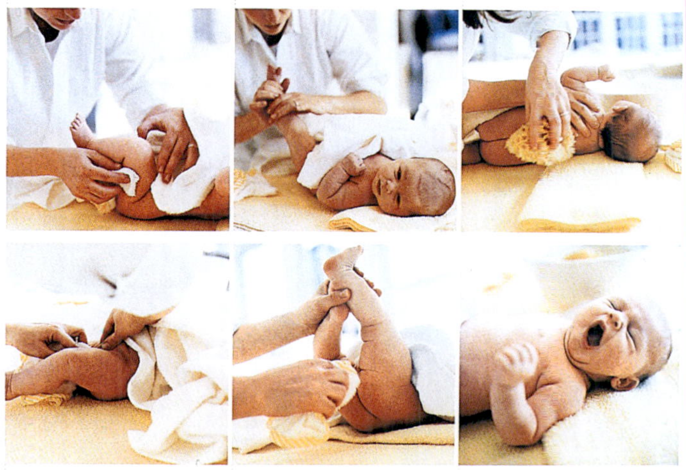

4. Wash the neck and ears with a washcloth or moistened cotton ball. Wash gently around and behind the outer ear. Use a little soap to wash these areas, as milk can collect behind the ear and in the creases of the neck.

5. Wash belly, underarms, arms, and hands. Clean inside all skin folds and creases. Use an alcohol wipe to clean gently around the edge of the umbilical cord. Dry the baby, and keep her body covered with a towel.

6. Babies love massages. Your gentle, reassuring voice and eye contact are as important as the motions of your hands. Place both hands lying flat at the center of the baby's chest, push out toward the edges of her torso, sweeping in and finishing at the baby's navel.

10. Wash genitals and groin, front to back. For girls, open the vulva with your thumb and index finger. Clean gently. For boys, clean the outside of the penis. Do not pull back the foreskin on an uncircumcised penis. On a circumcised penis, use a warm wet cotton ball. Lift testicles, and clean.

11. Wash the buttocks with a motion moving away from the genital area. Rinse, and pat dry.

12. Swaddle the baby in a dry warm towel. Well done!

SPREAD 3

HANAJIKAN AUGUST 1999 JAPAN PB: Kadokawa Shoten Publishing Co., Ltd. E: Fumiko Sugamoto AD: Issen Okamoto D: Naoko Onoda / Michiko Kobayashi

CATALOG カタログ

ACTUS STYLE BOOK VOL.5 2000 JAPAN

CL: ACTUS CD,AD,D: Masanori Araki / Toru Ohshige P: Keiji Ishiuchi / Yoshikazu Watase / Nobuyoshi Mori
CW: Yuko Ito / Masumi Yanagisawa

ROJAK VOL.0 1998 JAPAN CL: IDÉE Co., Ltd. AD,D: Takuji Nomoto D: Osamu Misawa P: Mamoru Minamiura / Masayuki Hayashi

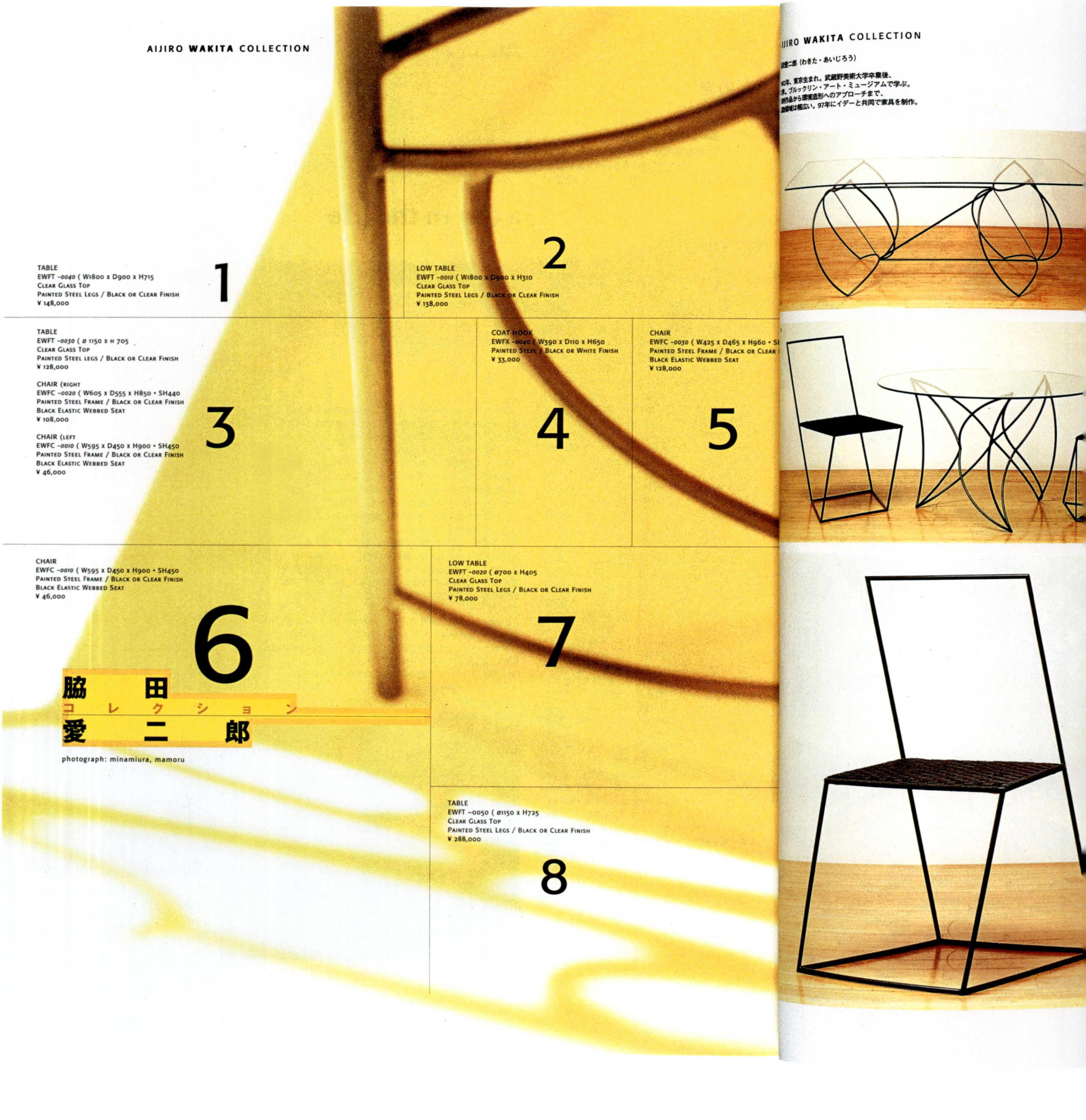

AIJIRO **WAKITA** COLLECTION

1
TABLE
EWFT -*0040* (W1800 x D900 x H715
Clear Glass Top
Painted Steel Legs / Black or Clear Finish
¥ 148,000

2
LOW TABLE
EWFT -*0010* (W1800 x D900 x H310
Clear Glass Top
Painted Steel Legs / Black or Clear Finish
¥ 138,000

3
TABLE
EWFT -*0030* (ø 1150 x H 705
Clear Glass Top
Painted Steel legs / Black or Clear Finish
¥ 128,000

CHAIR (right
EWFC -*0020* (W605 x D555 x H850 • SH440
Painted Steel Frame / Black or Clear Finish
Black Elastic Webbed Seat
¥ 108,000

CHAIR (left
EWFC -*0010* (W595 x D450 x H900 • SH450
Painted Steel Frame / Black or Clear Finish
Black Elastic Webbed Seat
¥ 46,000

4
COAT HOOK
EWFX -*0040* (W390 x D110 x H650
Painted Steel / Black or White Finish
¥ 33,000

5
CHAIR
EWFC -*0030* (W425 x D465 x H960 • S
Painted Steel Frame / Black or Clear
Black Elastic Webbed Seat
¥ 128,000

6
CHAIR
EWFC -*0010* (W595 x D450 x H900 • SH450
Painted Steel Frame / Black or Clear Finish
Black Elastic Webbed Seat
¥ 46,000

7
LOW TABLE
EWFT -*0020* (ø700 x H405
Clear Glass Top
Painted Steel Legs / Black or Clear Finish
¥ 78,000

8
TABLE
EWFT –0050 (ø1150 x H725
Clear Glass Top
Painted Steel Legs / Black or Clear Finish
¥ 288,000

脇田愛二郎 コレクション

photograph: minamiura, mamoru

IJIRO **WAKITA** COLLECTION

田愛二郎（わきた・あいじろう）

40年、東京生まれ。武蔵野美術大学卒業後、
米。ブルックリン・アート・ミュージアムで学ぶ。
制作品から環境造形へのアプローチまで、
動領域は幅広い。97年にイデーと共同で家具を制作。

(SPREAD 1 / 2) LIFE WITH IDÉE VOL.2 1997 JAPAN CL: IDÉE Co., Ltd. AD: Kaoru Watanabe D: Katsunori Hironaka P: Mamoru Minamiura

(SPREAD 3) LIFE WITH IDÉE VOL.3 1999 JAPAN CL: IDÉE Co., Ltd. AD,D: Kaoru Watanabe D: Miya Nishio P: Masayuki Hayashi / Noboru Morikawa / Mamoru Minamiura

SPREAD 1

SPREAD 2

SPREAD 3

CATALOG カタログ

LIFE WITH IDÉE NEW MODEL LINE UP ISSUE 1998 JAPAN

CL: IDÉE Co., Ltd. AD,D: Osamu Misawa
P: Masayuki Hayashi / Shoji Miyamoto / Yutaka Sakano / Mamoru Minamiura ST: Masayo Motegi

36-A Fractal Sofa
フラクタルソファ
To Order/受注生産
designed by Ross Lovegrove (ロス・ラヴグローヴ)
W760*D840*H1090, SH450
Injected foam seat and back elements
(grey, yellow, turquoise).
背座：モールドウレタンフォーム
(グレー、イエロー、ターコイズ)
White painted steel frame.
フレーム：スチールパイプ ホワイト塗装
¥ 380,000~
Ross Lovegrove
1958 Born, Wales, England.
1983 Graduated RCA, joined frog design, Germany.
1988 Opened London studio.
ロス・ラヴグローヴ
1958ウェールズ・イギリス生まれ
1983RCA卒業、フロッグデザインのスタッフとして活動
1988ロンドンにて多数のプロジェクトを手掛ける。
IDÉE page >36
IDÉE page >37

IDÉE
chair
IDÉE
table
shelf
etc.
IDÉE page 28
IDÉE page 29

COLORS 34 STATUS SYMBOLS OCTOBER-NOVEMBER 1999 ITALY PB: Colors Magazine S.r.l. Editorial Director: Oliviero Toscani Creative Editor: Richard Christiansen AD: Tetsuya Tamano

show it off
faire enterrer dans sa réplique en bois
s, beaucoup en possèdent une, volée en
nationale kenyane, il existe un mot pour
evenue l'attribut: ce sont les *wabenzi*. Et il
"En un mois, nous en vendons entre dix et
sponsable des ventes chez D.T. Dobie &
Mercedes-Benz de Nairobi. (Malgré la
ntes restent stables.) Les wabenzi forment
ncontrent aussi bien hommes d'affaires et
es du gouvernement. "Comme notre chef
ent la Mercedes au pouvoir et à la réussite,
rée est grosse, plus on gagne en prestige."
, mais je fais tout pour." A ce jour, Waki est
re la meilleure voiture du monde."
27

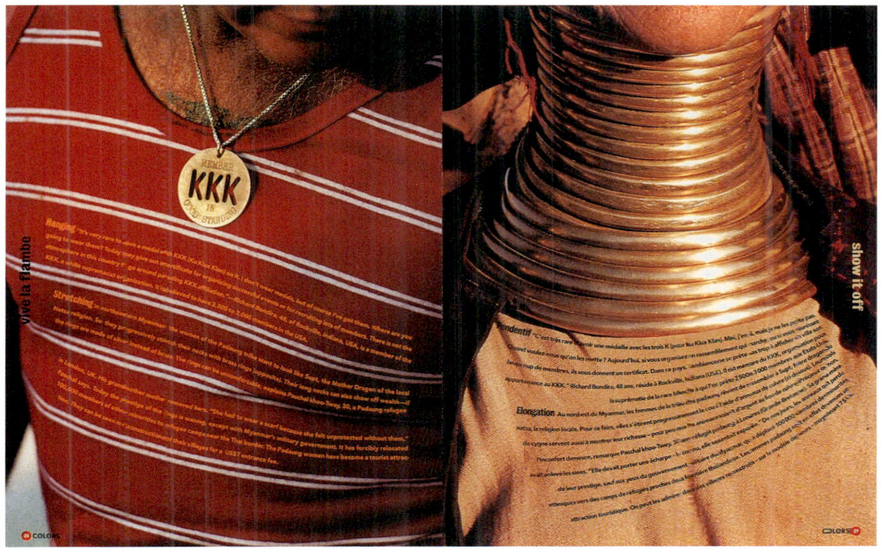
KKK
vive la flambe
show it off
COLORS

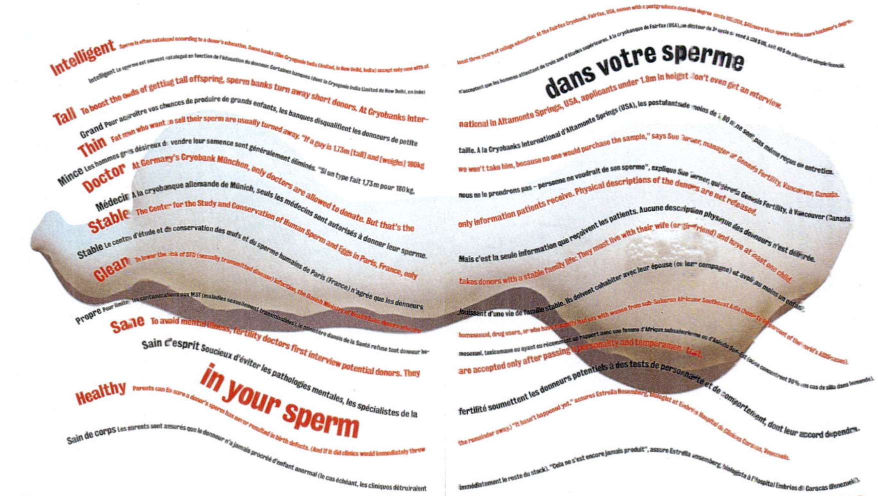
Intelligent
Tall
Thin
Doctor
Stable
Clean
Safe
Healthy
in your sperm
dans votre sperme
COLORS

in your sperm
dans votre sperme
COLORS

COLORS 26 TIME APRIL-MAY 1998 ITALY PB: Colors Magazine S.r.l. Editorial Director: Oliviero Toscani E: Adam Broomberg AD: Thomas Hilland

COLORS 30 HEART FEBRUARY-MARCH 1999 ITALY PB: Colors Magazine S.r.l. Editorial Director: Oliviero Toscani E: Antonio Otálvaro AD: Thomas Hilland

No.26 COVER

No.30 COVER

MAGAZINE 雑誌

COLORS 33 VENICE　AUGUST-SEPTEMBER 1999　ITALY　PB: Colors Magazine S.r.l.　Editorial Director: Oliviero Toscani　Creative Editor: Richard Christiansen
D: Tetsuya Tamano / Tony Linkson / Franca Pauli

No.33 COVER

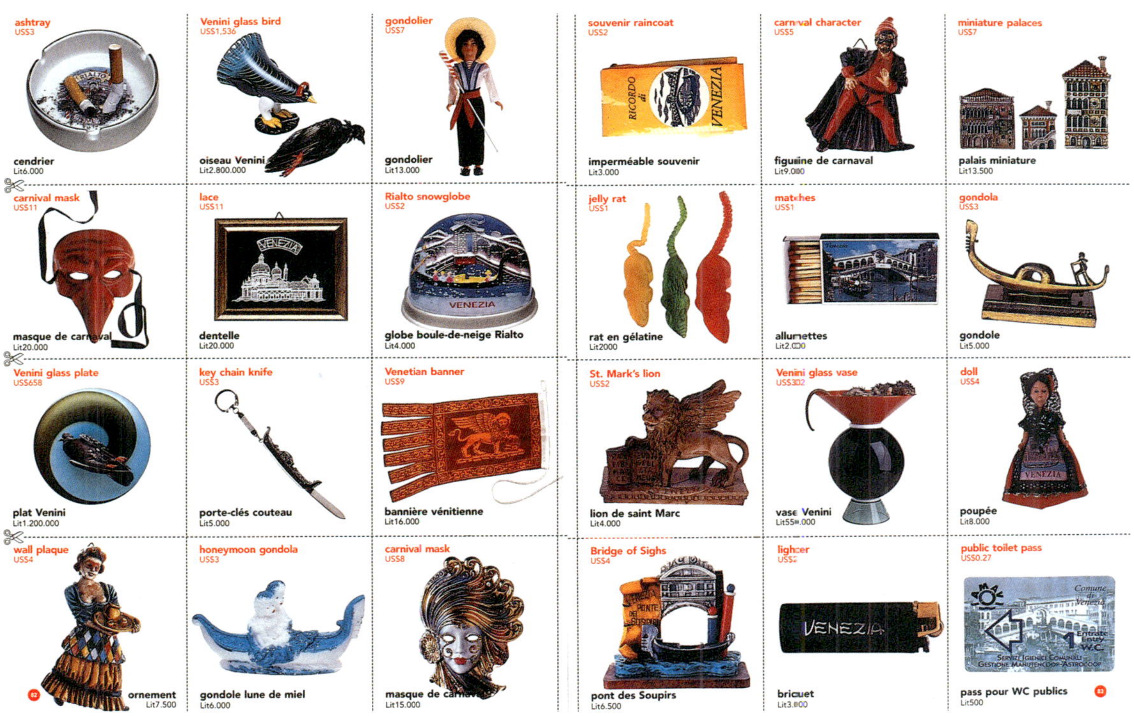

PAMPHLET パンフレット

KUNSTFEST AM KULTURFORUM 1999 GERMANY CL: Berliner Festspiele AD,D,CW,DF: Cyan

BROCHURE ブローシャー

AMOEBA CAPABILITIES BOOKLET 1999 CANADA CL,DF: Amoeba Corp. CD,CW: Mikey Richardson CD,D: Michael Kelar AD,D: Jason Darbyson D: Noël Nanton P: Janet Bailey

AMOEBA CORP.

VISUAL EXPERIMENTS

CLIENT YTV CANADA, INC.

DESCRIPTION PROGRAMMING MEDIA KIT

PURPOSE TO PRESENT YTV'S NEW SHOW LINEUP IN A HUMOUROUS, TONGUE-IN-CHEEK MANNER UTILIZING THE AESTHETIC OF THEIR NEW PRINT + ON-AIR CAMPAIGN.

METHOD GRAPHIC DESIGN/2D + 3D ILLUSTRATION

WORKER(S) I.D. A-01/A-03.7/A-04/A-05

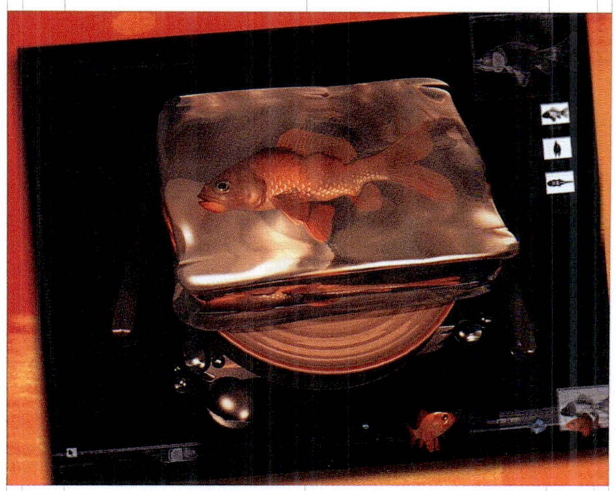

AMOEBA CORP.

VISUAL EXPERIMENTS

TITLE FROZEN DINNER

DESCRIPTION POSTER

PURPOSE TO CREATE A VISUAL PUN BY ILLUSTRATING THE LITERAL MEANING OF A COMMON TERM, FROZEN DINNER.

METHOD 3D ILLUSTRATION/GRAPHIC DESIGN

WORKER(S) I.D. A-04

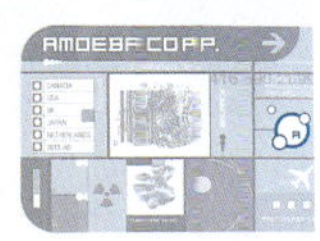

COVER

ANNUAL REPORT アニュアルレポート

SUGEN 1997 ANNUAL REPORT 1998 USA CL: Sugen CD,AD: Bill Cahan D: Sharrie Brooks P: Robert Schlatter CW: Carol Melis DF: Cahan & Associates

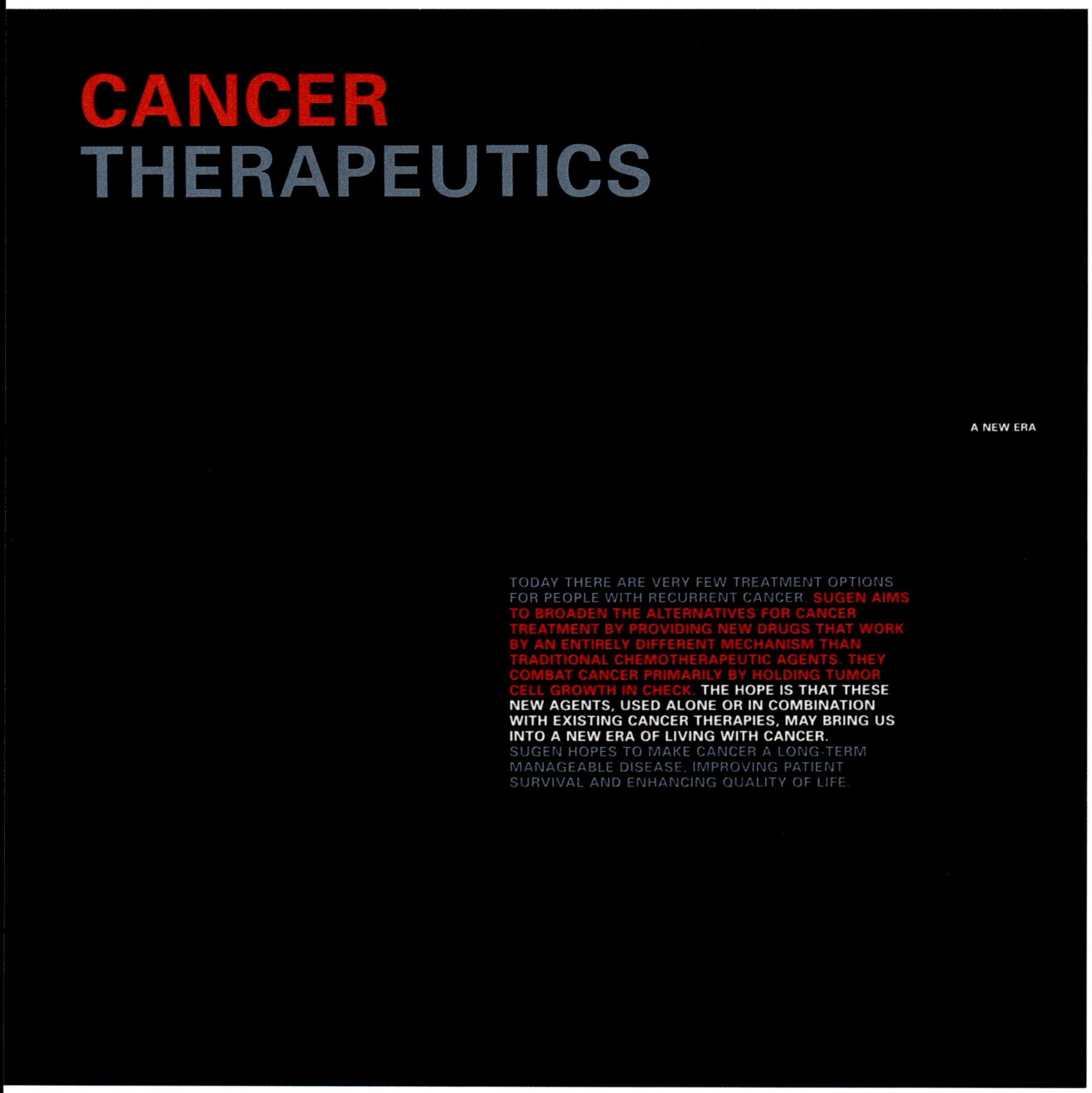

COVER

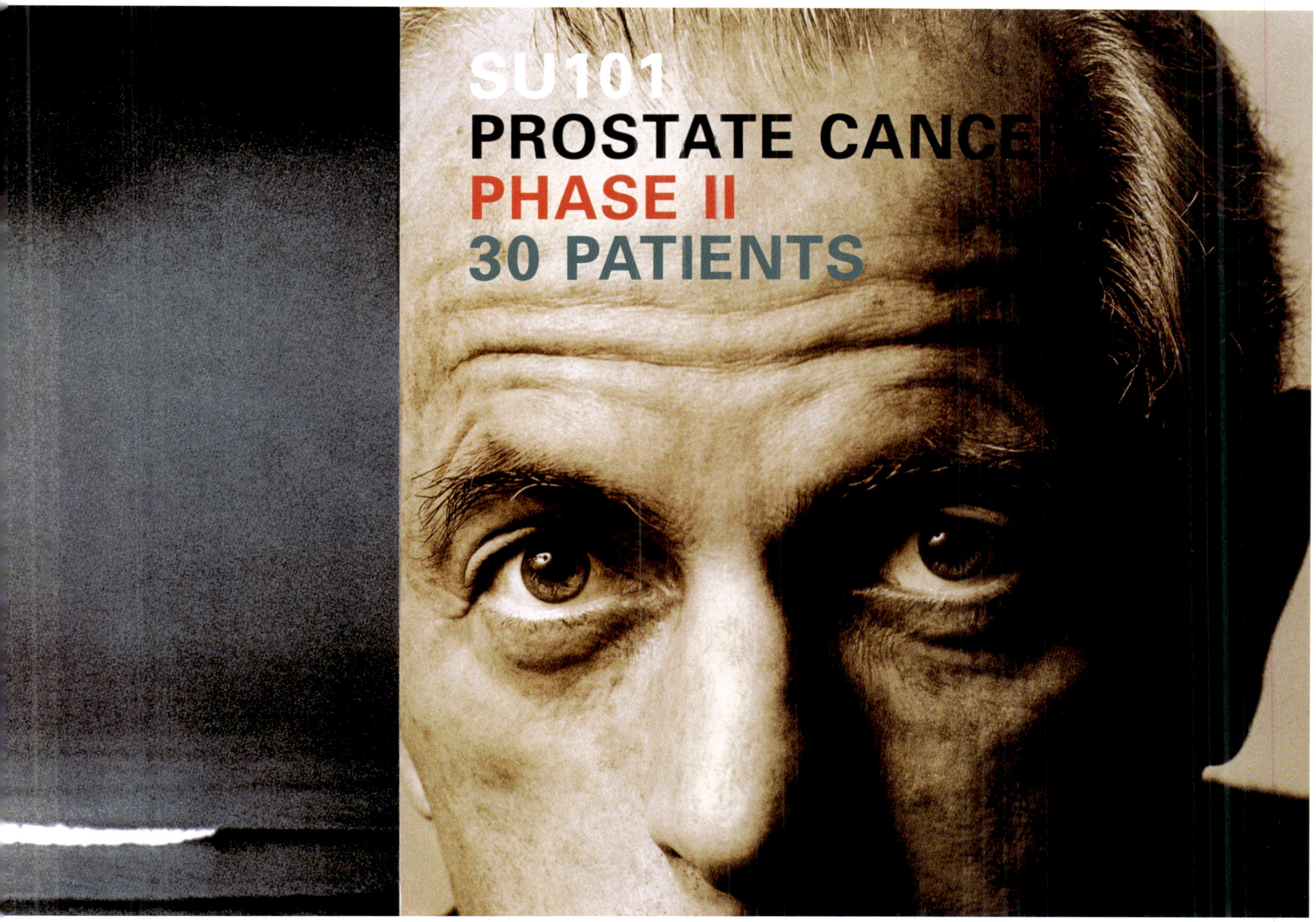
SU101
PROSTATE CANCE
PHASE II
30 PATIENTS

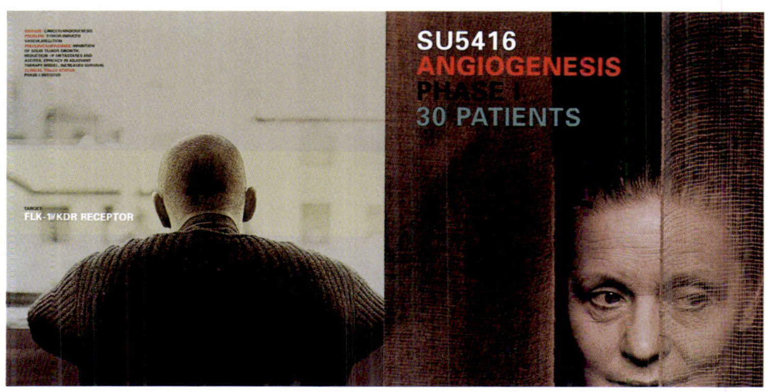
SU5416
ANGIOGENESIS
PHASE I
30 PATIENTS
FLK-1/KDR RECEPTOR

BROCHURE ブローシャー

A PHOTOGRAPH IS NOTHING WITHOUT SOMEONE TO LOOK AT IT 1999 NETHERLANDS CL, P: NEL CD: Erik Kessels / Johan Kramer AD: Karen Heuter CW: David Bell DF: Kesselskramer

COVER

1:marie-jose jongerius---2:menno kok---3:menno kok---4:menno kok---5:tom van heel---6:martien mulder---7:menno kok---8:martien mulder---9:edel verzijl---10:anna tiedink---11:carmen freudenthal---12:wendelien daan---13:tom van heel---14:marie-jose jongerius---15:marie jose jongerius---16:tom van heel---17:anna tiedink---18:anna tiedink---19:wendelien daan---20:carmen freudenthal---21:carmen freudenthal---22:wendelien daan---23:edel verzijl---24:tom van heel---25:martien mulder---26:edel verzijl---27:martien mulder---28:marie-jose jongerius---29:edel verzijl---30:anna tiedink---31:carmen freudenthal
concept, interviews, design: karen heuter, dave bell, pauline berkhout @ kesselskramer amsterdam
300-line screen, waterless printed by Equipage, Assendelft
lithography: PrePress Center, Assendelft
paper: Satimat Club, produced by Arjo Wiggins and delivered by Grafisch Papier b.v.
Special thanks to: Suleyman Demir, Alex wan der Steen, Fedde, Ingrid Boekel, Evelien Reich, Arjan Huffels, Radana, Caroline Fuchs, Sil, Winnie, Jochem, Doris + Yoeri, Flying Barber, Guus Bakker, Daantje .K., Homeboy Paul .DB., Ome Ko, Elle Verhagen, Taco Stuiver, Pieter Jeroense, Annemiek, Saskia van Drimmelen, SFEQ 3000, Kasia Gatkowska, Kuno, Roosje, Boot-Casting, Sandra Mercey, Boekers, Ulla, House of Orange, Name models, Modelmakers, Viva, Dutch: Peter Eemsing, Artview.
And everybody else who helped us.

29.
<It's mysterious. This is the first cigarette she's having after sex.>
Ellen van de Woestijne, 26, Interior Architect, Frozen Fountain, Amsterdam.

30.
<Beautiful, very science-fiction like. I like the glove where I can just see a peep of her hand.>
Koos Blokker, 50, Bus Driver, Amsterdam.

nel---nelleke strijkers---ruysdaelstraat 92-94hs---1071 xh amsterdam---the netherlands---tel+31 (0)20 470 29 44---fax+31 (0)20 470 29 45
e-mail:nelnl@xs4all.nl---internet:www.nel.nl

THE FACE OF THE CENTURY 1999 NETHERLANDS PB: do Publishing CD,AD,D: Erik Kessels P: Julian Germain CW: Martin Herron / David Bell DF: Kesselskramer

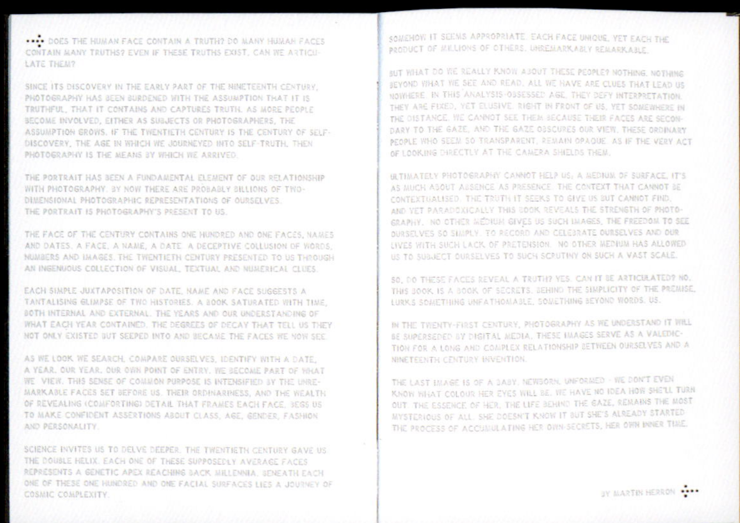

DOES THE HUMAN FACE CONTAIN A TRUTH? DO MANY HUMAN FACES CONTAIN MANY TRUTHS? EVEN IF THESE TRUTHS EXIST, CAN WE ARTICULATE THEM?

SINCE ITS DISCOVERY IN THE EARLY PART OF THE NINETEENTH CENTURY, PHOTOGRAPHY HAS BEEN BURDENED WITH THE ASSUMPTION THAT IT IS TRUTHFUL, THAT IT CONTAINS AND CAPTURES TRUTH. AS MORE PEOPLE BECOME INVOLVED, EITHER AS SUBJECTS OR PHOTOGRAPHERS, THE ASSUMPTION GROWS. IF THE TWENTIETH CENTURY IS THE CENTURY OF SELF-DISCOVERY, THE AGE IN WHICH WE JOURNEYED INTO SELF-TRUTH, THEN PHOTOGRAPHY IS THE MEANS BY WHICH WE ARRIVED.

THE PORTRAIT HAS BEEN A FUNDAMENTAL ELEMENT OF OUR RELATIONSHIP WITH PHOTOGRAPHY. BY NOW THERE ARE PROBABLY BILLIONS OF TWO-DIMENSIONAL PHOTOGRAPHIC REPRESENTATIONS OF OURSELVES.
THE PORTRAIT IS PHOTOGRAPHY'S PRESENT TO US.

THE FACE OF THE CENTURY CONTAINS ONE HUNDRED AND ONE FACES, NAMES AND DATES. A FACE, A NAME, A DATE. A DECEPTIVE COLLUSION OF WORDS, NUMBERS AND IMAGES. THE TWENTIETH CENTURY PRESENTED TO US THROUGH AN INGENUOUS COLLECTION OF VISUAL, TEXTUAL AND NUMERICAL CLUES.

EACH SIMPLE JUXTAPOSITION OF DATE, NAME AND FACE SUGGESTS A TANTALISING GLIMPSE OF TWO HISTORIES. A BOOK SATURATED WITH TIME, BOTH INTERNAL AND EXTERNAL. THE YEARS AND OUR UNDERSTANDING OF WHAT EACH YEAR CONTAINED. THE DEGREES OF DECAY THAT TELL US THEY NOT ONLY EXISTED BUT SEEPED INTO AND BECAME THE FACES WE NOW SEE.

AS WE LOOK WE SEARCH, COMPARE OURSELVES, IDENTIFY WITH A DATE, A YEAR. OUR YEAR. OUR OWN POINT OF ENTRY. WE BECOME PART OF WHAT WE VIEW. THIS SENSE OF COMMON PURPOSE IS INTENSIFIED BY THE UNREMARKABLE FACES SET BEFORE US. THEIR ORDINARINESS, AND THE WEALTH OF REVEALING (COMFORTING) DETAIL THAT FRAMES EACH FACE, BEGS US TO MAKE CONFIDENT ASSERTIONS ABOUT CLASS, AGE, GENDER, FASHION AND PERSONALITY.

SCIENCE INVITES US TO DELVE DEEPER. THE TWENTIETH CENTURY GAVE US THE DOUBLE HELIX. EACH ONE OF THESE SUPPOSEDLY AVERAGE FACES REPRESENTS A GENETIC APEX REACHING BACK MILLENNIA. BENEATH EACH ONE OF THESE ONE HUNDRED AND ONE FACIAL SURFACES LIES A JOURNEY OF COSMIC COMPLEXITY.

SOMEHOW IT SEEMS APPROPRIATE. EACH FACE UNIQUE, YET EACH THE PRODUCT OF MILLIONS OF OTHERS. UNREMARKABLY REMARKABLE.

BUT WHAT DO WE REALLY KNOW ABOUT THESE PEOPLE? NOTHING. NOTHING BEYOND WHAT WE SEE AND READ. ALL WE HAVE ARE CLUES THAT LEAD US NOWHERE. IN THIS ANALYSIS-OBSESSED AGE, THEY DEFY INTERPRETATION. THEY ARE FIXED, YET ELUSIVE. RIGHT IN FRONT OF US, YET SOMEWHERE IN THE DISTANCE. WE CANNOT SEE THEM BECAUSE THEIR FACES ARE SECONDARY TO THE GAZE, AND THE GAZE OBSCURES OUR VIEW. THESE ORDINARY PEOPLE WHO SEEM SO TRANSPARENT, REMAIN OPAQUE. AS IF THE VERY ACT OF LOOKING DIRECTLY AT THE CAMERA SHIELDS THEM.

ULTIMATELY PHOTOGRAPHY CANNOT HELP US; A MEDIUM OF SURFACE, IT'S AS MUCH ABOUT ABSENCE AS PRESENCE. THE CONTEXT THAT CANNOT BE CONTEXTUALISED. THE TRUTH IT SEEKS TO GIVE US BUT CANNOT FIND. AND YET PARADOXICALLY THIS BOOK REVEALS THE STRENGTH OF PHOTOGRAPHY. NO OTHER MEDIUM GIVES US SUCH IMAGES, THE FREEDOM TO SEE OURSELVES SO SIMPLY. TO RECORD AND CELEBRATE OURSELVES AND OUR LIVES WITH SUCH LACK OF PRETENSION. NO OTHER MEDIUM HAS ALLOWED US TO SUBJECT OURSELVES TO SUCH SCRUTINY ON SUCH A VAST SCALE.

SO, DO THESE FACES REVEAL A TRUTH? YES. CAN IT BE ARTICULATED? NO. THIS BOOK IS A BOOK OF SECRETS. BEHIND THE SIMPLICITY OF THE PREMISE, LURKS SOMETHING UNFATHOMABLE. SOMETHING BEYOND WORDS. US.

IN THE TWENTY-FIRST CENTURY, PHOTOGRAPHY AS WE UNDERSTAND IT WILL BE SUPERSEDED BY DIGITAL MEDIA. THESE IMAGES SERVE AS A VALEDICTION FOR A LONG AND COMPLEX RELATIONSHIP BETWEEN OURSELVES AND A NINETEENTH CENTURY INVENTION.

THE LAST IMAGE IS OF A BABY. NEWBORN, UNFORMED - WE DON'T EVEN KNOW WHAT COLOUR HER EYES WILL BE. WE HAVE NO IDEA HOW SHE'LL TURN OUT. THE ESSENCE OF HER, THE LIFE BEHIND THE GAZE, REMAINS THE MOST MYSTERIOUS OF ALL. SHE DOESN'T KNOW IT BUT SHE'S ALREADY STARTED THE PROCESS OF ACCUMULATING HER OWN SECRETS, HER OWN INNER TIME.

BY MARTIN HERRON

R E V E N U E

Q•MEDIA'S EXCELLENT PERFORMANCE IN FISCAL 1999

CAPPED FIVE YEARS OF OUTSTANDING GROWTH.

ANNUAL REVENUES HAVE GROWN FROM $2.1 MILLION

IN FISCAL 1994 TO OVER $100 MILLION THIS YEAR.

1999	1998	1997	1996	1995
$101.8	$45.8	$28.7	$15.9	$7.2

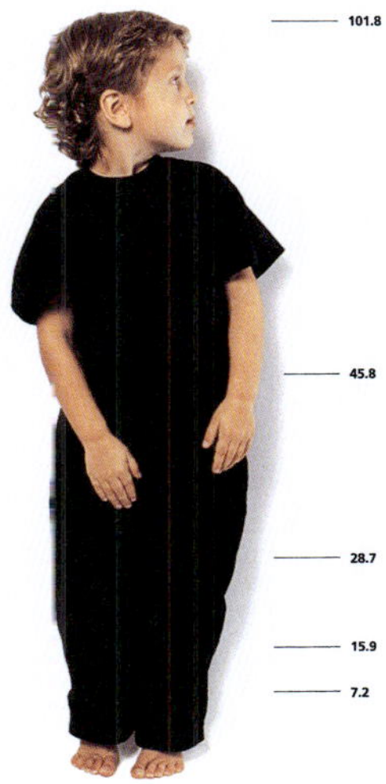

M E A S U R I N G O U R G R O W T H

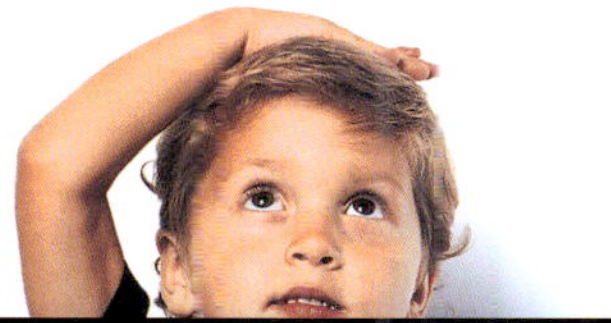

COVER

G R O S S M A R G I N

DISCIPLINE IN THE OPERATION OF OUR BUSINESS

WAS KEY TO IMPLEMENTING LOWER COSTS AND MORE

EFFICIENT SOLUTIONS FOR OUR CUSTOMERS.

1999	1998	1997	1996	1995
$26.6	$14.2	$8.1	$4.5	$1.9

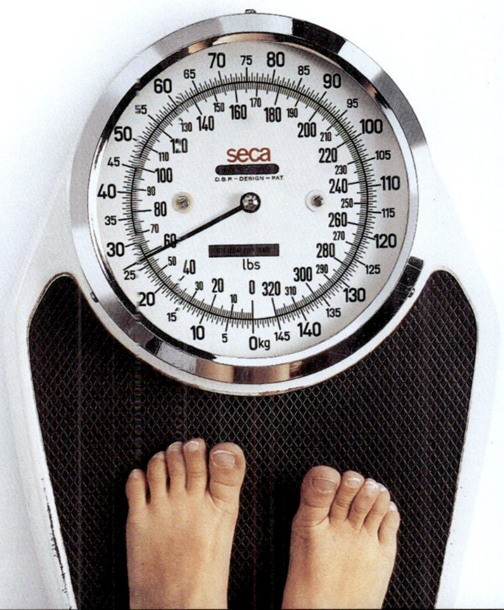

PALM DESERT SUMMER 1999 USA PB,DF: Emigre E,AD,D,P,TY: Rudy Vanderlans

67

Palm Desert
sages abound.
So head your head to the
ground
round

Meanwhile in the wild west of Hollywood
age is losing hold.
75

BROCHURE ブローシャー

ESM BROCHURE 1999 USA CL,P: ESM Consulting Engineers CD,AD,D,P: Dale Hart D: Christopher Downs / Jacqueline Smith P: Scott Areman CW: John Koval DF: The Traver Company

COVER

Realizing your project from the ground down.
"ESM has always been ahead of the curve with the latest technology. Our policy is to put great tools into creative hands. Do that, and you'll get outstanding work."
LARRY PETERSEN
president

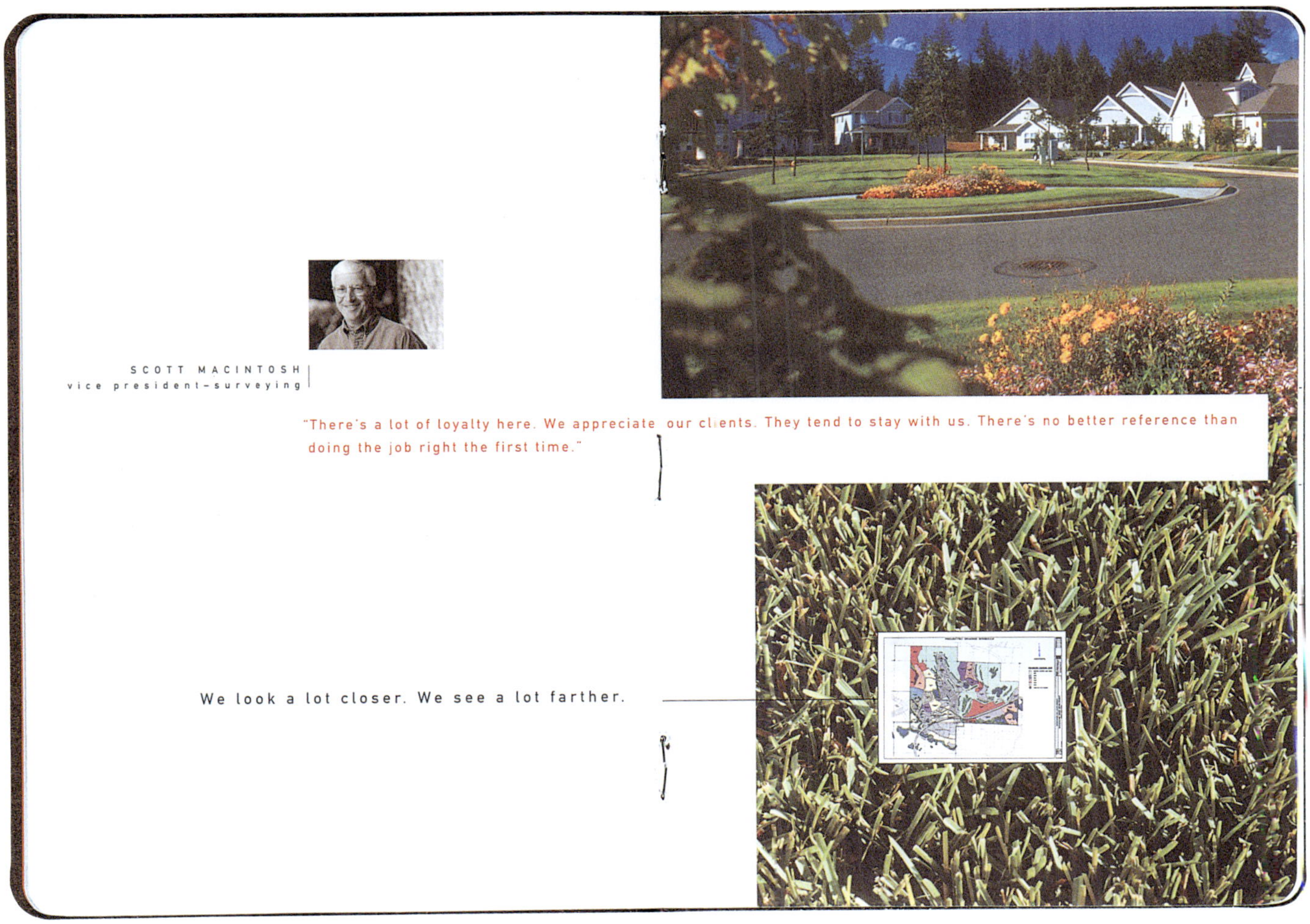
SCOTT MACINTOSH
vice president–surveying
"There's a lot of loyalty here. We appreciate our clients. They tend to stay with us. There's no better reference than doing the job right the first time."
We look a lot closer. We see a lot farther.

LINE SPRING 2000 UK

PB: TIME Life Entertainment Group Ltd. E: Tyler Brûlé / Tim Clark CD: Herbert Winkler AD: Richard Spencer Powell D: Sam Wilson TY: Fidel Peugeot@RGB107-6.com P: Wenner Hinniger (PAGE 1) / Magnus Winter (PAGE 2) ST: Sabine Feichtner (PAGE 2) Grooming: Karim Amerchih (PAGE 2)

sports news, engineering, design and trends **START**LINE

TRUNK CALL. A German triathlete in the locker room after a workout at Leipzig's Institute for Applied Training Science

CREDITS
Photographer: Wenner Hinniger

REDGOLD

The GDR might have been referred to as the German Doping Republic, but it wasn't only steroid-packed syringes that brought the country its gold medal glory. *Richard Hinzel* visits the curiously demure workshop that churns out champions and buffs up on his technical skills

LINE 35

PAGE 1

BLINE

MED AND BOARD. ***He wears*** **ski jacket, from a selection, by** Peak Performance, **from** Ski 47 Degrees. **Leather ski gloves, from a selection, by** Bogner. **Goggles, from a selection, by** Alpina, **from** Sport Kaap. **Striped knitted hat, from a selection by** Aveco, **from** Sport Kaap. ***She wears*** **Thermolite jacket, from a selection, by** Peak Performance, **from** Ski 47 Degrees. **Goggles, from a selection, by** Alpina, **from** Sport Kaap. **Knitted fleece-lined hat, from a selection, by** Bogner

CREDITS
Photographer: Magnus Winter. Photographer's assistant: Adriana Meneses von Ramin
Fashion styling: Sabine Feichtner. Grooming: Karim Amerchih. Models: Moyrick Cook and Camilla Astor
Special thanks: Hotel Albergo, Beirut and MEA

PURDAHSPORT

Like the Riyadh Bierfest, Libyan luge or Chad hosting the Americas Cup, there's something quite absurd about the idea of skiing in Lebanon. Finding good powder in the sun-seared sand bowl that is the Middle East – and only a snowball's throw from the Mediterranean – seems utterly implausible. Suspecting a mirage, *Edward Peacock* dons his Moncler flak jacket and sets out from Beirut

LINE 109

PAGE 2

MAGAZINE 雑誌

LINE SPRING 2000 UK

PB: TIME Life Entertainment Group Ltd. E: Tyler Brûlé / Tim Clark CD: Herbert Winkler AD: Richard Spencer Powell D: Sam Wilson
TY: Fidel Peugeot@RGB107-6.com

(SPREAD 1) P: Azim Haidaryan Hair: Johnny Walker Make-up: Cheryl Platt
(SPREAD 2) P: Sven Banziger ST: Caterina Soldani HM: Matthew Monzon

SPREAD 1

SPREAD 2

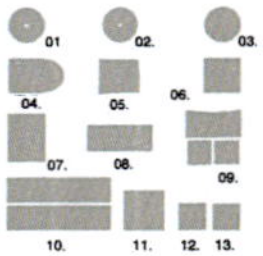

01. Artist: **Chamber**
Title: **Thrust**
Product: **12" Label**
Design & Art Direction: **Yacht Associates**
Photography: **Barnabys**
Client: **Hydrogen Dukebox**

02. Artist: **Slab**
Title: **Funked Up Kid**
Product: **12" Label**
Design & Art Direction: **Yacht Associates**
Client: **Hydrogen Dukebox1.**

03. Artist: **Bernard Butler**
Title: **Friends & Lovers**
Product: **10" Picture Disc**
Design & Art Direction: **Yacht Associates**
Illustration: **Jasper Goodall**
Client: **Creation**

04. Artist: **Blur**
Title: **On Your Own**
Product: **CD Single**
Design & Art Direction: **Yacht Associates**
Photography: **Miss Ella Louise Fortune**
Client: **Parlophone**

10. Artist: **Bernard Butler**
Title: **Friends & Lovers**
Product: **CD Album Inside**
Design & Art Direction: **Yacht Associates**
Illustration: **Jasper Goodall**
Client: **Creation**

11. Artist: **Bernard Butler**
Title: You **Must Go On**
Product: **CD Single Wallet**
Design & Art Direction: **Yacht Associates**
Illustration: **Jasper Goodall**
Client: **Creation**

12. Artist: **Bernard Butler**
Title: **You Must Go On**
Product: **7" Special Folding Vinyl**
Design & Art Direction: **Yacht Associates**
Illustration: **Jasper Goodall**
Client: **Creation**

13. Artist: **Bernard Butler**
Title: **Friends & Lovers**
Product: **10" Special Folding Vinyl**
Design & Art Direction: **Yacht Associates**
Illustration: **Jasper Goodall**
Client: **Creation**

05. Artist: **Blur**
Title: **Tender**
Product: **Foil Promo Single**
Design & Art Direction: **Yacht Associates**
Illustration: **Graham Coxon**
Client: **Parlophonee**

06. Artist: **Blur**
Title: **Blur**
Product: **CD Album**
Design & Art Direction: **Yacht Associates**
Photography: **Tony Stone Images**
Client: **Parlophone**

01.

02.

03.

04.

05.

06.

07.

08.

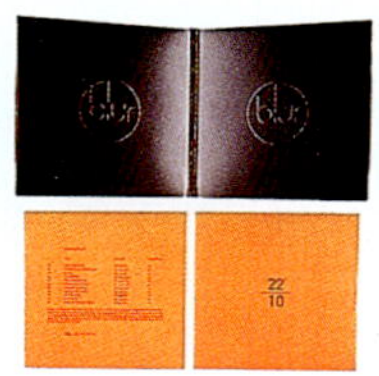
09.

10.

11.

12.

13.

+81: あの犬の写真はどうやって見つけたんですか？ C: スポーツライブラリーで見つけたんだ。ウィリアムヒル(=ロンドンの街中にたく

interview with

yacht associates / Richard Bull and Chris Thomson /

t Associates

08. Artist: **Blur**
Title: **Song 2**
Product: **Mailer Postcard**
Design & Art Direction: **Yacht Associates**
Photography: **Paul Postle**
Client: **Parlophone**

09. Artist: **Blur**
Title: **10/22**
Product: **Boxset Promo**
Design & Art Direction: **Yacht Associates**
Client: **Parlophone**

SPREAD 2

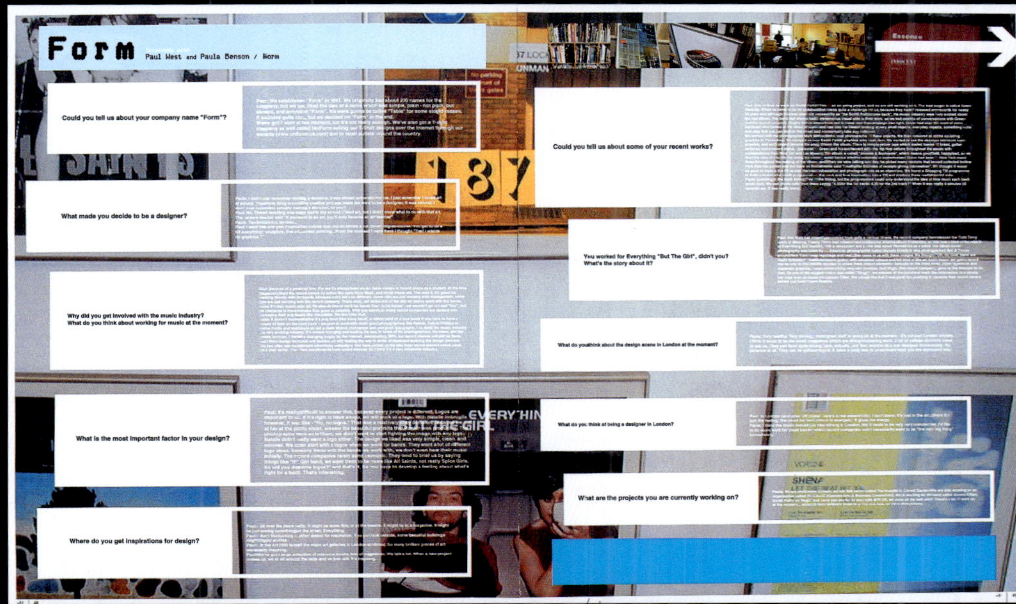

SPREAD 3

FREEPAPER フリーペーパー

LAFORET'S EYE VOL.4 1998 JAPAN CL: Laforet Harajuku CD: Tomoyuki Tanaka / Yataro Matsuura AD: Eisaku Ono P: Shinji Miyata I: Momoko Hirose

COVER

FREEPAPER フリーペーパー

LAFORET'S EYE VOL.7 1998 JAPAN CL,CD: Laforet Harajuku Matsuyama AD: Cap F: Masato Kawai CW: Teppei Kawakami / Ayumu Koike

●●●Laforet's EYE vol.007 '98 SUMMER

005
B・B・S BF 932−4201
キャミソール ¥6900
スカート ¥8900 バック ¥6900

YUKARI
今年のビーバップスタジオは、フリルや迷彩を「ハード&ラブリー」でかわいく着こなせるアイテムが超充実。

006
MARY QUANT 2F 933−3205
水着（チルデンニット） ¥18000
水着（チノクロス） ¥19000

AYA
マリーの水着は水着としてだけではもったいない。アウター感覚で着れるので、ぜひコーディネイトに加えてみて下さい。

007
アトリエメイク BF 932−9552
ワンピース ¥17800

恵
やさしくて、ナチュラルなライフスタイルが全体のイメージ。スズランプリントや刺繍入りキャミ&キャミワンピがおすすめ。

008
PAGE BOY BF 941−7858
ブラウス ¥8900
スカート ¥11800 キャミソール ¥3900

百恵
ページボーイはこの夏かわいいアイテム充実満載！ラブリー系から定番物まで全部そろうよ。（ちなみにマイブームはガ・ル・ボ）

009
45rpm BF 933−5895
半袖スウェット ¥7800

恵子
このスウェットは本当はバックプリントですが、前に着てもOK！今夏も45rpmならではのこだわりのある、着心地良い服が充実です。

010
pou dou dou BF 933−1886
シャツ¥7900 ストレッチデニム¥8900
リバーシブルハット¥5900

ヨッシー
天然素材を中心に、着心地の良い服が盛りたくさん！！あつーい夏にたくさん汗をかいても、さわやかに乗り切れます。

011
Set in BF 945−3735
ワンピース ¥17800 バスケット ¥4200

ゆき
かわいいキャミソールがいっぱい揃ってます。バックや帽子など、おしゃれな小物もお見逃しなく

012
BETTY'S BLUE BF 945−0799
ワンピース ¥15900 スカート ¥13900

Oちゃん
ベティの夏のテーマは"GIRLISH MIX"。あなたにピッタリのアイテムを探しに来てね。（ちなみに私は夏に向けて車の免許を取ります。ドライブ行くぞ！）

出会いと別れ、
本当のようなノロケ話
●松浦弥太郎（M&CO,booksellers）

それは肌寒いニューヨークでの出来事。「うー、サブー」とつぶやきながらポケットに手を突っ込んで、毎度ながら僕はブラブラと古本探しにでかけた。

勝手知らずの街では毎朝ホテルの窓から道行く人を眺めることで今日は厚着をしたほうがいいか、薄着でいいかを決めるのだが、その日はしっかり裏切られてしまった次第である。「しょうがない、スリフト・ショップでセーターでも買おう」なんて背中を丸めて街を徘徊していた僕はふと"何か"を感じて足を止めた。

こんなことはモノを探しているときによくあることで、僕はこれを「お告げ」と呼んでいる。英語でいうと「ハッピーサイン」。僕はその「お告げ」には素直に従うと何か幸せな出会いがあると信じている。用も無いのに感じるまま道を曲がってみたり、さっき行ったばかりの店なのにもう一度行ってみたり、すると必ず「やっぱり！ウフッ」と笑みを浮かべること度々。いつも何かを探してやろうという性分がある方には思い当たる節があるでしょ。

その時の「お告げ」の先はある古本屋

Laforet's EYE
vol.007 '98 summer

COVER

●●●Laforet's EYE vol.007 '98 SUMMER

045
パジャマジャ BF 933−0282
キャミセット ¥3000

陽子
パジャマジャには、安くてかわいい物がいっぱい。来てくれた方にはどんどんお買い得商品をおすすめしますので、ぜひぜひ来て下さいね。

046
Ready Steady Go! 3F 934−2155
ブルゾン ¥28000
パンツ ¥27000 シューズ ¥26800

ロン毛
ロリコンです！！

047
Vert Dense 1F 934−8595
ワンピース ¥12800
サンダル ¥13800 カーディガン ¥8900

えな
ロマンティックカジュアルを目指すならヴェールダンスへ…。デニムから刺繍入りキャミソールワンピまで何でも揃ってます。

048
島村楽器 5F 947−7337
アコースティックギター ¥75000
アンプ付ギター ¥55000
ポータブルプレーヤー ¥17800

黒田 智光（25歳）
スタッフの中で「迫力がある顔」と評判の私ですが、もうギターは3本目。やまほど魅力的なギターがあるので、もう1本…。みんな、俺とセッションしようぜ！！

049
coup de tat 4F 934−2133
ワンピース¥11900
キャミソール¥2900 バンビぬいぐるみ¥7900

涼子
クーデターの人気者バンビのぬいぐるみが登場 限定商品だから早めにGet！他にもかわいい小物や洋服がもりだくさんなので遊びに来てね。

050
CLUTCH&Heretic−goes−round
4F 933−2712
デニムパンツ ¥13800 カットソー ¥5900
ポータブルプレイヤー ¥17800

サザエさん
新人の是澤です。この夏のクラッチのオススメ商品は、コウモリデザインのアイテムです。（大洲から毎日通ってるので、是非松山で泊めてくれる人募集中です。よろしくね。）

051
ATELIER SAB for men 3F 943−3708
シャツ ¥10800
ショートパンツ ¥10800 サンダル ¥12800

セイジ
シンプルでありながら、素材使いや加工技術で遊び心を加えた98夏物が勢揃い。

EVENT Information

ラフォーレ原宿 松山15周年&CLUB BIBROS1周年記念
ラ☆マヒストラル produced by UNDER GROUND DJ'S

●DATE:6/12(Fri) ●PLACE:CLUB BIBROS ●FEE:前売り¥3500 当日¥4000（1DRINK付）
●DJ:ARATA・KIRI・CINCI・MITSU and UNDER GROUND DJ'S ●GUEST:Ed Tsuwaki

アラタ・キリ・チンチ・ミツゥの人気モデル4人がDJを務め、初防衛戦となった東京恵比寿「みるく」にておこなわれたイベントも、見事KO! 最大級の盛り上がりを見せた「ラ☆マヒストラル」。初遠征って感じで松山でも開催決定! 地元で積極的に活動している「UNDER GROUND DJ'S」のサポート&スペシャルゲストの参加で、超盛り上がり間違いなし。絶対見逃せない夜になるゾ。
●問い合わせ先：ラフォーレ原宿 松山運営室（943-4151） HAZARD・TURN-TABLE(932-1681)

Laforet's News

●この夏、Laforetオリジナルフィギュア登場！
今年はラフォーレ原宿松山の15周年を記念していろんなイベントが予定されてるけど、イメージ広告「NUDE OR LAFORET」をテーマに、ラフォーレオリジナルフィギュアも制作中。もちろん洋服にも手抜きはなし。みんな大好きブランド「ヒステリックグラマー」「スーパーラバーズ」「ベティーズブルー」「W&LT」などなど、人気ブランド別注の洋服とセットで登場！もちろん全国でもラフォーレでしか手にはいりません。8月頃にはラフォーレにお目見えするので要チェック。この夏も、ラフォーレから目がはなせないね。
（詳しいお問い合わせは、ラフォーレ原宿 松山運営室まで。各ショップへの問い合わせはご遠慮下さい。）

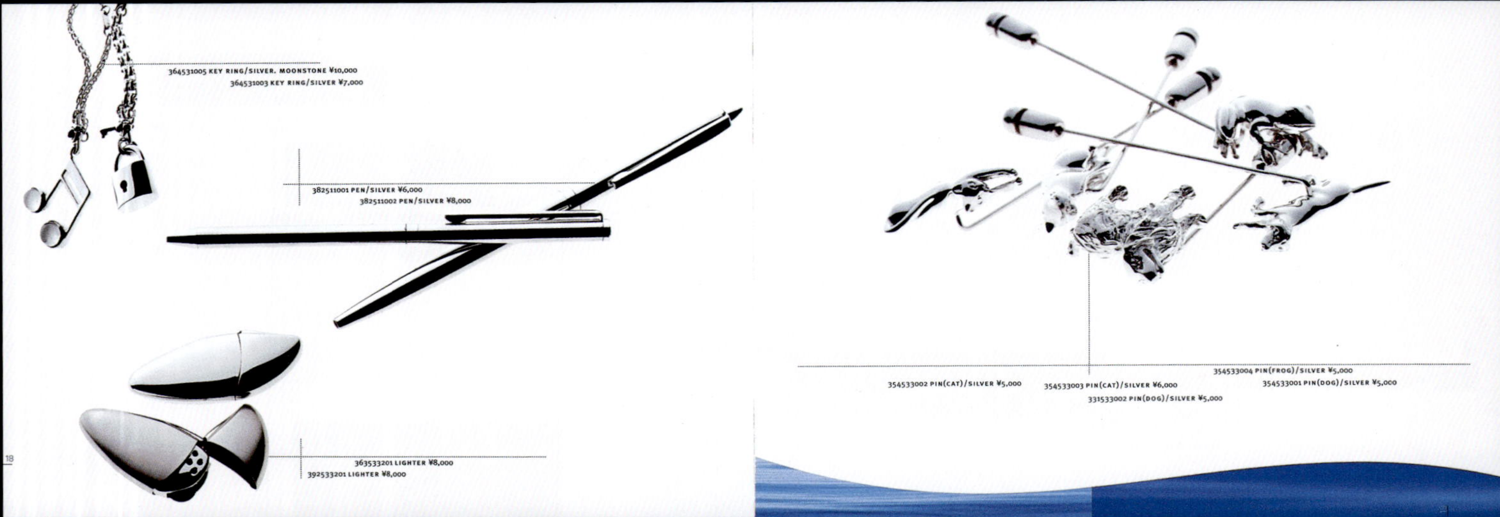
364531005 KEY RING/SILVER. MOONSTONE ¥10,000
364531003 KEY RING/SILVER ¥7,000
382511001 PEN/SILVER ¥6,000
382511002 PEN/SILVER ¥8,000
18
363533201 LIGHTER ¥8,000
392533201 LIGHTER ¥8,000
354533004 PIN(FROG)/SILVER ¥5,000
354533002 PIN(CAT)/SILVER ¥5,000
354533003 PIN(CAT)/SILVER ¥6,000
354533001 PIN(DOG)/SILVER ¥5,000
331533002 PIN(DOG)/SILVER ¥5,000

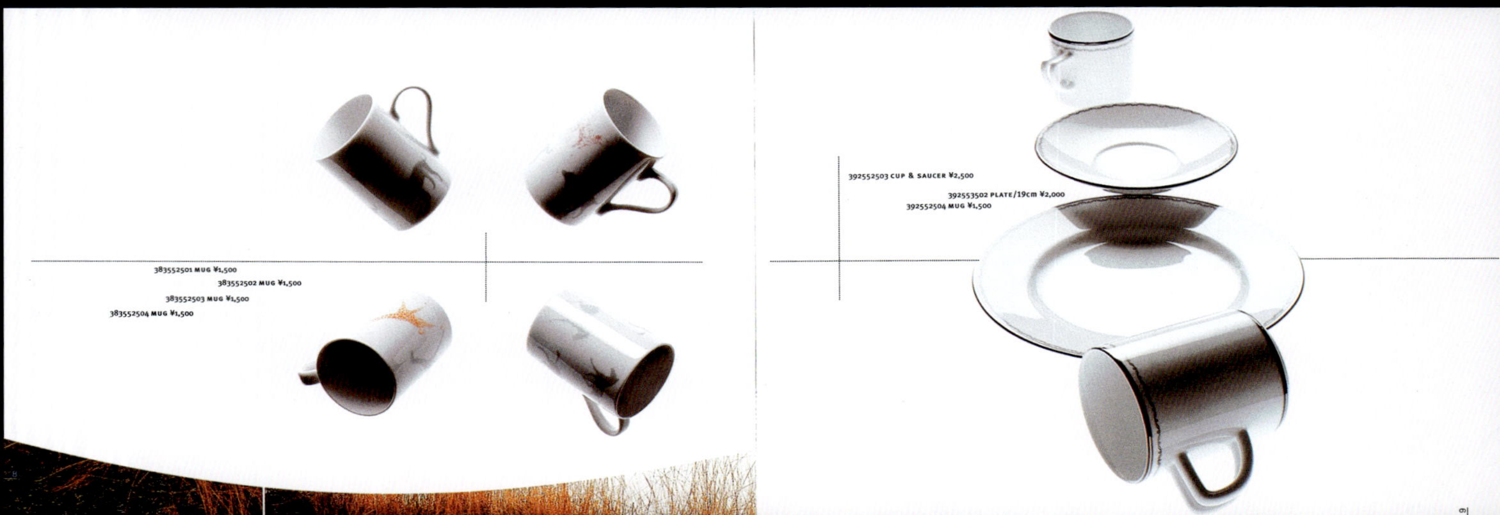
383552501 MUG ¥1,500
383552502 MUG ¥1,500
383552503 MUG ¥1,500
383552504 MUG ¥1,500
392552503 CUP & SAUCER ¥2,500
392553502 PLATE/19cm ¥2,000
392552504 MUG ¥1,500

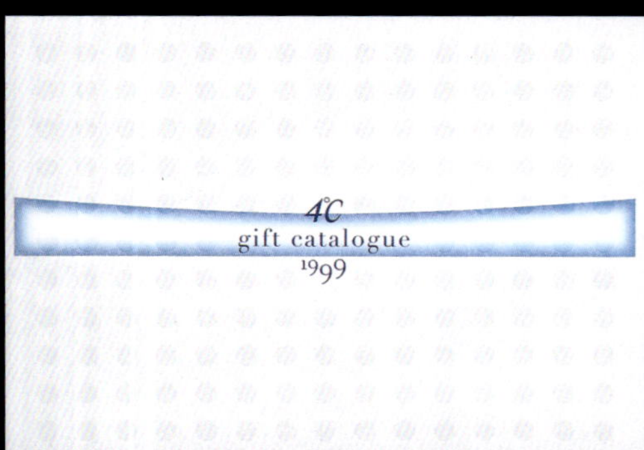
4C
gift catalogue
1999

COVER

about 2ℓ

018-02/LACQUERED LOVE LIP RING

Lungs Choker 

Heart Ring 

Liver Brooch 

Stomach Pin 

Large Intestines Bracelet 

Small Intestines Necklace 

Penis Ring 

about 60%

018-03/SILVER TORSO

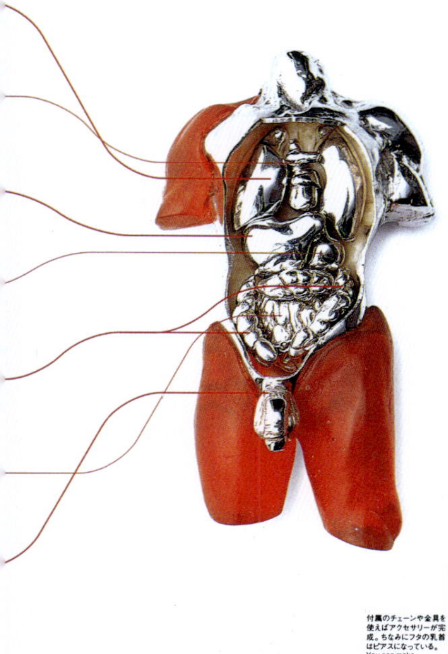

付属のチェーンや金具を使えばアクセサリーが完成。ちなみにフタの乳首はピアスになっている。
You can make accessories with a chain and metal fittings. The nipple-shaped lids of the case are earrings.

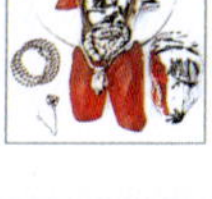

お茶する、薬を飲む、食事するなどの行為によって、人は1日に約2リットルの水分を摂取している。また、血液、汗、涙、体液などを含めると人体の約60%は水分。体重50Kgの人であれば毎日、30Kgにも及ぶ水を背負っていることになり、もしその水を失えばヒトの体温は100℃近くにまで上昇してしまう。水なくしては成り立つことも、維持することもできない人体の神秘、美しさ。それは神が創った、自然の造形美。唇、乳房、内臓の一つひとつにいたるまで、生命力にあふれ、力強く躍動するその輝きには決してどんな高価な宝石もかなわないだろう。
018-01・02/妖艶な唇型リングは01がシルバー、02はシルバーの上に漆でコーティング。018-03/ シルバーの人体ケースに、さまざまな内臓型のパーツを内蔵。心臓はリングに大腸はブレスレットに。

People consume about two liters of water a day by drinking tea, taking medicine, and eating. About 60% of the human body is water; including blood, sweat, tears, and other body fluids. The human body is about 60% water. This means that for a person who weighs 50 kilograms, about 30 kilograms is water. If all the water were to be removec from a human body, the body temperature would go up to 100 degrees Celsius. Humans cannot survive without water. The mysterious and beautiful human body is a natural plastic art-work that God made. No precious gem can compare with the energy and brilliant life-force of each part of a human body, such as lips, breast, and organs.
018-01・02 / This fascinating lip-shaped ring, '01', is silver. '02' is covered with lacquer.
018-03/ This silver human-body case has various organ-shaped parts. The heart is a ring. The colon is bracelet.

018
SILICON BABY >>P132

WATER PLANET STORE
purchasing information P.136

018-01 Love Lip Ring	¥10,000
018-02 Lacquered Love Lip Ring	¥18,000
018-03 Silver Torso	¥600,000

01●素材／Silver925 ●サイズ／W30 D30 H30 ●受注制作 ※サイズは12号〜20号のみ

02●素材／Silver925・漆塗り ●サイズ／W30 D30 H30 ●カラー／赤・ベージュ ●受注制作 ※サイズは12号〜20号のみ ※こちらの商品は漆の完全乾燥のため、到着後最低3ヵ月間はご使用できません。また、アレルギー体質の方にはお薦めしかねます。

03●素材／Silver925,950・アクリル樹脂 ●サイズ／W70 D150 H50 ●セット内容／人体型ケース×1＋choker×1＋ring×2＋brooch×1＋pin×1＋bracelet×1＋necklace×1＋取付け金具×1 ●受注制作限定10個

MAGAZINE 雑誌

RELUCKS 1999 JAPAN E: Chokkaku Shibuya / Shogo Kawabata / Masaru Kato AD,D: tgb design

MR. HIGH FASHION JUNE 2000 JAPAN

PB: Bunka Shuppankyoku E: Toshiko Taguchi / Kazuhiro Kikuchi D: Kei Nihongi (3.4.5.) P: Junji Hata (COVER) / Yosio Kato (B P.B.)
Model: Ryuhei Matsuda (COVER) ST: Tomoki Sukezane (COVER) HM: Ryoji Inagaki (Maroon brand) (COVER)

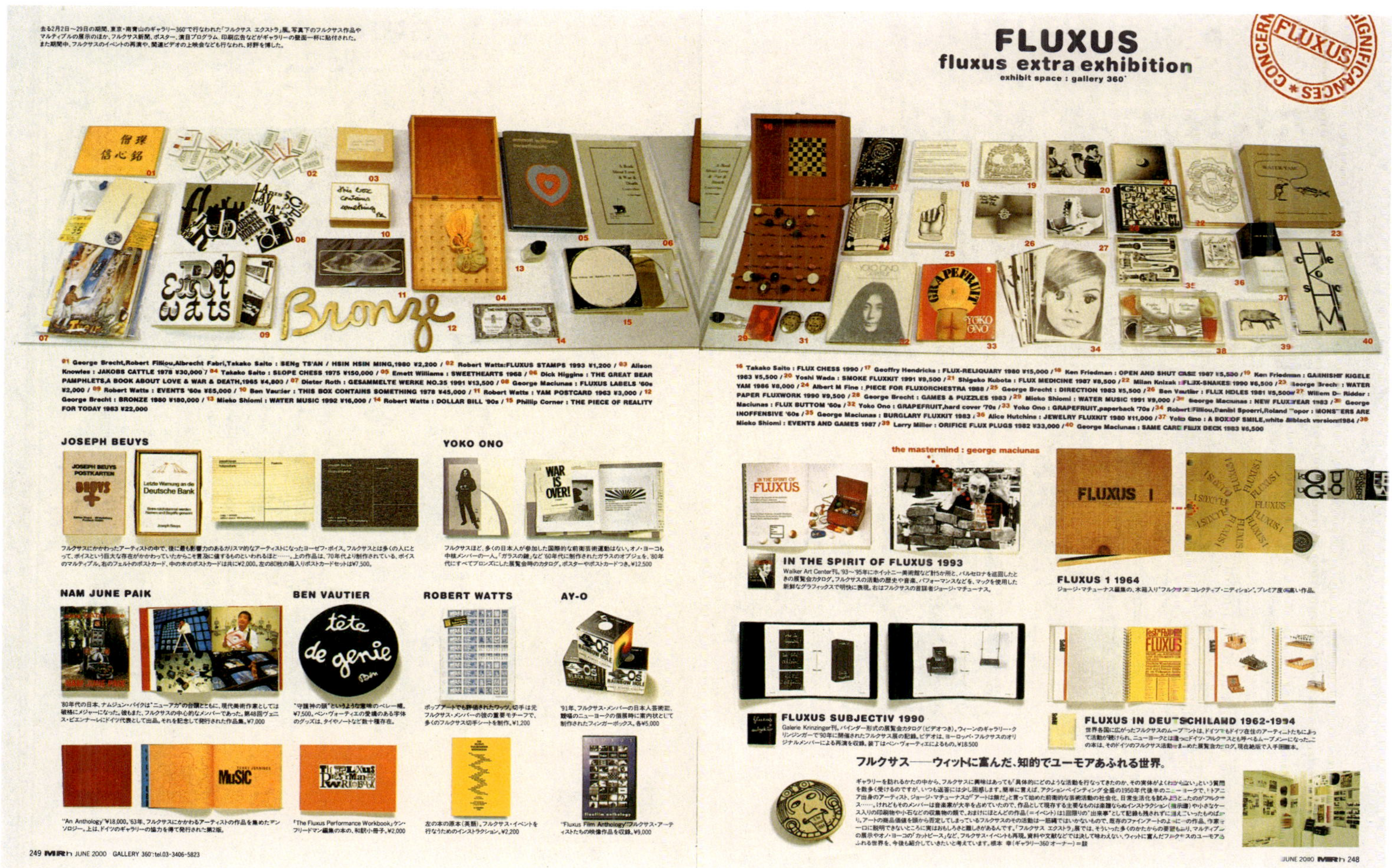

COVER

FIGURE/PLATE CAPTIONS

MAGAZINE 雑誌

MR. HIGH FASHION　JUNE 2000　JAPAN

PB: Bunka Shuppankyoku　E: Toshiko Taguchi / Mami Aiko　CD: Kazuhiro Kikuchi　D: Kei Nihongi (3.4.5.)
P: Futoshi / Yasuo Matsumoto　HM: Katsumi Nagatsuka (Heads)　ST: Yoshitomo Ochi (Cab)

TOKION NO.18 MAY 2000 JAPAN PB: Knee High Media Japan E: Kaori Sakura AD,D: Takaya Toyama P: Yasuhide Kuge I: Kenichi Watanabe

As I lie on the verge of a peaceful sleep in my bed made of cypress, children in the southern part of America play cards together in a tree house.

檜のベッドの上で心地よい眠りについている時、アメリカ中南部に住む少年は小さなツリーハウスの中で友達とトランプをしている。

As I water a red pine bonsai which decorates the window sill, a weaver enjoys an afternoon nap under the shade of a large tree in Iran.

窓辺に飾られた小さな赤松の盆栽にじっくり水をあげている時、イランの織物職人は大きな木の木陰で食後の一服を満喫している。

As people celebrate under a cherry tree on the banks of a river, harvested lumber is stacked neatly in the back of a truck in Norway.

川沿いの桜並木の下で盛大な宴が行われている時、ノルウェーの木こりは伐採したての材木をトラックに積んでいる。

We fold our hands together at a temple where the fragrance from the cedar trees floats in the air. At the same time a large family in Madagascar gazes up at the stars from under a baobab tree.

杉の香りが漂う森の神社でゆっくり手を合わせている時、マダガスカルの大家族はバイバブの木の間から夜空の星を眺めている。

Our countries, words and environments are all a little different, but we share a singular thought: "Trees are soooo nice." At any given moment in any given place that thought is running through someone's mind.

国も言葉も環境も、みんなそれぞれ違うのに、思うことはひとつだけ。「木はいいなあ」いつもどこかでそんな思いがグルグルグルグルまわってる。

Woody Life

Photography: YASUHIDE KUGE

Illustration: KENICHI WATANABE

Special Thanks: MASAMITSU SAITO, MINERVA

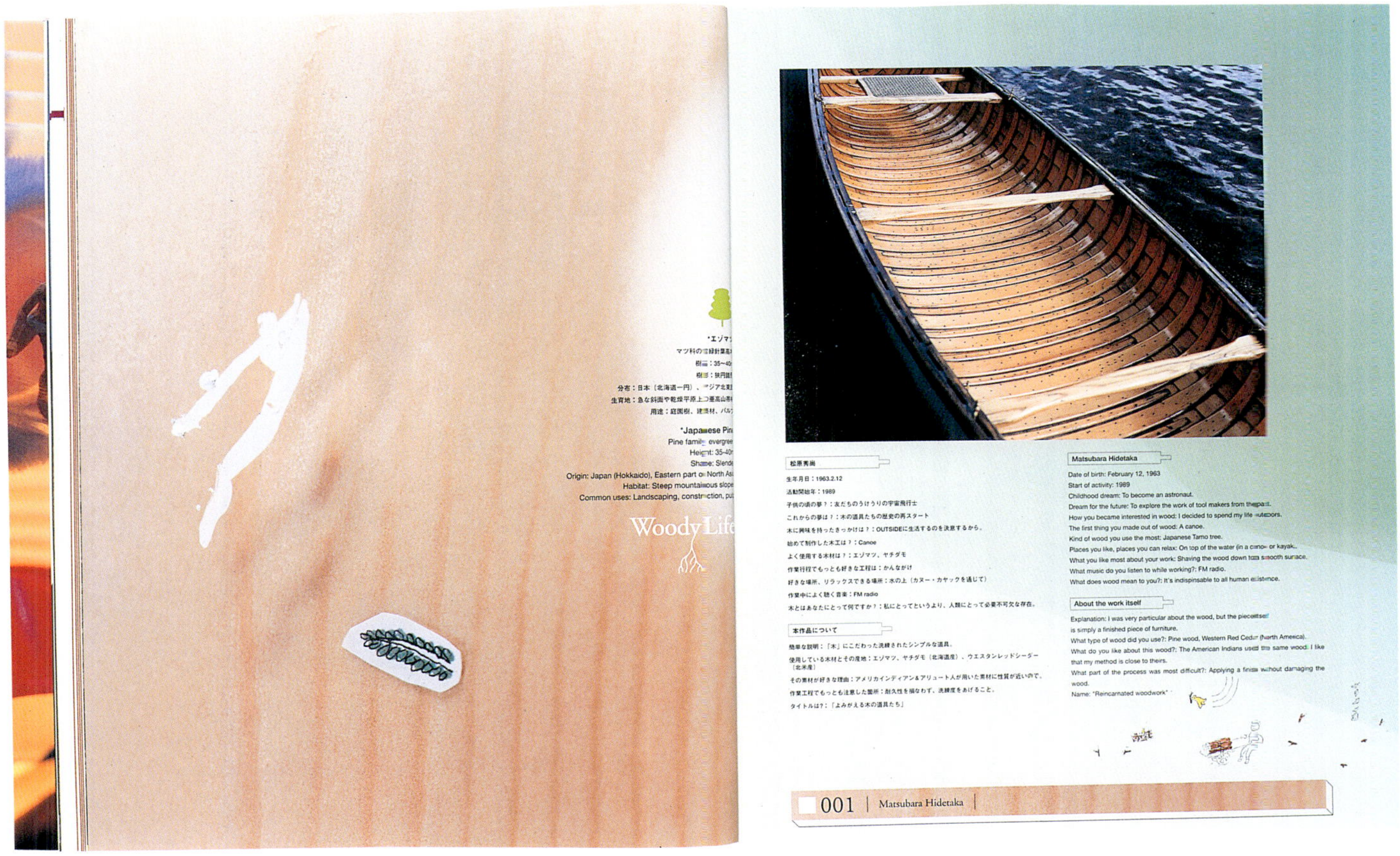

松原秀尚

生年月日：1963.2.12

活動開始年：1989

子供の頃の夢？：友だちのうけうりの宇宙飛行士

これからの夢は？：木の道具たちの歴史の再スタート

木に興味を持ったきっかけは？：OUTSIDEに生活するのを決意するから。

始めて制作した木工は？：Canoe

よく使用する木材は？：エゾマツ、ヤチダモ

作業行程でもっとも好きな工程は：かんながけ

好きな場所、リラックスできる場所：水の上（カヌー・カヤックを通じて）

作業中によく聴く音楽：FM radio

木とはあなたにとって何ですか？：私にとってというより、人類にとって必要不可欠な存在。

本作品について

簡単な説明：「木」にこだわった洗練されたシンプルな道具。

使用している木材とその産地：エゾマツ、ヤチダモ（北海道産）、ウエスタンレッドシーダー（北米産）

その素材が好きな理由：アメリカインディアン&アリュート人が用いた素材に性質が近いので。

作業工程でもっとも注意した箇所：耐久性を損なわず、洗練度をあげること。

タイトルは?：「よみがえる木の道具たち」

Matsubara Hidetaka

Date of birth: February 12, 1963

Start of activity: 1989

Childhood dream: To become an astronaut.

Dream for the future: To explore the work of tool makers from the past.

How you became interested in wood: I decided to spend my life outdoors.

The first thing you made out of wood: A canoe.

Kind of wood you use the most: Japanese Tamo tree.

Places you like, places you can relax: On top of the water (in a canoe or kayak).

What you like most about your work: Shaving the wood down to a smooth surface.

What music do you listen to while working?: FM radio.

What does wood mean to you?: It's indispinsable to all human existence.

About the work itself

Explanation: I was very particular about the wood, but the piece itself is simply a finished piece of furniture.

What type of wood did you use?: Pine wood, Western Red Cedar (North America).

What do you like about this wood?: The American Indians used the same wood. I like that my method is close to theirs.

What part of the process was most difficult?: Applying a finish without damaging the wood.

Name: "Reincarnated woodwork"

001 | Matsubara Hidetaka

CATALOG カタログ

SUNDOG 1995 USA CL: SunDog, Inc. AD,D: Jack Anderson D: David Bates P: Darrell Peterson I: Todd Connor CW: Julie Huffaker DF: Hornall Anderson Design Works, Inc.

COVER

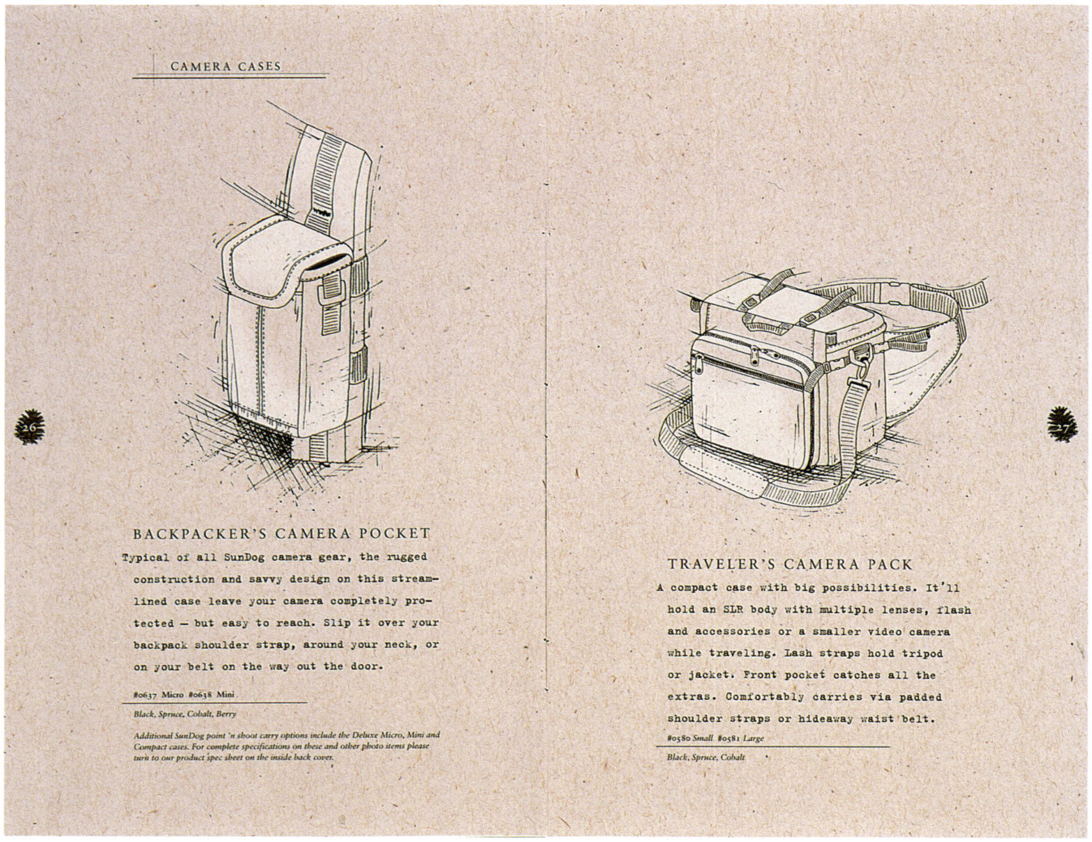

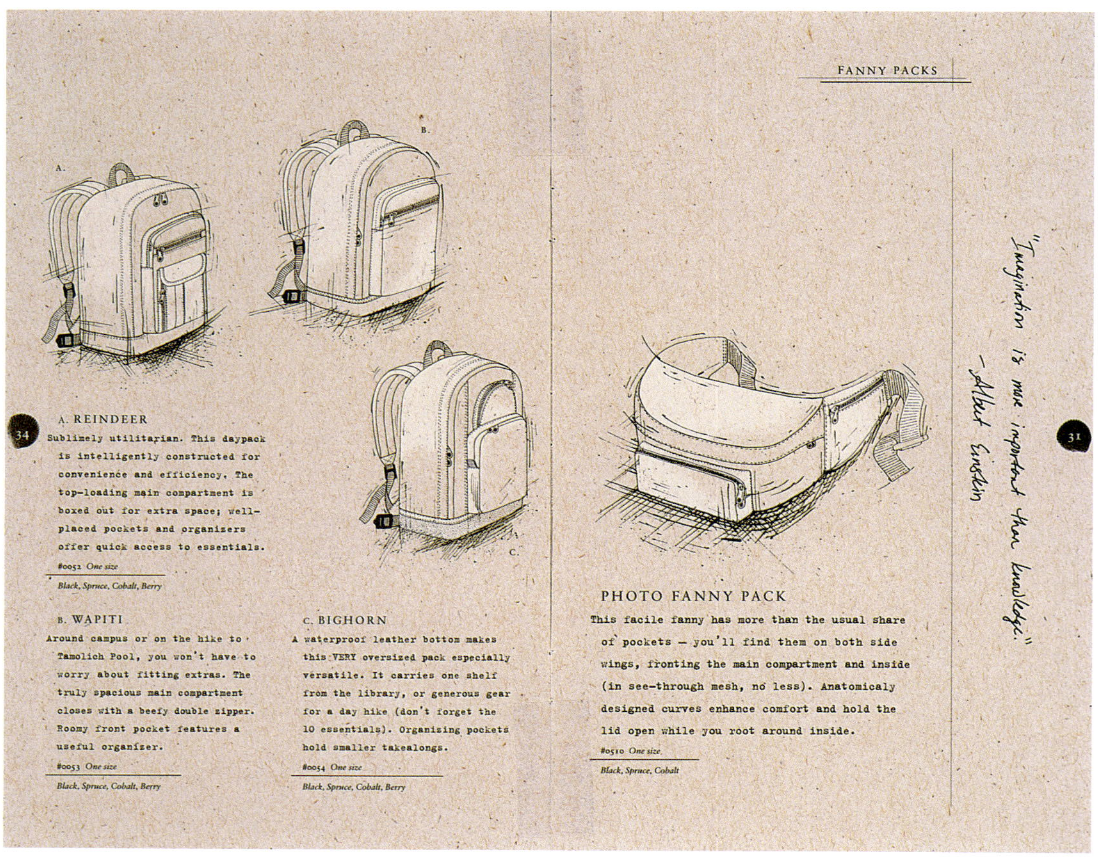

CATALOG カタログ

LEATHERMAN 1997 USA CL,CW: Leatherman Tools AD: Jack Anderson AD,D: David Bates D: Lisa Cerveny P: Condit Studio I: Jack Unruh
DF: Hornall Anderson Design Works, Inc.

COVER

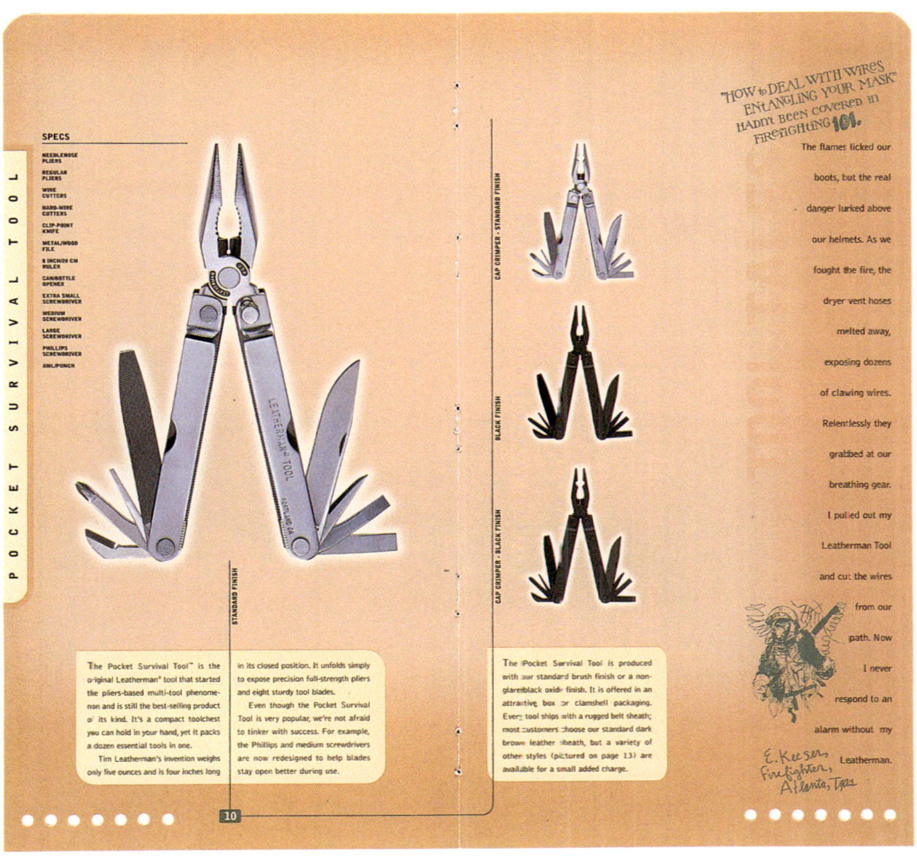

SUPERHUMAN CREW 1999 USA CL: J. Paul Getty Museum D: Markus Brilling P: Lou Meluso DF: J. Paul Getty Trust Publication Services

COVER

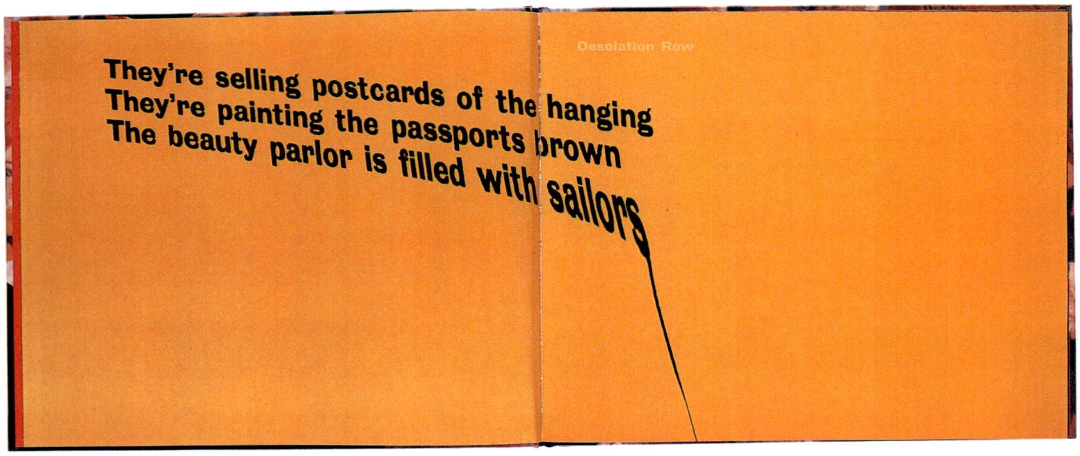

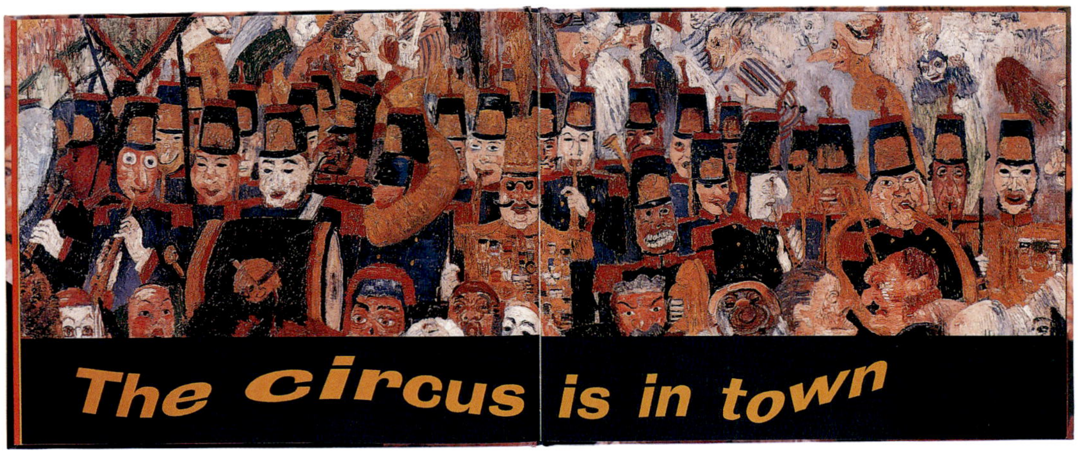

BOOK 書籍

WHAT'S THE STORY? 1999 AUSTRALIA/USA CL: Stewart, Taboli & Chang D: Annie Schwebel I: Matthew Johnstone

COVER

COULTER 1997 ANNUAL REPORT 1998 USA CL: Coulter Pharmaceutical CD,AD: Bill Cahan D,CW: Kevin Roberson P: Robert Schlatter CW: Sylvia Wheeler DF: Cahan & Associates

COVER

FIRST-LINE STAGE

INTERIM DATA ON 24 PATIENTS FROM A PHASE II TRIAL OF NEWLY-DIAGNOSED PATIENTS TREATED WITH BEXXAR DEMONSTRATED A 100 PERCENT OVERALL RESPONSE RATE, WITH 71 PERCENT OF PATIENTS EXPERIENCING COMPLETE REMISSION OF THEIR DISEASE.

REFRACTORY STAGE

DATA FROM A MULTI-CENTER, PHASE II TRIAL OF 45 PATIENTS WITH ADVANCED-STAGE DISEASE REVEALED THAT 31 PERCENT OF PATIENTS EXPERIENCED A COMPLETE REMISSION FOLLOWING BEXXAR THERAPY.

100 %
97.5%
95.0%
92.5%
90.0%
87.5%
85.5%
80.5%
77.5%
75.0%
72.5%
71.0%
67.5%
65.0%
62.5%
60.0%
57.5%
55.0%
52.5%
50.0%
47.5%
45.0%
42.5%
40.0%
37.5%
35.0%
32.5%
31.0%
27.5%
25.0%
22.5%
20.0%
17.5%
15.0%
12.5%
10.0%
07.5%
05.0%
02.5%
00.0%

71%

complete remission

31%

complete remission

3

BOOK 書籍

YOUR MOST VALUABLE POSSESSION 1999 NETHERLANDS CL: PANL CD,AD: Erik Kessels CD: Johan Kramer D: Harmine Louwé CW: Franklin Neuteboom DF: Kesselskramer

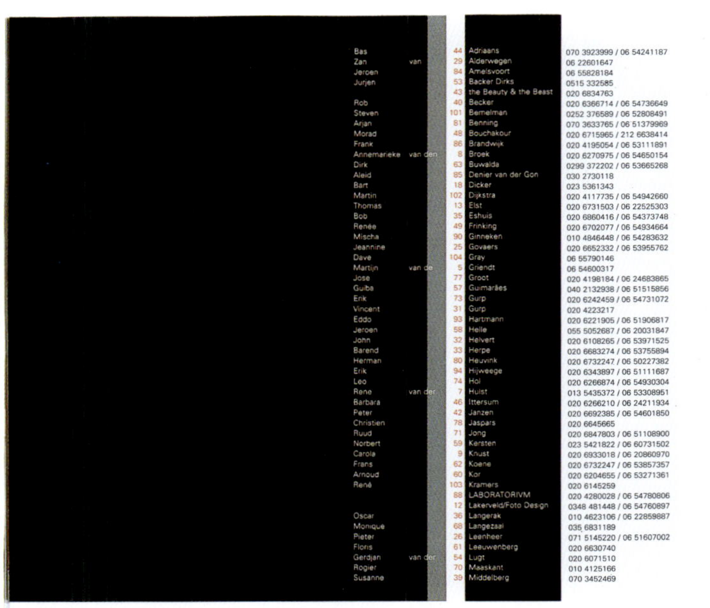

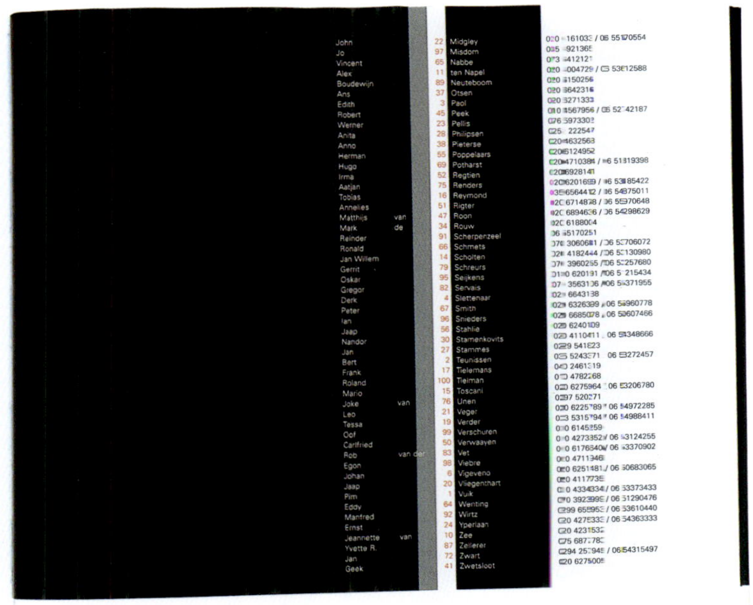

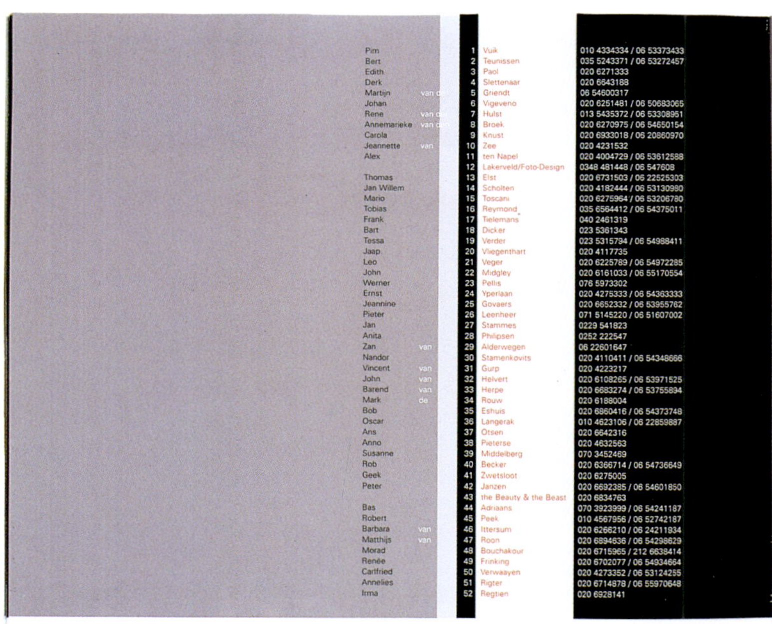

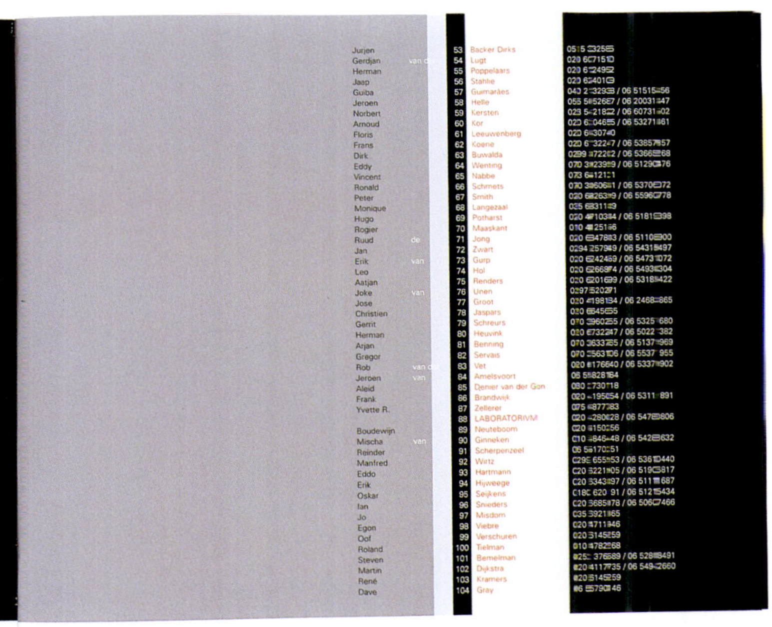

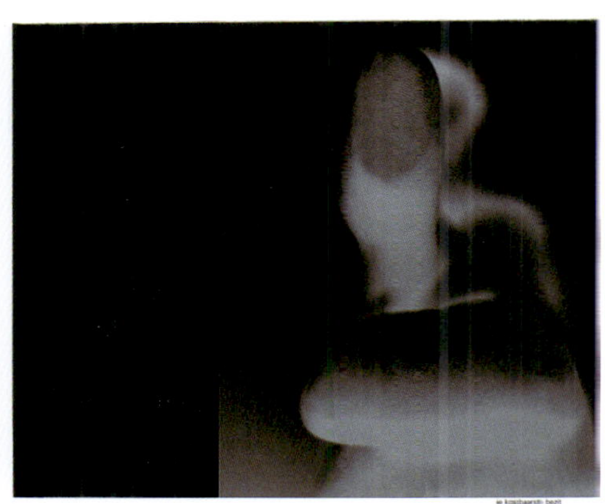

COVER

ZEUM BROCHURE 1998 USA CL: ZEUM CD,AD: Bill Cahan D,CW: Ben Pham CW: Suzanne Tuchler DF: Cahan & Associates

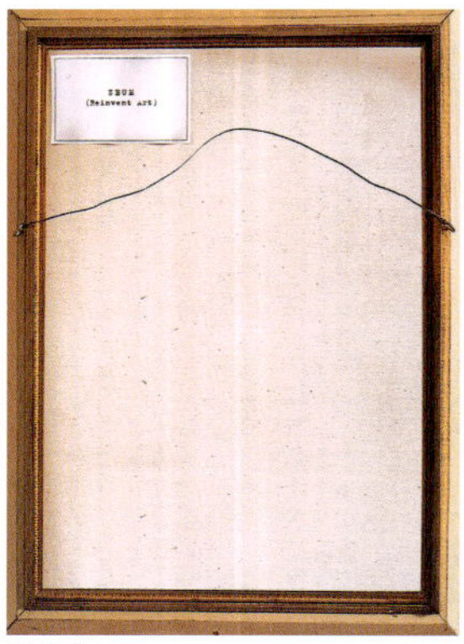

COVER

PROGENITOR 1997 ANNUAL REPORT 1998 USA CL: Progenitor CD,AD: Bill Cahan D,I,CW: Bob Dinetz P: Jay Blakesberg CW: Carrie Wick DF: Cahan & Associates

COVER

7 >>>

FY97 Accomplishments

Accomplishment	Month YEAR
Functional genomics collaboration formed with Vanderbilt University	10 96
Functional genomics collaboration formed with the National Jewish Center	10 96
Leptin receptor licensing agreement formed with Amgen Inc.	12 96
T7T7 nonviral gene delivery system patent issued	01 97
Asthma DNA chip collaboration formed with Affymetrix, Inc.	02 97
EPM1 epilepsy gene licensed from Stanford University	02 97
Mercator acquisition agreement	02 97
Bioinformatics collaboration formed with Pangea Systems, Inc.	03 97
Gene expression collaboration formed with University of Cambridge	04 97
Functional genomics collaboration formed with Ontario Cancer Institute	05 97
First US patent for leptin receptor issued	07 97
Initial public offering	08 97
Relocation and consolidation of facilities in Menlo Park, CA	09 97
HH gene licensing agreement formed with SmithKline Beecham	09 97
High-throughput genomic sequencing patent issued	09 97

MOLECULAR BIOSYSTEMS 1998 ANNUAL REPORT 1998 USA CL: Molecular Biosystems Inc. CD,AD: Bill Cahan D,CW: Kevin Roberson P: Ken Probst / Various CW: Bob Giargiari DF: Cahan & Associates

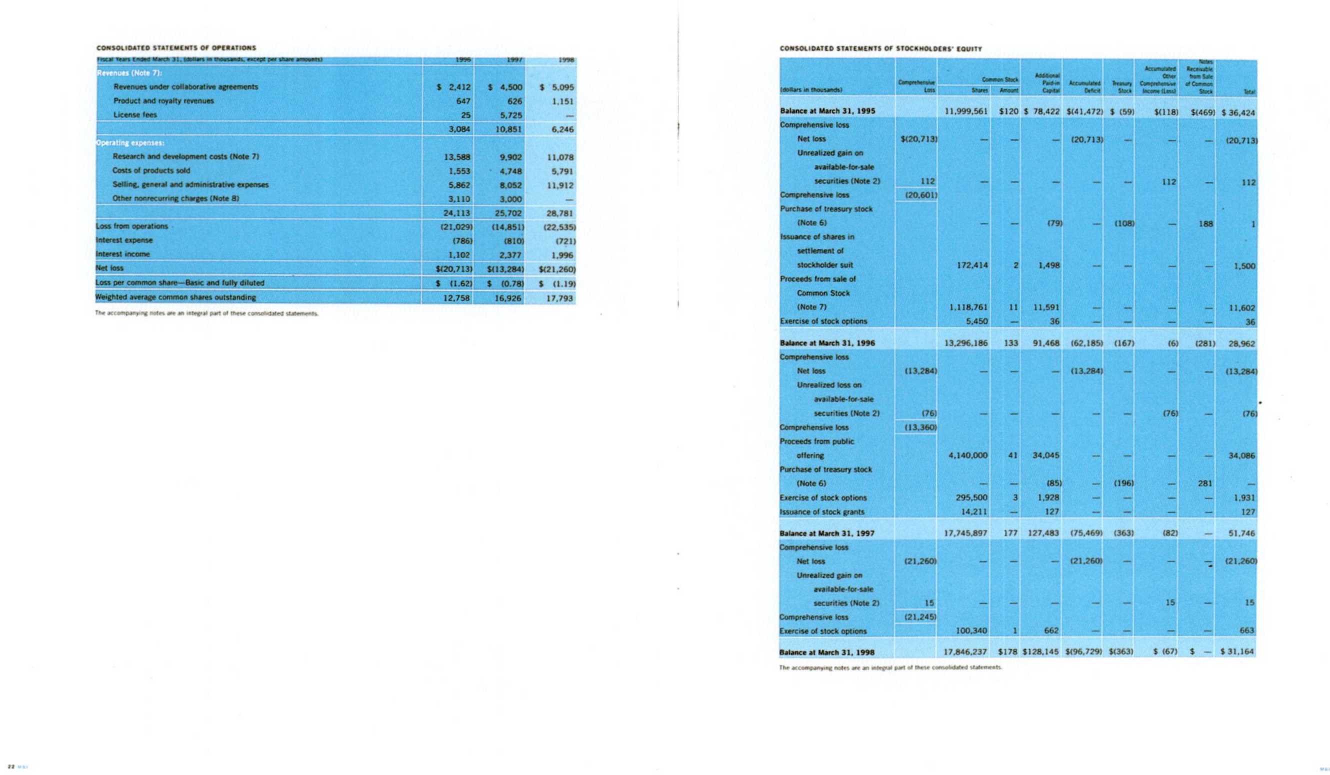

CONSOLIDATED STATEMENTS OF OPERATIONS

Fiscal Years Ended March 31, (dollars in thousands, except per share amounts)	1996	1997	1998
Revenues (Note 7):			
Revenues under collaborative agreements	$ 2,412	$ 4,500	$ 5,095
Product and royalty revenues	647	626	1,151
License fees	25	5,725	—
	3,084	10,851	6,246
Operating expenses:			
Research and development costs (Note 7)	13,588	9,902	11,078
Costs of products sold	1,553	4,748	5,791
Selling, general and administrative expenses	5,862	8,052	11,912
Other nonrecurring charges (Note 8)	3,110	3,000	—
	24,113	25,702	28,781
Loss from operations	(21,029)	(14,851)	(22,535)
Interest expense	(786)	(810)	(721)
Interest income	1,102	2,377	1,996
Net loss	$(20,713)	$(13,284)	$(21,260)
Loss per common share—Basic and fully diluted	$ (1.62)	$ (0.78)	$ (1.19)
Weighted average common shares outstanding	12,758	16,926	17,793

The accompanying notes are an integral part of these consolidated statements.

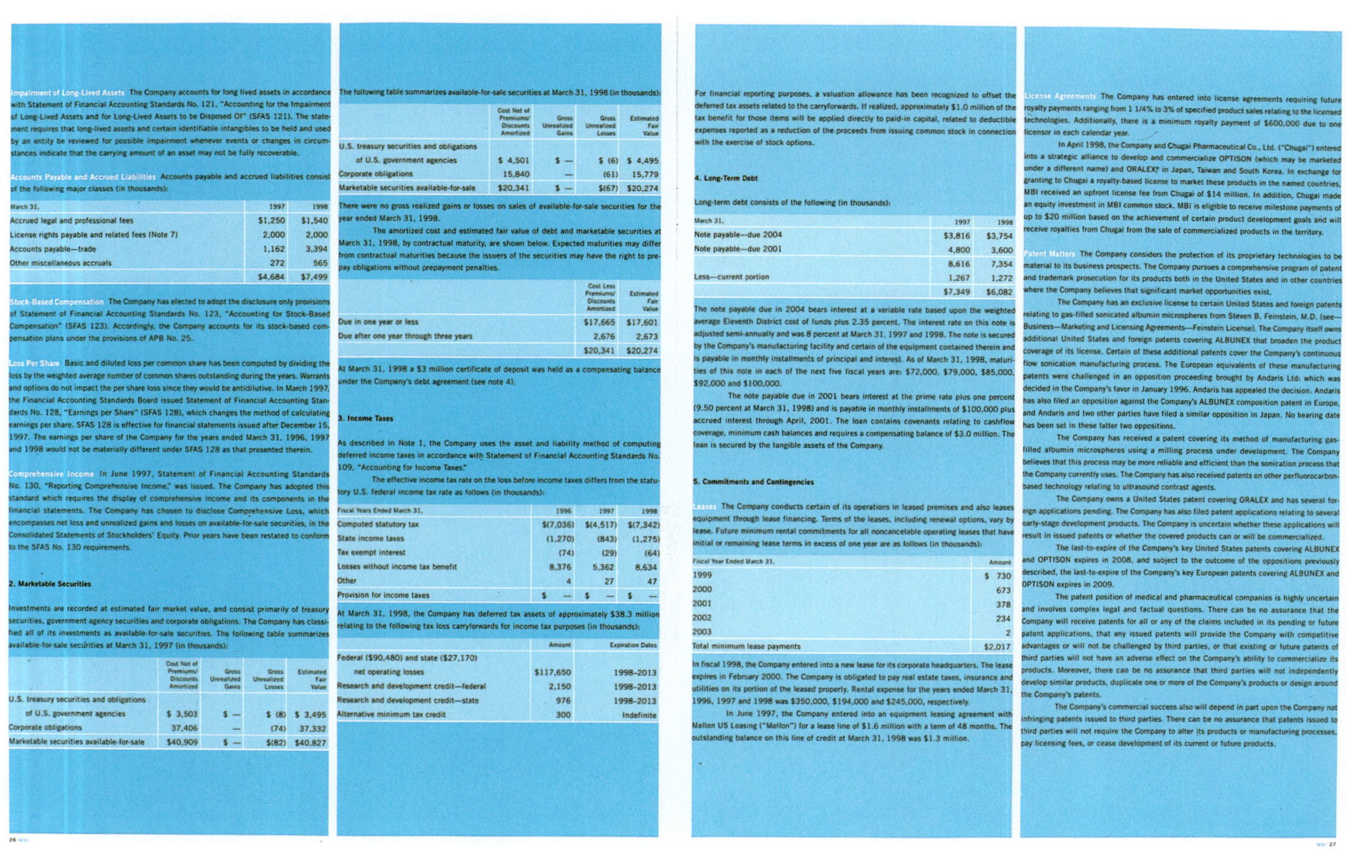

GILEAD SCIENCES 1997 ANNUAL REPORT 1998 USA

CL: Gilead Sciences CD,AD: Bill Cahan D,I: Lian Ng P: Daniel De Sousa CW: Lana Lauher / Susan Hubbard
DF: Cahan & Associates

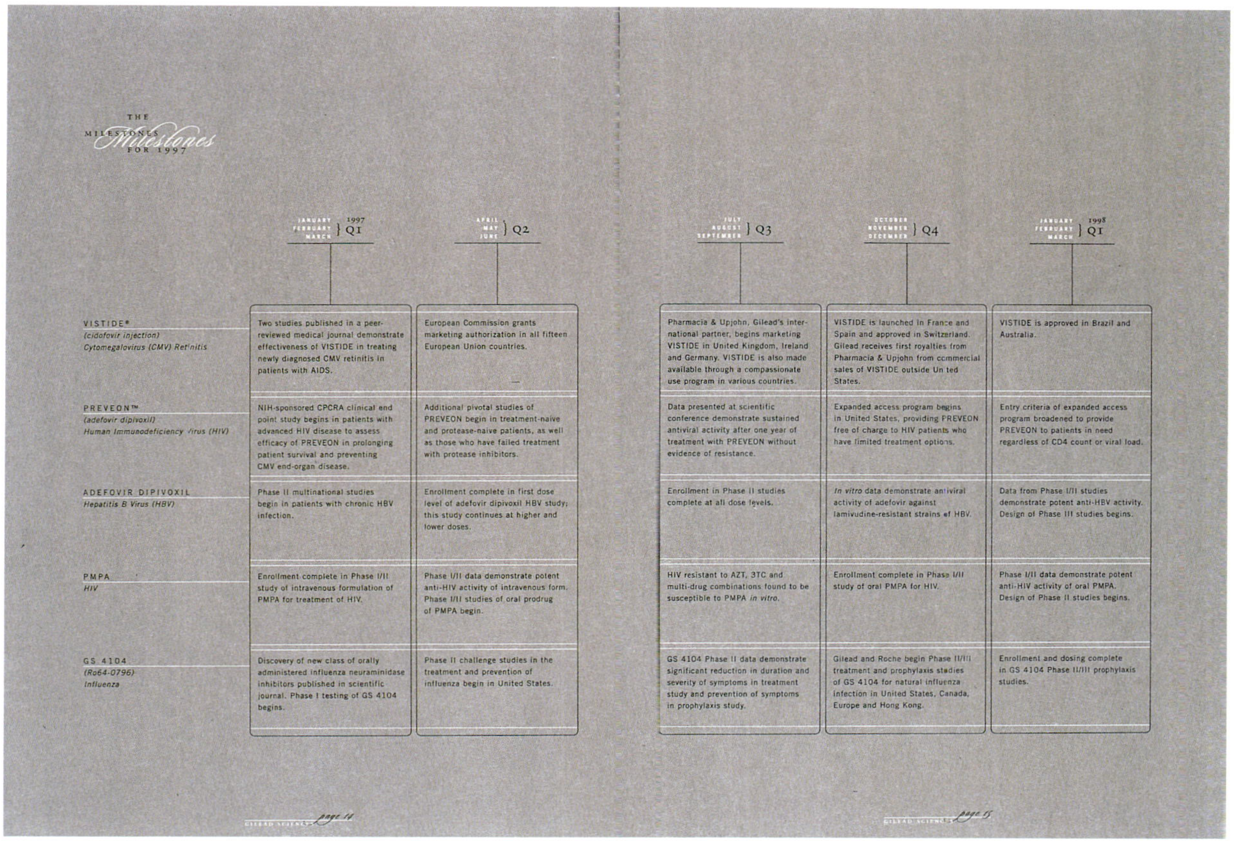

THE MILESTONES *Milestones* FOR 1997

	JANUARY FEBRUARY MARCH } Q1 1997	APRIL MAY JUNE } Q2	JULY AUGUST SEPTEMBER } Q3	OCTOBER NOVEMBER DECEMBER } Q4	JANUARY FEBRUARY MARCH } Q1 1998
VISTIDE® *(cidofovir injection)* *Cytomegalovirus (CMV) Retinitis*	Two studies published in a peer-reviewed medical journal demonstrate effectiveness of VISTIDE in treating newly diagnosed CMV retinitis in patients with AIDS.	European Commission grants marketing authorization in all fifteen European Union countries.	Pharmacia & Upjohn, Gilead's international partner, begins marketing VISTIDE in United Kingdom, Ireland and Germany. VISTIDE is also made available through a compassionate use program in various countries.	VISTIDE is launched in France and Spain and approved in Switzerland. Gilead receives first royalties from Pharmacia & Upjohn from commercial sales of VISTIDE outside United States.	VISTIDE is approved in Brazil and Australia.
PREVEON™ *(adefovir dipivoxil)* *Human Immunodeficiency Virus (HIV)*	NIH-sponsored CPCRA clinical end point study begins in patients with advanced HIV disease to assess efficacy of PREVEON in prolonging patient survival and preventing CMV end-organ disease.	Additional pivotal studies of PREVEON begin in treatment-naive and protease-naive patients, as well as those who have failed treatment with protease inhibitors.	Data presented at scientific conference demonstrate sustained antiviral activity after one year of treatment with PREVEON without evidence of resistance.	Expanded access program begins in United States, providing PREVEON free of charge to HIV patients who have limited treatment options.	Entry criteria of expanded access program broadened to provide PREVEON to patients in need regardless of CD4 count or viral load.
ADEFOVIR DIPIVOXIL *Hepatitis B Virus (HBV)*	Phase II multinational studies begin in patients with chronic HBV infection.	Enrollment complete in first dose level of adefovir dipivoxil HBV study; this study continues at higher and lower doses.	Enrollment in Phase II studies complete at all dose levels.	*In vitro* data demonstrate antiviral activity of adefovir against lamivudine-resistant strains of HBV.	Data from Phase I/II studies demonstrate potent anti-HBV activity. Design of Phase III studies begins.
PMPA *HIV*	Enrollment complete in Phase I/II study of intravenous formulation of PMPA for treatment of HIV.	Phase I/II data demonstrate potent anti-HIV activity of intravenous form. Phase I/II studies of oral prodrug of PMPA begin.	HIV resistant to AZT, 3TC and multi-drug combinations found to be susceptible to PMPA *in vitro*.	Enrollment complete in Phase I/II study of oral PMPA for HIV.	Phase I/II data demonstrate potent anti-HIV activity of oral PMPA. Design of Phase II studies begins.
GS 4104 *(Ro64-0796)* *Influenza*	Discovery of new class of orally administered influenza neuraminidase inhibitors published in scientific journal. Phase I testing of GS 4104 begins.	Phase II challenge studies in the treatment and prevention of influenza begin in United States.	GS 4104 Phase II data demonstrate significant reduction in duration and severity of symptoms in treatment study and prevention of symptoms in prophylaxis study.	Gilead and Roche begin Phase II/III treatment and prophylaxis studies of GS 4104 for natural influenza infection in United States, Canada, Europe and Hong Kong.	Enrollment and dosing complete in GS 4104 Phase II/III prophylaxis studies.

GILEAD SCIENCES *page 14*

GILEAD SCIENCES *page 15*

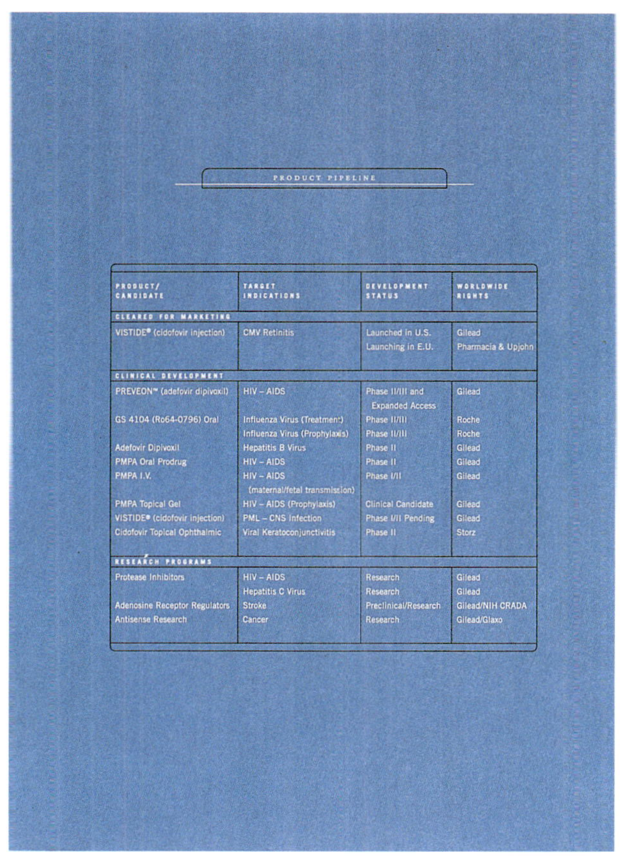

PRODUCT PIPELINE

PRODUCT/ CANDIDATE	TARGET INDICATIONS	DEVELOPMENT STATUS	WORLDWIDE RIGHTS
CLEARED FOR MARKETING			
VISTIDE® (cidofovir injection)	CMV Retinitis	Launched in U.S. Launching in E.U.	Gilead Pharmacia & Upjohn
CLINICAL DEVELOPMENT			
PREVEON™ (adefovir dipivoxil)	HIV – AIDS	Phase II/III and Expanded Access	Gilead
GS 4104 (Ro64-0796) Oral	Influenza Virus (Treatment)	Phase II/III	Roche
	Influenza Virus (Prophylaxis)	Phase II/III	Roche
Adefovir Dipivoxil	Hepatitis B Virus	Phase II	Gilead
PMPA Oral Prodrug	HIV – AIDS	Phase II	Gilead
PMPA I.V.	HIV – AIDS (maternal/fetal transmission)	Phase I/II	Gilead
PMPA Topical Gel	HIV – AIDS (Prophylaxis)	Clinical Candidate	Gilead
VISTIDE® (cidofovir injection)	PML – CNS Infection	Phase I/II Pending	Gilead
Cidofovir Topical Ophthalmic	Viral Keratoconjunctivitis	Phase II	Storz
RESEARCH PROGRAMS			
Protease Inhibitors	HIV – AIDS	Research	Gilead
	Hepatitis C Virus	Research	Gilead
Adenosine Receptor Regulators	Stroke	Preclinical/Research	Gilead/NIH CRADA
Antisense Research	Cancer	Research	Gilead/Glaxo

BROCHURE ブローシャー

FRANK RUSSELL COMPANY 1999 LIFEPOINTS BROCHURE 1999 USA

CL,CW: Frank Russell Company AD: Jack Anderson AD,D: Lisa Cerveny
D,I: Margaret Long / Holly Craven / Michael Brugman / Alan Florsheim
D: Mary Hermes / Kaye Farmer P: Rosanne Olson / Robin Bartholick
I: Heidi Favour / Otto Steininger / Don Stayner DF: Hornall Anderson Design Works

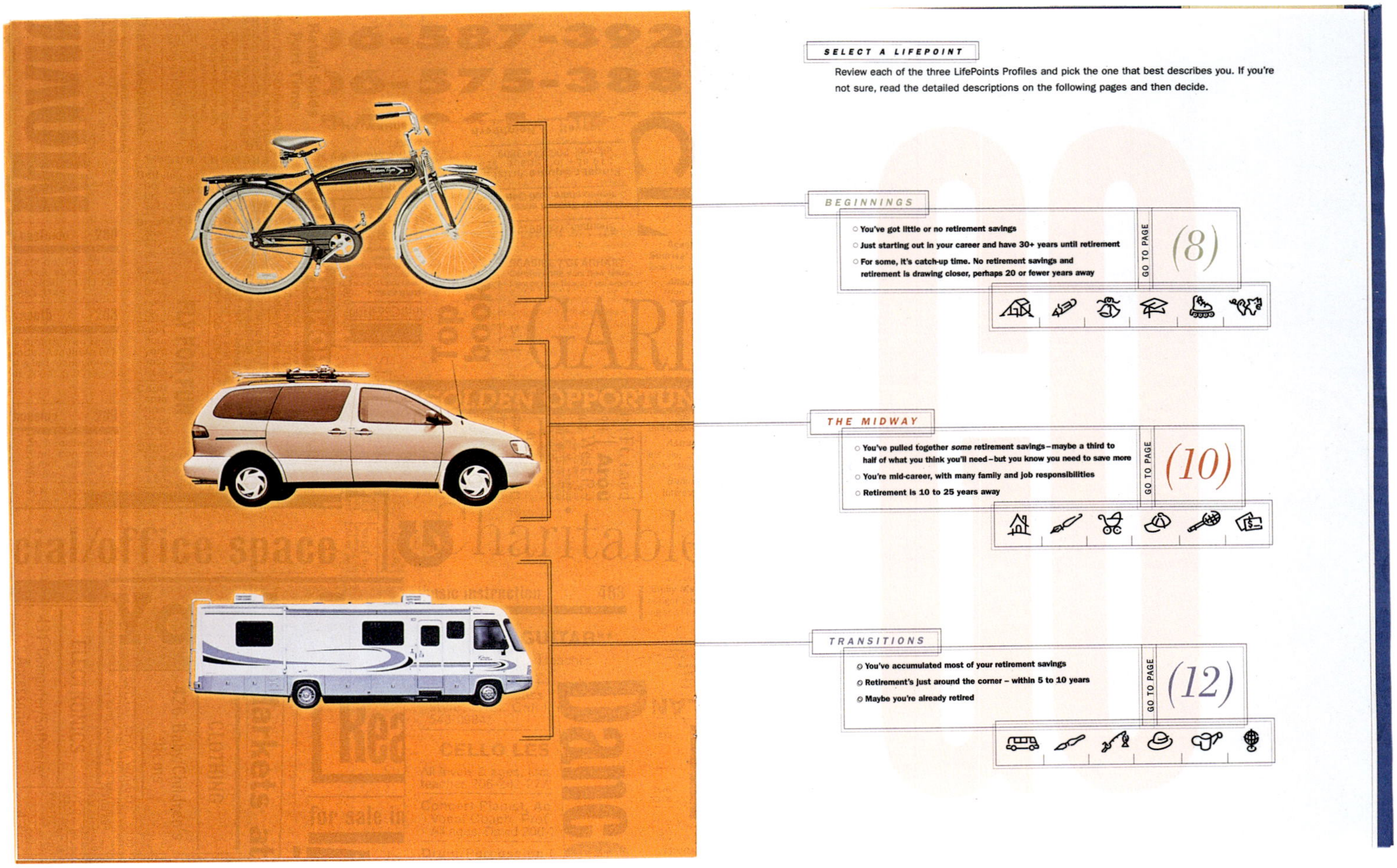

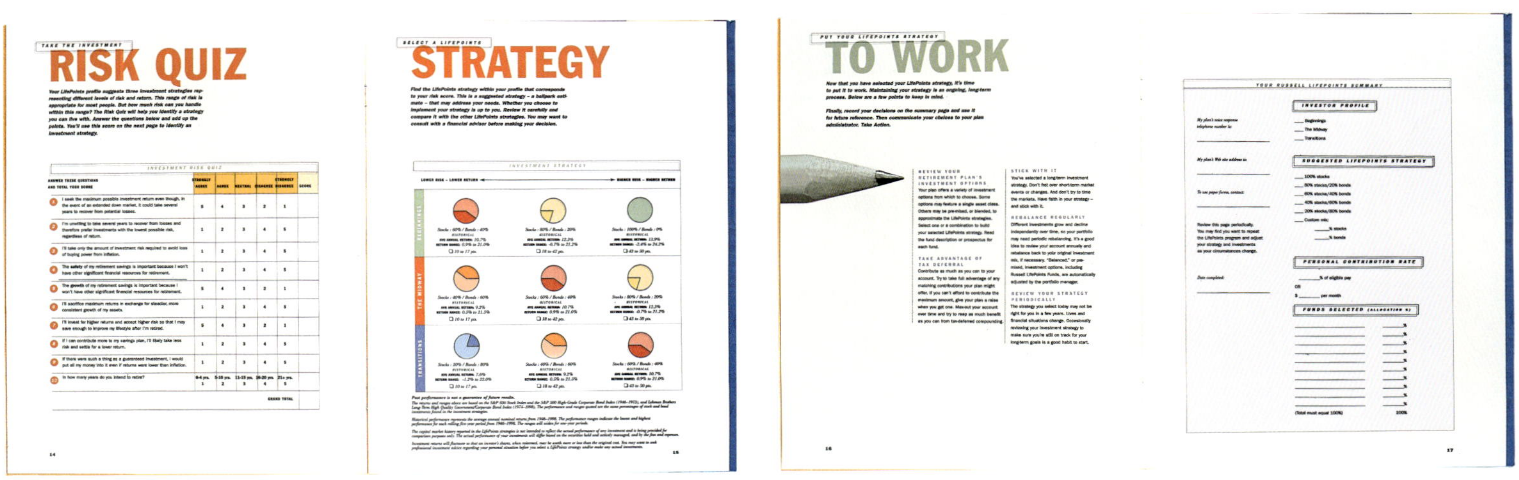

BROCHURE ブローシャー

A MANDATE FOR LEADERSHIP 1999 USA CL: Federal Reserve System D,I: Wempy Ping Homeric DF: Federal Reserve Bank of Chicago, Graphics Department

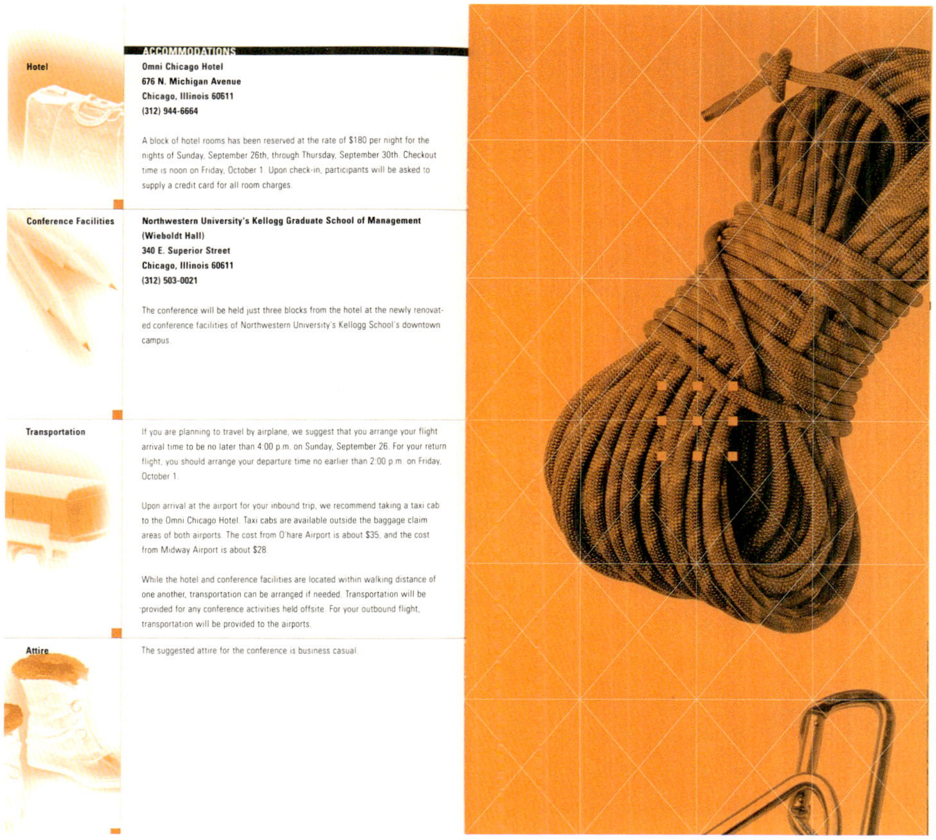

ACCOMMODATIONS

Hotel

Omni Chicago Hotel
676 N. Michigan Avenue
Chicago, Illinois 60611
(312) 944-6664

A block of hotel rooms has been reserved at the rate of $180 per night for the nights of Sunday, September 26th, through Thursday, September 30th. Checkout time is noon on Friday, October 1. Upon check-in, participants will be asked to supply a credit card for all room charges.

Conference Facilities

Northwestern University's Kellogg Graduate School of Management
(Wieboldt Hall)
340 E. Superior Street
Chicago, Illinois 60611
(312) 503-0021

The conference will be held just three blocks from the hotel at the newly renovated conference facilities of Northwestern University's Kellogg School's downtown campus.

Transportation

If you are planning to travel by airplane, we suggest that you arrange your flight arrival time to be no later than 4:00 p.m. on Sunday, September 26. For your return flight, you should arrange your departure time no earlier than 2:00 p.m. on Friday, October 1.

Upon arrival at the airport for your inbound trip, we recommend taking a taxi cab to the Omni Chicago Hotel. Taxi cabs are available outside the baggage claim areas of both airports. The cost from O'hare Airport is about $35, and the cost from Midway Airport is about $28.

While the hotel and conference facilities are located within walking distance of one another, transportation can be arranged if needed. Transportation will be provided for any conference activities held offsite. For your outbound flight, transportation will be provided to the airports.

Attire

The suggested attire for the conference is business casual.

COVER

ANNUAL REPORT アニュアルレポート

HOW DOES IT GO... FACTS AND FIGURES 1998/1999 1999 NETHERLANDS

CL: ONVZ Zorgverzekeraar CD,AD,D,I: Tirso Francés / Ron Faas
AD,D,I: Sybren Kuiper / Martijn Engelbregt CW: Frans van Rijn / Vincent Huizing
DF: Dietwee / -Syb-grafich ontwerp

COVER

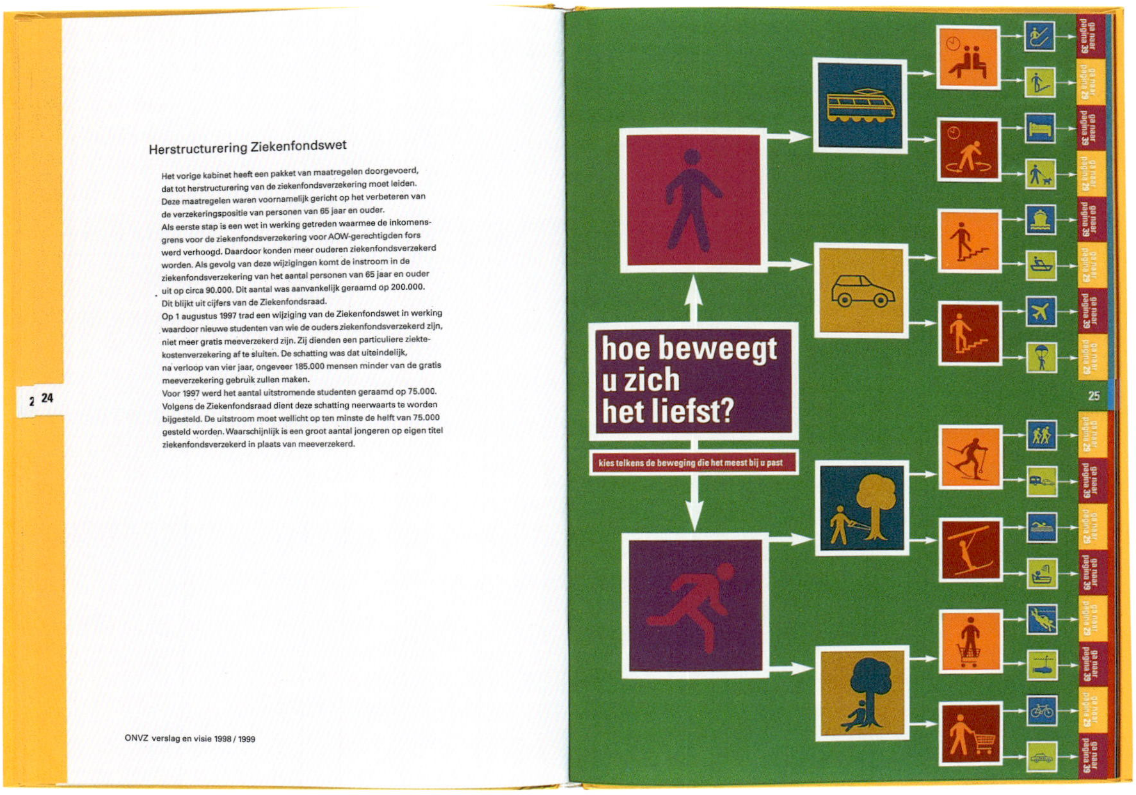

Herstructurering Ziekenfondswet

Het vorige kabinet heeft een pakket van maatregelen doorgevoerd, dat tot herstructurering van de ziekenfondsverzekering moet leiden. Deze maatregelen waren voornamelijk gericht op het verbeteren van de verzekeringspositie van personen van 65 jaar en ouder.
Als eerste stap is een wet in werking getreden waarmee de inkomensgrens voor de ziekenfondsverzekering voor AOW-gerechtigden fors werd verhoogd. Daardoor konden meer ouderen ziekenfondsverzekerd worden. Als gevolg van deze wijzigingen komt de instroom in de ziekenfondsverzekering van het aantal personen van 65 jaar en ouder uit op circa 90.000. Dit aantal was aanvankelijk geraamd op 200.000. Dit blijkt uit cijfers van de Ziekenfondsraad.
Op 1 augustus 1997 trad een wijziging van de Ziekenfondswet in werking waardoor nieuwe studenten van wie de ouders ziekenfondsverzekerd zijn, niet meer gratis meeverzekerd zijn. Zij dienden een particuliere ziektekostenverzekering af te sluiten. De schatting was dat uiteindelijk, na verloop van vier jaar, ongeveer 185.000 mensen minder van de gratis meeverzekering gebruik zullen maken.
Voor 1997 werd het aantal uitstromende studenten geraamd op 75.000. Volgens de Ziekenfondsraad dient deze schatting neerwaarts te worden bijgesteld. De uitstroom moet wellicht op ten minste de helft van 75.000 gesteld worden. Waarschijnlijk is een groot aantal jongeren op eigen titel ziekenfondsverzekerd in plaats van meeverzekerd.

24

ONVZ verslag en visie 1998 / 1999

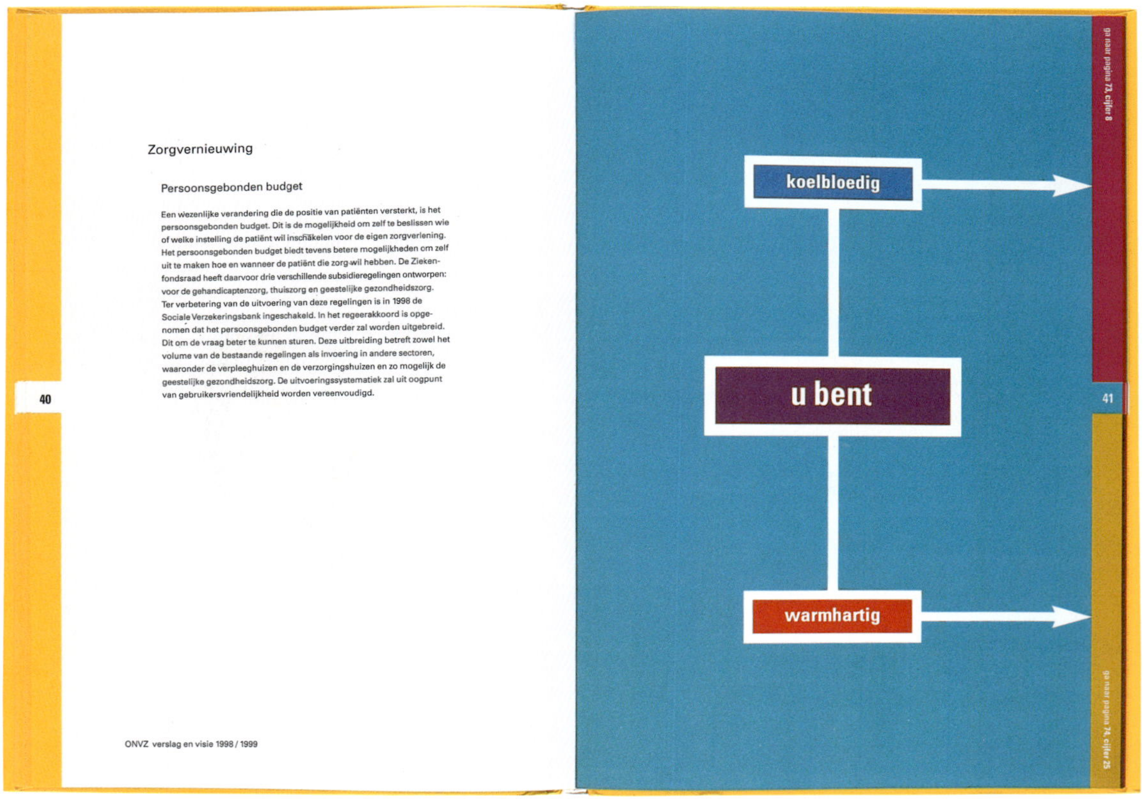

Zorgvernieuwing

Persoonsgebonden budget

Een wezenlijke verandering die de positie van patiënten versterkt, is het persoonsgebonden budget. Dit is de mogelijkheid om zelf te beslissen wie of welke instelling de patiënt wil inschakelen voor de eigen zorgverlening. Het persoonsgebonden budget biedt tevens betere mogelijkheden om zelf uit te maken hoe en wanneer de patiënt die zorg wil hebben. De Ziekenfondsraad heeft daarvoor drie verschillende subsidieregelingen ontworpen: voor de gehandicaptenzorg, thuiszorg en geestelijke gezondheidszorg. Ter verbetering van de uitvoering van deze regelingen is in 1998 de Sociale Verzekeringsbank ingeschakeld. In het regeerakkoord is opgenomen dat het persoonsgebonden budget verder zal worden uitgebreid. Dit om de vraag beter te kunnen sturen. Deze uitbreiding betreft zowel het volume van de bestaande regelingen als invoering in andere sectoren, waaronder de verpleeghuizen en de verzorgingshuizen en zo mogelijk de geestelijke gezondheidszorg. De uitvoeringssystematiek zal uit oogpunt van gebruikersvriendelijkheid worden vereenvoudigd.

40

ONVZ verslag en visie 1998 / 1999

MEGABIOS 1998 ANNUAL REPORT 1998 USA CL: MEGABIOS CD,AD: Bill Cahan D: Sharrie Brooks CW: Bennet Weintraub DF: Cahan & Associates

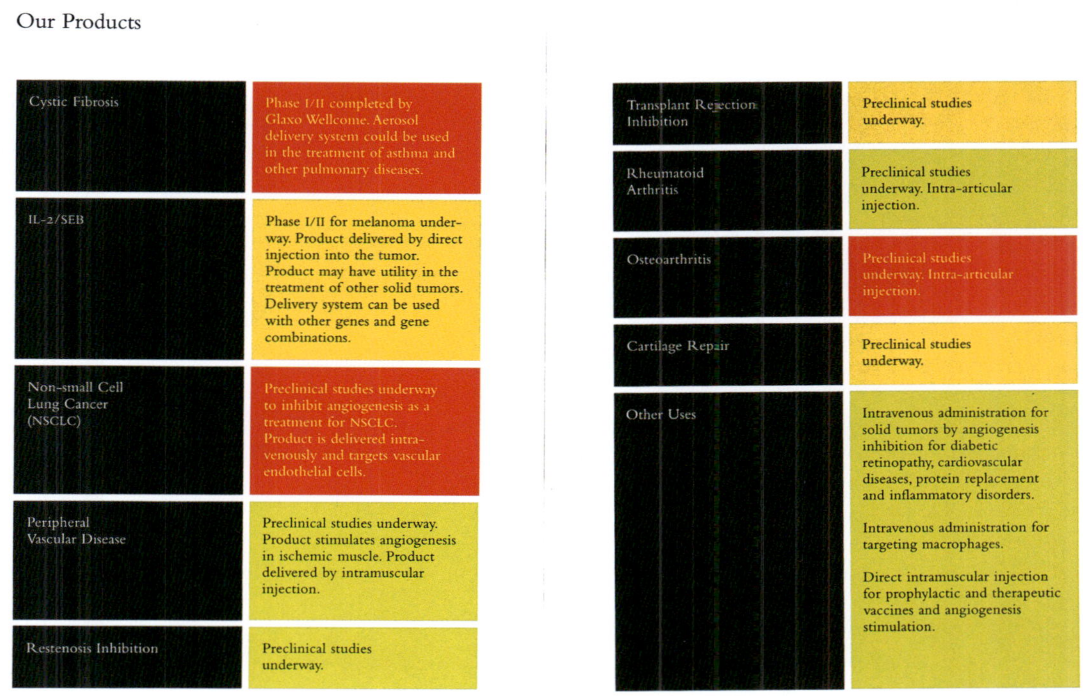

Our Products

Cystic Fibrosis	Phase I/II completed by Glaxo Wellcome. Aerosol delivery system could be used in the treatment of asthma and other pulmonary diseases.
IL-2/SEB	Phase I/II for melanoma underway. Product delivered by direct injection into the tumor. Product may have utility in the treatment of other solid tumors. Delivery system can be used with other genes and gene combinations.
Non-small Cell Lung Cancer (NSCLC)	Preclinical studies underway to inhibit angiogenesis as a treatment for NSCLC. Product is delivered intravenously and targets vascular endothelial cells.
Peripheral Vascular Disease	Preclinical studies underway. Product stimulates angiogenesis in ischemic muscle. Product delivered by intramuscular injection.
Restenosis Inhibition	Preclinical studies underway.
Transplant Rejection Inhibition	Preclinical studies underway.
Rheumatoid Arthritis	Preclinical studies underway. Intra-articular injection.
Osteoarthritis	Preclinical studies underway. Intra-articular injection.
Cartilage Repair	Preclinical studies underway.
Other Uses	Intravenous administration for solid tumors by angiogenesis inhibition for diabetic retinopathy, cardiovascular diseases, protein replacement and inflammatory disorders. Intravenous administration for targeting macrophages. Direct intramuscular injection for prophylactic and therapeutic vaccines and angiogenesis stimulation.

COVER

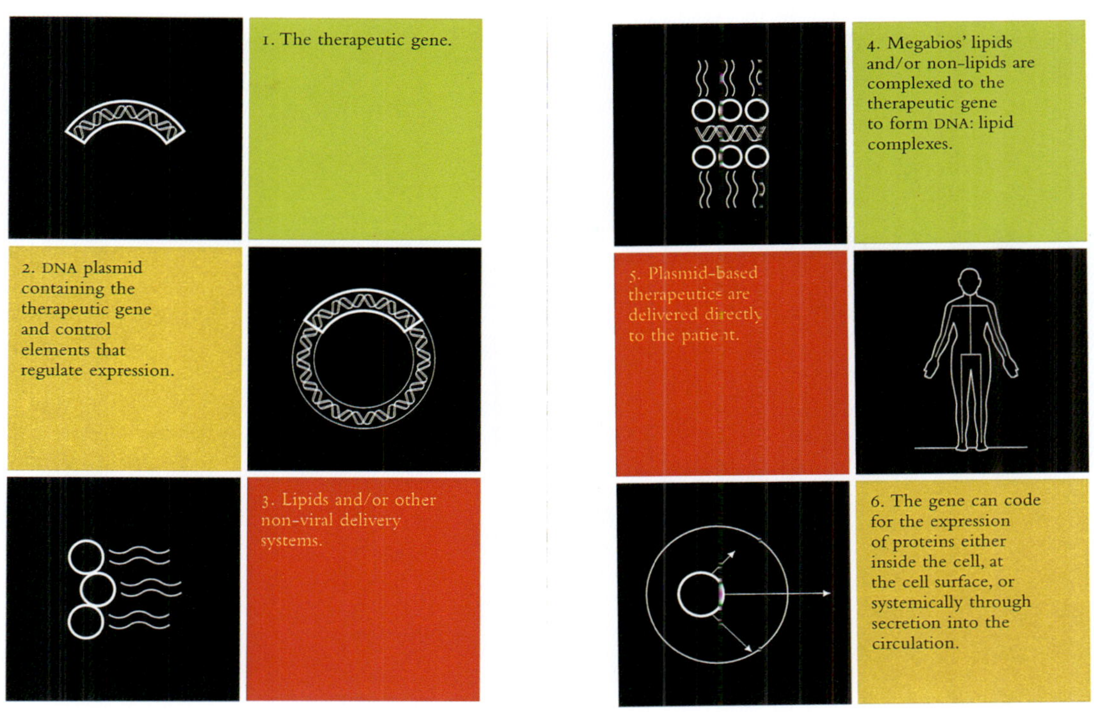

FOOD NUTRITION & HEALTH 1999 FRANCE CL: Actia CD,AD,D: Anne-Lise Dermenghem

COVER

Network of european focal points

Le réseau des points focaux européens

Name	Organization	Address	Postal Code	City	Country	Telephone
ANZJON Siri	The Research Council of Norway	Stensberggata 26	0131	Oslo	Norway	+ 47/22 037 098
BOELSKOV Marjon	EuroCenter Danish Agency of Trade and Industry	Raadhuspladsen 14	1550	Copenhagen V	Denmark	+ 45/33 765 842
CARLSSON-ULIN Monika	NUTEK Dept. of Energy and Environmental Technology	Lilgeholmvagen 32	11786	Stockholm	Sweden	+ 46/8 681 9 336
COTILLON Christophe	ACTIA - Association de coordination technique pour l'industrie agro-alimentaire	19, avenue du Maine	75732	Paris	France	+ 33/1 454 98 985
D'HULSTER Freddy	Vlaams Instituut voor de Bevordering van het Wetenschappelijk	Bisschoffsheimlaan 25	1000	Brussels	Belgium	+ 32/2 223 0 033
DI MAGGIO Diassina	APRE	piazza G. Marconi 25	00144	Rome	Italy	+ 39/6 591 1 817
DIJKSTRA Robert	EG Liaison	Grote Marktstraat 43 Postbus 30732	2500 GS	Den Haag	The Netherlands	+ 31/703 610 250
EVRARD Jacques	Bruxelles Technopole ASBL	r. G.-Petit 4, Boîte 12	1080	Brussels	Belgium	+ 32/2 422 0 025
GARRIDO Margarida	JNICT Agencia de Inovacao Centro Value	av. D.-Carlos I, 126	1200	Lisboa	Portugal	+ 351/1 397 9 021
GRÖNROOS Ari	TEKES	POB 526	20101	Turku	Finland	+ 358/10 521 5333
HEDINSDOTTIR Ragnheidur	Federation of Icelandic Industries	Hallveigarstigur 1	121	Reykjavik	Iceland	+ 354/511 5 555
HERLITSCHKA Sabine	BIT - Bureau for International Research and Technology Cooperation	Wiedner Hauptstraße 76	1040	Vienna	Austria	+ 43/1 581 16 16 - 103
HOWELL Richard	Department Agriculture & Food, Agriculture House 6E	Kildare Street	2	Dublin	Ireland	+ 353/1 607 2 572
LOWERY Duncan	Beta Technology Limited	Riverside House, Weedon Street	S9 2 FT	Sheffield	England	+ 44/114 242 20 04
PETROHILOU Ioanna	ETAT S. A. Food Industrial Research and Technolocial Development Company	80 Vouliagmenis avenue	11743	Athens	Greece	+ 30/1 927 0 040
PONCELA Maria Luisa	Subdirectora Gén. de Promocion de la Innov. Ind. Ministerio de Ind. y Energia	Po de la Castellana, 160 - 10 piso, 21 bureau	28046	Madrid	Spain	+ 34/91 349 43 39
SCHLESSER Gilles	Luxinnovation	7, rue A. de Gasperi	1615	Luxembourg	Luxembourg	+ 352/436 263
VETTER Joachim	BEO Forschungszentrum Jülich	PT BEO 13	52425	Juelich	Germany	+ 49/246161 48 41
ZÜND Marianne	KBF - Koordinationsstelle für schw. Beteiligungen an int. Forschungsprojekten	c/o VSM, Kirchenweg 4, PO Boox	CH-8032	Zurich	Switzerland	+ 41/1 384 48 44

CATALOG カタログ

MORISAWA FONT CATALOG 1997 JAPAN CL: Morisawa & Company Ltd. AD, D: Shinnoske Sugisaki D: Jun Itadani CW: Shiho Sugisaki DF: Shinnoske Inc.

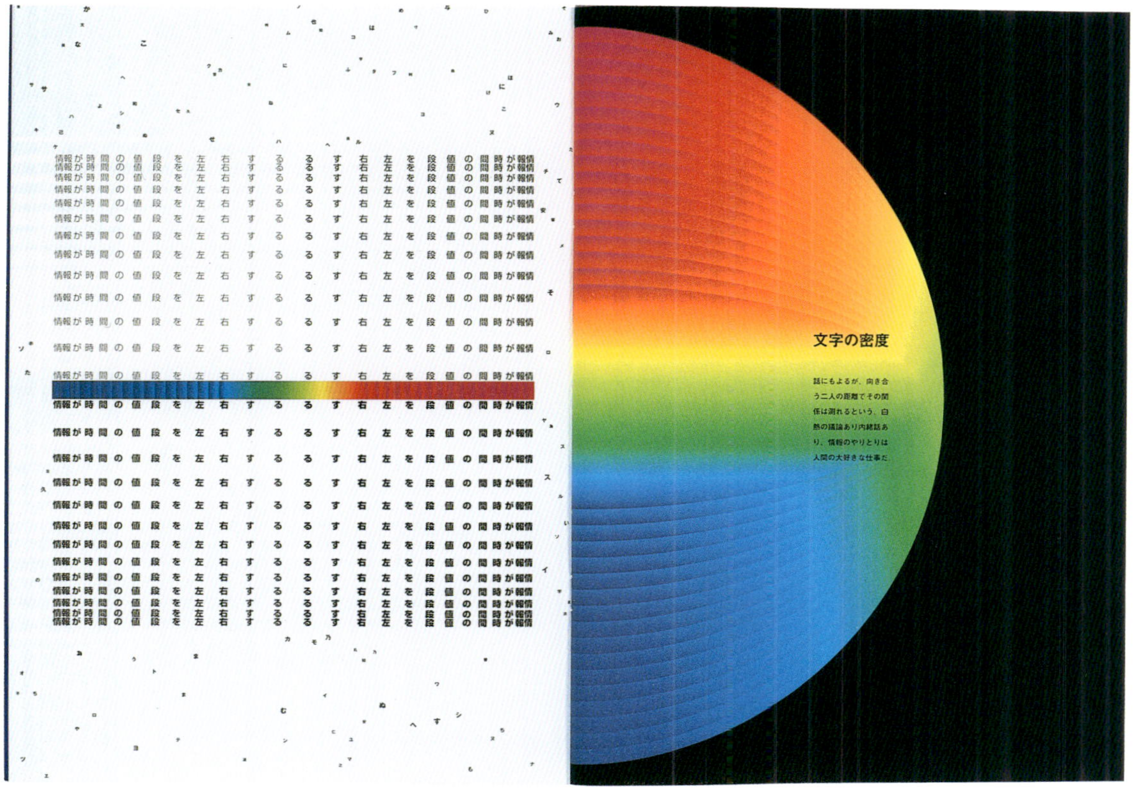

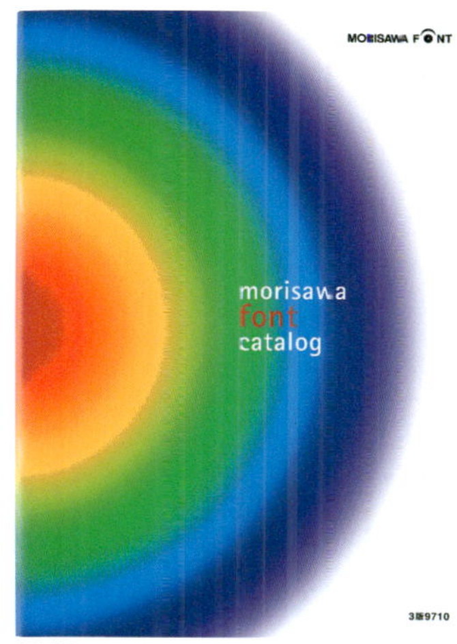

COVER

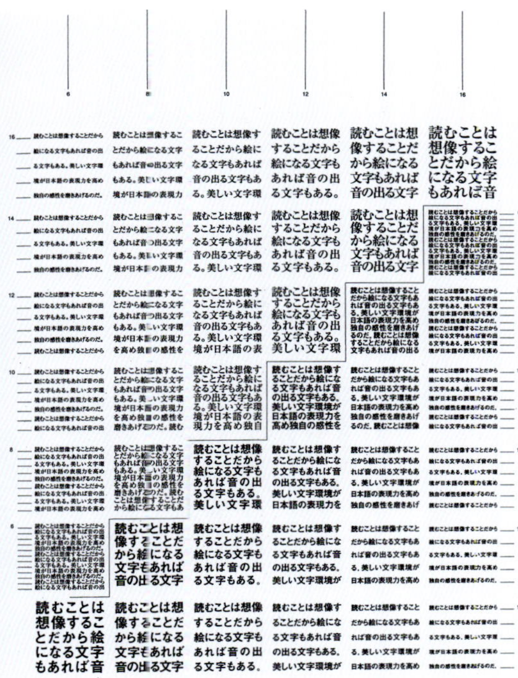

GO HEINRICH GO! 1997 NETHERLANDS CL: Nike Europe CD,CW: Johan Kramer CD,AD,D: Erik Kessels CW: Tyler Whisnand DF: Kesselskramer

COVER

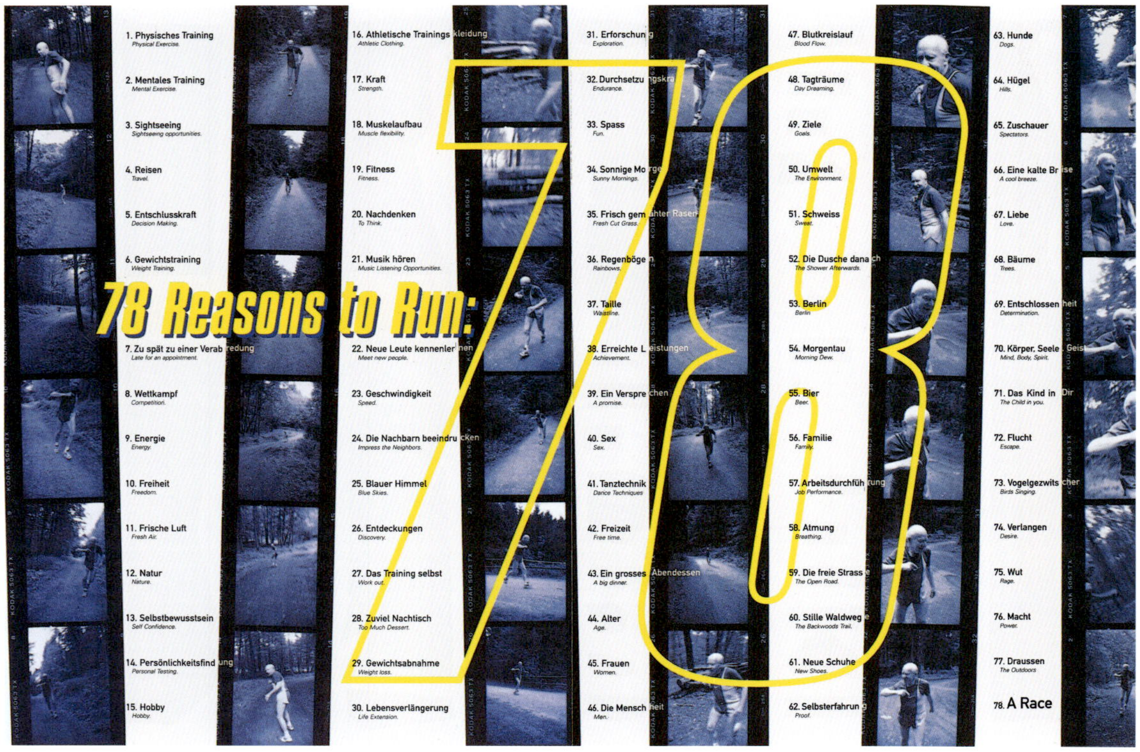

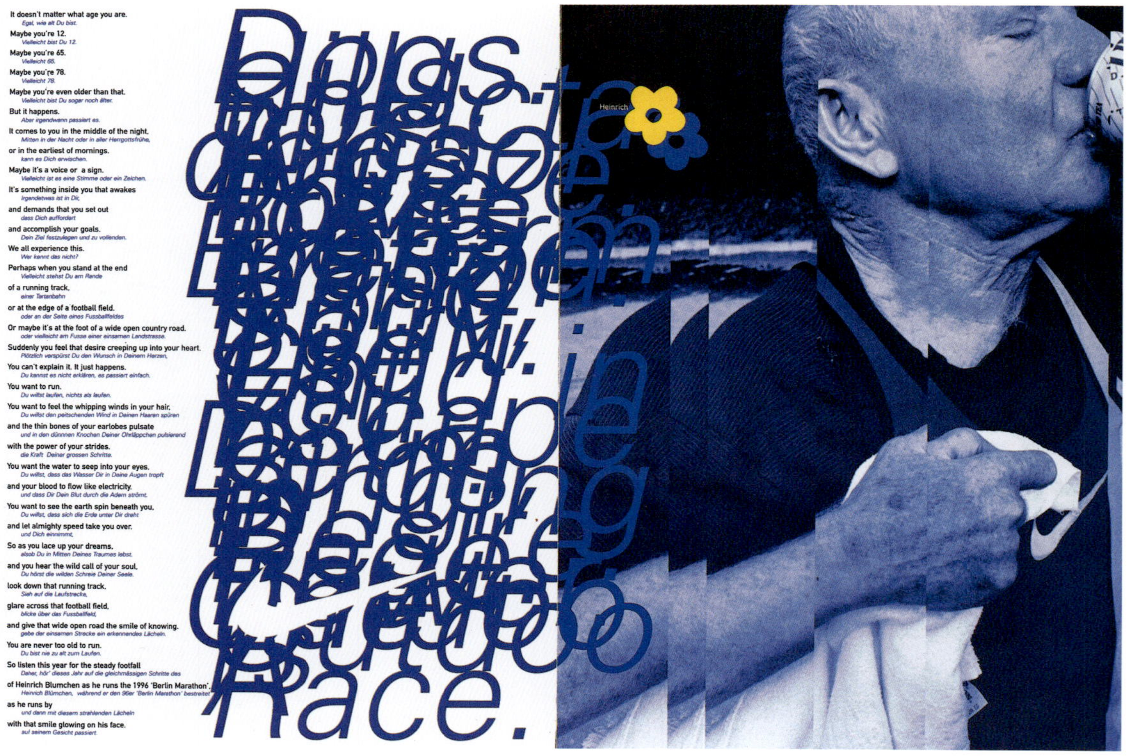

FREEPAPER フリーペーパー

FLYING POSTMAN PRESS 1999 JAPAN PB: Flip Co., Ltd. CD,AD,D: Kazunobu Kitakoga P: Ryoichi Imagawa CW: Urara Hamada DF: Medio Co., Ltd.

COVER

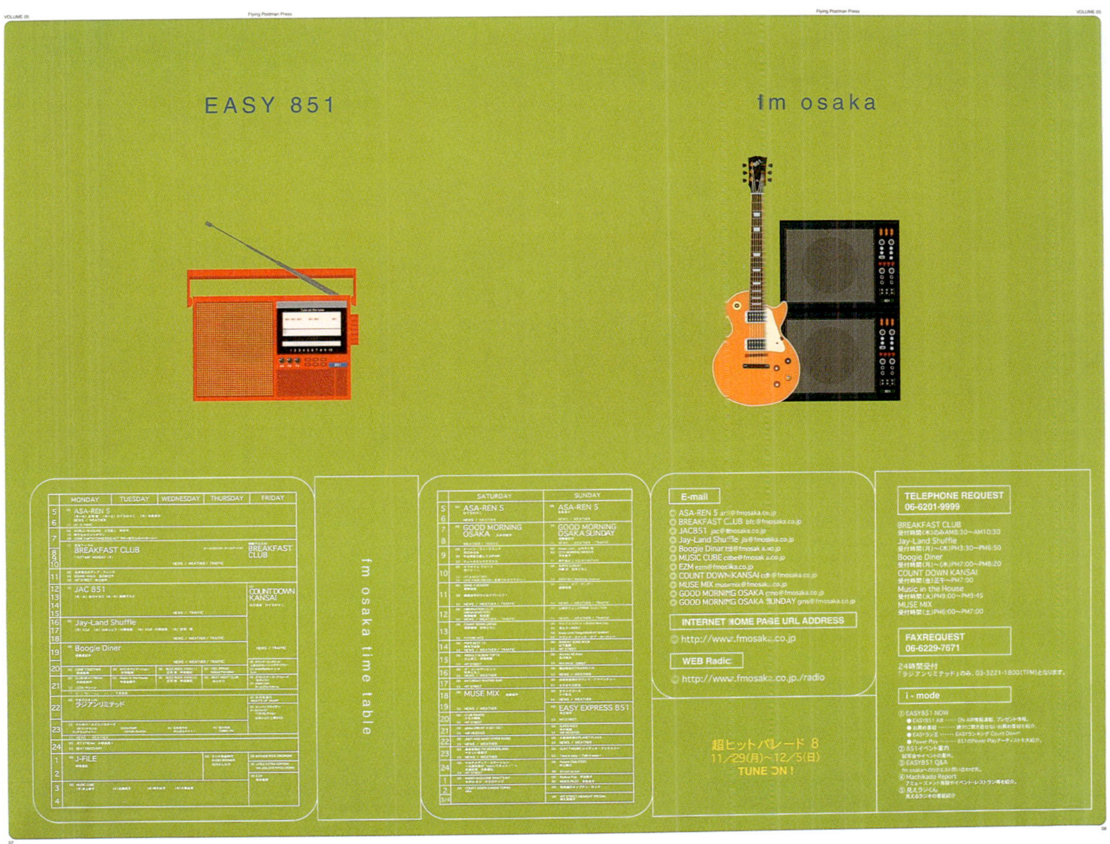

COVER

FREEPAPER フリーペーパー

TADADAH! 1998-99 JAPAN CL: Space Shower Network AD,D: ASYL design Inc.

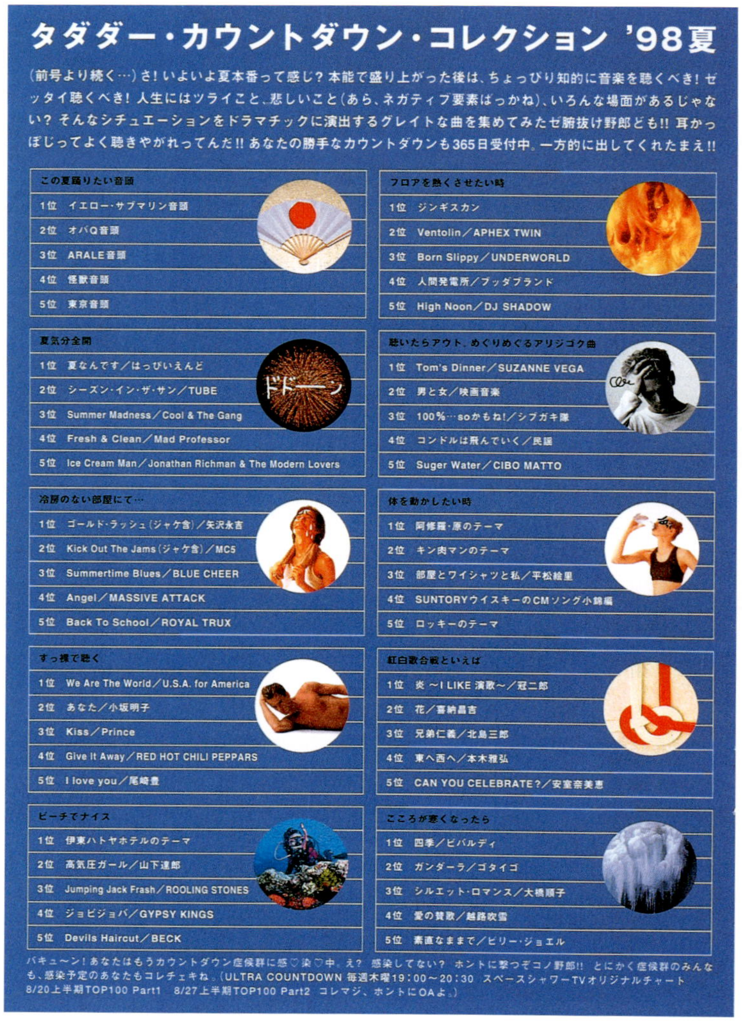

タダダー・カウントダウン・コレクション '98夏

（前号より続く…）さ！いよいよ夏本番って感じ？本能で盛り上がった後は、ちょっぴり知的に音楽を聴くべき！ゼッタイ聴くべき！人生にはツライこと、悲しいこと（あら、ネガティブ要素ばっかね）、いろんな場面があるじゃない？そんなシチュエーションをドラマチックに演出するグレイトな曲を集めてみたゼ腑抜け野郎ども!! 耳かっぽじってよく聴きやがれってんだ!! あなたの勝手なカウントダウンも365日受付中。一方的に出してくれたまえ!!

この夏踊りたい音頭
1位 イエロー・サブマリン音頭
2位 オバQ音頭
3位 ARALE音頭
4位 怪獣音頭
5位 東京音頭

フロアを熱くさせたい時
1位 ジンギスカン
2位 Ventolin／APHEX TWIN
3位 Born Slippy／UNDERWORLD
4位 人間発電所／ブッダブランド
5位 High Noon／DJ SHADOW

夏気分全開
1位 夏なんです／はっぴいえんど
2位 シーズン・イン・ザ・サン／TUBE
3位 Summer Madness／Cool & The Gang
4位 Fresh & Clean／Mad Professor
5位 Ice Cream Man／Jonathan Richman & The Modern Lovers

聴いたらアウト、めぐりめぐるアリジゴク曲
1位 Tom's Dinner／SUZANNE VEGA
2位 男と女／映画音楽
3位 100％…soかもね!／シブガキ隊
4位 コンドルは飛んでいく／民謡
5位 Suger Water／CIBO MATTO

冷房のない部屋にて…
1位 ゴールド・ラッシュ（ジャケ含）／矢沢永吉
2位 Kick Out The Jams（ジャケ含）／MC5
3位 Summertime Blues／BLUE CHEER
4位 Angel／MASSIVE ATTACK
5位 Back To School／ROYAL TRUX

体を動かしたい時
1位 阿修羅・原のテーマ
2位 キン肉マンのテーマ
3位 部屋とワイシャツと私／平松絵里
4位 SUNTORYウイスキーのCMソング小錦編
5位 ロッキーのテーマ

すっ裸で聴く
1位 We Are The World／U.S.A. for America
2位 あなた／小坂明子
3位 Kiss／Prince
4位 Give It Away／RED HOT CHILI PEPPARS
5位 I love you／尾崎豊

紅白歌合戦といえば
1位 炎 ～I LIKE 演歌～／冠二郎
2位 花／喜納昌吉
3位 兄弟仁義／北島三郎
4位 東へ西へ／本木雅弘
5位 CAN YOU CELEBRATE?／安室奈美恵

ビーチでナイス
1位 伊東ハトヤホテルのテーマ
2位 高気圧ガール／山下達郎
3位 Jumping Jack Frash／ROOLING STONES
4位 ジョビジョバ／GYPSY KINGS
5位 Devils Haircut／BECK

こころが寒くなったら
1位 四季／ビバルディ
2位 ガンダーラ／ゴダイゴ
3位 シルエット・ロマンス／大橋順子
4位 愛の賛歌／越路吹雪
5位 素直なままで／ビリー・ジョエル

バキューン！あなたはもうカウントダウン症候群に感♡染♡中。え？ 感染してない？ ホントに撃つぞコノ野郎!! とにかく症候群のみんなも、感染予定のあなたもコレチェキね。（ULTRA COUNTDOWN 毎週木曜19：00～20：30 スペースシャワーTVオリジナルチャート 8/20上半期TOP100 Part1 8/27上半期TOP100 Part2 コレマジ、ホントにOAよ。）

COVER

COVER

GASBOOK 6 1999 JAPAN PB: DesignEXchange Co., Ltd. CD,AD: Akira Natsume D: Hideki Inaba

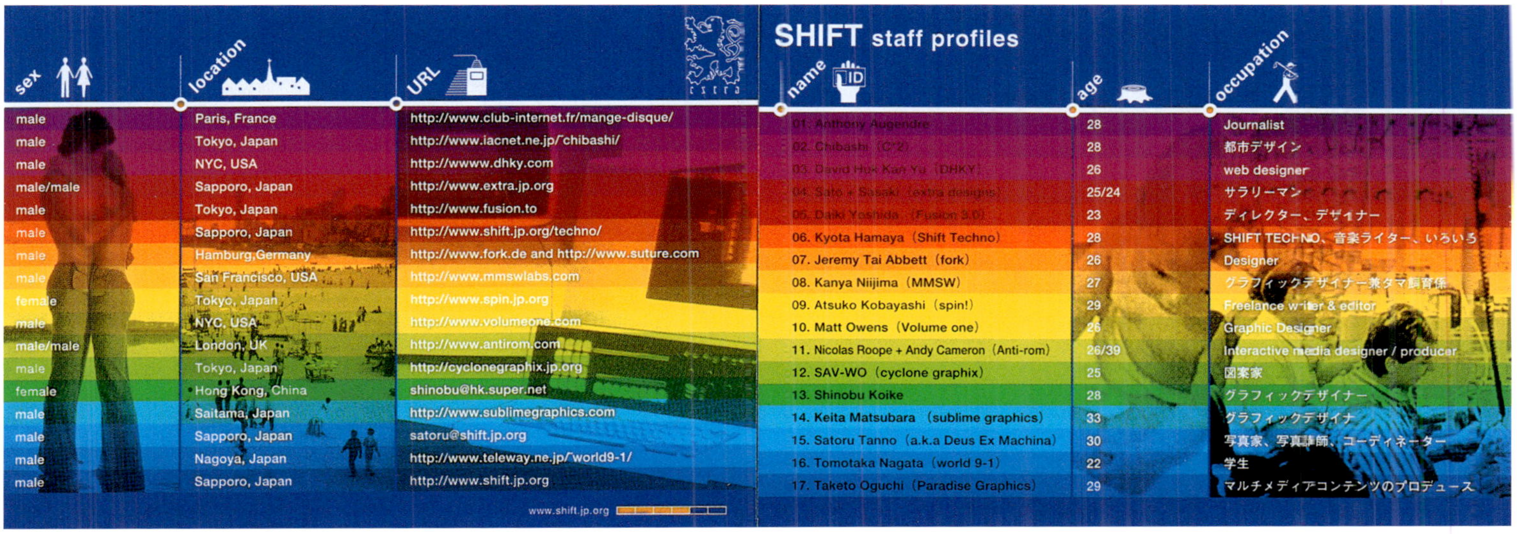

sex	location	URL
male	Paris, France	http://www.club-internet.fr/mange-disque/
male	Tokyo, Japan	http://www.lacnet.ne.jp/~chibashi/
male	NYC, USA	http://wwww.dhky.com
male/male	Sapporo, Japan	http://www.extra.jp.org
male	Tokyo, Japan	http://www.fusion.to
male	Sapporo, Japan	http://www.shift.jp.org/techno/
male	Hamburg,Germany	http://www.fork.de and http://www.suture.com
male	San Francisco, USA	http://www.mmswlabs.com
female	Tokyo, Japan	http://www.spin.jp.org
male	NYC, USA	http://www.volumeone.com
male/male	London, UK	http://www.antirom.com
male	Tokyo, Japan	http://cyclonegraphix.jp.org
female	Hong Kong, China	shinobu@hk.super.net
male	Saitama, Japan	http://www.sublimegraphics.com
male	Sapporo, Japan	satoru@shift.jp.org
male	Nagoya, Japan	http://www.teleway.ne.jp/~world9-1/
male	Sapporo, Japan	http://www.shift.jp.org

www.shift.jp.org

SHIFT staff profiles

name	age	occupation
01. Anthony Augendre	28	Journalist
02. Chibashi (C*2)	28	都市デザイン
03. David Hux Kan Yu (DHKY)	26	web designer
04. Sato + Sasaki (extra designs)	25/24	サラリーマン
05. Daiki Yoshida (Fusion 3.0)	23	ディレクター、デザイナー
06. Kyota Hamaya (Shift Techno)	28	SHIFT TECHNO、音楽ライター、いろいろ
07. Jeremy Tai Abbett (fork)	26	Designer
08. Kanya Niijima (MMSW)	27	グラフィックデザイナー兼タマ飼育係
09. Atsuko Kobayashi (spin!)	29	Freelance writer & editor
10. Matt Owens (Volume one)	26	Graphic Designer
11. Nicolas Roope + Andy Cameron (Anti-rom)	26/39	Interactive media designer / producer
12. SAV-WO (cyclone graphix)	25	図案家
13. Shinobu Koike	28	グラフィックデザイナー
14. Keita Matsubara (sublime graphics)	33	グラフィックデザイナ
15. Satoru Tanno (a.k.a Deus Ex Machina)	30	写真家、写真講師、コーディネーター
16. Tomotaka Nagata (world 9-1)	22	学生
17. Taketo Oguchi (Paradise Graphics)	29	マルチメディアコンテンツのプロデュース

SHIFT the online magazine

世界は少しづつ複雑に、そして身近になってきている。センスを共有する事が出来れば世界中に友人を持つ事も可能な時代になってきた。
あなたが今のPOPカルチャーに少しでも興味があれば、それはすでにもう知っている事だろう。でもなかなかそれを実体験として理解する事は難しい。
ここで紹介するE-ZINE(インターネットの雑誌)「SHIFT」は世界と日本が同軸上に繋がっている事を確認出来る日本では数少ないサイト。
デザイン、ファッション、アート、ミュージック、オタクなどのエッジカルチャーを中心に、世界中に散らばるスタッフがその時々の気になる情報を伝えてくれる。
GASBOOKでは彼等とのコラボレーションからいくつかのタイトルを作りだしてきた。
世界中に散らばるSHIFTスタッフのデータを集める事で、「SHIFT」の内部を紹介をしてみよう。

COVER

SMART THINKING 1998 AUSTRALIA CL: Integral Energy CD,AD,D: Annie Schwebel P: Neil Billington DF: Kathy Wong Creative Design

COVER

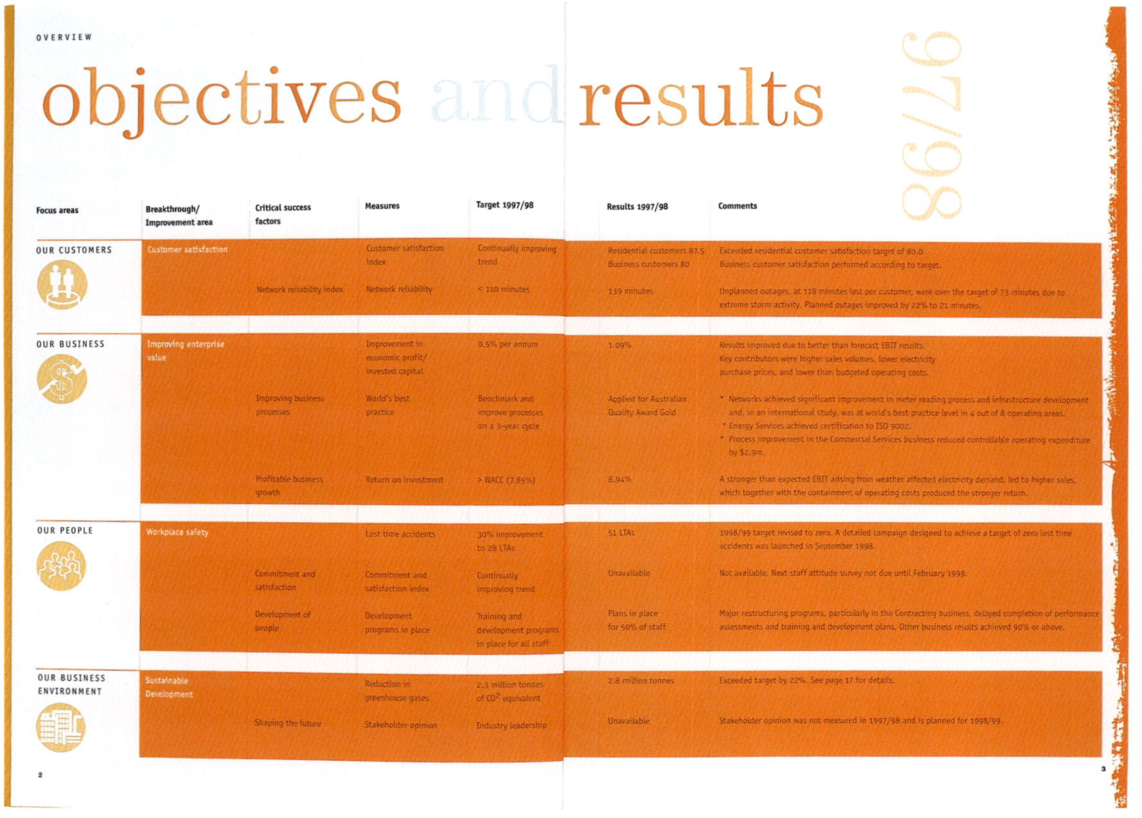

OVERVIEW

objectives and results 97/98

Focus areas	Breakthrough/ Improvement area	Critical success factors	Measures	Target 1997/98	Results 1997/98	Comments
OUR CUSTOMERS	Customer satisfaction		Customer satisfaction index	Continually improving trend	Residential customers 87.5 Business customers 80	Exceeded residential customer satisfaction target of 80.0 Business customer satisfaction performed according to target.
		Network reliability index	Network reliability	< 110 minutes	139 minutes	Unplanned outages, at 118 minutes lost per customer, were over the target of 73 minutes due to extreme storm activity. Planned outages improved by 22% to 21 minutes.
OUR BUSINESS	Improving enterprise value		Improvement in economic profit/ invested capital	0.5% per annum	1.09%	Results improved due to better than forecast EBIT results. Key contributors were higher sales volumes, lower electricity purchase prices, and lower than budgeted operating costs.
		Improving business processes	World's best practice	Benchmark and improve processes on a 3-year cycle	Applied for Australian Quality Award Gold	* Networks achieved significant improvement in meter reading process and infrastructure development and, in an international study, was at world's best practice level in 4 out of 8 operating areas. * Energy Services achieved certification to ISO 9002. * Process improvement in the Commercial Services business reduced controllable operating expenditure by $2.9m.
		Profitable business growth	Return on investment	> WACC (7.85%)	8.94%	A stronger than expected EBIT arising from weather affected electricity demand, led to higher sales, which together with the containment of operating costs produced the stronger return.
OUR PEOPLE	Workplace safety		Lost time accidents	30% improvement to 28 LTAs	51 LTAs	1998/99 target revised to zero. A detailed campaign designed to achieve a target of zero lost time accidents was launched in September 1998.
		Commitment and satisfaction	Commitment and satisfaction index	Continually improving trend	Unavailable	Not available. Next staff attitude survey not due until February 1999.
		Development of people	Development programs in place	Training and development programs in place for all staff	Plans in place for 50% of staff	Major restructuring programs, particularly in the Contracting business, delayed completion of performance assessments and training and development plans. Other business results achieved 90% or above.
OUR BUSINESS ENVIRONMENT	Sustainable Development		Reduction in greenhouse gases	2.3 million tonnes of CO^2 equivalent	2.8 million tonnes	Exceeded target by 22%. See page 17 for details.
		Shaping the future	Stakeholder opinion	Industry leadership	Unavailable	Stakeholder opinion was not measured in 1997/98 and is planned for 1998/99.

2 3

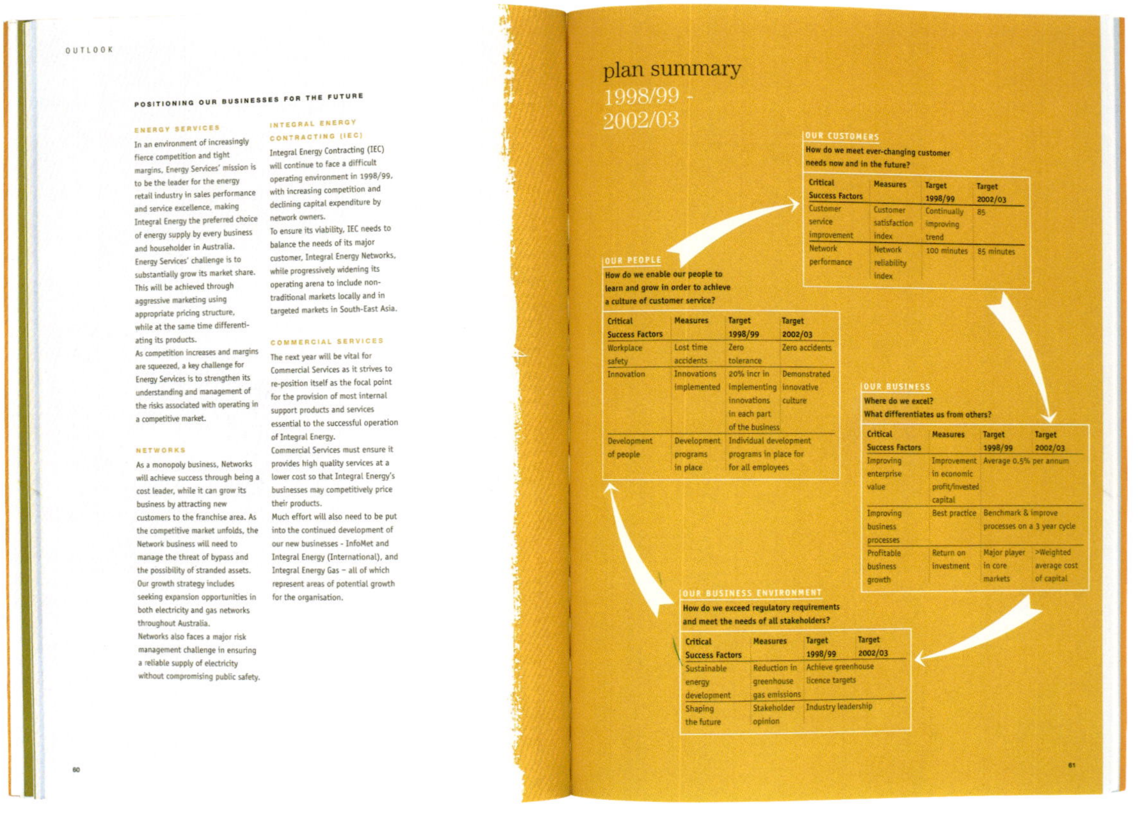

OUTLOOK

POSITIONING OUR BUSINESSES FOR THE FUTURE

ENERGY SERVICES

In an environment of increasingly fierce competition and tight margins, Energy Services' mission is to be the leader for the energy retail industry in sales performance and service excellence, making Integral Energy the preferred choice of energy supply by every business and householder in Australia.

Energy Services' challenge is to substantially grow its market share. This will be achieved through aggressive marketing using appropriate pricing structure, while at the same time differentiating its products.

As competition increases and margins are squeezed, a key challenge for Energy Services is to strengthen its understanding and management of the risks associated with operating in a competitive market.

NETWORKS

As a monopoly business, Networks will achieve success through being a cost leader, while it can grow its business by attracting new customers to the franchise area. As the competitive market unfolds, the Network business will need to manage the threat of bypass and the possibility of stranded assets.

Our growth strategy includes seeking expansion opportunities in both electricity and gas networks throughout Australia.

Networks also faces a major risk management challenge in ensuring a reliable supply of electricity without compromising public safety.

INTEGRAL ENERGY CONTRACTING (IEC)

Integral Energy Contracting (IEC) will continue to face a difficult operating environment in 1998/99, with increasing competition and declining capital expenditure by network owners.

To ensure its viability, IEC needs to balance the needs of its major customer, Integral Energy Networks, while progressively widening its operating arena to include non-traditional markets locally and in targeted markets in South-East Asia.

COMMERCIAL SERVICES

The next year will be vital for Commercial Services as it strives to re-position itself as the focal point for the provision of most internal support products and services essential to the successful operation of Integral Energy.

Commercial Services must ensure it provides high quality services at a lower cost so that Integral Energy's businesses may competitively price their products.

Much effort will also need to be put into the continued development of our new businesses - InfoMet and Integral Energy (International), and Integral Energy Gas – all of which represent areas of potential growth for the organisation.

80

plan summary 1998/99 - 2002/03

OUR CUSTOMERS

How do we meet ever-changing customer needs now and in the future?

Critical Success Factors	Measures	Target 1998/99	Target 2002/03
Customer service improvement	Customer satisfaction index	Continually improving trend	85
Network performance	Network reliability index	100 minutes	85 minutes

OUR BUSINESS

Where do we excel? What differentiates us from others?

Critical Success Factors	Measures	Target 1998/99	Target 2002/03
Improving enterprise value	Improvement in economic profit/invested capital	Average 0.5% per annum	
Improving business processes	Best practice	Benchmark & improve processes on a 3 year cycle	
Profitable business growth	Return on investment	Major player in core markets	>Weighted average cost of capital

OUR BUSINESS ENVIRONMENT

How do we exceed regulatory requirements and meet the needs of all stakeholders?

Critical Success Factors	Measures	Target 1998/99	Target 2002/03
Sustainable energy development	Reduction in greenhouse gas emissions	Achieve greenhouse licence targets	
Shaping the future	Stakeholder opinion	Industry leadership	

OUR PEOPLE

How do we enable our people to learn and grow in order to achieve a culture of customer service?

Critical Success Factors	Measures	Target 1998/99	Target 2002/03
Workplace safety	Lost time accidents	Zero tolerance	Zero accidents
Innovation	Innovations implemented	20% incr in implementing innovations in each part of the business	Demonstrated innovative culture
Development of people	Development programs in place	Individual development programs in place for all employees	

81

THE PARTNERS' FORMULA BOOK 1999 CANADA CL: The Partners' Film Company CD,AD,D: Vanessa Eckstein D: Frances Chen P: Don Miller DF: Book Design

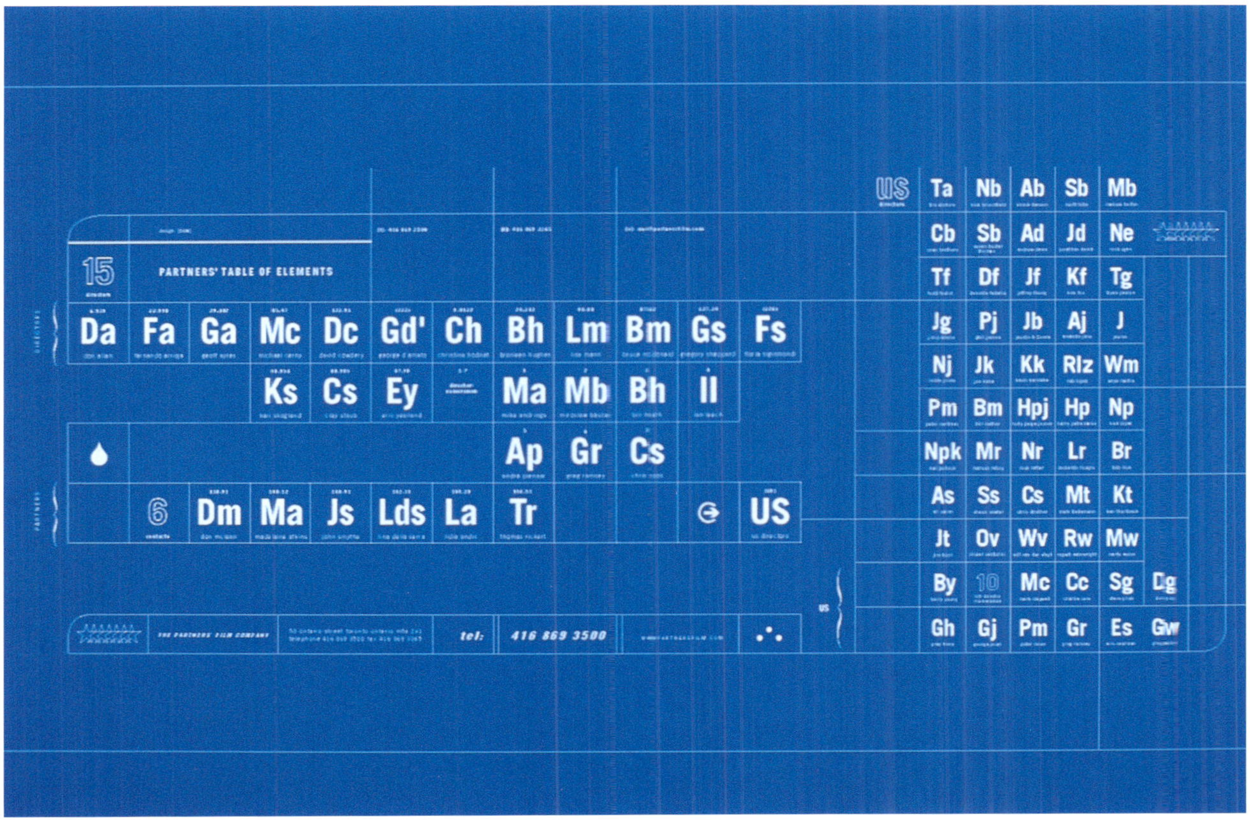

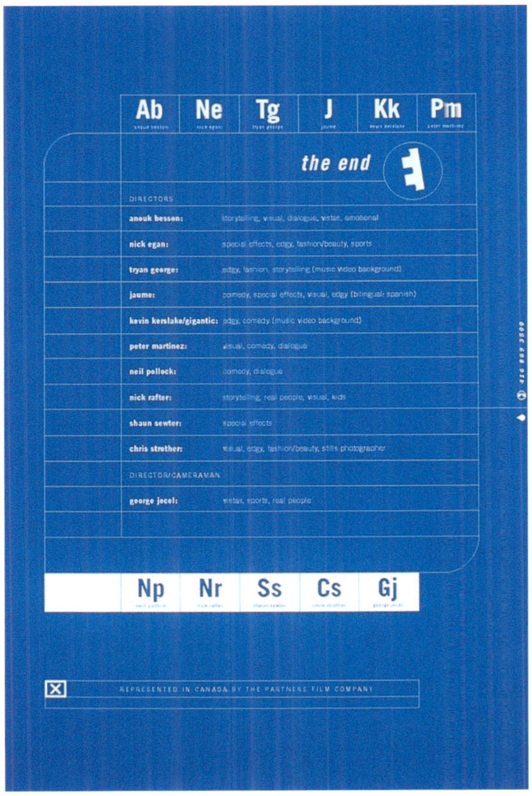

How to order?

WATER PLANET STORE

■作品のご購入方法とご注意

お気に入りのアート作品は、少しでも早く手に入れたいもの。でも、「WATER PLANET STORE」では、いろんな作家の皆さんに直接作品を販売してもらうので、制作や販売のスタイルも様々。一般的な通販とは少しスタイルが違います。そこで、皆さんに安心してご利用いただくためにも、ご購入前にぜひ知っておいてもらいたいお約束をご紹介します。※販売エリアは、日本国内に限らせていただきます。

1 ご購入前に

「WATER PLANET STORE」で紹介される作品のほとんどが、限定ものなど、この本でしか買うことのできない作品です。しかも、他の通販雑誌などで販売される商品のように大量に生産されるものではありません。一点一点が作家の創作活動から生まれる貴重な作品。ですから、お届けするのに時間がかかったり、写真で見るものとは微妙に違っていたりすることがあるかも知れません。ご購入いただく方は、まずそのことをご理解ください。

2 作品購入の申し込み方法は?

掲載作品のご注文は、本誌付属の専用ハガキに必要事項をご記入の上お申し込みください。

3 「限定販売」&「受注制作」とは?

作品が既存の場合は「限定販売」。注文後に作品を制作するのが「受注制作」です。※「限定販売」は数に限りがあるため売り切れ次第、受付を終了いたします。また、「受注制作」は、作品をお送りするまでに多少日数がかかりますので予めご了承ください。

4 作品についての問い合わせは?

掲載作品ついてのお問い合わせについては、編集部では一切対応いたしませんのでご了承ください。

5 代金の支払い方法は?

代金の支払い方法は、ご購入お申し込み受付後に作家または販売代理店よりご連絡しますので指定の方法に従ってください。

6 送料はいるのでしょうか?

作品のご購入には、掲載されている作品の代金に加えて、送料及び梱包料が必要となります。なお送料及び梱包料は作家によって輸送システムが異なる上、地域、作品の大きさや重量などによって違いますのでご了承ください。また、一部の作品については消費税5%が必要となります。

7 作品は、いつ届くのでしょうか?

販売作品の納期は、作家及び作品ごとに異なりますが、受注制作によるハンドメイドの作品については、お送りするまで2週間〜1ヵ月程度かかりますのでご了承ください。

8 返品は可能でしょうか?

ご購入のお申し込みをされた作品のキャンセル及び、作品ご購入後の返品・お取り替えは、原則的にお断りいたします。
※やむをえずお客様のご都合でキャンセルされる場合は、キャセル料金が必要となる場合がありますのでご注意ください。なお、作家責任による作品の不良については、作品到着後に3日以内に作家までご連絡ください。

9 掲載作品の販売期間は?

本誌で掲載されている作品のご購入お申し込み受付は、平成12年6月20日(火)までです。それ以降は受付をいたしませんのでご了承ください。

■レシート表示の読み方

```
WATER PLANET STORE
purchasing information P.136
000-01  WATER PLANET  ¥1,900
01●素材/紙・水・ビニール ●サイズ/W00 D00 H00 ●セット内容/本・水・袋 ●限定00組 ※送料込み
```

Ⓐ WATER PLANET STOREのレシートがついている作品はすべてご購入いただけます。お申し込みハガキにレシートに記載の作品番号・作品名・価格・サイズ等をご記入ください。

Ⓑ 頭の3桁は作家番号で、P.128〜P.135の作家紹介ページで作家情報をご覧いただけます。末の2桁は商品番号で、いずれもご購入申し込み時に必要となります。

Ⓒ 表示の価格は作品の価格です。別途消費税が必要となる場合があります。

Ⓓ サイズ(表示はmm単位、またM、L表示など)やカラーはお申し込みの際には必ずご記入ください。、また限定販売、受注制作など各商品についての情報を記載しています。

■掲載の作品について

- ●掲載作品の多くはハンドメイドです 同じ作品でもカタチや表情が微妙に違いますのでご了承ください
- ●掲載作品は、作家の都合で止む無く制作を中止することがありますのでご了承ください。
- ●印刷の都合上、色や質感が実際の作品と異なる場合がありますのでご了承ください。
- ●掲載作品の無断転載・複製を禁じます

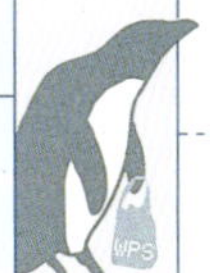

⚠ This application form is available until June 20 2000 only in Japan.

この作品購入の申し込みは平成12年6月20日まで有効です
オーダーは日本国内のみ有効です

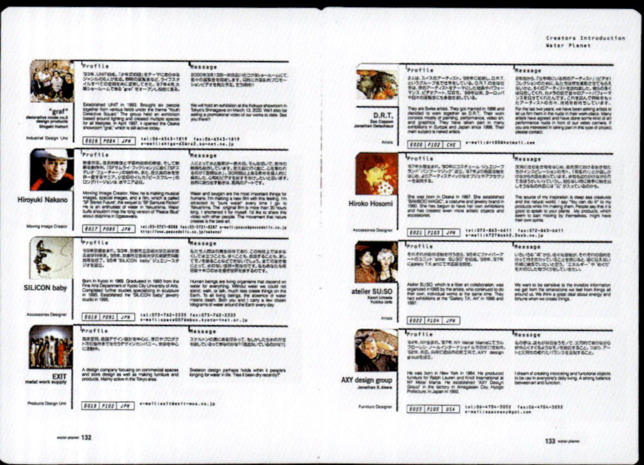

mimi

mimiは、インテリアと花を愉しむためのフリースタイルのラウンジスクール。
毎日の暮らしが楽しくなるようなインテリアのアイディアや、暮らしの中にもっと気軽に取り入れられる花あしらいを、
自由な雰囲気の中で提案したい。その時どきの、流行や季節感なども大切にして、mimiならではのスタイルを、
集まってくださる皆さんといっしょに考えていきたいとも思っています。勉強する、なんてかたっ苦しい雰囲気ではなく、
あくまでもみんなが楽しめること。それを一番大切にしていきたいと考えています。

teacher

小澤（おざわ）典代（のりよ）（インテリア）
雑誌や広告などのスタイリング。著者に「気持ちいい雑貨たち」リブロポート刊、「a styling in the life」メディアファクトリー刊

井出（いで）綾（あや）（花）
雑誌や広告のフラワーアレンジ、ガーデンデザイン。ウェディングの花をてがける。「Bouqet de Soleil」主宰。

course

ラウンジスクールmimiではインテリアと花の基本知識をいろいろな場面を基にレクチャーおよびデモンストレイションしていきます。春夏秋冬の4コース。どのコースから始めてもこの1年間で最低限必要なそれぞれの基本と楽しく暮らすアイディアをお伝えできると考えています。

spring 4/5/6 春コース

- 基本的なディスプレイの構成やカラーコーディネイトなどをレクチャー。実際に物を飾ったり家具を配置したりするための基本の知識をレッスン。
- 花色のカラーコーディネイトを中心に器やインテリア空間と花や植物の色あわせをレクチャー。

summer 7/8/9 夏コース

- いろいろなおもてなしのアイディアとテーブルコーディネイトを紹介。
- グリーン（葉もの）の役割をとおして夏の暑い時期に役立つフラワーアレンジのヒントとテーブルフラワーをレッスン。

autumn 10/11/12 秋コース

- 壁面を効果的に飾る方法をスタディ。
- 植物や自然の物を使って壁を飾るアイディアを紹介。この季節の代表的なクリスマスリースを作ってみます。

winter 1/2/3 冬コース

- 生活にかかせない収納を楽しみながらオシャレにするにはどうすればいいのか。オープン棚を使って飾りながらの収納方法を。
- 植物の選び方や器の選び方を通してインテリアのひとつの要素として花を飾る方法をレクチャー。

class

＊金曜クラス
pm7:30～pm9:00

＊土曜クラス
pm6:00～pm7:30

各コースとも第2金曜、第2土曜、計2クラス開設
上記の2クラスから、好きなクラスを選べます。
同じ月の中での振替も可能です。
また、都合により日時など変更する場合もあります事をご了承ください。

curriculum

1st.
インテリアを中心にした内容で進めます。
基本的なインテリアコーディネートのコツを資料やスライドを見ながらレクチャーします。
実際に雑貨や花を使ったデモンストレーションも行います。

2nd.
フラワーコーディネートを中心にした内容で進めます。
雑貨感覚で楽しめるフラワーアレンジをレクチャー。
アレンジのコツやアイディアをデモンストレーション。

3rd.
実際にコーディネート。
第1回、第2回のレクチャーをふまえて、みんなでスタイリング。
それぞれのアイディアをディスカッションしてみましょう。

3回を通して、必ずフリートークの時間を設けます。この時間には、みんなが今気になっていることを話し合ったり、講師に対する質問なども気軽にできるような時間にしたいと考えています。とにかく楽しいクラスを目指しましょう。

price

1クール：月1回×3ヶ月　¥20,000　1class：20名

place

BORN FREE WORKS ボーンフリーワークス　担当：馬詰
〒158-0081 東京都世田谷区深沢1-14-6
telephone & facsimile : 03-3701-5489　handyphone : 090-4621-4475
access : 東急東横線、自由ヶ丘駅より東急コーチバス　深沢1丁目下車　徒歩1分

COVER

FREEPAPER フリーペーパー

LIMITLESS LUXURY 1999 JAPAN CL: Baycrew's Co., Ltd. CD: Go Public AD,D: Trade Mark P: Takashi Noguchi

COVER

	Spick & Span	IÉNA	DEUXIÈM CLASSE	JOURNAL STANDARD	ÉDIFICE	B.C STOCK
Coat	Jacket, ¥58,000	Coat, ¥49,000	Coat, ¥34,000	Jacket, ¥21,000	Coat, ¥68,000 (SARTORIA SCUDERI)	Jacket, ¥12,800 (British Outdoors)-men's
Knit	Knit, ¥8,800	Knit, ¥13,000 (sese)	Knit, ¥170,000 (MARC JACOBS)	Knit, ¥22,800 (John Molloy)	Knit, ¥110,000 (CLEMENTS RIBEIRO)	Knit, ¥6,800 (Lancho Diseno)-ladies
Maffler	Muffler, ¥4,800-each (f's hers)	Muffler, ¥19,000-each (Lucien Pellat-Finet)	Stole, ¥12,800-each	Muffler, ¥9,800 (INVERLLAN)	Muffler, ¥4,800 (BENSIMON)	Cape, ¥8,800 -ladies
Accessory	Hair pin, ¥2,300-each (Patch)	Ring, ¥8,500-men's, ¥8,000-ladies (IENA Eclat des Etiles)	Choker, ¥18,000-each (Johnny Moke)	Choker, ¥48,000 (ERICKSON BEAMON)	Bracelet, ¥118,000 (YASUNAO WADA) Necklace, ¥25,000 (YASUNAO WADA)	Bracelet, ¥9,800-each (Evatini) -ladies
Bag	Bag, ¥11,000 (INCA)	Bag, ¥23,000 (Glenalmond)	Bag, ¥25,000 (MICHIRU ABE)	Bag, ¥14,800	Bag, ¥118,000 (FELISI)	Bag, ¥9,800 (TENAX) -ladies
Shoes	Shoes, ¥19,000 (Attitude)	Shoes, ¥24,000 (Zamagni)	Shoes, ¥26,000 (Collection Privée?)	Boots, ¥42,000 (SENDRA)-ladies	Shoes, ¥29,000 (PASSENGER'S)	Shoes, ¥14,800 (MORARA) -men's
	Spick & Span	IÉNA	DEUXIÈM CLASSE	JOURNAL STANDARD	ÉDIFICE	B.C STOCK

Limitless Luxury: ITEM

FICTION CATALOG 1999 CANADA CL: Prototype Design CD,D: Stephen Parkes AD D: Troy Bailly AD,I: David Papineau P: Steven Carty I: Neil Singh DF: Prototype Design

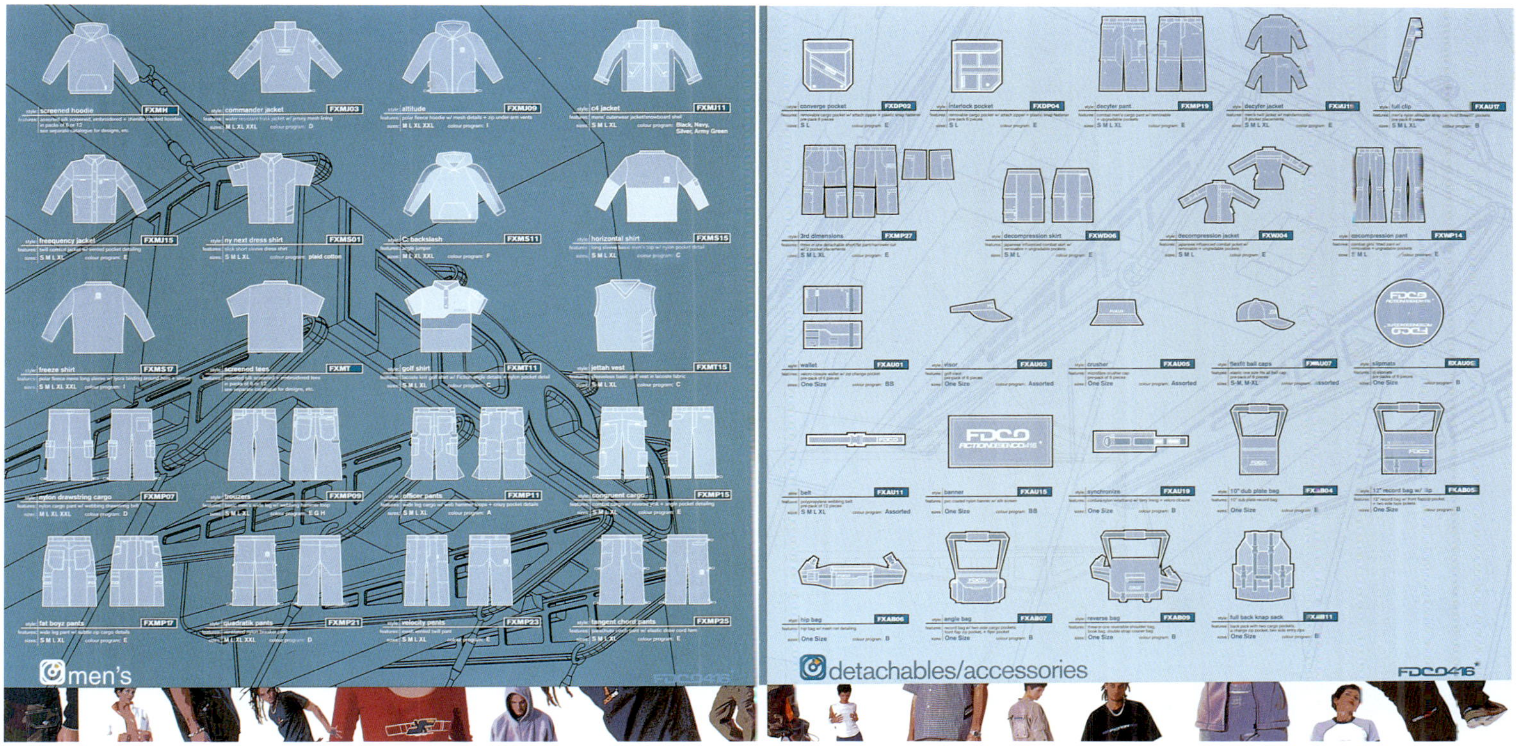

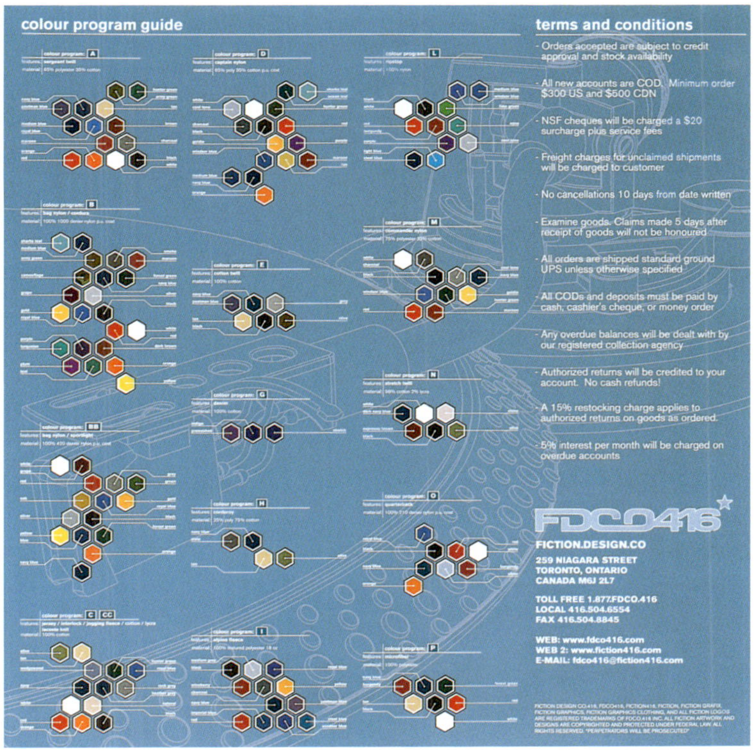

COVER

BOOK 書籍

MARKON PRODUCE SOLUTIONS 1999 USA CL: Markon Cooperative, Inc. CD,AD,D: Jerry Takigawa D: Jay Galster P: Batista Moon Studio / Patrick Tregenza CW: Deena Ensworth DF: Jerry Takigawa Design

Index of Contributors

Typographic Composition

TEXT & TABLE LAYOUT DESIGN CONTENTS PAGES · TEXT PAGES FIGURE/PLATE CAPTIONS · TABLES

Art Direction & Design: Yutaka Ichimura

Design: Akiko Shiba

Editor: Maya Kishida

Photographer: Kuniharu Fujimoto

Translator: Pamela Miki

Publisher: Shingo Miyoshi

2000年9月13日　初版第1刷発行
印刷・製本（株)サンニチ印刷

定価　本体13,000円＋税

発行所　ピエ・ブックス
〒170-0003　東京都豊島区駒込4-14-6-301
編集Tel: 03-3949-5010 Fax: 03-3949-5650 e-mail: editor@piebooks.com
営業Tel: 03-3940-8302 Fax: 03-3576-7361 e-mail: sales@piebooks.com

ISBN4-89444-136-5 C3070

Printed in Japan

THE P·I·E COLLECTION

ポスター グラフィックス 2
好評！業種別ポスター・コレクション、第2弾
Pages: 256 (192 in Color) ¥16,505+Tax
国内外のトップ・クリエイター、有名企業から集められたポスター700作品を業種別に一挙掲載！各業種、各企業のデザイン傾向、コンセプトを比較してみることができる今回の企画はかつて類を見ず、まさに待望の1冊です。

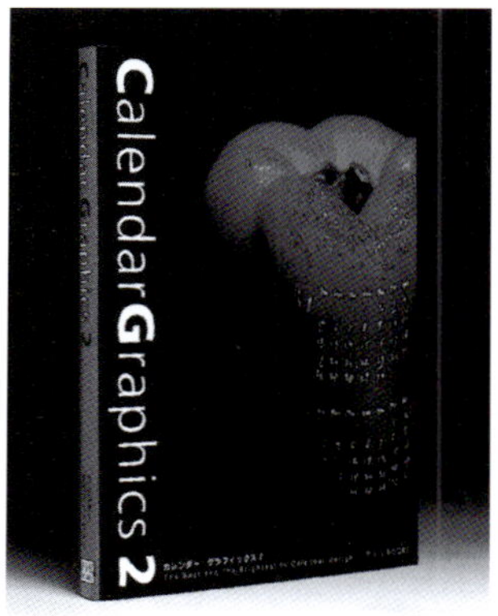

カレンダー グラフィックス 2
好評カレンダー・デザイン集の決定版、第2弾
Pages: 224 (192 in Color) ¥15,534+Tax
好評のカレンダー・デザイン集、第2弾の登場です。'94年、'95年向けの作品を中心に世界各国の最新デザインを約250点収録しました。市販品はもちろん、普段目にする機会が少ない企業のＰＲカレンダーも数多く掲載しています。

ブローシャー & パンフレット コレクション 4
好評！業種別カタログ・コレクション、第4弾
Pages: 224 (Full Color) ¥15,534+Tax
大好評シリーズの第4弾です。カタログ、パンフレットを12業種別に一覧。個性的かつ斬新なデザイン展開で商品を効果的にプロモートする力作を数多く集めました。カタログデザインの今を伝えるクリエイター必携の1冊です。

カタログ グラフィックス
衣·食·住のセールスカタログ特集
Pages: 224 (Full Color) ¥15,500+Tax
販売を目的とした実用性の高いカタログ&パンフレット約200作品を収録。商品の具体的な説明や図、価格、オプション、注文書等が記載された作品は消費者の購買意欲を一歩踏み込んで刺激するカタログ作りに欠かせない1冊です。

カンパニー ブローシャー コレクション 3
業種別(会社·学校·施設)案内グラフィックス、第3弾
Pages: 224 (Full Color) ¥15,500+Tax
メーカー、流通、サービス業…様々な業種の事業・入社案内から大学、専門学校等の入学案内、ホテル、スポーツクラブなどの各種施設案内まで、今まで紹介されることの少なかった案内カタログを業種別に見やすく紹介しています。

コーポレイト プロファイル グラフィックス 3
大好評！世界の会社案内グラフィックス、第3弾
Pages: 224 (Full Color) ¥13,500+Tax
世界各国から集まった最新の会社・学校・施設案内カタログから、デザインの質の高い作品ばかり約200点を業種別に分類。構成、コンセプト、レイアウトを十分に堪能できるように、カバーから中ページまで見やすく紹介しています。

コーポレイト プロファイル グラフィックス 2
世界の会社案内グラフィックス、第2弾
Pages: 224 (Full Color) ¥15,534+Tax
大好評の国内編／業種別案内グラフィックスに続く世界編の第2弾です。世界各国から寄せられた数多くの案内カタログの中から約200点を厳選し紹介しています。学校案内や団体・施設案内まで盛り込んだ充実した内容の1冊。

ニュータイポ グラフィックス 2
世界の最新タイポグラフィックスをコレクション！
Pages: 224 (Full Color) ¥15,500+Tax
シンプルかつモダンなデザイン、刺激的なビジュアル、実験的なタイポグラフィ、可読性への挑戦と美的追求…ドイツ、スイス、オランダ、イギリス、アメリカを中心に、国内外より集めた刺激的な最新作品約400点を紹介します。

イベント フライヤー グラフィックス
世界のイベントフライヤー·コレクション
Pages: 224 (Full Color) ¥15,534+Tax
好評、世界のチラシ·グラフィックスからイベントだけを特集しました。国内外の音楽、映画、アート、舞台芸術など様々なジャンルからフライヤーを収集し紹介。若者のサブ·カルチャー·テキストとしても貴重な1冊です。

アドバタイジング フライヤー グラフィックス
衣·食·住·遊の商品チラシ特集
Pages: 224 (Full Color) ¥15,534+Tax
消費者へ向けて最もスタンダードな広告媒体の1つであるフライヤーを様々な業種から収集し、ファッション・グルメ・ホーム・レジャーと消費者の目的別に紹介します。新しいフライヤーの可能性を発見するための1冊です。

トラベル & レジャー グラフィックス
ホテル&旅行 案内グラフィックス
Pages: 224 (Full Color) ¥15,534+Tax
ホテル·旅館の施設案内／ツアー·観光地ガイド／交通機関案内からアミューズメントの施設案内まで…パンフレットを中心にポスター、DMなど約400点を一挙掲載！！現地に行かなければ入手困難な内容が盛りだくさんの1冊。

ニューロゴ & トレードマーク デザイン
業種別 世界の最新ロゴ&トレードマーク特集
Pages: 272 (Full Color) ¥15,500+Tax
世界中から集めた最新ロゴマークの決定版！！オーソドックスなデザインから個性的で独創的な若手デザイナーの作品まで数多く収録。様々な業種のCIから商品、イベントロゴまで幅広いジャンルを網羅し業種別に分類した必携の1冊。

1&2カラー グラフィックス
効果的にデザインされた1色&2色 デザインの大特集
Pages: 224 (Full Color) ¥15,534+Tax

限定された色数で効果的にデザインされたもの、目を引く意外な色の組み合わせ、また色数を抑えることによってさらに印象的な作品など…見るものに、より強烈なイメージとアイデアを与える作品を世界中から紹介しています。

ビジネス ステーショナリー グラフィックス 2
世界のレター・ヘッド・コレクション、第2弾
Pages: 224 (176 in Color) ¥15,534+Tax

好評！第2弾は世界各国の企業やショップで使用されているレターヘッド、封筒、名刺を中心に様々なステーショナリーを業種別に幅広く紹介しています。触発する様々な工夫を凝らした個性的で新鮮な作品群にご期待ください。

ファッション ラベル&タグ 3
最新ファッションブランドのラベル&タグ コレクション
Pages: 216 (Full Color) ¥15,500+Tax

レディース、メンズ、ユニセックスからキッズやジーンズ、スポーツブランドまで、個性的なラベルとタグを約1000点厳選しアイテム別に紹介。ファッションにおけるグラフィック表現の可能性を広げるデザイナー待望の１冊です。

プライベート グリーティングカード
季節の挨拶状、個人的な案内状・招待状の大特集
Pages: 224 (Full Color) ¥15,500+Tax

クリスマスカード、年賀状などの季節の案内状をはじめ移転通知、出産通知、展示会・結婚式の招待状を世界中のクリエイターからコレクション。厳選した450作品を一挙掲載。プライベートならではの楽しい作品がいっぱいです。

ビジネス パブリケーション グラフィックス 2
大好評！業種別ＰＲ誌の集大成、第２弾
Pages: 224 (Full Color) ¥15,534+Tax

大好評の業種別PR誌の特集、第2弾。様々な業種から集められた情報誌・フリーペーパーの中から厳選した約200作品を、各号の表紙、中ページとともに紹介していますので企画・コンセプトの流れがつかめ、活用できる貴重な１冊です。

ポストカード グラフィックス 4
世界の業種別ポストカード・コレクション
Pages: 224 (192 in Color) ¥15,534+Tax

好評"POSTCARD GRAPHICS" シリーズが装いを新たに新登場。世界中から寄せられた個性あふれる斬新な作品の中から企業、ショップのＤＭを中心にプライベートなグリーティングカードまでバリエーション豊かに約1000作品を紹介。

シーズン キャンペーン グラフィックス
デパート・ショップのシーズン別キャンペーン広告特集
Pages: 224 (Full Color) ¥15,534+Tax

デパート・ファッションビル・ショップ・ファーストフード業界がシーズンごとまたは年間を通して展開するセールや様々なキャンペーンの特集です。季節を感じさせ、インパクトある作品約600点を厳選し季節ごとに分類し紹介します。

ショッピングバッグ グラフィックス
世界の最新ショッピングバッグ・デザイン集
Pages: 224 (Full Color) ¥15,534+Tax

東京、ニューヨーク、ロサンジェルス、ロンドン、パリ、ミラノ…世界の主要都市の百貨店・ブティック・雑貨店・菓子店などの様々な業種から集められた個性豊かな最新ショッピング・バッグ 約500点を一挙掲載！

マガジン アドバタイジング グラフィックス
業種別 世界の独創的な雑誌広告デザイン特集
Pages: 224 (Full Color) ¥13,500+Tax

世界19ケ国から厳選されたコンセプチュアルで独創性に富む雑誌広告は斬新でインパクトのあるビジュアルと消費者の心を捉えるコピーを兼ね備え（効果的コピーは日英翻訳付）成功するプロモーションの在り方を考えさせます。

プレゼンテーション グラフィックス
発想から完成までのプレゼンテーション特集
Pages: 192 (Full Color) ¥15,500+Tax

世界８ヶ国31名のクリエイターによるデザイン制作の発想から完成までを、アイデアスケッチ、カラーカンプ、デザイナーのコメントとともに紹介します。今まで見ることのできなかった制作の裏側を紹介した貴重な１冊です。

マガジン エディトリアル グラフィックス
洗練された世界のエディトリアル・デザイン特集
Pages: 224 (Full Color) ¥15,500+Tax

アバンギャルドなイギリス、ニュースタイルのフランス、パワー溢れるアメリカ…世界9ヶ国より選りすぐった話題の79冊に紹介するトップクリエイター達のグラフィックワークはまさにニューエイジのクリエイションバイブルです。

プロモーショナル グリーティングカード
世界の案内状&ダイレクトメール集大成
Pages: 224 (Full Color) ¥15,534+Tax

世界中のクリエイターたちから届いたシックで美しいカードや、アイデアたっぷりの楽しいカードなど約500点を厳選して掲載。企業の展示会案内、商品案内はもちろん、結婚・出産のプライベートなカードまで幅広く用途別に収録。

ダイレクトメール グラフィックス 1
業種別世界のDMコレクション
Pages: 224 (176 in Color) ¥15,534+Tax
デザイン性だけでなくセールス効果の高いDMをコレクションした待望のデザイン集です。厳選した約100業種、350作品を業種別に紹介。この時代にこそ重要なダイレクトマーケティング・デザインのノウハウを知る貴重な1冊。

パリコレクション／インビテーション カード
パリ・コレクションの招待状グラフィックス
Pages: 176 (Full Color) ¥13,398+Tax
過去10年間、世界のトップ・ファッションブランドがパリコレクションのために制作した案内状、招待状の特集です。大胆なアイデアとユニークなデザイン約400作品を厳選した本書はまさに見て楽しめるアイデアの宝庫です。

ファッション & コスメティック グラフィックス
Pages: 208 (192 in Color) ¥15,534+Tax
流行の先端をいく世界各国の アパレル、アクセサリー、コスメティック・ブランドのグラフィック集がついに登場。カタログを中心にラベル、タグ、DM … etc. 約40ブランドのトレンドを先取りした広告アイテム約800点を掲載。

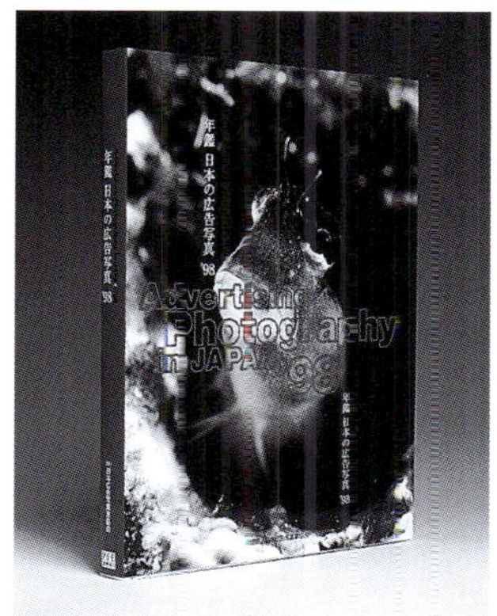

年鑑 日本の広告写真 '98
待望の広告写真年鑑、第7弾
Pages: 224 (Full Color) ¥14,500+Tax
広告は時代の証言者だ！過去4年間の傑作、話題の広告写真の中から高い水準で選び抜かれた作品425点を一挙収録。広告の枠に縛られないハイクオリティな内容です。日本広告写真家協会監修、4年ぶりの待望の年鑑、第7弾。

ピエ・ブックス
〒170-0003 東京都豊島区駒込4-14-6-301
TEL: 03-3940-8302 FAX: 03-3576-7361

P·I·E BOOKS
#301, 4-14-6,komagome, Toshima-ku, Tokyo 170-0003 JAPAN
TEL : 03-3940-8302 FAX : 03-3576-7361

THE BUSIEST BEAVER

For my dearest Swaggers
(and for everyone else who thinks like Nora).
You make my world a better place . . . LF x

For Beatrice and Rory – KH

SIMON & SCHUSTER
First published in Great Britain in 2025 by Simon & Schuster UK Ltd
1st Floor, 222 Gray's Inn Road, London WC1X 8HB

The authorised representative in the EEA is Simon & Schuster Netherlands BV,
Herculesplein 96, 3584 AA Utrecht, Netherlands. info@simonandschuster.nl

A CIP catalogue record for this book is available from
the British Library upon request

ISBN: 978-1-3985-1515-4 (HB)
ISBN: 978-1-3985-1514-7 (PB)
ISBN: 978-1-3985-1516-1 (eBook)

Printed in China
1 3 5 7 9 10 8 6 4 2

THE BUSIEST BEAVER

LU FRASER KATE HINDLEY

SIMON & SCHUSTER
London New York Amsterdam/Antwerp Sydney/Melbourne Toronto New Delhi

In a far-away forest of tall twisty trees,
Where the dragonflies glitter and glide on the breeze,
There's a river of beavers all chomping and gnawing,

And one busy beaver who's drilling and sawing . . .

Now Nora did LOTS of things beavers should do,
But she *also* thought thinkings
quite different and new . . .

She asked lots of questions like
'How?', 'Where?' and 'Why?'

And invented inventions . . .
. . . and gave things a try.

She could stick things and make things
and carve things from wood
And build things with hammers that
no one else could.

But . . .

"That's quite enough sawing!" the beavers all said.
"Try being a little more beaver instead.

More gnawing!

More nibbling!

More paddling, too!

And *try* not to do things that beavers *don't* do!"

"But what if," frowned Nora, "a beaver can be,
A little like you . . . OR a little like ME?

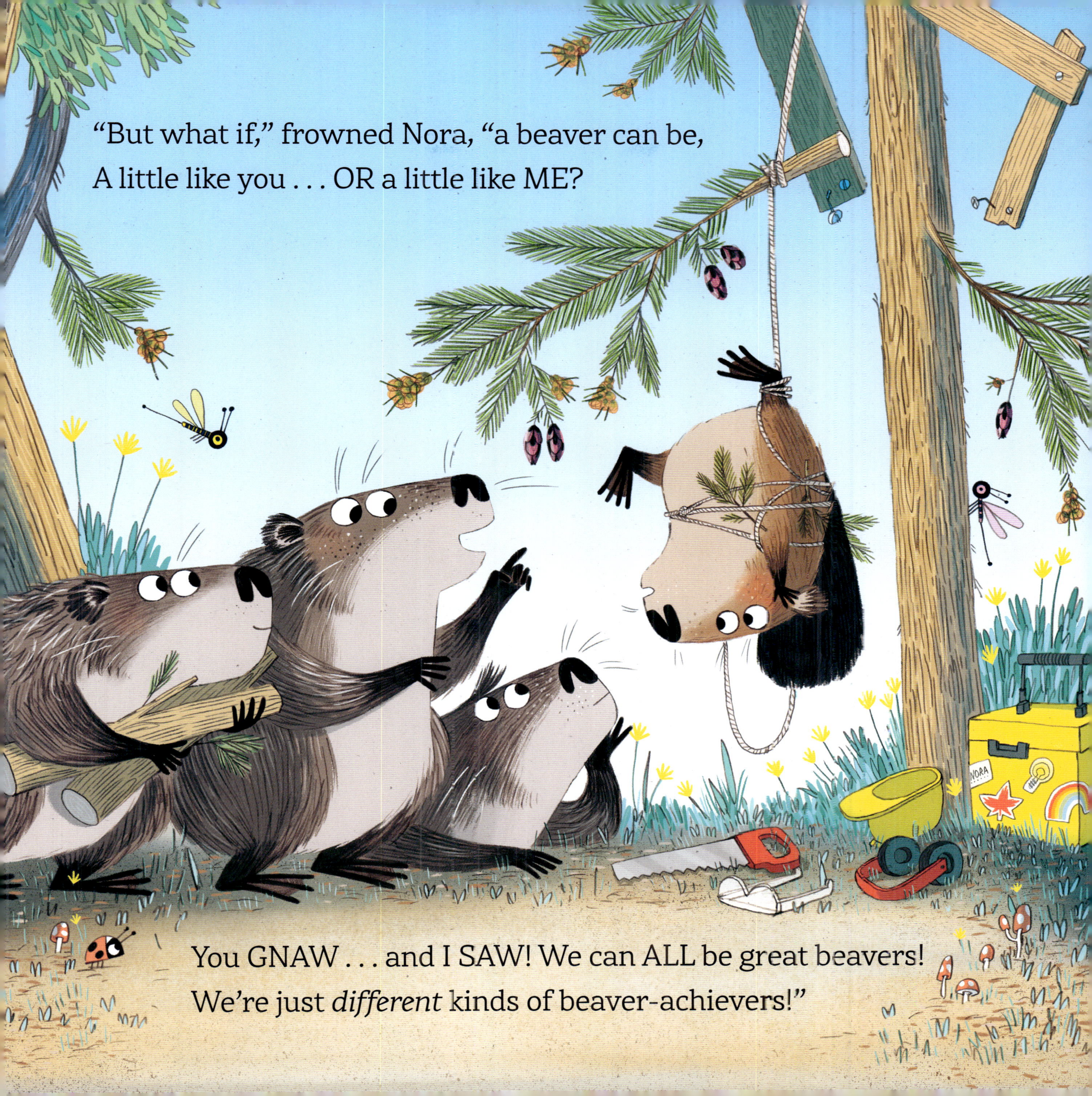

You GNAW . . . and I SAW! We can ALL be great beavers!
We're just *different* kinds of beaver-achievers!"

But the beavers looked puzzled,
"That's *not* beaver thinking!"
Nora looked at her toolbox,
her furry heart sinking . . .

"No more inventing,"
she whispered, "for me?
Maybe Grandad can help?"
Nora nodded, "Let's see . . ."

“Oh, Nora,” smiled Grandad,
“You must *always* be . . . YOU!
Don’t ever stop seeing this world as you do!
Think things and build things – be happy each day!

And be your own beaver . . . your own beaver way.”

But as Nora skipped home,
something went PLOP!
The first of the raindrops
that soon wouldn't stop.

Then it drizzled . . . it showered . . . it TORRENTED down!
"Where does rain *go*?" Nora asked with a frown.

So she opened her toolbox . . .
and pulled out a book,
Then she peered in the river
and took a long look.

She counted . . . then pondered,
her little paws clasped,

Then she wrote it all down and
. . . "OH, NO!" Nora gasped!

“Beavers!” cried Nora, “I’ve *spotted* a thing!
I’ve measured our river with long bits of string.
I’ve used lots of numbers, and watched how it’s flowing,
And I’m *sure* that it’s FILLING with raindrops and . . .

GROWING!”

But the beavers all blinked . . . then the beavers all sighed,
"Not *again*, Nora!" the beavers all cried!
"Be more like US! No more numbers! NO STRING!"

And into the river they dived with a spring . . .

"But my thinkings are *right*!" Nora whispered, "It's true!
This river is RISING! Oh, what should I do?"

Then she thought about Grandad and what he would say . . .

"I must be my *own* beaver," she gulped,
"my *own* way!"

So, with jottings and plottings and plans in her head,
Off Nora scampered to Grandad's old shed . . .

SWISH! went the pencil
as Nora was drawing!

PING! went her tape measure!
ZZRRR! went the sawing!

She chiselled and sanded
and measured and weighed
’Til hammer by hammer-blow,
something . . . was made!

Then she HOISTED and HEAVED
and she HAULED and she HUFFED!

"Oh, I hope I'm in time!" Nora panted and puffed.

But . . .

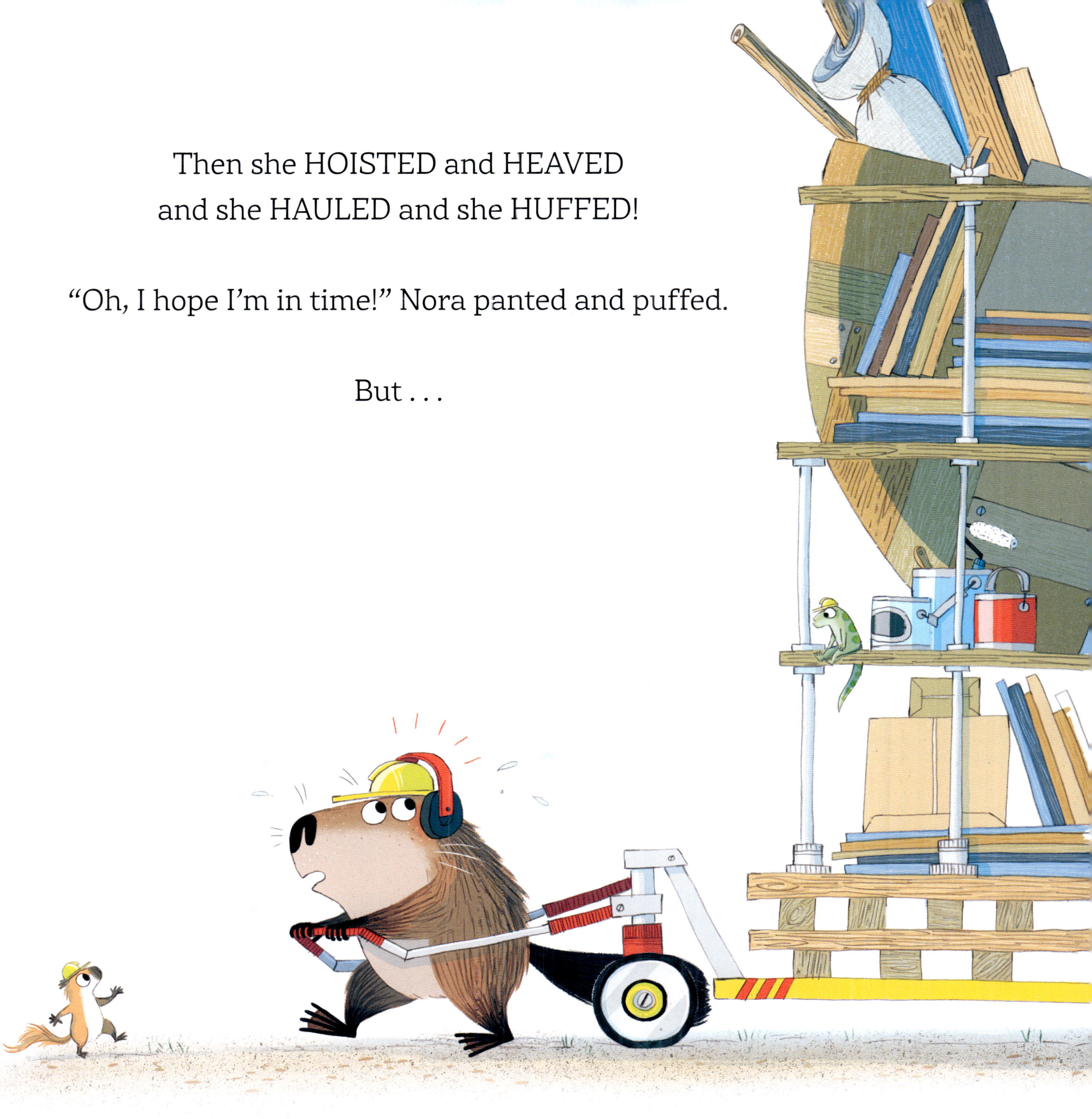

. . . something was mumbling! Something was humming!
Something was grumbling and rumbling and . . . COMING!
First came a GLUG! Then a burbling BUBBLE!
"Oh dear," Nora frowned, "I think we're in trouble!"

And, just as her little tape measure had shown,
Their river had STRETCHED!
It had SPREAD!

It had GROWN!

"LOOK OUT!"
Nora called across slip-slidey mud,

"Time to leave, Beavers!
Here comes a . . .

. . . FLOOD!”

"EEK!" squeaked the beavers, "Nora was right!
Oh, our river's too BIG and too FAST! Hold on tight!"
But something ASTONISHING zoomed into view . . .

"NORA?!" the beavers all cried, "Is that . . .

. . . YOU?!"

"AHOY THERE!" cried Nora, "I'll keep us afloat!
We'll make our escape in my BIG BEAVER BOAT!"
And dropping the ladder she cried, "Up you climb!"
Then the boat full of beavers set sail, just in time.

"Whiskers UP! Paddles DOWN!
Beavers, let's HURRY!"

And away they were washed in a watery flurry . . .

SWOOSH! went the bobbing boat, WHOOSHING! and WHIZZING!
As the tumbling river was LEAPING! and FIZZING!

And each time they sailed alongside someone wet,
Nora scooped them aboard with a big swishy net.

Furry friends, scaly friends, friends great and small,
"There's plenty of room," Nora called, "for us ALL!"

UP swirled the animals!
DOWN they all dipped!
'Til . . .

. . . their bob-along boat into gentleness slipped.
And, softly, the tired little river below
Rocked them safely to shore in the setting sun's glow.

"THREE CHEERS FOR NORA!" they clapped. "Now we see
How **brilliant** thinking like Nora can be!"

Then, squeezing her paw, Grandad looked very wise
As they turned to gaze up at the sparkling skies . . .

"Every star is a part of the shimmering night,
Each one is different . . . but each one shines bright!
So never forget for a moment, each day,
You light up this world in your own unique way . . ."

And there, side by side, in the star-glow they stood,
"Yes, my thinkings *are* different," smiled Nora, "but good!
And so," she smiled brightly, "that's just how I'll stay . . .

. . . I'll be my own beaver
my **own**
beaver way."